WHO'S AFRAID OF ACADEMIC FREEDOM?

WHO'S AFRAID OF ACADEMIC FREEDOM?

EDITED BY
AKEEL BILGRAMI
& JONATHAN R. COLE

COLUMBIA UNIVERSITY PRESS
NEW YORK

Columbia University Press
Publishers Since 1893
New York   Chichester, West Sussex
cup.columbia.edu
Copyright © 2015 Columbia University Press
All rights reserved

Library of Congress Cataloging-in-Publication Data

Who's afraid of academic freedom? / edited by Akeel Bilgrami and Jonathan R. Cole.
pages cm
Includes bibliographical references and index.
ISBN 978-0-231-16880-9 (cloth : alk. paper)
1. Academic freedom—United States. 2. Academic freedom—Moral and ethical
aspects—United States. 3. Teaching, Freedom of—United States.
I. Bilgrami, Akeel, 1950– II. Cole, Jonathan.

LC72.2.W48 2015
378.1'213–dc23

2014014722

Jacket Design: Jordan Wannemacher
Jacket Image: ©National Geographic Creative/Bridgeman Images

References to websites (URLs) were accurate at the time of writing. Neither the
author nor Columbia University Press is responsible for URLs that may
have expired or changed since the manuscript was prepared.

For those, past and present, who have suffered because of the absence of free inquiry.

CONTENTS

INTRODUCTION

T HE TITLE OF this volume, despite its associative distractions, is meant quite literally. A primary achievement of the essays in the pages that follow is to identify and analyze different groups and tendencies in our society that fear academic freedom and attempt to thwart it, sources as diverse in range and generality as intellectual orthodoxy, intellectual obscurantism, the interests of donors, institutional review board licensing, Israeli and other pressure groups, U.S. legislation and government policy, and actions taken within universities such as speech codes and restrictions on research . . .

As a value within the academy, it is arguable that freedom of inquiry is unique and may be given a lexicographical priority over other values because it is an *enabling* value. It enables the pursuit of *other* values and, therefore, it cannot be weighed on the same scale as the values it enables, whether these be "truth" in the outcome of inquiry, or more generally "excellence" in the pursuit of inquiry, or simply the peace of mind of inquirers . . . We have said it is "arguable" that this is so. It cannot complacently be assumed to be so. Some of the essays in the volume try to provide the arguments by which it may be established, addressing considerations that are sometimes raised to question this priority of academic freedom, considerations that appeal to the very values that it claims to enable.

Such lexicographical priority is, of course, often granted to freedom of speech and discussion *outside* the academy as well, so much so that it is enshrined as a familiar and fundamental law of the land. There are essays here that wrestle with the question: Is academic freedom just a name for the practice, within universities, of the political freedom guaranteed by the U.S. Constitution, or is it, for reasons having to do with the specific nature of the academy, set apart from that more general freedom?

That question needs to be considered in conceptual and analytic terms, but also historically. One of the curious features of the value of academic freedom is how little it has evolved since the American Association of University Professors (AAUP) first articulated the value in its formal statement in 1915, which was reinforced and somewhat expanded in 1940. The value has not evolved over time the way the interpretation and scope of the First Amendment has. While there have been essays and books written about academic freedom since 1940, it may well be time for a more detailed and considered articulation of what exactly academic freedom protects and what it does not— and whether we should reconsider its original intent, which was (as Robert Post has claimed in a number of essays) that academic freedom is distinguishable from First Amendment rights and has more to do with the "contract" that exists between faculty members and others, including trustees, academic administrators, and outside authorities. Some essays here make an attempt to give some historical grounding to this issue, while others dispute it by showing its extreme restrictiveness.

Though questions of academic freedom affect all of society and not just the society of scholars, though its fruits are reaped by everyone and by most institutions, a specific group that is most affected by its presence or absence is the faculty in universities with their special duties of teaching and research. With this in mind, the editors decided to carry out an empirical pilot survey of Columbia University full-time faculty opinion on a wide variety of questions revolving around the academic freedom they enjoy and expect but which is sometimes under question and threat. The survey is presented here with an analysis by Jonathan R. Cole and his collaborators. One question that is derived from the results of the survey relates to the hierarchy of values in a university: Is academic freedom seen by the faculty as a special enabling value, or is it considered by most contemporary faculty members as one among a set of contenders for priority? The fourteen vignettes contained in the empirical study, which in some cases asked faculty members to choose among competing university values (one of which was always free inquiry or academic freedom, although that was never explicitly mentioned in the survey), suggest that most faculty view academic freedom as essentially freedom of speech.

The survey also suggests an erosion of certain core values within the academy. Is academic freedom one of them, as apparently are values like disinterestedness (exemplified in, among other things, the normative prohibition against faculty members profiting from their discoveries)? The pilot study raises more questions than it answers, one of which is whether different major universities and colleges place different weights on these various values. It is fair to say that ever since John Coulter in a celebrated address stressed the value of *Lehrfreiheit* to the idea of the modern research university, followed several decades later by the equally and rightly celebrated Kalven committee report, the University of Chicago has been something of a pioneer in this country on the matter of the centrality that academic freedom came to have in higher education. A comparison of other universities with the University of Chicago on the question of freedom of inquiry may therefore be one way to assess these differential weights. Two essays here that focus on the University of Chicago may provide a start in helping to make such a comparative study possible.

Taken together, these essays powerfully convey how no freedom can be taken for granted even in the most well oiled of functioning formal democracies. It is in the nature of power to resist the possession and exercise of freedom by those over whom it exercises power. And power, as we also know, does not threaten freedom always by coercion or, to put it differently, the opposite of freedom is not necessarily always coercive *agents* and policies and institutions but the presence of much less easily identifiable *tendencies*. The modern university is not a medieval cloister and is as subject to the political and economic interests that generate these tendencies and threaten freedom as most, if not all, other institutions. (One extraordinary, up-to-the-minute example of this is the very recent amendment to a budget bill by Senator Tom Coburn (R-OK), which was passed by a voice vote and signed into law by President Obama. The amendment, or rider, to the bill ordered the National Science Foundation to refrain from funding any political science research "except for research projects that the [NSF director] certifies as promoting national security or the economic interests of the United States." Not since former president Ronald Reagan's effort to eliminate all social science funding by the NSF has there been such a blatant attack by Congress on free inquiry and research judged as superior by the members of NSF panels of experts.) In analyzing the nature of these tendencies, their sometimes hidden sources, and their detailed and widespread implications, the essays presented here are exercises in and for democracy.

What follows is a set of very brief summaries of each essay in the book to steer the reader to specific interests and points of focus in the volume.

Geoffrey Stone provides us with "A Brief History of Academic Freedom," which traces the origins and evolution of academic freedom from Athens to the present. It explores the many battles that have been fought over the years to give meaning and content to that freedom; examines its meaning today; and considers the political, economic, and cultural challenges academic freedom continues to face now and in the future.

Akeel Bilgrami finds a celebrated argument in John Stuart Mill appealing to human fallibility to be both fallacious on its own terms and unnecessary to make the case for freedom of inquiry. He rejects such metaphors as "the marketplace of ideas" and "balance in the classroom" that are encouraged by Mill's argument and provides an alternative analysis for what it is in dogmatism that threatens freedom of inquiry.

David Bromwich articulates the case *against* the sort of sequestering of academic freedom from the more generally articulated political freedom enshrined in the Constitution that has recently been put forward by both Robert Post and Stanley Fish, and in doing so raises a question about the extent to which their position reflects (and feeds) the increasing transformation in our societies of knowledge into a form of "expertise."

Jonathan R. Cole's essay deploys the ideals and logic of the Kalven committee report as a point of departure for his analysis of the logic and limits of academic freedom. He suggests that the threats against academic freedom are very much still with us and proposes how great universities ought to respond in certain ways that are consistent with this value. He outlines the nature of the threats and the roles that the university and its faculty ought to play in responding to them. Indeed, he argues that great universities cannot be created or continue to exist without a vigilant defense of this value, upon which is built most of the rest of the structure of a great university. He argues, as does the Kalven committee report, that the best of our universities are by design meant to be unsettling—to be critical of our society's weaknesses, as a source for new, even radical ideas (in all disciplines) that must also meet the test of extreme methodological rigor. The essential tension with the university is between the acceptance to listen to the most radical ideas and simultaneously to apply the most stringent methodological criteria for establishing fact or truth.

Joan Scott exposes the weaknesses in conventional efforts at making and maintaining a distinction between politics and scholarship by appeal to a notion of "objectivity," and thinks the consequences of this through for the diverse use that is made of notions of "academic responsibility" to restrict academic freedom.

Jon Elster's polemical essay is on how tolerance of two broad tendencies in academic disciplines that he finds "obscurantist" can be a threat to academic freedom. At first sight, this would seem to be an argument for there being *too much* academic freedom. But that is not his view. He distinguishes between freedom of thought and freedom of speech and claims that "excessive politeness" toward obscurantism undermines the former. The essay should raise an interesting question for the reader. Suppose even that we put aside the protest that one person's obscurantism is another person's depthful clarity, and grant him that we have permitted a great deal of obscurantism in the academy. The interesting question is: Why is this a form of academic *unfreedom*? Obscurantism, if and where it exists, is no doubt a wrong, but why should all wrongs be the same wrong? Should we count it as the same wrong as academic unfreedom, as promoting the same wrong as coercion or dogmatism does, or as a different sort of malaise in the university?

Michele Moody-Adams addresses conflicting values as they affect questions of academic freedom. As she notes, academic freedom can have culturally and politically unsettling consequences, particularly when practices of intellectual exclusion that are central to academic freedom and define academic life conflict with values of inclusion that we deem important to democratic institutions. Her essay considers the causes and implications of such conflicts, as well as broader cultural sources of unease about academic freedom, to show that the benefits of protecting academic freedom far outweigh any potential dangers.

As we said above, Robert Post has written extensively in the past on aspects of the history and practice of academic freedom in the United States, and has made a clear and sharp distinction between the concepts of academic freedom and the First Amendment clause protecting freedom of speech. He has argued that academic freedom grew out of an effort to redefine the relationship between academics and their employers in an era (the first two decades of the twentieth century). His is an argument that academic freedom protects the rights of experts from disciplines to make a series of decisions about the quality of scholarship and the organization of how to evaluate it without external interference. In the current essay found here, Post makes a structural argument that the constitutional law of academic freedom, properly speaking, protects neither professors as individuals nor universities as institutions, but the disciplinary norms which define the scholarly profession and which universities exist to nourish and reproduce.

Philip Hamburger explores conflicting norms in his essay where he argues that the use of institutional review boards, or IRBs, violates the principles of academic freedom. He argues that licensing of speech or the press was a method of controlling the press employed by the Inquisition and the Star Chamber, and the First Amendment unequivocally barred it. Nonetheless, the federal government has revived licensing through the regulation of human-subjects research. Although federal regulations provide for academics and students to get permission for "research," which sounds like mere conduct, both the text and the effect of the regulations reveal that they provide for licensing of speech and the press—initially in academic inquiry and then in its publication. Of course, research on human subjects can be harmful, and the government aims to prevent that, but the harms prevented by the human-subjects research regulations are minimal compared to the harm caused by suppression of speech. Particularly in medical research and its publication, the suppression evidently causes several thousands of deaths each year. Hamburger juxtaposes these two norms of the academy, while arguing that, in fact, the federal regulations are unconstitutional. Indeed, the resulting censorship is the most widespread and systematic assault on the freedom of speech and the press in the nation's history.

Richard Shweder's essay seeks first to define the ancient Socratic ideal of freedom of thought and the application of the methods of critical reason as the ultimate ends of academic life. According to this view the university is primarily an intellectual, not a moral, political, or commercial, institution. What makes a great university great is its commitment and willingness to nurture and protect the ardor and fearlessness of autonomous minds to following the argument where it leads regardless of moral, political, or commercial interests or popular opinion. Is this antiquarian conception a foolish ideal in the contemporary academic world? To what extent does a self-consciously neo-antiquarian academic institution such as the University of Chicago live up to the standard? Would Socrates be welcome and thrive within the halls of the modern university or would he slowly suffer death by a thousand cuts?

Robert Zimmer examines some of the history and context of academic freedom and its meaning, fastening particularly on the uses of that history at the University of Chicago as a case study. He examines the nature and role of the Kalven committee report, which reflects long-standing views within the University on the subject of academic freedom and the critical role that the report played in the implementation of this value. The essays by Zimmer and Shweder, and to some extent Stone's as well, are understandably rooted in issues that arose at the University of Chicago. This is not merely because they are all professors there but because, as we have said, that university was one of the earliest sites where the issue of academic freedom was aired and documented.

Matthew Goldstein and his coauthor Frederick Schaffer are particularly well suited to explore the core issues their paper raises: How is academic freedom to be viewed from the point of view of the relative roles that faculty members and academic administrators ought to play in the governance structure of universities that are seeking to transform themselves? The division of academic labor has become very much entrenched, and as much as most outsiders believe that faculty members at our great universities are diehard liberals, those who have tried to "move" universities from one position to another know that when you bring two or more faculty members together they can be extremely conservative. This skepticism about change and novel ideas has its upside, since it tends to dismiss the many fads and fashions that would envelop the university. Yet when there is need for meaningful structural or substantive reform, which potentially includes the closure of some units of a university or a dramatic shift in its curricular orientation, the faculty members often are deeply offended by initiatives taken by academic administrators. Goldstein and Schaffer open up an important area for further thought and investigation: In times that require change at universities, what should be the relative roles of faculty members and administrators in initiating and carrying out that change? Does administrative initiative, with faculty consultation, violate principles of academic freedom and the roles that have been carved out over the decades for the two groups?

Stanley Fish and Judith Butler take opposing sides on the relation between academic freedom and the academic boycott politics surrounding the Israeli occupation of Palestinian lands. While Fish takes this particular issue as yet another location to argue for his view that the academy is a relatively narrow and isolated enterprise whose pursuits must not be contaminated by larger political struggles, Butler makes an argument that academic freedom is a *conditioned* value, a value that can only be implemented under certain conditions that are *necessary* for it, and if those conditions are being manifestly abrogated by the Israeli government's policies and practices, then it cannot be a threat to academic freedom, as is sometimes thought, to propose an academic boycott of the sort that some would wish to impose on Israel.

John Mearsheimer looks at the variety of ways in which the "Israel lobby" adversely affects the freedom of the academy in the United States, from smear tactics against professors who are critics of Israel and working toward excluding such critics from visiting and speaking on campuses to co-opting students to support Israel and discouraging donations to universities that do not internally subdue criticism of Israel.

Noam Chomsky expands the canvas of these issues from Mearsheimer's narrower interest in the intrusive presence of the Israel lobby on campuses to the much more generalized voluntary subservience of university administrators and intellectuals to state power, with some telling details of the recent history of this form of subservience as it relates to American foreign policy toward the Middle East.

Finally, little is known about what faculty members at major universities feel about the principle of academic freedom, especially when it may conflict with other values and norms at the institution. With his coauthors Stephen Cole and Christopher Weiss, Jonathan R. Cole explores the faculty reactions to fourteen hypothetical situations (that were, in fact, based upon actual academic freedom and free inquiry cases). The pilot study polled full-time Columbia University faculty, asking them to assess certain actions of a fictional professor (although each was based on actual academic freedom and free inquiry cases) and to tell us whether and/or how much the professor should be sanctioned for her or his actions. The results of the study are presented in this essay as a first step in an effort to stimulate the gathering of more empirical evidence about faculty members' attitudes and values surrounding academic freedom.

Two essays in this volume, the ones by Chomsky and Bilgrami, were presented as lectures on occasions whose context is not entirely detachable from some of the substance of what they have to say. The same may be said of Jonathan R. Cole's essay, which appeared previously in an issue of *Daedalus*. The editors have therefore retained references to the context in those essays.

Modern social life is everywhere characterized by the undue demands that are made on individuals in the occupations that they choose or are landed with and by the brief and distracting release from such demands in recreation. Life in a thoroughly professionalized academy cannot be counted as an exception to this. There is scarce time and energy remaining for serious critical reflection on what one does in living such a life, and this often induces an unwilled complacence about what one may have allowed as fundamental threats to the basic liberties that enable the pursuits of inquiry. But, as even these brief summaries of the essays in this volume display in gratifying abundance, there are also pockets of determined resistance against such complacence. In inviting and presenting them, we have sought both thematic range and historical depth in identifying and diagnosing the threats to freedom of inquiry, but above all we have sought to exemplify the spirit of controversy that many of the contributors believe universities should protect, indeed encourage.

WHO'S AFRAID OF
ACADEMIC
FREEDOM?

1

A BRIEF HISTORY
OF ACADEMIC FREEDOM

GEOFFREY R. STONE

A S COLUMBIA UNIVERSITY professor and former provost Jonathan R. Cole observed in his work *The Great American University*, "the protection of ideas and expression from external political interference or repression became absolutely fundamental to the university."[1] Indeed, it is in no small measure our deep commitment to academic freedom that has allowed American universities to be "great."

It is imperative, though, that we never take academic freedom for granted, for the freedom of thought and inquiry we enjoy today in the academy is the product of centuries of struggle, and in the first part of this essay I will briefly trace the history of academic freedom, because unless we know how we got to where we are today we may not understand just how unique and potentially fragile our academic freedom really is. In the final part of this essay, I will offer a few thoughts about the challenges of the future.

Although the struggle for academic freedom can be traced at least as far back as Socrates's eloquent defense of himself against the charge that he corrupted the youth of Athens, the modern history of this struggle, as it has played out in the university context, begins with the advent of universities, as we know them today, in the twelfth century.

In the social structure of the Middle Ages, universities were centers of power and prestige. They were largely autonomous institutions, conceived in the spirit of the guilds. Their members—whom we today would describe as their faculty—elected their own officials and set their own rules.

There were, however, sharp limits on the scope of scholarly inquiry. There existed a hard core of authoritatively established doctrine that was made obligatory on all scholars and teachers. It was expected that each new accretion of knowledge would be consistent with a single system of truth, anchored in Christian dogma.

As scholars and teachers gradually became more interested in science and began to question some of the fundamental precepts of religious doctrine, the conflict between scientific inquiry and religious authority grew intense. When Galileo published his heretical telescopic observations, for example, he was listed as a suspect in the secret books of the Inquisition, threatened with torture, compelled publicly to disavow his views, and imprisoned for the remainder of his life.

Throughout the seventeenth century, university life remained largely bounded by the medieval curriculum. Real freedom of thought was neither practiced nor professed. As one statement of the then prevailing ideal put the point, the teacher was "not to permit any novel opinions to be taught," nor was he to teach "anything contrary to prevalent opinions."[2]

This was the general attitude in America, as well as in Europe, and freedom of inquiry in America was severely limited by the constraints of religious doctrine until well into the nineteenth century. In 1654, for example, Harvard's president was forced to resign because he denied the scriptural validity of infant baptism.

The latter part of the eighteenth century saw a brief period of relative secularization of the American college as part of the Enlightenment. By opening up new fields of study and by introducing a note of skepticism and inquiry, the trend toward secular learning began gradually to liberate college work. The teacher of science introduced for the first time the discovery, rather than the mere transmission, of knowledge into the classroom.

This shift was short-lived, however, for the opening decades of the nineteenth century brought a significant retrogression. This was due largely to the rise of religious fundamentalism in the early years of the nineteenth century, which led to a sharp counterattack against the skepticism of the Enlightenment and a concerted effort on the part of the Protestant churches to reassert their control over intellectual life.

As a result of this development, the American college in the first half of the nineteenth century once again found itself deeply centered in tradition. It looked to antiquity for the tools of thought and to Christianity for the laws of living. It was highly paternalistic and authoritarian. Its emphasis on traditional subjects, mechanical drill, and rigid discipline stymied free discussion and squelched creativity.

Three factors in particular stifled academic freedom in this era. First, the college teacher was regarded first and foremost as a teacher. Because academic honors hinged entirely on teaching, there was no incentive or time for research. Indeed, it was generally agreed that research was positively harmful to teaching. In 1857, for example, the trustees of Columbia College attributed the low state of the college to the fact that some of its professors "wrote books."

Second, educators of this era generally regarded the college student as intellectually naive and morally deficient. "Stamping in," with all that phrase implies, was the predominant pedagogical method, and learning was understood to mean little more than memorization and repetitive, mechanical drill.

Third, freedom of inquiry and teaching was smothered by the prevailing theory of "doctrinal moralism," which assumed that the worth of an idea should be judged by its moral advantages, an attitude that is anathema to scholarly inquiry.

The most important moral problem in America in the first half of the nineteenth century was, of course, slavery. In both the North and the South, colleges rigidly enforced their views on this subject. By the 1830s, the mind of the South had closed on this issue. When it became known, for example, that a professor at the University of North Carolina was sympathetic to the 1856 Republican presidential candidate, the faculty repudiated his views, the students burned him in effigy, and he was discharged by the trustees. The situation in the North was not much better. The president of Franklin College was dismissed because he was not an abolitionist, and Judge Edward Loring was dismissed from a lectureship at the Harvard Law School because, in his capacity as a federal judge, he had enforced the fugitive slave law.

Between 1870 and 1900, there was a genuine revolution in American higher education. Dramatic reforms, such as graduate instruction and scientific courses, were implemented, and great new universities were established at Cornell, Johns Hopkins, Stanford, and Chicago. New academic goals were embraced. To criticize and augment, as well as to preserve the tradition, became an accepted function of higher education. This was an extraordinary departure for a system that previously had aimed primarily at cultural conservation. Two forces in particular hastened this shift. The first was the impact of Darwinism. The second was the influence of the German university.

By the early 1870s, Darwin's theory of evolution was no longer a disputed hypothesis within the American scientific community. But as scientific doubts subsided, religious opposition rose. Determined efforts were made exclude proponents of Darwinism whenever possible. The disputes were often quite bitter.

This conflict brought together like-minded teachers, scientists, scholars, and philosophers who believed in evolution and who developed new standards of academic inquiry. In their view, to dissent was not to obstruct, but to enlighten.

The great debate over Darwinism went far beyond the substantive problem of whether evolution was true. It represented a profound clash between conflicting cultures, intellectual styles, and academic values. It pitted the clerical against the scientific; the sectarian against the secular; the authoritarian against the empiricist; and the doctrinalist against the naturalist. In these conflicts, science and education joined forces to attack both the principle of doctrinal moralism and the authority of the clergy.

A new approach to education and intellectual discourse grew out of the Darwinian debate. To the evolutionists, all beliefs were tentative and verifiable only through a continuous process of inquiry. The evolutionists held that every claim to truth must submit to open verification; that the process of verification must follow certain rules; and that this process is best understood by those who qualify as experts.

In the attack upon clerical control of universities, the most effective weapon was the contention that the clergy were simply incompetent in science. The result of this attack was the almost complete disappearance of the clergy as a serious academic force. In 1860, 39 percent of the members of the boards of private colleges were clergymen; by 1900, the percentage had dropped to 23 percent; by 1930, it had dwindled to 7 percent.

The other factor that played a critical role in the transformation of American higher education in the late nineteenth century was the influence of the German university. The modern conception of a university as a research institution was in large part a German contribution.

The object of the German university was the determined, methodical, and independent search for truth. Such a vision of the research university attracted individuals of outstanding abilities, rather than mere pedagogues and disciplinarians. The German professor enjoyed freedom of teaching and freedom of inquiry. The German system held that this freedom was the distinctive prerogative of the academic profession and that it was the essential condition of a university.

Indeed, the single greatest contribution of the German university to the American conception of academic freedom was the assumption that academic freedom defined the true university. As William Rainey Harper, the first president of the University of Chicago, observed in 1892: "When for any reason . . . the administration of [a university] attempts to dislodge a professor because of his political or religious sentiments, at that moment the institution has ceased to be a university."[3]

Although American universities borrowed heavily from the German in this era, there evolved two critical differences between the American and German conceptions of academic freedom. First, whereas the German conception encouraged the professor to convince his students of the wisdom of his own views, the American conception held that the proper stance for professors in the classroom was one of neutrality on controversial issues. As President Charles Eliot of Harvard declared at the time: "The notion that education consists in the authoritative inculcation of what the teacher deems true . . . is intolerable in a university."[4]

Second, the German conception of academic freedom distinguished sharply between freedom within and freedom outside the university. Within the walls of the academy, the German conception allowed a wide latitude of utterance. But outside the university, the German view assumed that professors were obliged to be circumspect and nonpolitical.

American professors rejected this limitation. Drawing upon the more general American conception of freedom of speech, they insisted on participating actively in the arena of social and political action. American professors demanded the right to express their opinions even outside the walls of academia, even on controversial subjects, and even on matters outside their scholarly competence.

This view of academic freedom has generated considerable friction, for by claiming that professors should be immune not only for what they say in the classroom and in their research but also for what they say in public debate, this expanded conception empowers professors to engage in outside activities that can inflict serious harm on their universities in the form of disgruntled trustees, alienated alumni, and disaffected donors.

These issues were brought to a head in the closing years of the nineteenth century, when businessmen who had accumulated vast industrial wealth began to support universities on an unprecedented scale. For at the same time that trusteeship in a prestigious university was increasingly becoming an important symbol of business prominence, a growing concern among scholars about the excesses of commerce and industry generated new forms of research, particularly in the social sciences, that were often sharply critical of the means by which these trustee-philanthropists had amassed their wealth.

The moguls and the scholars thus came into direct conflict in the final years of the nineteenth century. For example, a professor was dismissed from Cornell for a pro-labor speech that annoyed a powerful benefactor, and a prominent scholar at Stanford was dismissed for annoying donors with his views on the silver and immigration issues. This tension continued until the beginning of World War I, when it was dwarfed by an even larger conflict.

During the Great War, patriotic zealots persecuted and even prosecuted those who questioned the war or the draft. Universities faced the almost total collapse of the institutional safeguards that had evolved up to that point to protect academic freedom, for nothing in their prior experience had prepared them to deal with the issue of loyalty at a time of national emergency.

At the University of Nebraska, for example, three professors were discharged because they had "assumed an attitude calculated to encourage . . . a spirit of [indifference] towards [the] war."[5] At the University of Virginia, a professor was discharged because he had made a speech predicting the war would not make the world safe for democracy. And at Columbia, the board of trustees launched a general campaign of investigation to determine whether doctrines that tended to encourage a spirit of disloyalty were being taught at the university.

Similar issues arose again, with a vengeance, during the age of McCarthy. In the late 1940s and 1950s, many if not most universities excluded those accused of Communist sympathies from participation in university life. The University of Washington fired three tenured professors, the University of California dismissed thirty-one professors who refused to sign an anti-Communist oath, and Yale president Charles Seymour boasted that "there will be no witch hunts at Yale, because there will be no witches. We will not hire Communists."[6] At many universities, faculty members were actively complicit in the campaign to purge their institutions of alleged subversives.

Most recently, the first Bush administration tortured academic freedom in the 1990s by restricting research into certain "sensitive" areas; implementing restrictive visa policies for prospective researchers, students, and speakers; prohibiting the use of federal funds for embryonic stem cell research, essentially on religious grounds; and manipulating the nation's peer review system for political ends.

So, what can we learn from this very quick survey of the history of academic freedom? Several themes emerge. First, and perhaps most important, academic freedom is *not* a law of nature. It is a practical, highly vulnerable, hard-bought acquisition in the struggle for intellectual freedom.

Second, the real threat to academic freedom comes not from the isolated incident that arises out of a highly particularized dispute, but from efforts to impose a pall of orthodoxy that would broadly silence all dissent.

Third, every form of orthodoxy that has been imposed on the academy— whether religious, political, patriotic, scientific, moral, philosophical, or economic—has been imposed by groups who were completely convinced of the *rightness* of their position. With the benefit of hindsight, however, every one of these groups has come to be viewed by most thoughtful people as inappropriately intolerant, at best, and as inappropriately intolerant and wrong, at worst.

Finally, what should be our concerns for the future? For the most part, they are mere extensions of the challenges we have faced—not always very well—in the past. Let me give just four examples.

First, and most obviously, there is the corrupting temptation of money. From the very beginning of the modern university, the need for resources has generated a dangerous conflict. How much should we bend our values to please or avoid alienating our donors?

I was at a university several months ago at which the most generous benefactor in the university's history, who had not yet paid off his very large pledge, met regularly with the president and provost to make sure the university was headed in the "right" direction. There is no doubt they were pandering to his ill-informed whims. I was appalled, but this sort of thing, usually in a less gross form, occurs at universities all too often.

The fact is that universities require vast amounts of financial support from individuals, foundations, corporations, and governments. Too often, these donors want a say—they want to select the students who receive their scholarships; to remove from their professorship a faculty member who has said or written something that offends them; to insist that the program they support must use their products; and on and on and on.

At what point does a dean, provost, or president say, "Never mind. We won't take your money." This poses an especially serious dilemma in the sciences, particularly in the realm of medical research, where both the costs and the stakes are very high. As Bill Clinton said on another subject, when it comes to the future of academic freedom, "it's the economy, stupid."

Second, we live in an era of political correctness in which accusations of racism, sexism, anti-Semitism, homophobia, neocolonialism, and terrorism chill discourse to the bones. It is impossible to take certain positions without inviting a torrent of abuse, protest, and ostracism. In this respect, students are often the worst violators. Silencing too often is preferred to debate. But universities must stand for debate over repression. We must teach our students about the importance of tolerance, civil discourse, and academic freedom. In this, we too often have failed.

Third, as we saw, the rise of religious fundamentalism in the first half of the nineteenth century—the so-called Second Great Awakening—had a devastating effect on free inquiry in institutions of higher learning. We may now be in the opening years of a Third Great Awakening, as we experience a new and perhaps even more aggressive rise in religious fundamentalism.

We see this today in the political realm on such issues as abortion, creationism, stem-cell research, and same-sex marriage. The same pressures that now bear on the political process will likely be felt in universities as well. This is perilous, for religion and academic freedom do not mix.

Fourth, universities must understand that at the very core of academic freedom is institutional neutrality. The role of the university is not to take positions on matters political, moral, legal, economic, social, religious, or international. For universities to promote academic freedom, they cannot themselves participate in the debate. Our responsibility is to create the conditions for free and open debate, and we cannot fulfill that responsibility if we take sides.

Too often, trustees, president, provosts, deans, faculty, alumni, and students want their universities to stand up and be counted. During the Vietnam War, when I was a student, I wanted my university to condemn the war as immoral. I was furious that it would not do so. I was wrong—deeply, profoundly, and dangerously wrong.

Universities should never stand up and be counted. They should not endorse candidates, condemn policies, embrace causes, or advocate positions not integrally related to higher education itself. If a university takes sides, it undermines its own neutrality, stifles free and open discourse, and makes itself a target for others who will want it to take sides more often. To paraphrase William Rainey Harper from more than a century ago, a university that takes sides is not a "university."

NOTES

1. Jonathan R. Cole, *The Great American University: Its Rise to Preeminence, Its Indispensable National Role, Why It Must Be Protected* (New York: Public Affairs, 2010), 45.
2. *The Role of Scientific Societies in the Seventeenth Century* (Chicago, 1938), 215.
3. University of Chicago, *The President's Report, July, 1892–July, 1902* (Chicago: University of Chicago Press, 1903), 1:xxii.
4. *The New York Teacher, and the American Educational Monthly* (New York: J. W. Schermerhorn, 1870), 7:19.
5. Richard Hofstadter and Walter Metzger, *The Development of Academic Freedom in the United States* (New York: Columbia University Press, 1955), 498.
6. Cole, *The Great American University*, 361.

2

TRUTH, BALANCE, AND FREEDOM

AKEEL BILGRAMI

1

THOUGH THERE IS much radical—and often unpleasant—disagreement on the fundamental questions around academic freedom, such disagreement tends to be between people who seldom find themselves speaking to each other on an occasion such as this or even, in general, speaking to the same audience. On this subject, as in so much else in the political arena these days, one finds oneself speaking only to those with whom one is measurably agreed, at least on the *fundamental* issues. As proponents of academic freedom, we all recognize who the opponents of academic freedom are, but we seldom find ourselves conversing with them in academic conferences. We only tend to speak to them or *at* them in heated political debates when a controversy arises, as for instance at Columbia University over the promotion of faculty in Middle Eastern studies or in those states where the very idea of a curricular commitment to modern evolutionary biology is viewed with hostility. I will not be considering such controversial cases of overt political influence on the academy. This is not because they are not important. The threats they pose are very real, when they occur, and the need for resistance to these threats is as urgent as anything in the academy. But they raise no interesting intellectual issues at a fundamental level over which anyone here is likely to be in disagreement. If there is disagreement in a forum of the kind at which we are presently gathered, it is likely to be on relatively *marginal* questions, such as, for instance, whether academic freedom is a special case of the more basic constitutional right to free speech or whether it is instead a distinct form of freedom tied to the specific mission of universities.

What might a philosopher contribute to these more marginal questions? In this essay, I would like to make a fuss about a standard argument for a conception of academic freedom that we all seem to subscribe to when it is coarsely described but which, when we describe it more finely and look at the arguments more closely, is quite implausible and leads indirectly to thoroughly confused ideas about displaying "balance" in our classrooms and our pedagogy quite generally. I will then use some of the points and distinctions I make in this critique to explore the exact nature of more subtle and interesting (and actually more pervasive) kinds of threat to academic freedom than the obviously controversial ones I mentioned previously, which all of us, I assume, find an abomination, and which, as I said, raise no interesting issues for any of us, even if they ring urgent alarms. At the very end, I will venture to advocate imbalance of a very specific kind in the "extramural" domain, when it is neither inquiry nor classroom curriculum that is at stake but the effort to engage the intellectual and political culture at large.

2

No matter which stand is taken on the marginal question as to whether academic freedom is a special case of the constitutional right to free speech or something special and apart, there is a great and recurring tendency in the literature on the subject to appeal to the same broad arguments and metaphors and intuitions to present the justifications for academic freedom as is done for the justification for freedom of speech in general. And it takes roughly the following lines. First, there is a statement of purpose or *goal*: academic institutions are sites for intellectual inquiry and research and therefore one of their chief goals is the pursuit of truth and the pedagogical project of conveying the truth, as one discovers it and conceives it in one's research, to students and to set students on the path of discovering further truths in the future on their own. And then second, there is a statement of the *conditions for the pursuit of that goal*: this pursuit of truth is best carried out, it is said, under conditions wherein a variety of opinions are allowed to be expressed on any subject, even if one finds some of them quite false, since it is possible that they might be true and one's own view might turn out to be false. Often, the metaphor used to capture this ethos and its efficacies in the matter of truth is that truth surfaces in a *"marketplace of ideas."*

When Justice Oliver Wendell Holmes first put that phrase into the air, he was not particularly thinking about the academy but quite generally about the shape of a free society.[1] In fact, as two Columbia historians (Richard Hofstadter and Walter Metzger) pointed out,[2] Holmes was really expressing in more intuitive and metaphorical terms the justification for tolerance in speech quite generally, for which John Stuart Mill had earlier in *On Liberty* given a more structured argument with premises and a conclusion.[3] So even if one thought that academic freedom was set apart from the articulations of the First Amendment, the structure of the *underlying* philosophical argument is the same as to be found in Mill's more general argument for liberty of speech as a fundamental principle of the polity at large. I want to spend some time on this underlying argument, but before I do, it is worth emphasizing that it is not just given by professional and lay philosophers, it is found in the case law of this country in which universities have figured repeatedly. Thus for instance, in *Keyishian v. Board of Regents of the State University of New York*, the language of the Supreme Court of this country explicitly cites the phrase "marketplace of ideas" and talks of the "robust exchange of ideas which discovers truth out of a multitude of tongues." That is just one example. There are literally scores of cases in the lower courts as well that appeal to Millian considerations, and they too begin by defining the goal of universities as being one of seeking the truth in intellectual inquiry.

What is Mill's argument and why does it have such a strong appeal for law, philosophy, and even our everyday understanding of the justifications for academic freedom? Its appeal is the appeal of a certain fallibilist epistemology that widely underlies the classical and orthodox liberal mentality. Curiously, this form of fallibilism clashed starkly with the pragmatist epistemology of American thinkers like Charles Sanders Peirce and also with the heterodox form of liberalism that one finds in American thinkers like John Dewey. Yet the American courts and American quotidian opinion cite Holmes and Mill like a mantra.

Mill's argument has two premises and a conclusion. The premises are:

> Premise 1: Many of our past opinions, which we had held with great conviction, have turned out to be false.
> Premise 2: So, some of our current opinions that we hold with great conviction may also turn out to be false.

From these premises, he drew a conclusion about tolerance and free speech:

> Conclusion: Therefore, let us tolerate dissenting opinions just in case our current opinions are wrong and these dissenting opinions are right.

The idea is that the marketplace of ideas keeps us honest. Since we can never be sure that we are right, a marketplace of opinions, many of which may oppose our own opinions, may well throw up the truth, displacing our own convictions about it. Metzger and Hofstadter make this connection between Holmes and Mill explicit, and there is no doubt that something like this justification, if true, would hold for free speech in the academy with particular force, even if we saw the academy as standing apart from constitutional contexts for free speech, because the academy is specially geared to pursue the truth in its various disciplinary pursuits.

Let us, then, stare at the argument for a while.

Mill's argument is based on an induction. It is often called Mill's "meta-inductive argument." The induction is found in the transition from the first premise to the second. It is called a *meta*-induction presumably because whereas most inductions go from observations about the *world* in the past to conclusions about the future, his induction goes from an observation about our past *beliefs* about the world to a conclusion about our present and future *beliefs* (viz., that they may be false).

There is an extraordinary ambition in this argument. It hopes to persuade us of a value, the value of free speech as something for a polity or a university to embrace, on the basis of something that is pure rational argument. By this I mean that it does not aim to convince us to adopt a value (the value of free speech) *on the basis of any other moral or political values*. It hopes to convince us on grounds that are, in that sense, value free. It does not matter what moral or political values we have, so long as we are capable of induction, we are supposed to see the force of the argument. And since inductive capacities, like deductive capacities, are part of general rational capacities possessed by all (adult, undamaged) human beings, if the argument is right, everyone should see the value in free speech just by virtue of their rationality. To fail to do so, therefore, is nothing less than irrational. Mill gives quite other arguments for free speech in that careless masterpiece—such as, for instance, that free speech is a value to live by, because it encourages diversity as well as creativity in society, and that a willingness to submit to the clash of ideas is essential to the moral courage of human beings and prevents their mental pacification. But such an argument is inherently less ambitious. Its appeal is confined to those who value individual creativity or variety or what Blake called "mental fight." There is a risk in any argument that comes to an evaluative conclusion by appealing to another value. Values are things that have variable appeal. And so those who do not subscribe to the other value will not be convinced by it. The meta-inductive argument, by contrast, if successful, is supposed to knock us down with a much more general logical force: induction.

But is it successful? The incessant sloganeering about the marketplace of ideas depends centrally on its success. Deep though it goes in liberal culture and sensibility, I think Mill's argument is a numbing fallacy.

To begin with, even at a cursory glance, it will be apparent that the judgment in the first premise is made from the point of view of one's current opinions and convictions. It is from our present point of view, from what we *currently take to be true*, that we are able to say that our past opinions are false. But the judgment in the second premise is telling us that our current point of view may contain false views and therefore we should be unsure and diffident about them. Now, if we are unsure about our current beliefs, and our judgment in the first premise is made on the basis of our current beliefs, then to that extent we must be unsure of our first and basic premise. Any conclusion based on it therefore is bound to be, to that extent, itself shaky and uncertain.

There is another more fundamental internal problem with the argument.

In characterizing it, I have said that it comes to a value conclusion on the basis of premises that appeal merely to an induction and not on the basis of any other political or moral value. But the fact is that although it appeals to no moral and political values, it does appeal to a cognitive value, the value of truth. Since it says that one should adopt free speech because it creates a marketplace of ideas from which the truth, even if it goes against one's convictions, will emerge, one is assuming at least that there is value in pursuing the truth. So it *does* appeal to another value (the cognitive value of truth) to justify the value of free speech. It is only because we value truth and have it as a goal that we will be moved by the idea that a marketplace of ideas engendered by freedom of speech is something we should adopt.

But now, if that is so, there is something internally peculiar about an argument that appeals to the value of truth and the goal of pursuing the truth, as it does, while also implying, as the second premise does, that we can never know we have achieved the truth. How can we claim to have a goal we can never know we have achieved when we have achieved it? What sort of goal is that? It is not perhaps as peculiar as having a goal we know we can never achieve? That is outright incoherent. You cannot coherently strive to achieve what you know to be impossible. But to allow that we can achieve a goal and yet insist we can never *know* we have achieved it when we have, though not perhaps outright incoherent, is a very peculiar understanding of what goals are.

To put it explicitly, the internal tension is this: The argument's second premise says that beliefs whose truth we are utterly convinced about may turn out to be false. This strictly implies we can never be sure we have achieved the goal of truth, not even when we are quite convinced we have. And yet the argument presupposes that the pursuit of truth is a value and that we have it as a goal to pursue. If the goal of inquiry into the truth that all academic institutions embrace is really to pursue in this way something we never can be sure we have achieved, then we must be assuming that what we do in pursuing it is a bit like sending a message in a bottle out to sea. We never know what comes of it; we never know it has arrived. What sort of epistemological project is that? It is a conception of inquiry in which we have no control over its success. If inquiry is successful, that success is, from our hapless point of view as inquirers, necessarily some sort of bonus or fluke.

The argument demands that our point of view of inquiry have a built-in diffidence: We are supposed to be diffident even about our most well-established claims. But such diffidence yields no instruction. The doubt expressed by the thought "for all one knows even our strongest convictions as to what is true might be false" is an idle form of doubt. Consider the paradox of the preface, in which the author says coyly, "Something or other that I say in the next four hundred pages is bound to be erroneous or false" (and then typically adds, "for those errors I alone am to blame and not all these nice people I have just acknowledged as having aided my thought and argument"). The author's declaration of impending falsity in the pages to come is idle, because it gives him or her no instruction about what to do to remedy things. It is not as if the author knows what it is that is bound to be false, and why. Like Mill and Holmes, he just thinks that that is the tentativeness and diffidence with which we must hold the views he has written down. But a doubt that gives no instruction in his practice of writing is a doubt that does not make any epistemic difference. And as pragmatists say, something that makes no difference to practice (not even to cognitive practice, as in this case) makes no difference to inquiry and epistemology at all.[4] Any argument that arrives at a commitment to free speech on the basis of a conception of inquiry that has such precarious coherence hardly deserves the centrality it has been given in the liberal tradition of political thought.

In the immediate context of the political controversies in which we in university life find ourselves, the conception of academic freedom based on such a classical liberal form of argument leads *directly* to the advice we often get, sometimes even from university presidents, about how we should be *balanced* in what we say in our classrooms, showing consideration to all points of view, even those that from our point of view we confidently know to be wrong. This directive wholly fails to understand what sort of role the ideal of "balance" ought to play in the academy. It is a worthy ideal, but we have to understand the right place and context for it in the academy.

Let us go along, as we have been doing, with the assumption that a primary aim of universities is to pursue the truth in our various disciplinary inquiries and that the point of pedagogy is to try and present the truth we have found by presenting evidence and argument for it. Now if balance has any role to play in all this, its role is entirely *nested within* this primary goal, *not* something *independent* of this goal. And within this primary goal, the only thing that "balance" *could* mean is that one must look at *all* the evidence available to one in our inquiries. (This is the cognitive counterpart to what decision theorists call the *total evidence requirement*.) What "balance" cannot possibly mean is the nonsensical thing the directive we are considering tells us, namely, the equal presentation in the classroom of two contradictory views. No educator with any minimal rationality would do that on the elementary grounds that if there are two contradictory views, only one can be right. Of course if she cannot make up her mind on the evidence as to which one is right, she might present the case for both views evenhandedly. But presumably such undecidedness is an *occasional* phenomenon. If so, balance cannot be put down as a *requirement* for pedagogy in the classroom. Hence, the constant demand that we always present both sides of a disagreement presupposes a conception of education as a sort of chronic dithering. It is far more sensible to say that balance allows that an educator presents her judgment with complete conviction, because balance in the academy is nothing other than a synonym for the idea that we must look at *all* the evidence before coming to our convictions. It has no other role or meaning. Attempts to give it another meaning (as in the directive with which I am finding fault) are drawn from a fault line that has its beginnings in the canonical Millian form of liberal argument for free speech.[5]

3

I have been inveighing against a very standard liberal argument and a metaphor that it yields about truth emerging from a marketplace of ideas, which goes deep in the sensibility of our self-understanding in the academy and in the courts that have pronounced judgment in controversial cases the academy has thrown up. This may have given the impression that I am recommending more dogmatism regarding our own convictions than a commitment to academic freedom can allow. That impression would be wrong.

The criticisms I have just made of Mill's argument are quite compatible with the view (which is my own view) that there is far too much dogmatism in the academy, especially in the social sciences and even in the humanities. (And if it is less so in the natural sciences, still, as Kuhn pointed out almost five decades ago, there is some there too.) As a matter of fact, my view is that if we could characterize more or less exactly what this dogmatism is, we would have identified the most pervasive as well as the most insidious and interesting form of threat to academic freedom.

As I said at the outset, this paper is going to raise a typical philosopher's fuss about how to rigorously characterize the arguments by which we justify academic freedom, and I have said that I find Holmes's metaphor and Mill's argument less than exact and plausible, and this implies that theirs is not the way to understand the dogmatism that thwarts academic freedom. To be fussy is to demand that one gets certain distinctions carefully right. And I am claiming that to diagnose and combat the far too high levels of dogmatism in the academy, we do not have to assume a fallibilist notion of diffidence and doubt. It is one thing to be undogmatic in the way that academic freedom demands, quite another to have the sort of notion of inquiry suggested by Millian and classical liberal arguments for academic freedom.

Let me convey what I have in mind by the dogmatism that constitutes a threat to academic freedom by returning to the paradox of the preface. This paradox offers us a site for locating a useful taxonomy via which we can identify what sort of dogmatism amounts to such a threat.

I had said about the paradox that the *generalized*, that is to say, the *unspecific* form of doubt that is stated in the preface ("something or other in what follows in these pages may not be true," echoing Mill's argument that our strongest convictions may turn out to be false) gives the author no instruction as to what to do about it. He cannot possibly be moved to do anything about his text by a doubt such as this. What the author will be moved and instructed by is not this sort of doubt but, rather—if he is not dishonest and not obtuse— by some *specific* evidence or argument that is provided against one or other of his *specific* conclusions or claims. Now, both these qualifications—"if he or she is not dishonest and not obtuse"—are revealing.

They show that there is no direct relevance of this issue I have just raised (about ignoring *specific* counterevidence and counterargument presented to one) to the question of academic freedom. Suppose someone failed to recognize counterevidence presented to him. That would be a sign of obtuseness. Suppose again that someone did recognize that counterevidence had been presented to him by some colleague and he simply ignored it. That would be a sign of intellectual dishonesty. But both these things are quite *separate* kinds of wrong from thwarting academic freedom. Now it is true that sometimes those who are dishonest in this way are caused by this dishonesty to suppress or hound out someone who presented that evidence and that would, of course, be threatening to academic freedom; but suppressing or hounding someone out is a matter quite separable from what we are concerned with, the ignoring of evidence that is provided against what one takes to be the truth.

If this is right, we have identified so far three different phenomena. *First*, there is academic *dishonesty*—to recognize evidence or argument that goes against one's conclusions but ignore it. This in itself is *not* academic unfreedom. *Second*, there is the inability to even recognize the force of counterevidence and counterargument. Let us call this academic or intellectual *obtuseness*. And even more obviously, that is not a case of academic unfreedom either. *Third*, there is the suppression of those who present counterevidence and counterargument that one has recognized to be so and one has dishonestly evaded. This, I have said, *is* a case of academic unfreedom. But, as I said at the beginning of this essay, it is a very obvious case and not a very interesting one, so I will simply put such cases aside, because they raise no difficult questions. It is not even clearly characterizable as a case of dogmatism, although it bears some relation to dogmatism.

We then still do not have the kind of academic unfreedom that is genuinely and clearly also a case of dogmatism. So now, finally *fourth* in our taxonomy, I want to present that kind of dogmatism and show why it is a far more interesting and unobvious and also a more pervasive threat to academic freedom than is identified in the third; and in this presentation, it will become clear what its relation is to the first and second phenomena in the taxonomy, from which it is also important to distinguish it, especially from the first phenomenon, with which it is too often conflated.

The dogmatism that interests me is found in submerged forms of academic *exclusion* when we circle the wagons around our own frameworks for discussion so that *alternative frameworks* for pursuing the truth simply will not even become visible on the horizon of our research agenda. This form of dogmatism is distinguishable from the first of our four phenomena, academic dishonesty of the kind that refuses to accept counterevidence and counterargument presented in refutation of some specific conclusion of our inquiry. Why? Because alternative frameworks *do not refute our conclusions directly* with counterevidence or counterarguments, so much as point to other, possibly deeper and more interesting ways of looking at what we are studying. And here is the crucial point. *If they *do* contain counterarguments and counterevidence to our own claims and convictions, those will only surface further downstream, well after the frameworks are recognized by us upstream as possibly fruitful forms of investigation. But it is this recognition upstream that the dogmatist in us finds so hard to confer, and it is in this failure that academic unfreedom (rather than intellectual dishonesty) is located.

These are cases in which a discipline discourages the development of frameworks outside of a set of assumptions on which there is mainstream consensus—and the political influence on the formation and maintenance of these exclusive assumptions, where it exists, is very indirect indeed, so indirect that it would need a fair amount of diagnostic work to reveal it, since the *practitioners themselves are often quite innocent of the influence*. (On the other hand, it is not as if this is a rare or unusual phenomenon. It is widespread and is quite well known and many of my listeners at the lecture on which this essay is based know it closely, since what has made the New School one of the most valuable institutions of higher learning in this country is that it has valiantly housed—indeed it has been something of a hospice for—those suffering from an exclusion of unorthodox frameworks for thinking about a range of themes in a range of different disciplines.)

Dogmatism of this kind is also distinguishable from the third sort of flaw, obtuseness. To be dogmatic in this way is not at all to be lacking in the acuity that would recognize the force of counterevidence and counterargument. If one has failed to recognize any counterevidence (downstream, in my metaphor), that is because one has (further upstream) not even so much as recognized the possibility of the framework from which it flows. It is not as if the counterevidence is there for us to see downstream and we are not perceptive enough to see it. Rather it is not there for us to see downstream because we have not recognized the framework upstream from within which it is visible. And this last failure is a kind of dogmatism, not stupidity.

Among disciplines, economics provides the most gorgeous examples of this. It is perhaps the worst offender in inuring itself against alternative frameworks of thought and analysis. In fact, I will frankly say that I have never come across a discipline that combines as much extraordinary sophistication and high-powered intellect and intelligence with as much demonstrable falsehood. So, for instance, some of the most brilliant intellectuals I have known to this day make claims about the trickle down of wealth in capitalist economies and present them with the most sophisticated quantitative methods, despite the plain fact that wealth has not trickled down (at least not to the places where it needs to trickle down) *anywhere in the world in the entire history of capitalist political economy.* If a physicist were to make some of the claims that economists have made and that have been falsified as repeatedly as they have, he would not only have his career terminated, he would properly be the laughingstock of the profession. Now there is no direct political influence that forces this sort of refusal to question, let alone give up, one's assumptions in a discipline such as economics. The regulation is wholly *within* the discipline's profession and even there, there may be very little browbeating or intellectual bullying, that is to say, very little *explicit* regulation. It is largely unconscious self-censorship—often done with career advancement in mind—that threatens academic freedom in such a discipline.

On the very evening after I wrote these words, I was over at a dinner at my economist colleague Joe Stiglitz's apartment, and I impertinently told him that I was going to raise this point in a lecture I was to give at a conference on academic freedom at the New School the next day. His response was memorable. "Akeel, I agree with you about economists, but I don't understand why you are so puzzled. One would only be puzzled if one were making the wrong assumption about economics. What you should be assuming is that—as it is done by most economists—economics is really a religion. And so why should you be puzzled by the fact that they cling to and never give up their views despite their frequent falsification?" So I will rephrase my point: one apparently makes one's way up in a church hierarchy by clinging fast to the orthodox faith.

But there is the following difference. The church has had a history of explicit and rigid regulation of what may or may not be said and pursued in its fold. But as I said, if there is political (or corporate) influence in play in the sort of dogmatism I have described in economics, it is not obviously visible and direct, and the protagonists in economic inquiry in universities would be quite genuinely clueless about it and, with no dishonesty, deny its influence. Sometimes, as in my own subject of analytic philosophy, where there is a great deal of exclusion of alternative frameworks for discussion, there is no political influence, *however indirect*, in play. If there is a question of power and politics involved it is entirely internal to the discipline, the power that is felt and enjoyed simply in keeping certain ways of thinking out of the orbit of discussion, forming small coteries of people referring to one another's work with no concern that the issues they discuss are issues that have no bearing on anything of fundamental concern to any of a number of disciplines with which philosophy had always been concerned before, say, even fifty years ago, and from which it has now managed to isolate itself for the most part. Richard Rorty had tried to raise Kuhnian questions for the discipline of analytic philosophy and spoke with eloquence about its insularity, and he was certainly right to notice just how exclusionary the subject had become, the more it had become a profession in universities.[6]

Moving away from specific disciplinary examples, the general point that emerges from these examples can be made if one recalls that Tocqueville famously said: "I know of no country where there is so little independence of mind and real freedom of discussion as in America." And here is a wildly curious thing. At the same time, it is America that has more free institutions (including academic institutions) than anywhere else in the world. How can this extraordinarily paradoxical duality coexist? What explains this paradox? I cannot possibly try to provide an explanation here,[7] but whatever it is that explains it will provide a very good sense of the deep, that is to say submerged, forms of academic unfreedom that exist in this country. When the freest academic institutions coexist with some of the highest levels of academic unfreedom in the democratic world, the sources of unfreedom are bound to be far subtler than is captured by the standard vocabulary of "suppression," "brainwashing," "political pressure," "manipulation," and so on. That is why this fourth phenomenon, this pervasive sort of dogmatism, is a far more interesting case of academic unfreedom than the third phenomenon in our taxonomy. When a person working with unorthodox frameworks of research is looked upon with *perfect sincerity* by professionals as someone unfortunate and alienated and to be pitied as irrelevant or outdated rather than bullied and hounded, we know not only that the political influences on these professionals are not even easily identified, let alone easily confronted, we also know that this kind of thwarting of academic freedom needs a quite different descriptive vocabulary than I used in describing the third phenomenon.

Equally, I would insist that it is different from the first phenomenon of academic dishonesty as well, because to accuse these professionals of *dishonesty* (rather than in their dogmatism unconsciously perpetrating academic *unfreedom*) would be to be glibly moralistic, since (if I am right in making the upstream/downstream metaphor) it is not *honesty* that requires that people should be willing to allow frameworks of investigations other than their own. At any rate, it is not honesty in the sense that it is required to admit that one's views have been refuted when one has been shown evidence against them and one is not too obtuse to recognize the evidence. To insist that they are both a case of dishonesty would be to perpetrate a (not very good) pun.

The interest and subtlety of this exclusionary phenomenon, then, lies in its distinguishabilty from all of the other three in our quartet: academic dishonesty, academic stupidity, and straightforward and obvious forms of academic suppression. Despite its subtlety, it *is* a recognizable assault on academic freedom, and it is the more important to analyze in detail precisely because there is nothing as obvious (or infrequent) about it as there is about the efforts at external influence of Christian groups on science curricula or of Zionist groups on Middle East studies departments in some universities. Being much more subtle it is also much more pervasive than these more obvious phenomena—and much harder to resist. Different people feel it differently at different times. Frameworks for serious research in race and gender felt it constantly for decades till as late as the seventies of the last century. Quite possibly more old-fashioned forms of humanistic scholarship in a range of literary disciplines began feeling it in the late eighties and nineties of that century. And I daresay, research programs that pursue seriously socialist forms of analysis feel it more than ever today in economics departments . . .

I have tried in this essay to shift attention away from the fallibilist episte-mological presuppositions of metaphors such as the "marketplace of ideas" and its classical Millian arguments for academic freedom, and I have tried to focus instead on the need to diagnose the sorts of unconscious attitudes that make for unwitting disciplinary mandarins and gatekeepers, "normal scientists" as Kuhn called them. One does not need to be diffident in the conviction with which one holds one's views in order to resist such attitudes. We should allow alternative frameworks not because we have some general-ized doubt that we ourselves might be holding false views. We should allow alternative frameworks for quite different kinds of reasons, also found in Mill's writing on liberty, having to do with the fact that if we allow for frameworks of investigation other than our own, we make for an attractively diverse intel-lectual ethos and in doing so allow the creativity of different sorts of people and minds to flower. These sorts of consideration in favor of academic free-dom, unlike Mill's argument considered in section 2, which appeals to all those capable of inductive reasoning and in pursuit of the truth, give rise to a picture of academic freedom that appeals *only* to those who think there is value in creativity and diversity in the academy. The appeal therefore is frankly disadvantaged by its less than universal reach. But on the other hand, the picture can claim the advantage of not being landed with a bizarre con-ception of inquiry presupposed by Mill's more ambitious argument and the metaphorical cliché it has yielded about the marketplace of ideas.

The vital point I want to repeat in marking this difference from Holmes's metaphor, and from Mill's meta-inductive argument on which that metaphor is based, is that if considerations about truth and falsity enter this picture, it is only, as I said, further downstream when something other frameworks deliver might claim to be a truth that clashes with ours and provides some evidence or argument for us to give up some of our own convictions. But since those considerations do not surface upstream, where we are pursuing the goal of inquiring into the truth in our investigations, that goal of pursuing the truth need never be conceived of as a goal whose success is necessarily opaque to its seekers, as in Mill's argument for freedom. In our own pursuits toward the truth, we may be as confident in the truth of the deliverances of our investi-gations as is merited by the evidence in our possession, and we need feel no unnecessary urge to display balance in the classroom if we have shown bal-ance and scruple in our survey of the evidence on which our convictions are based, the only place where balance is relevant in the first place.

4

Having said that, I should like to conclude with a point that rotates the angle a bit on the question of balance.

One of the questions that has most exercised scholars of academic freedom is the extent to which the concept and the policy apply to the utterances of a scholar not within the university but in what is called the *extramural* context. Is a professor free to say things outside the university in public forums that would be unsuitable for one reason or another in the classroom or at official university events? There is a lot of interesting writing on this subject, some of the most interesting by scholars of the law. But I want to say something here that is a bit off that beaten track.

When it is not classroom curriculum and intellectual inquiry in the university but political debate in general outside the study and the classroom that is in question, there are good reasons why the views one expresses can and often should be substantially *im*balanced. And by imbalance here, I do not just mean that they should speak with conviction for one side of a disagreement, if that side has the preponderance of evidence on its side. That form of imbalance is what my critique of Mill and Holmes has tried to establish as perfectly appropriate in the classroom. But for extracurricular and extramural public speech by academics, I have in mind the moral appropriateness of a *further* and more *willful* kind of imbalance. To conclude in one's thought what the evidence in one's investigations dictates is not really a matter of choice or will.[8] The evidence *compels* us, as it were. But to be imbalanced in the *further* way I am about to mention *is* a matter of will and moral decision. Let me explain.

I find it not only understandable but honorable, if someone speaking and writing in America finds it important to *stress much more* the wrongs of the American government and its allies and clients, like Israel, Saudi Arabia, Egypt, Pakistan, now even India, Indonesia under Suharto, Chile under Pinochet, rather than speak obsessively, as is so often done, about the wrongs done by Muslim terrorists or Islamic theocratic regimes or, for that matter, Cuba and North Korea. But if the same person were speaking or writing, say, in the Palestinian territories or in Arab newspapers, it would be far more admirable if he or she were to criticize Hamas or Islamic regimes like Iran's. So also, unlike the many who were abusive toward him for not doing so, I find it entirely honorable that Sartre, living in Paris in the Cold War ethos, refused to spend his time criticizing the Soviet Union and instead criticized Western governments for the most part.

It is said that whenever Sakharov criticized the Soviet Union's treatment of dissidents in the fifties, he was chastised by his government for showing an imbalance and not speaking out against the treatment of blacks in the American South. That is precisely the kind of imbalance that courageous academics are going to be accused of by the enemies of intellectual freedom in this country, and I hope that all of us will have the courage to continue being imbalanced in just this way.

NOTES

This is the text of a lecture given at the New School in New York.

1. Actually, it was the idea and not the expression that Holmes put into the air in his dissenting opinion in Abrams v. United States, 250 U.S. 616 (1919). His own expression was "free trade in ideas." The expression "marketplace of ideas" was first used in the language of the Supreme Court in Keyishian v. Board of Regents, 385 U.S. 589, 603 (1967).
2. R. Hofstadter and W. P. Metzger, *The Development of Academic Freedom in the United States* (New York: Columbia University Press, 1955), 527.
3. John Stuart Mill, *On Liberty* (London: Longman, Roberts and Green, 1869), chap. 2.
4. To be more precise and detailed, the pragmatist—Peirce, for instance, in his remarkably profound and original paper "The Fixation of Belief," in *Collected Papers of Charles Sanders Peirce*, vol. 5, ed. Charles Hartshorne and Paul Weiss (Cambridge, Mass.: Harvard University Press)—makes a distinction within inquiry between our settled beliefs and our hypotheses. See also Isaac Levi, *The Enterprise of Knowledge* (Cambridge, Mass.: MIT Press, 1986), for an elaborate and interesting deployment of this distinction to construct a theory of the dynamics of knowledge or what is sometimes called a theory of "belief revision." Hypotheses do not command our confidence in the same way our beliefs do. Mill might be right to ask us, as inquirers, to have some diffidence in the way we hold our hypotheses to be true since, unlike a settled belief, a hypothesis, even by our own lights, is still up for grabs; it is not something we have decisively counted as having the full prestige of "truth." But making this distinction and granting that he has a point about diffidence for one-half of the distinction (hypotheses), does not help with Mill's meta-inductive argument *for liberty*. The distinction merely says that unlike a settled belief (such as, say, his or her belief that the earth is not flat), a scientist today might make a hypothesis that he or she is hoping to have confirmed by the evidence. He will hold the latter with diffidence, but not the former. But if the former is held without diffidence, then Mill's argument for liberty does not hold for such settled beliefs. That is

absurd, from Mill's point of view. He would not have wanted flat-earthers to be tyrannized and suppressed, so he would not have been prepared to restrict his argument for liberty to just hypotheses. He would have wanted freedom of speech and discussion to apply to the expression and discussion of *all* beliefs, settled *and* hypothetical. The trouble with his argument is that he extrapolates fallaciously from the diffidence that is properly advocated for hypotheses to *all* beliefs, even settled ones. And he *must* do so, since liberty presumably will apply to the expression of all beliefs. That is why I am suggesting that one should simply abandon this argument, with its fallibilist appeal to diffidence, as providing the basis for free speech. It is the wrong basis for liberty. We should be looking for entirely different grounds and arguments for liberty, some of which Mill himself provides elsewhere in that work.

5. It might be thought that there is no very direct link between the broad liberal mentality toward freedom of speech and academic freedom that I am situating in Mill's argument and this talk of "balance" in the university. After all, for those interested in protecting Israel from the justifiably harsh criticisms of its actions toward Palestinians, there are much more straightforward political motives for insisting on "balance" in the way contemporary Middle Eastern politics is taught. If both sides are constantly being presented equally, as is demanded by balance, then the force of such decisive criticism can be softened. I do not deny that there are these political motives for demanding balance in cases of this kind as well as in other cases. But we cannot forget that many political motives of this kind are cloaked in high-sounding intellectual arguments so that their nakedness, qua political motives, is hidden. Just think of the way slaves were said to be not quite persons by ideologues rationalizing slave ownership or the way natives were said to be lacking rationality by colonists. These philosophical arguments are a constant factor in the pursuit of political motives. Millian forms of liberalism similarly often underlie (as rationalizations) the political motives for demands for balance in pedagogy.

6. Richard Rorty, *Philosophy and the Mirror of Nature* (Princeton, N.J.: Princeton University Press, 1981).

7. Noam Chomsky and Edward Hermann, in their rightly celebrated *Manufacturing Consent* (New York: Pantheon, 2002), have addressed this subject with the focus primarily on the media in this country, and I am hoping that Jonathan R. Cole in his forthcoming magnum opus on the research university in America will—among the many other things about the American academy that that book is ambitiously intended to address—speak to this issue with the focus on the universities in this country.

8. I realize that it *is* a matter of will whether one *presents* in a classroom (or indeed in one's research) what one has evidence for. That is why failing to do so is to be described as "dishonesty." I am only saying here that when the evidence compels us to draw a conclusion, the will is not in play, it is not a matter of choice, even though coming to believe something on the basis of evidence is in the realm of the intentional.

3

ACADEMIC FREEDOM AND ITS OPPONENTS

DAVID BROMWICH

T HE ARGUMENT I will be making requires a single premise: the limits of academic freedom should not be narrower than the limits of intellectual freedom.[1] It is the right of the scholar to think, write, and speak whatever he or she wants to think, write, and speak. (I leave out the obvious limit on that freedom: it does not extend to immediate and threatened harm to other people, or the raising of an imminent physical threat to the institution that houses the scholar. We have laws to protect us from that menace, and a code of freedom should not be used to lighten the burden of proof on those who enforce the laws.) Understood in its broad and libertarian sense, academic freedom is a category of political freedom. It belongs to the larger class of rights enjoyed by citizens of a free society. The experience of teachers confirms that this is what academic freedom is in practice and what it has been for some time.

To defend academic freedom with the vigor the task demands, we have to see it as a result of following a principle. This means that we ought to resist appeals for "balance." Equally, we ought to resist the narrower and more profession-centered definitions of academic freedom that have arisen in recent years — above all, the view that academic freedom can be practiced only relative to a disciplinary consensus. Such a tacit redefinition plucks freedom from the conscience of the individual scholar and lodges it in an official locus of oversight, a professional corporate body. The result can be no freer than the internal inhibitions of the corporate body allow. On the contrary: it is only by seeing academic freedom as an instance of political freedom that we can understand the good it makes possible and the evil it may counteract. The knowledge to which this freedom applies may be recondite and intricate, but the reason for supporting the freedom itself is simple. It is a tributary right of the public good in democracy.

■ ■ ■ ■

The liberty to speak one's mind on matters of general interest is apt to be used more conspicuously in a university and to surprise listeners there more often than happens in other settings. The startling effects of free speech in an educational institution may be strongly felt, in particular, when students from a homogeneous protected background are brought into contact with the uncircumscribed (not necessarily uncalibrated or immoderate) judgments of their teachers. More rarely, but often enough, the shock of surprise goes the other way, from students to teachers. The teacher who startles a class by saying that the *Genealogy of Morals* seems true as psychology, whatever its truth as history, is answered by the student who, without any previous exposure to Nietzsche, says, "He seems to hate Jesus as much as he hates Socrates."

Is this freedom subject to abuse? It is certainly liable to lead to the expression of views that are demonstrably false or that are felt by the society to be damaging to the harmony and well-being of society itself. To promulgate in a classroom in the American South in the 1950s the doctrine that "Negroes are not biologically inferior to white people" would have created a discordance that made the idea unwelcome in spite of its truth. To affirm that "unregulated markets are self-correcting" in almost all economics classrooms in America during the years 2001–2008 was to sustain a mythology whose destructive consequences are now evident. Yet it was possible and remains possible, as it should be, to inculcate such views without fear of reprisal. That a disconcerting truth or a demonstrable falsehood may on occasion be taught is a possible cost of all freedom of speech and expression, and academic freedom can claim no exemption here. Its expressions usually are, but they need not be, more polite or presentable than those that come from the freedom of the political stump. *Wild* manifestations of academic freedom have been rare in our time, but they are likely to draw particular notice in universities, because that is where speech can be heard that comes from people who are informed, articulate, and self-confident (not always in the happiest proportions). Also, these are people who are apt to be quoted, because they are accepted as authorities by the general public and presented as such by journalists and other mediators of opinion.

What shall we make of the fact that university scholars are taken as authorities? If we think of the prestige that goes with such status as a *privilege*, we may come to feel that circumscription of academic speech is warranted in order to prevent abuse of the privilege. This reservation, I think, betrays a paternally overprotective fear that people in a democracy are susceptible to *wrong authorities*. That perception in turn leads fearful persons to exaggerate the need for laws to protect us from the effects of popular credulity. One might, of course, suggest a family of similar laws to penalize false statements or the suppression of inconvenient facts by politicians, advertisers, and corporate heads, but we are satisfied with a much looser regimen of laws in those areas: public opinion is trusted to do its work, at whatever speed, of winnowing out falsehood and shrinking the numbers of the credulous.

Professors come to be considered as authorities in part because they are licensed by a qualified parochial community of scholars in a given field of study. They are not licensed as political authorities, and when they speak of political matters, their opinions ought to carry only the same weight and to enjoy the same protection as the opinions of ordinary citizens. No more, no less. The fact that their scholarly authority belongs to a different curriculum than their political pronouncements, however, does not in itself invite political abuse unless they subject to a *political* test the students over whom they have *educational* authority. It is indeed an abuse of academic freedom for a teacher to mark down or rule out arguments that are well reasoned and supported by good evidence but that the teacher dislikes. To use the authority of the classroom in this way is to exercise a kind of censorship that weakens education. Yet actual occurrences of such abuse are rare. The vast majority of suspicious reports on Internet academic watch sites do not concern cases of evident reprisal by teachers for the expression by students of forbidden opinions, but rather internalized inhibition among students themselves, who confess they are made "uncomfortable" by the idea of saying things they fear their teachers would disapprove of.

A student's liberty of thought and action is not much impaired even by manifest abuse, unless the teacher is the only available one and the course is required for the completion of a major or the attainment of a degree. Where that is the case, a variety of sanctions are plausible. The most important is the dissemination of evidence of bad conduct so as to render the teacher deplorable. Overt demonstrations may also be useful to register disapproval of intellectual bigotry. But what counts as abuse of the power of the classroom does not include the expression of strong opinions that oppose what students are used to hearing elsewhere. Again, complaints of this sort are so rare that, in a search of watch sites several years ago, I found dozens of interesting cases but not one involving the prohibition or punishment of contradictory opinions.

There remains a broad public concern in American culture, especially among people who trust the schools to do almost all the educating of children, that the young in our society should be taught fairly. Here we come up against a characteristic anxiety of democratic culture: strong judgments, if they are unfamiliar, are felt to be uncouth, unpleasant, biased. (This prejudice crosses political lines.) Reasoned consecutive argument that arrives at unexpected and possibly obnoxious conclusions is not a usual component of our culture. It is more common in the universities. Accordingly, it has been supposed that a proper way to bring the criteria of public judgment to bear on academic conduct is the monitoring and enforcement of a "balance of opinions."

The demand for balance exemplifies a misjudged adaptation of common sense and springs from an error about the nature of free inquiry. The relevant freedom for a professor of the sciences or the arts and letters is the freedom of the inquirer to search and speak about a given subject without impediment. This must also mean the freedom to do so without prior consultation or oversight by people who represent a cooperative norm to which one's views are expected to adhere. A university constituted by scholars who cannot exert effectual pressure on one another, but who teach as individually as they think, is a free university. The only necessary assurance of freedom is the actual existence of this multiplicity of uncoerced individuals. One might add that in a country as heterogeneous as the United States, the reality of freedom is supported by the multiplicity of institutions. You can find an economics department of a certain temper and emphasis at the University of Chicago, and one of a different sort entirely at the University of Massachusetts at Amherst. The fact that each, by the other's lights, propagates error, does not render either side guilty of indoctrination or a breach of the etiquette of freedom. There is no such etiquette.

Cultivating a fear of imbalance has generally been a political tactic of persons who want a different political emphasis, but it has in recent years fostered the expectation that there should be an academic *requirement* of balance. Thus, a teacher of biology in Kansas may be asked to incorporate the findings of Genesis as a second opinion to challenge Darwin on natural selection. Besides the wish for a balance of perspectives, one sees—often more subtly enforced—a wish for balance of coverage. An author of a short book on American philosophy may be advised to include a woman and a black philosopher in his table of contents if he wants to be taken seriously. The falseness of the idea of balance is plain to any teacher who has ever had a surprising thought and been impelled to speak a truth related to that thought. Intellectual candor is not a halfway point between truth and error.

So much for the demand of balance. A different answer to the scandal of intellectual freedom has come from within the scholarly disciplines, or rather from administrators who believe their duty has been discharged when once they invoke the reality of the disciplines. You are free, on this view, to say whatever you think within your discipline, by virtue of the license conferred by disciplinary training and the possession of a corresponding expertise. Your license is considered to be indefinitely renewable and, at moments of political exposure, instantly revocable. Professors are rewarded for the "production of knowledge"—that is the phrase the licensers especially favor. The argument was originated by the American Association of University Professors (AAUP) in response to the Red Scare after 1917. Recent refinements have been offered by Stanley Fish, Robert Post, and others. So long (the argument says) as you go on producing knowledge by the current lights and prevailing understandings of your discipline, you retain the right to make whatever assertions you please. But when you step out of the bounds of your productive province, you forfeit all protection. If a scholar's expertise is shown to be contaminated by moral or political interests external to the discipline, academic freedom no longer applies to that scholar's utterances and publications.

This definition of academic freedom, which turns on licensed expertise, owes its seductiveness to its apparent simplicity. It also flatters the wish of scholars outside the sciences to be considered as scientists of some sort—the most irreproachable vocation in America except for businessmen and military officers. The solution is tidy, and it defers to a seemingly impersonal authority. Let us call it the administrative solution. Its attraction, in a problem-solving culture, is obvious. Yet the administrative solution gets its air of convenience by ignoring a condition of teaching and scholarship whose real strangeness we should not underrate.

There are few other walks of life in which men and women engage in work that is not connected with specified goals or measurable utility. And this anomaly of academic scholarship can become an embarrassment. The licensed-expert idea of freedom rids us of the embarrassment of getting paid for work that lacks a utilitarian rationale. It does away at a stroke with the vagaries of unproductive thought. Instead, the disciplinary argument for the freedom of scholarship marks off a zone of security for the scholar within a designated expertise. The permission to work freely loses its force at the exact boundary of the expertise. The intent is to purify, and at the same time to limit, the conditions that allow free inquiry to be counted as a right.

Academic freedom is apparently strengthened yet actually narrowed by vesting in disciplinary and professional bodies the exclusive right to grant that freedom. You are licensed to say what you say by the previous and ever-to-be-renewed consensus of experts in the field. Knowledge turns into the name of something commanded by administrators and produced by professors. As long as professors keep their side of the bargain, they can connect the dots of knowledge in the ways they like. If they stray from the production of what is called knowledge, they are seen to be abusing academic freedom. They are then producing mere opinion or conjecture and, by implication (even if they never mention their title or status), they are using their license (and the prestige and authority that come with it) to gain a hearing in matters on which their expertise has not been solicited and their status as experts is not recognized.

But who exactly is an expert on the public good? In what department or program shall we look for its permitted espousers?

And there is a direr question for the licensers. What if the things produced or disclosed in a given field of study are not, properly speaking, knowledge but rather insights or interpretations—intellectual perceptions (let us call them) whose characteristic virtue is accuracy of imagination? The result may be statements of a kind that are to be judged not true or false so much as interesting or arid, well observed or ill observed.

Much of what used to be called the arts and letters—what is now called the humanities—has been built on statements of this kind. To realize the peculiarity of that fact may prompt a nonexpert reservation, namely that a large exception to the model of knowledge production exists in fields of study that do not even pretend to fulfill one of the major desiderata of science. The knowledge or truth they convey is *not progressive*. Yet I take it that among the things that universities make students conscious of, as part of the discovery of a freedom of the mind, are those human powers that occur irregularly and are not reducible to technique or product. The result, very often, of the discovery of such powers is not satisfaction, as at the finding of a useful object, but the gradual understanding of a way to watch or attend. Insight is not the name of a field of study. Nor is it an interdisciplinary field. It is, nevertheless, one of the possible experiences of human life, and one that a university ought to encourage.

■ ■ ■ ■

I can offer two examples of insight from the field of literature. D. H. Lawrence in his *Study of Thomas Hardy* says that the hero of *Jude the Obscure* "is only Tess turned round about. Instead of the heroine containing two principles, male and female, at strife within her one being, it is Jude who contains them both, whilst the two women with him take the place of the two men to Tess. Arabella is Alec d'Urberville, Sue is Angel Clare. These represent the same pair of principles."[2] It is an ordinary insight, from one point of view, only extraordinary if you are a reader of Hardy's novels who has ever wondered at their secret. Still, if a man in a realistic novel is the same as a woman in another novel, or if he might as well be a woman himself—I am stating the innocent and thunderstruck reaction to Lawrence's comment— then novels become to that extent less helpful in arriving at a measureable idea of character in fiction and perhaps in life. Is this a regrettable feature of the insight? We can admit anyway that there never will be a body vested with a disciplinary expertise capable of saying what kind of knowledge Lawrence was producing here.

Or consider the observation by an academic critic, Harold Goddard—in lectures he gave at Swarthmore College from the early 1920s onward—that the "demons" in *The Turn of the Screw* are not ghosts but fevered projections of the mind of the oppressed and dutiful governess who narrates the tale. James himself had implied in his preface to the story that the ghosts were real, and he seemed to confirm the explanation in several letters, though with elaborate evasions in his way of saying it. Most critics and biographers have agreed with James's apparent view of his own production. Goddard's interpretation might seem, on the face of it, extremely unsettling, since it appears to discredit the good faith of a parable about a decent woman's quest to defend innocent children from metaphysical molestation. Like the Freudian theory of hysteria, with which this reading of James's story shares some features, the insight undermines the credit we might otherwise bestow on a civic-minded witness of outlandish deeds. If the deep convictions of a person like the governess suggest a possible delusion, something in our common world is altered beyond the control of expertise. The judgment may affect the way we arrive at the disapproval or the discountenancing of wicked behavior. Further down the line, it might be felt to sap our confidence in the arrests and convictions we base on the productive science of criminology.

In their time, interpreters like Lawrence and Goddard were flouting the canons of expertise that govern the interpretation of narrative fiction; in doing so, they implicitly waived protection by the production-of-knowledge view of academic freedom. The originality of comments like theirs is appreciable mainly by those who share with the commentators a subject matter and certain points of reference. In the absence of such a common starting point, anomalous or transgressive insights are apt to elicit reactions of indifference or shock. You cannot know what the stakes are in an argument about a text in literature, or in philosophy or art, or in an argument about motives of action in history, unless you have an experience of the text or the problem with which to compare the statements of the scholar. Honest and telling disagreements become proportionately less likely when a field de-defines itself and no two members of a department are expected to share a methodology or acquaintance with a family of texts or exhibits. Even the starkest difference of view presumes a shared identification of the subject about which we are disagreeing. I point out this practical limitation because I suspect the sense it conveys is no longer well understood.

On August 29, 2009, the *New York Times* published a report by Motoko Rich, "A New Assignment: Pick Books You Like," about new methods of teaching critical reading in middle schools. To get students to read at all, Rich observes, some teachers have lately tried the experiment of letting every member of a class read a different book. Sheer interest was in this way increased: many who would have found the assigned text boring or abstruse were able to pick something else they wanted to read. And to the extent that the creation of an appetite for reading was the aim, that aim was clearly advanced. On the other hand, if informed discussion and the give-and-take of interpretation was the aim, twelve persons reading twelve different books were denied that experience. Under the all-elective curriculum of reading, the exposure of students to an argument about an assertion whose proof or refutation does not depend on easily discovered facts—the experience of an *interpretative argument in which reasons can be given*—now must be postponed indefinitely. Interpretation is a laudable goal but an evident inconvenience.

A certain fidelity to the artifice of subject matter therefore seems a primary virtue in education. That is not to say that occasional failures of fidelity involve the breach of an educational contract. Students enroll in a course because they want to learn about a stated subject. If the professor goes off track habitually, the students will learn something useful, namely what it is to be preoccupied, as this professor is unhappily preoccupied. They will not be introduced to the subject they had in mind to learn about. If they are clever, they can drop the course. If they are not clever, they will gradually learn to avoid one sort of distracted teacher early on. To discourage such misfires, we have sanctions already in place that have nothing to do with disciplinary licensing. A teacher who cannot teach a subject up to a certain standard of decency will not be asked to teach it again; or if he or she is asked again, the enrollment will be sparse.

Granted, the natural curb on bad teachers at any level, like the curb on bad lawyers, bad doctors, and bad shopkeepers, will never be sufficient. The K–12 teacher who holds a monopoly on a subject and fails to impart mechanical mastery of algebra or chemistry is as recurrent an example of civic irresponsibility as the real-estate lawyer whose last-minute addenda on contracts throw a wrench in the works. Yet there is a danger (fatigue apart) in trying to weed out the insalubrious specimens by ever more intricate trials of licensing and relicensing. The danger becomes more vivid in cases—they occur all the time in the classroom—where it would be hard to name the relevant competence for a given observation. If I teach a course on the career of Edmund Burke, and if, coming to his charges against the East India Company (which he called "a state in the disguise of a merchant"[3]), I bring to mind a comparison with Halliburton contracts in Iraq, should I hesitate before offering the analogy because I was hired to teach a course on a British political thinker cross-listed in English and political science and not a course on South Asia in the eighteenth century or on comparative imperialism? The apt analogy drawn from contemporary life is as constant a phenomenon in teaching as is the mistaken analogy. There is no way to prohibit such improvisations, short of an agreement not to use the range of our minds; yet that is the agreement that the devisers of the regime of freedom-as-expertise ask us to enter into.

Why do they do it? Because (they say) we academics need a way to justify ourselves to the sponsors of higher education. The donors and the taxpayers and the loyal alumni will trust our product only so long as the instruments of expertise are mystified; that is, so long as they feel reasonably sure that they do not understand what is being said, or so long as they can respect us on the model of a guild whose rituals and honors are properly opaque to an outside view. The peril, to democracy and education, of this deliberate removal of the scene of learning from public discussion will emerge plainly from a final example.

■　■　■　■

Eight months after Israel's December 2008 attack on Gaza, the Israeli political scientist Neve Gordon, who teaches at Ben-Gurion University of the Negev, published an editorial in the *Guardian* entitled "Time to Boycott Israel." Gordon stated a political view and gave his reasons for holding it. He believes that a boycott is the only way to bring his country to its senses. As it happens, he supports the existence of a Jewish state, and to that extent falls within the national consensus in Israel; but to call for a boycott against your own country is a radical position for anyone to take in any country at any time. If proof of this claim were needed, on July 11, 2011, the Knesset passed the Boycott Prohibition Law. Any person or body of persons calling for boycott of "the State of Israel, one of its institutions, or an area under its control" may now be sued for civil damages. Besides discountenancing the political uses of the boycott—an accepted form of democratic protest from the American colonies in the eighteenth century to British India in the twentieth—the anti-boycott enactment operates as a gag law to discourage public discussion. Thus, for an Israeli citizen to advocate the boycott now incurs a palpable risk of punishment. In 2009 the risk was already substantial, but Gordon nonetheless felt a moral obligation to support the protest movement. He took his stand as a parent and a citizen, and not as a scholar of politics: "For the sake of our children, I am convinced that an international boycott is the only way to save Israel from itself." His academic status was mentioned nowhere in his column.

Now, it is possible without any stretching of definitions to support a scholar's right to publish his political views in a country where academic freedom is understood as an aspect of political freedom. But as soon as a duty is invoked toward the *consensus* of one's colleagues in an educational institution or the *consensus* of one's neighbors in a nation, the accusation may be leveled against any dissident that he or she is breaching an unwritten protocol of the public good. Thanks to the existence of the right of political speech in Israel, that charge could not be made against Neve Gordon in 2009. There are others besides him who have taken a similar stand. But note: it was political freedom and not academic freedom (narrowly defined) that gave him the necessary protection.

His column drew a reply, "Neve Gordon's Divisive Op-Ed," published ten days later in the *Los Angeles Times* by the president of Ben-Gurion University, Rivka Carmi. President Carmi spoke paternalistically on behalf of the university, which found itself assailed for harboring such a professor. Gordon's unseemly and provocative article, she suggested, might spur a de facto boycott of the university by potential donors within Israel itself. Meanwhile, in assisting the criticism of Israel by other nations, Gordon was indirectly working to deprive Ben-Gurion University of its livelihood. And yet, she confessed, his slander could not be prosecuted because Gordon enjoyed the political right of free speech.

Here the feebleness of the professional-expert idea of academic freedom comes into glaring exposure. Carmi rightly perceived that the weakest point in Gordon's imaginable defense was the assumption of expertise that went with his possession of tenure as a university professor. She did not cite but might have cited the AAUP's 1940 revision of its 1925 Conference Statement on Academic Freedom: "Teachers are entitled to freedom in the classroom in discussing their subject, but they should be careful not to introduce into their teaching controversial matter which has no relation to their subject."[4] Should they not then be just as "careful" about silent use of their academic prestige to "introduce" into public discussion materials for which they lack an expert license? Though declaring herself open to "the wide diversity of opinions within our academic faculty and their right to free speech, no matter how controversial their writings may be," Carmi soon worked around to the view that Gordon "oversteps the boundaries of academic freedom" because his political views have "nothing to do with" the free expression of his ideas in his expert field. "Academic freedom," she went on to say, "exists to ensure that there is an unfettered and free discussion of ideas relating to research and teaching and to provide a forum for the debate of complicated ideas that may challenge accepted norms. Gordon, however, used his pulpit as a university faculty member to advocate a personal opinion, which is really demagoguery cloaked in academic theory." So an insufficiently careful use of academic privilege is seen as vulgar politics in the classroom, while an insufficiently careful venture into the public sphere by a professor yields "demagoguery cloaked in academic theory."

In fact, Gordon in his column presumed no specialized knowledge of political theory or its terms of art; though even supposing he had, the political principle of free speech would have allowed him to say what he said. But if we remove every controversy to the ground of expertise—the knowledge production approved by one's educational compatriots—then the avowal of support for a boycott can be redescribed as a demagogic stepping outside the bounds of academic disciplines. Carmi's response was at once elaborate and incoherent, compared with Gordon's article, but her propositions were made to serve a practical conclusion: by abusing freedom in order to betray his country, Gordon had "forfeited his ability to work effectively within the academic setting." The specific warrant for the charge that Gordon deployed his academic license for demagogic ends appears to have been President Carmi's belief that he used the word "apartheid" unscientifically.

In America, antilibertarian practice has received a new impetus from the efforts of employers to enforce surveillance of their employees. This warrant for repression seems natural to technocrats in the most various settings. It was brought into public view on March 17, 2011, when the Republican Party of Wisconsin invoked the Open Records Law in a letter to the University of Wisconsin demanding scrutiny of all the 2011 e-mails of the historian William Cronon. The Republican Party hoped to discredit Cronon's published appeal against the recent actions of the Republican governor of Wisconsin, Scott Walker. The stratagem failed in this case—the university defended the right of the professor to speak his mind, as well as the propriety of his conduct—but there are likely to be other such attempts, and it is worth asking what the politicians thought they stood to gain. Evidently, they believed that their request might uncover in Cronon's mail (1) political judgments or opinions of some sort or (2) discussion of matters unrelated to his academic work. These assumptions were easy to make, since (1) Cronon has the reputation of being an activist on environmental issues, and (2) many academics, like many professional people, owners of small businesses, and political party operatives have been known to use workplace e-mails for unofficial business. But note the additional assumption: that the forming of judgments or opinions on public affairs could never in any honorable way be related to the professional calling of an American historian. It is a paralyzing idea when you think about it. Yet this was a view the political grievance collectors for the moment shared with defenders of the expert-licensing version of academic freedom.

There is such a thing as angry knowledge. If academic freedom has ever meant anything, it has meant to guard against political persecution for the dissemination of such knowledge. Political pressures may operate, of course, to discourage and weaken the exercise of freedom of speech in any setting, but my argument has been that those pressures are increased and given legalistic shelter by a definition of academic freedom that renders it purer than mere freedom and at the same time helplessly vulnerable to abuse. On the licensing argument, a dissident like Neve Gordon, because he is a professor, actually has less freedom than a member of the security industry or a worker on a farm or a police officer. All of those people can speak as citizens. Whereas, when a professor speaks, the automatic aura of expertise is taken to confer an ulterior authority on his or her views. The disciplinary limits on academic freedom suffice to turn anything the professor says about politics into a demagogic disguise; and by means of that reversal, the defenders of academic freedom become the keenest inquisitors on behalf of its restriction. We should not want to breathe the air of this theological paradox. Certification of expertise in the disciplines, as in the professions, is good for the purpose it was invented to serve, the declaration of a desired competence, but it was never meant to limit or disqualify the work the mind may perform in the world. The way to uphold the principle of academic freedom is simply to treat it as part of the ordinary freedom that is the birthright of citizens in a democracy.

NOTES

1. This essay was first published in *Raritan* (Winter 2012).
2. D. H. Lawrence, *Study of Thomas Hardy and Other Essays* (Cambridge: Cambridge University Press, 1985), 101.
3. Edmund Burke, *Edmund Burke: Selected Writings and Speeches* (Washington, D.C.: Regnery, 1963), 474.
4. Wilson Smith and Thomas Bender, *American Higher Education Transformed 1940–2005: Documenting the National Discourse* (Baltimore: Johns Hopkins University Press, 2008), 455.

4

ACADEMIC FREEDOM UNDER FIRE

JONATHAN R. COLE

TODAY, A HALF century after the 1954 House Un-American Activities Committee held congressional hearings on Communists in American universities, faculty members are witnessing once again a rising tide of anti-intellectualism and threats to academic freedom.[1] They are increasingly apprehensive about the influence of external politics on university decision making. The attacks on professors like Joseph Massad, Thomas Butler, Rashid Khalidi, Ward Churchill, and Edward Said, coupled with other actions taken by the federal government in the name of national security, suggest that we may well be headed for another era of intolerance and repression.

The United States paid a heavy price when the leaders of its research universities failed in the 1950s to defend the leader of the Manhattan Project J. Robert Oppenheimer; the double Nobel Prize–winning chemist Linus Pauling; and the China expert Owen Lattimore. But a wave of repression in American universities today is apt to have even more dramatic consequences for the nation than the repression of the Cold War.

Compared with today, universities during the McCarthy period were relatively small institutions that were not much dependent on government contracts and grants. In the early 1950s, Columbia University's annual budget was substantially less than $50 million. Its annual budget is now roughly $3.5 billion, and more than a quarter of this comes from the federal government, leaving research universities like it ever more vulnerable to political manipulation and control.

Universities today are also more deeply embedded in the broader society than ever before. They are linked to industry, business, and government in multiple ways. Their links to the larger society inevitably lead to public criticism of the university when faculty members or students express ideas or behave in ways that some in the public find repugnant.

Can the leaders and the tenured faculty of our great research universities rise to the challenge of rebutting such criticism? Can we do better at defending academic freedom than our predecessors did in the 1950s?

To do so, we must convince the public that a failure to defend dissenting voices on the campus places at risk the greatest engine for the creation of new ideas and scientific innovation the world has ever known. We must explain that one can never know the true worth of an idea unless one is free to examine it. We must explain that such freedom of inquiry is a key to innovation and progress over the long term in the sciences as well as the humanities. Above all, we must show that a threat to academic freedom poses a threat as well to the welfare and prosperity of the nation.

The preeminence of American universities is an established fact. It was recently reaffirmed in a 2004 study conducted in China at Shanghai Jiao Tong University that evaluated five hundred of the world's universities. The United States has 80 percent of the world's twenty most distinguished research universities and about 70 percent of the top fifty. We lead the world in the production of new knowledge and its transmission to undergraduate, doctoral, and postdoctoral students. Since the 1930s, the United States has dominated the receipt of Nobel Prizes, capturing roughly 60 percent of these awards.

Our universities are the envy of the world, in part because the systems of higher education in many other countries—China is a good example—do not allow their faculty and students the extensive freedom of inquiry that is the hallmark of the American system. As a consequence, our universities attract students from all over the world who either remain in this country as highly skilled members of our society or return home to become leaders in their own countries and ambassadors for the United States. The advanced graduates of the American research university populate the world's great industrial laboratories, its high-tech incubator companies, and its leading professions. Many of the emerging industries on which the nation depends to create new jobs and maintain its leading role in the world economy grow out of discoveries made at the American research university.[2] The laser, the MRI, the algorithm for

Google searches, the global positioning system, the fundamental discoveries leading to biotechnology, the emerging uses of nanoscience, the methods of surveying public opinion, even Viagra—all these discoveries and thousands of other inventions and medical miracles were created by scholars working in the American research university.

Unfortunately, most leaders of higher education have done a poor job of educating the public about the essential values of the American research university. They have also failed to make the case for the research university as the incubator of new ideas and discoveries. As a consequence, when a professor comes under attack for the content of his or her ideas, the public has little understanding of why the leader of a research university, if he or she is to uphold the core principle of academic freedom, must come to the professor's defense.

Attacks on academics follow a clear pattern: A professor is singled out for criticism. This is followed by media coverage that carries the allegations to larger audiences. The coverage is often cursory and sometimes distorted. Some citizens conclude that the university harbors extremists who subvert our national ideals. Pressed by irate constituents, political leaders and alumni demand that the university sanction or fire the professor. This is an all too familiar story in our nation's history.

The recent attack on Professor Joseph Massad of Columbia University offers a perfect example of how this process unfolds. The drama began with a group called the David Project, which was launched in 2002 "in response to the growing ideological assault on Israel." The project subsequently produced a one-sided twenty-five-minute film, *Columbia Unbecoming*, in which former students accused Professor Massad of inappropriate behavior in his elective course, Palestinian and Israeli Politics and Societies. One former student alleged on camera that Massad used "racial stereotypes" and "intimidation tactics . . . in order to push a distinct ideological line on the curriculum"; another asserted that Massad had crossed the line "between vigorous debate and discussion, and hate."[3]

The David Project distributed this film to the media, and one-sided stories soon began to appear in conservative publications such as the *New York Sun*. This triggered follow-up stories in *The New York Times*; *The Chronicle of Higher Education*; and other local, national, and international news outlets. One, appearing in the November 21, 2004, Sunday edition of the *New York Daily News*, bore the headline HATE 101.

Not every story about Massad was this crude. A correspondent for *The Jewish Week*, for example, interviewed an Israeli student at Columbia who strongly defended Massad. "The class was an incredible experience," this student reported. "It wasn't fun to be the only Israeli in class, but I never felt intimidated. Passionate, emotional, but not intimidated."

Unfortunately, these nuanced accounts could not compete with strident headlines about hate. At one point, Congressman Anthony D. Weiner, a New York Democrat, asked Columbia's President Lee Bollinger to fire the untenured Professor Massad as a way of demonstrating Columbia's commitment to tolerance. The irony was seemingly lost on Mr. Weiner, who had the audacity to write, "By publicly rebuking anti-Semitic events on campus and terminating Professor Massad, Columbia would make a brave statement in support of tolerance and academic freedom."

Weiner's Orwellian ploy of calling intolerance "tolerance" must be seen in a broader context. There is a growing effort to pressure universities to monitor classroom discussion, create speech codes, and more generally, enable disgruntled students to savage professors who express ideas they find disagreeable. There is an effort to transmogrify speech that some people find offensive into a type of action that is punishable.

There is of course no place in the American research university classroom for physical intimidation, physical assault, or violations of the personal space of students. There is no place for faculty members to use their positions of authority to coerce and cow students into conforming to their own point of view. No university will protect a professor's use of a string of epithets directed toward a particular student in a gratuitous manner that is unrelated to the substance of the course. There are workplace rules in place at universities that govern and control such forms of behavior. And there must be, by law, mechanisms for students or others at the university to lodge complaints against professors who violate these rules. This basic commitment to civility and professional responsibility is part of the code of conduct at Columbia and at every other major American research university.[4]

But the codes that place limits on conduct must never be directed at the content of ideas—however offensive they may be to students, faculty, alumni, benefactors, or politicians.

Critics of the university, such as those affiliated with the David Project, tend to blur the distinction between speech and action. They accuse professors of inappropriate action and intimidation when they are actually trying to attack the content of the professors' ideas. They also tend to expropriate key terms in the liberal lexicon, as if they were the only true champions of freedom and diversity on college campuses.

Consider Students for Academic Freedom (SAF), an organization launched by veteran conservative activists. The group's very name implies a commitment to a core liberal value, just as the group's tactics promise to empower aggrieved students. Currently, the SAF is encouraging students nationwide to organize and lobby university leaders, alumni, and members of state legislatures to adopt a "student bill of rights."

But SAF's language and tactics are misleading. Under the banner of seeking balance and diversity in the classroom, these students are trying to limit discussion of ideas with which they disagree. They want students to become judges, if not final arbiters, of faculty competence. They have supported the campaign against Massad at Columbia and have urged students to report "unfair grading, one-sided lectures, and stacked reading lists" as abuses of student rights.

While I was provost at Columbia there were many efforts by outside groups to influence university policy and to silence specific members of the faculty. Repeated efforts were made to defame and discredit the renowned literary critic and Palestinian advocate Edward Said. External groups tried, but failed, to have Columbia deny an appointment to an eminent Middle East historian, Rashid Khalidi. Sixty-two members of Congress wrote to Columbia calling on us to fire Nicholas De Genova, a professor of anthropology, after he made inflammatory remarks at an antiwar teach-in prior to the most recent Iraq War—even though his remarks were immediately criticized at the same teach-in by other Columbia faculty members.

Even when nobody loses his or her job, these assaults take a toll. As Professor Massad explains on his website, "With this campaign against me going into its fourth year, I chose under the duress of coercion and intimidation not to teach my course [Palestinian and Israeli Politics and Societies] this year."

Most of the recent attacks on university professors have been leveled against social scientists and humanists. Many critics of the university seem to believe that sanctioning one group of professors will have no effect on those in other disciplines. This is dangerously naive, both in principle and in practice.

The stakes are high. The destruction of university systems has historically been caused by the imposition of external political ideology on the conduct of scholarly and scientific research. Defense of faculty members in the humanities and social sciences from external political pressure protects all members of the university community.

History suggests that the natural sciences, too, can be infected by political pressures to conform to ideological beliefs. German universities still have not recovered from the catastrophe of 1933, when Hitler began to dismantle German science and technology by purging those researchers who did "Jewish science." Japanese universities were damaged immeasurably in the 1930s by the purging of dissident intellectuals. Soviet biology never fully recovered from the imposition of Lysenkoism into the biological sciences.

Today, political pressure to include "creationism" and theories of "intelligent design" as alternatives to Darwinian evolution in the secondary school science curriculum has already led to a purging of Darwin's theory from the science curriculum in at least thirteen states. The National Academy of Sciences and the Union of Concerned Scientists have catalogued many examples of the George W. Bush administration's interference with research and education. Consider just a few examples: Foreign students and scholars from "suspect" nations are harassed and even denied entry into the United States without a scintilla of evidence that they are security risks. American professors are prevented from working with gifted foreign scientists and students. Open scholarly communication is impeded by policies designed to isolate nations supporting terrorism; library and computer records are searched; political litmus tests are used by the Bush administration to decide who will serve on scientific advisory committees; and scientific reports whose content is inconsistent with the Bush administration's ideology have been altered. Even though the National Institutes of Health supported the research, some members of Congress almost succeeded in rescinding funding for projects on HIV/AIDS. Another recent bill, House Resolution 3077, almost succeeded in mandating direct government oversight of university "area studies" programs (the bill passed the House but died in the Senate).

These attacks should be related to still other threats to scientific inquiry. The USA PATRIOT Act and the Bioterrorism Defense Act have, for example, led to the criminal prosecution of Dr. Thomas Butler, one of the nation's leading experts on plague bacteria. Butler faced a fifteen-count indictment for violating the Patriot Act's provision requiring reporting on the use and transport of specific biological agents and toxins that in principle could be used by bioterrorists. Butler was acquitted of all charges related to the Patriot Act, except for a minor one—his failure to obtain a transport permit for moving the bacteria from Tanzania to his Texas laboratory, as he had done for the past twenty years. However, while investigating Butler's work with plague bacteria, the FBI combed over everything in his lab at Texas Tech University, reviewed all of his accounts, and added on fifty-four counts of tax evasion, theft, and fraud unrelated to the Patriot Act. His conviction was based on the add-on counts. The upshot of all of this was that he lost his medical license, was fired from his job, and now, if he loses his appeal, faces up to nine years in jail.

In another case, Attorney General John Ashcroft publicly targeted Dr. Steven J. Hatfill of Louisiana State University as "a person of interest" in the anthrax scare that followed 9/11. Although Hatfill has never been charged with any crime, LSU fired him because of the accusation and intervention of the Justice Department. Other faculty members at other institutions have suffered through unannounced and intimidating visits from the FBI to their homes or campus offices.

These crude efforts to enforce the Patriot Act have already had some serious consequences. Robert C. Richardson, whose work on liquid helium earned him a Nobel Prize in Physics, has described the atrophy of bioterrorism research at Cornell:

> The Patriot Act, which was passed after 9/11, has a section in it to control who can work on "select agents," pathogens that might be developed as bioweapons. At Cornell [before 9/11], we had something like 76 faculty members who had projects on lethal pathogens and something like 38 working specifically on select agents. There were stringent regulations for control of the pathogens — certain categories of foreign nationals who were not allowed to handle them, be in a room with them or even be aware of research results. So what is the situation now? We went from 38 people who could work on select agents to 2. We've got a lot less people working on interventions to vaccinate against smallpox, West Nile virus, anthrax and any of 30 other scourges.[5]

Is our national security enhanced when the government turns our best immunology and biodefense laboratories into ghost towns?

In an atmosphere of growing fear and intimidation, we would be wise not to dismiss these attacks on the American research university as mere aberrations. Indeed, universities are fragile institutions, and they have historically caved in to external political pressure at key moments — as they did during the Red Scares that followed the two world wars.[6]

Periodically, often during times of national fear, political leaders and ideologues on the Right and the Left have silenced dissent and pressured universities to abandon their most fundamental values of free and open inquiry. Most university leaders and faculty members fell easily into line during the first Red Scare of 1919–1921 and during the reign of Joseph McCarthy. As historians Ellen Schrecker and Sigmund Diamond have shown, presidents and trustees of research universities often publicly espoused civil liberties, academic freedom, and free inquiry while privately collaborating with the FBI to purge faculty members accused of holding seditious political views.[7]

Some university leaders underestimated the gravity of the threat and bowed to wealthy benefactors who threatened to withdraw their support. Others dismissed professors out of fear of bad publicity. Still others supported these purges because they believed in them. For example, Cornell's president E. E. Day maintained that "a man who belongs to the Communist Party and who follows the party line is thereby disqualified from participating in a free, honest inquiry after truth, and from belonging on a university faculty devoted to the search for truth." Yale's President Charles Seymour proclaimed, "There will be no witch hunts at Yale because there will be no witches. We do not intend to hire Communists."

Robert Maynard Hutchins, chancellor of the University of Chicago, was one of the few great heroes during those perilous times. In 1949, testifying before a state commission investigating Communists on campus, he boldly argued for tolerance:

> The danger to our institutions is not from the tiny minority who do not believe in them. It is from those who would mistakenly repress the free spirit upon which those institutions are built. . . . The policy of repression of ideas cannot work and has never worked. The alternative is the long, difficult road of education.

On another occasion, Hutchins observed that the problem with witch hunts was "not how many professors would be fired for their beliefs, but how many think they might be. The entire teaching profession is intimidated."

Hutchins's boss, Laird Bell, chairman of the University of Chicago's board of trustees, was equally outspoken: "To be great," he declared, "a university must adhere to principle. It cannot shift with the winds of passing public opinion. . . . It must rely for its support upon a relatively small number of people who understand the important contributions it makes to the welfare of the community and the improvement of mankind: upon those who understand that academic freedom is important not because of its benefits to professors but because of its benefits to all of us."

What, then, are the defining principles that guide the work of the university? As scholars and scientists, we place a premium on openness, rigor, fairness, originality, and skepticism. We are part of an international community of scholars and scientists whose ideas transcend international borders. We collaborate and exchange ideas with Iraqis, Russians, Iranians, Chinese, and Israelis without considering politics or nationality. We hold that members of our community must always be free to dissent—to pursue and express new and even radical ideas in an environment of unfettered freedom.

By the same token, proponents of new ideas and their critics must be free to disagree. And this is especially true in the classroom, in which faculty and students must be free to explore and develop their ideas in robust and uninhibited debate. By encouraging independent thinking, no matter how preposterous or outrageous, the university promotes trust, creativity, collaboration, and innovation.

The goal is to establish an environment in which it is possible for the inquisitive mind to flourish. In contrast to private enterprise, the university places the welfare of the community above individual gain. The coin of the academic realm is the recognition that professors and students receive based on the quality of their contributions to the creation, transmission, and understanding of knowledge. The university is a meritocracy. Ideally, quality of mind expressed through teaching, research, and learning is rewarded without regard to race, religion, nationality, or gender.

This does not mean, of course, that real merit is always rewarded: like any complex institution, the modern university does not always function as it is meant to. But it is simply ridiculous to perpetuate the myth that research universities are rogue institutions that operate in an uncontrolled environment.

Most of them are probably more accountable for their products and for their financial transactions than most large American corporations.[8]

Universities are evaluating themselves from dawn to dusk. State and regional accrediting agencies are continually reviewing the academic quality of university programs and faculties. Federal funding agencies conduct extensive peer reviews of grant applications that evaluate the quality of applicants' prior work, the quality of the proposals submitted, and the potential value of the work when completed; they use site visits to review elaborate proposals before funding large centers or university institutes. Obsessed with knowledge about their reputation and quality, research universities use ad hoc or standing committees of experts to evaluate the quality of the curriculum, the quality of the faculty, and the quality of departments and schools. The scientific and scholarly papers and monographs of faculty members are peer reviewed before they are accepted for publication and are assessed in terms of the potential impact of this work on the field. The results of course evaluations by undergraduate and graduate students are part of the "teaching portfolios" that are used in deciding on the promotion and tenure of junior faculty members. Finally, there is accountability for personal conduct: students and colleagues can file grievances of discrimination with deans, department chairs, ombuds officers, the university senate, and the Equal Employment Opportunity Commission, among other outlets for claims of inappropriate behavior.

The governing role played by peers makes universities different from most other American institutions. The research university was founded on the idea that the professors should regulate their own affairs. This aspiration has never been fully realized. But it is plainly evident in the tradition that those who oversee the core academic work of the university—the president, the provost, the deans, and the department chairs—are themselves distinguished scholars and teachers who are respected members of the faculty. Moreover, university leaders govern by persuasive and delegated authority, not by the exercise of power.

Another essential feature of the American research university is that no one speaks "for" the university—not even its official leaders. While the president and the provost and the board of trustees have the responsibility and the authority to formulate and carry out university policies, the essence of a university lies in its multiplicity of voices: those of its faculty, its students, its researchers, its staff. Presidents and provosts are often asked questions of the following kind: "What is the university's position on the writings, or remarks, or actions of Professor X?"

In fact, there is no "university position" on such matters. The university does not decide which ideas are good and bad, which are right and wrong. That is up for constant debate, deliberation, and discourse among the faculty and students. For the university to take such positions would stifle academic freedom and alienate those whose views differ from those of the institution's leaders. The responsibility of these leaders is not to decide whose ideas are best, but to create an environment in which all ideas may be explored and tested.

First and foremost, the American research university is designed to be unsettling. Was this not Socrates's purpose as well? Because it is committed to the creation of new knowledge and the intellectual growth of its students, the university must nurture the expression of novel and sometimes startling ideas and opinions. Lionel Trilling, the preeminent literary critic, wrote in *Beyond Culture* about the contentious nature of the literature sometimes taught at the university: "Any historian of literature of the modern age will take virtually for granted the adversary intention, the actual subversive intention, that characterizes modern writing—he will perceive its clear purpose of detaching the reader from habits of thought and feeling that the larger culture imposes, of giving him a ground and a vantage point from which to judge and condemn, and perhaps revise, the culture that has produced him." Whether in 1965, when this was published and Trilling taught at Columbia, or today, the mission of the American research university is to encourage faculty and students to challenge prevailing values, policies, beliefs, and institutions. That is why the university will always have—and must welcome—dissenting voices and radical critics.

Researchers at America's universities do not generally investigate questions for which there are "right" or ready answers—answers at the back of a book. The goal of academic discourse is not merely to convey information, but to provoke, to stimulate ideas, and to teach students to think and provide them with the intellectual and analytical tools that will enable them to think well. Great teachers challenge their students' and colleagues' biases and presuppositions. They present unsettling ideas and dare others to rebut them and to defend their own beliefs in a coherent and principled manner. The American research university pushes and pulls at the walls of orthodoxy and rejects politically correct thinking. In this process, students and professors may sometimes feel intimidated, overwhelmed, and confused. But it is by working through this process that they learn to think better and more clearly for themselves.

Unsettling by nature, the university culture is also highly conservative. It demands evidence before accepting novel challenges to existing theories and methods. The university ought to be viewed in terms of a fundamental interdependence between the liberality of its intellectual life and the conservatism of its methodological demands. Because the university encourages discussion of even the most radical ideas, it must set its standards at a high level. We permit almost any idea to be put forward—but only because we demand arguments and evidence to back up the ideas we debate and because we set the bar of proof at such a high level.

These two components—tolerance for unsettling ideas and insistence on rigorous skepticism about all ideas—create an essential tension at the heart of the American research university. It will not thrive without both components operating effectively and simultaneously.

Here we must acknowledge an area in which the university today faces a real and difficult problem with the mechanisms it uses to evaluate the work of its scholars. For the threats to free inquiry do not come only from government policies, from local or national politicians, from external lobbying groups, or from lazy journalism. Some of the most subtle threats come from within the academy itself.

For example, an unspoken but widespread aversion to airing topics that are politically sensitive in various fields sometimes limits debates that ought to take place. The growth of knowledge is greatly inhibited when methodological thresholds for evidence are relaxed, and claims to truth are advanced on the basis of shoddy evidence or on the basis of supposedly possessing privileged insight simply as a result of one's race, gender, religion, or ethnicity.

Most scholars and scientists at leading universities would more than likely exercise their right to remain silent before placing on the table for debate any number of controversial ideas: for example, the idea that differences in educational performance between different racial groups are not a result of discrimination; that occupational differentiation by gender may be a good thing; that dietary cholesterol above and beyond genetic predispositions has only a minimal effect on coronary heart deaths; that the children of crack cocaine mothers will nevertheless experience normal cognitive development; or until recently, that prions, as well as bacteria or viruses, can cause disease.

I have suggested that we entertain radical and even offensive ideas at universities because we simultaneously embrace rigorous standards in determining the adequacy of truth claims. But if scholarly skepticism is sometimes compromised by a lack of courage or an intolerance for competing points of view, then the primary mechanisms by which universities ensure the quality of research will not always reliably function. To complicate matters, different disciplines have evolved somewhat differently in institutionalizing mechanisms to ensure that rigorous standards exist to evaluate ideas and the results of research.

Biologists may broadly agree that advocates of creationism are simply in error and that the theory they defend is unworthy of serious scientific debate, while social scientists are more likely, for example, to disagree about the scholarly merits of theories that stress the influence of socialization rather than innate abilities on individual achievement. As new areas of research and inquiry appear in the modern university and begin to dominate their disciplines, the definition of acceptable research questions may well change, as may definitions of what is acceptable methodology, acceptable evidence, acceptable standards of proof, and also acceptable peer reviewers (who in turn will judge whether a given scholar's methodology and use of evidence is acceptable). As a statistician might put it, whoever owns the "null hypothesis" often determines what is taken for fact.

When skepticism falters or fails, does the academic community, even in the longer run for which it is built, have the mechanisms to correct its errors?

This has to be an open question. Currently, there is broader agreement about the appropriate corrective mechanisms in the natural sciences than in the humanities and social sciences, although in periods of what Thomas Kuhn called revolutionary rather than normal science, we often also find sharp disagreements within natural science over standards of proof and truth claims. It is the very possibility of ongoing disagreement, however, that is a primary justification for protecting and promoting freedom of thought. John Stuart Mill put it this way:

> Truth, in the great practical concerns of life, is so much a question of the rec-onciling and combining of opposites, that very few have minds sufficiently capa-cious and impartial to make adjustment with an approach to correctness, and it has to be made by the rough process of a struggle between combatants fighting under hostile banners.[9]

Moreover, as Mill well knew, it is more important to tolerate an occasional error in the current appraisal of conflicting ideas than to risk compromis-ing free expression. For in the long run, it is unfettered freedom of inquiry that ensures innovation, intellectual progress, and the continued growth of knowledge.

I have defended the right of academic freedom within the community of scholars. But what, if any, right to freedom of expression does a student have as against his or her professor? The rise of groups like SAF raises this important question.

Students clearly have the right—indeed, the obligation—to enter the general debate within the university community. They have the right to express their ideas forcefully in the classroom and to argue against their professors' views. I have made the point that professors in the classroom must never discriminate against students on the basis of their ascribed characteristics—who they are in terms of their race, ethnicity, religion, or gender.

At the same time, there is a clear differentiation of roles between professors and students. We expect professors, not students, to offer their own best judgment on competing truth claims. A student may argue for creationism or intelligent design; but that does not oblige his or her biology professor to take his or her views seriously as a rival to the evolutionary accounts favored by virtually all contemporary biologists. Similarly, a professor of Jewish history is under no obligation to take seriously the arguments of a student who denies the Holocaust.

What, then, about a student who says he or she is being discriminated against by Professor Massad of Columbia, because Massad declares the student's position on the 1982 Shatila massacres in Lebanon to be factually erroneous. Is that student therefore entitled to level formal charges against Massad?

If we are going to allow the biology professor and the Jewish historian a right to offer their best judgment on competing truth claims, and because of those judgments to take some students more seriously than others, then do we not also have to grant this right to Joseph Massad?

In any case, we should remember that the proper goal of higher education is enlightenment—not some abstract ideal of "balance." Indeed, those who demand balance on some issues never demand it on others. The University of Chicago's school of economics is admired widely for its accomplishments. Must Chicago seek balance by forcing its economics department to hire scholars with contrasting points of view?

Occasionally, students have to do the hard work of seeking alternative points of view across institutional boundaries. They cannot always expect "balance" to be delivered in neat packages. It is the professor's pedagogical role that grants him or her the authority and the right to judge what are the scientific theories or historical facts presented in the classroom. We cannot deny the asymmetry in these roles. If we do, we fail to understand a legitimate goal of higher education: to impart knowledge to those who lack it. Of course, one can question the competence of a professor—that happens routinely in a good university. But the evaluation of that competence must be, and is, left to the professor's peers—not to students, and surely not to trustees, regents, congressional representatives, advocacy groups, or members of the press.

Over the past seventy-five years, the Supreme Court has expanded greatly the protection of free speech. Today, prevailing First Amendment doctrine holds that the government cannot restrict speech because of its content and that only forms of "low value" speech, such as "fighting words," libel, commercial advertising, or obscenity, can be regulated. Universities cannot act outside the law, but they can—and should—try to expand still further the limits placed on free expression, when those constraints hamper inquiry and debate.[10]

Expression in the classroom requires virtually absolute protection. Absent such protection, professors will hesitate to discuss sensitive topics out of fear of retribution, suspension, dismissal, or litigation.

The university cannot and should not attempt to decide what ideas or perspectives are appropriate for the classroom. For one student, a professor's ideas may represent repugnant stereotypes or efforts at intimidation; for another, the same ideas may represent profound challenges to ostensibly settled issues. For example, a professor's discussion of our culture's bias against female circumcision may seem to one student an affront to what is self-evidently a basic human right; but to another student, it may seem a provocative illustration of cultural imperialism, raising serious moral questions that ought to be put on the table for debate. Are we to take seriously those who would have us sanction the professor for raising this subject in a seminar? And if we did, who would be cast in the role of the "Grand Inquisitor"?

The broadest possible protection of freedom of expression is of a piece with another important aspect of the academy. We have understood for some time now that the university is not a place where we exclusively house or train the kind of scientist or scholar who advises the prince—those who currently control the government. There are members of the faculty who sometimes voluntarily give advice to the prince—and there may even be academic programs (such as Russian studies during the Cold War) that exist in part to inform government policy—but it is not the point or the rationale of universities to furnish such advice, nor to have the thematic pursuits of inquiry in the university shaped by the interests of the prince. That is why universities will often find in their midst those who air the most radical critiques of the prince and his interests. Were we to silence or even to inhibit such people, we would not only be undermining free inquiry, we would also gradually reinforce the countervailing power of conformism.

Despite the commitment of the American research university to freedom of thought, the natural tendency of professors and students, as we have seen, is to avoid expressing views that may offend others. But the responsibility of the university is to combat this tendency and to encourage, rather than squelch, freewheeling inquiry. The university must do everything it can to combat the coercive demand for political litmus tests from the Right and the Left and the pressure to conform with established academic paradigms.

By affording virtually absolute protection to classroom debate, the university under fire encourages the sort of open inquiry for which universities exist. Those members of the university community who are willing to take on prevailing beliefs and ideologies—be they the pieties of the academic Left or the marching orders of the politicians currently in power—need to know that the university will defend them unconditionally if they are attacked for the content of their ideas.

The defense of academic freedom is never easy.

It is understandable that university leaders will react to outside attacks with caution. There is always a risk that taking a public position on a controversial matter may alienate potential donors or offend one of the modern university's many and varied constituencies. In response to negative publicity, it is entirely natural for presidents and provosts—and for trustees and regents—to work feverishly "to get this incident behind us" and to reach for an accommodation that calms the critics and makes the problem go away.

However, to act on such understandable impulses would be a grievous mistake. There are few matters on which universities must stand on absolute principle. Academic freedom is one of them. If we fail to defend this core value, then we jeopardize the global preeminence of our universities in the production and transmission of new knowledge in the sciences, in the arts, indeed in every field of inquiry. Whenever academic freedom is under fire, we must rise to its defense with courage—and without compromise.

For freedom of inquiry is our reason for being.

NOTES

1. Many colleagues have provided useful comments on earlier drafts of this essay. I received particularly helpful comments from Akeel Bilgrami, David Cohen, Joanna L. Cole, Susanna Cole, Tom Goldstein, Eric Foner, James Miller, Richard Shweder, and Geoffrey Stone.
2. The role of industry is, of course, critical as well, but most of the great industrial laboratories are highly dependent on these same research universities for PhDs who join these companies. So universities have both a direct and an indirect influence on the production of innovation.
3. The film has been shown in at least four or five different versions; its content is continually changing.
4. "Academic freedom implies that all officers of instruction are entitled to freedom in the classroom in discussing their subjects: that they are entitled to freedom in research and in the publication of its results; and that they may not be penalized by the University for expression of opinion or associations in their private civic capacity; but they should bear in mind the special obligations arising from their position in the academic community." *The Faculty Handbook* (New York: Columbia University, 2000), 184.
5. Quoted in Claudia Dreifus, "The Chilling of American Science: A Conversation with Robert C. Richardson," *New York Times*, July 6, 2004, D2.
6. For an exceptionally fine discussion of these failures, see Geoffrey Stone, *Perilous Times: Free Speech in Wartime from the Sedition Act of 1798 to the War on Terrorism* (New York: Norton, 2004).
7. Reviewing the now available archival material at Harvard University, Robert N. Bellah has confirmed the accounts of Diamond and Schrecker. Bellah reports his findings in "McCarthyism at Harvard," letter to the editor, *New York Review of Books*, February 10, 2005, 42–43. *Daedalus* (Spring 2005).
8. I am not focusing here on financial accountability. In fact, universities have many ways of reviewing and accounting for their financial transactions. Fund accounting at universities allows auditors to review every research grant or contract in minute detail. Full-time federal auditors are fixtures at universities. Major accounting firms audit the books of the universities on an annual basis. Bonds floated by universities to finance construction projects are brought to market only after bond-rating agencies evaluate the creditworthiness of the university and rate the bonds. The ratings depend almost as much on qualitative factors of the quality of university schools and departments as on financial ratios and other indicators.
9. John Stuart Mill, *On Liberty* (Cambridge: Cambridge University Press, 1989), 49.
10. Here I am putting aside the distinction between public and private universities.

5

KNOWLEDGE, POWER, AND ACADEMIC FREEDOM

JOAN W. SCOTT

ALTHOUGH THE TERM academic freedom has come to seem self-evident—so often is it invoked to condemn egregious violations of the perceived rights of members of university communities—in fact, it is a complicated idea with limited application. In its origins in the United States at the turn of the last century, it pertained only to faculty—to those who produced and transmitted the knowledge necessary for the advancement of the common good. And not necessarily to tenured faculty, since the practice was virtually unknown then. Academic freedom was aimed at resolving conflicts about the relationship between power and knowledge, politics and truth, action and thought by positing a sharp distinction between them, a distinction that has been difficult to maintain. Rather than offer a pat definition, I want to look at some of the tensions that bedevil the concept of academic freedom, both as a theory of faculty rights and as a practice that can defend them.

THE BUSINESS OF THE UNIVERSITY

The American version of the doctrine of academic freedom, codified in the "1915 Declaration of Principles on Academic Freedom and Academic Tenure" of the American Association of University Professors (AAUP), was formulated during the Progressive era at a crucial moment in the history of higher education, one which saw the coming into prominence of the research university (AAUP 1915). The idea of academic freedom was premised not only on a sharp distinction between religious and secular institutions but also on the autonomy of the faculty of the new research university from the very forces that supported it: state legislatures and/or philanthropic businessmen. If the tension between what John Dewey referred to as sectarian discipleship and intellectual discipline seemed relatively easy to resolve (by the time of the AAUP's "Declaration," colleges were no longer exclusively training grounds for the ministry), the antagonism between corporate America and the American university persists to this day. As early as 1902 (in an essay called "Academic Freedom"), Dewey warned of the erosion of the educational mission by the need to curry favor with funders: "The great event in the history of an institution is now likely to be a big gift rather than a new investigation or the development of a strong and vigorous teacher" (Dewey [1902] 1976, 62–63). Dewey was not alone in his worry about the effects of money on the production of knowledge. Thorstein Veblen's trenchant critique of the business methods of universities, *The Higher Learning in America*, was published in 1916, followed in 1923, by Upton Sinclair's denunciation of the close ties between corporate America and universities, *The Goose-Step: A Study in American Education*. The passion and polemical tone of these books attest to the intensity of the conflict as it was felt in those years. These authors were responding to pressure from financial backers such as Clarence Birdseye, a lawyer and the father of the future frozen food magnate, who in 1907 compared "college standards" unfavorably with "business principles." He urged faculty and administrators to imitate "a good manufacturer" and alumni to "help introduce business methods into the work of your alma mater." Andrew Carnegie had no use for humanistic training, arguing that it was "fatal" to "the future captain of industry." And Frederick Winslow Taylor offered models of corporate efficiency for the reorganization of university life (Donoghue 2008, 4–5, 7–8, 1–23). Businessmen and politicians, then as now, have had little patience with the ideal of learning for its own sake and even less respect for faculty who often espouse ideas at odds with their views of the purpose and value of higher education. Today the sums may be larger and their impact on university research operations greater, but the pressure to bring universities in line with corporate styles of accounting and management persists.

The principle of academic freedom articulated a vision of the university that was at once immune to these powerful interests and that promised to serve them, however indirectly, by producing new knowledge for the common good. Indeed, academic freedom rested on the assumption that knowledge and power were separable; the pursuit of truth ought to have nothing to do with public conflicts of interest, even if new knowledge could weigh in on one side or another of one of those conflicts. The university was defined as "an inviolable refuge from [the] tyranny [of public opinion]. . . . An intellectual experiment station, where new ideas may germinate and where their fruit, though distasteful to the community as a whole, may be allowed to ripen . . . " (AAUP 1915, 32). Scientific and social progress depended on the nonconformity protected, indeed fostered, by the university. The "well-being" of the place came from its ability to support critical thinkers, those who would challenge prevailing orthodoxy and stir students to think differently, to become "more self-critical," hence more likely to bring about change.

The AAUP "Declaration" cited a university president who had eloquently stated this view: "Certain professors have been refused reëlection lately, apparently because they set their students to thinking in ways objectionable to the trustees. It would be well if more teachers were dismissed because they fail to stimulate thinking of any kind." The professor, he continued, ought to be "a contagious center of intellectual enthusiasm." "It is better for students to think about heresies than not to think at all; better for them to climb new trails and stumble over error if need be, than to ride forever in upholstered ease on the overcrowded highway" (AAUP 1915, 36). The university's function was to offer shelter to these intrepid explorers, to protect them from the cold winds of disapproval that inevitably greeted dissenting ideas.

The faculty considered to be at greatest risk were those in the emerging social sciences and humanities disciplines. In his 1902 essay, Dewey suggested that these areas most needed the protections of academic freedom:

> The sphere of ideas which has not yet come under recognized scientific control is, moreover, precisely that which is bound up most closely with deep-rooted prejudice and intense emotional reaction. These, in turn, exist because of habits and modes of life to which the people have accustomed themselves. To attack them is to appear to be hostile to institutions with which the worth of life is bound up. (Dewey [1902] 1976, 58)

It was precisely because they addressed the question of the moral and social needs of society, because their studies might be disturbing and transformative, that the social sciences most needed the protection of academic freedom. Unlike the mathematical and physical sciences, which, Dewey pointed out, "have secured their independence through a certain abstractness, a certain remoteness from matters of social concern,"

> political economy, sociology, historical interpretation, psychology . . . deal face-to-face with problems of life, not problems of technical theory. Hence the right and duty of academic freedom are even greater here than elsewhere. (Dewey [1902] 1976, 57)

Academic freedom, then, formulated as it was in the heyday of Progressivism, aimed to protect those perceived to be most radical, those who were on the front lines of movements of social criticism and social reform. For them, expert knowledge necessarily had an instrumental purpose. The historian/philosopher Michel de Certeau put it this way: "The social sciences born in modern times form a set of institutions that express ethical postulates through technical operations. For a long period, these special institutions organized 'new crusades' of a technical nature to perform ethical tasks" (Certeau 1986, 199). In the early twentieth century the "crusaders" were (ironically from today's perspective) overwhelmingly in the field of economics, making readily apparent the tension between critical professorial thinking (knowledge) and business-minded trustees (power). Two examples dramatically illustrate the tension: the experiences of Edward Ross at Stanford and Scott Nearing at the University of Pennsylvania's Wharton School of Business.

Ross was secretary of the American Economic Association when he arrived at Stanford. He believed that "the aim of big business was to throttle social criticism" of the kind he and his fellow Progressives practiced, and his encounters there proved his point (Metzger 1955, 438). Stanford's founder had been a Republican and a railroad magnate, whose business relied on cheap Chinese immigrant labor. Ross quickly (and probably deliberately) incurred the wrath of the founder's widow by supporting Socialist Eugene Debs, advocating municipal ownership of utilities, calling for an end to Chinese immigration, and defending the free silver platform of the Democratic party. Mrs. Stanford wrote to the president of Stanford, David Jordan, that Ross's political associations "play into the hands of the lowest and vilest elements of socialism" and bring "tears to my eyes." Later she insisted that "Professor Ross cannot be trusted, and he should go." Jordan's attempts at negotiation and his appeals to Ross for restraint came to naught, and in 1900, he acquiesced to Mrs. Stanford's wishes by dismissing Ross. In response, seven other faculty members resigned and a group of members of the American Economic Association launched an investigation into the case, "the first professorial inquiry into an academic freedom case," according to historian Walter Metzger, "and a predecessor, if not directly the parent, of the proceedings of Committee A [the Committee on Academic Freedom and Tenure] of the AAUP" (Metzger 1955, 442–3)

More than a decade later, economist Scott Nearing was forced to leave the Wharton School, after being attacked by influential alumni. An outspoken Socialist whose work addressed the abuses of industrial capitalism, Nearing was let go in 1915 by the president and the board of trustees despite positive recommendations from his department, his chairman, and his dean. He was considered an exceptional teacher, a good administrator, and someone skilled in "the maintenance of student discipline." Although his dean conceded that he had "not been so tactful as he might be," there was no question either about the fulfillment of his duties or of his "moral worthiness" (AAUP 1916, 132). Nor was he said to be lacking in "professorial gumption"—an ambivalent comment, damning in the eyes of a trustee but praising in the opinion of colleagues and students. Nearing's removal was at least in part the result of three years of campaigning by a group of influential alumni who objected to "the bizarre and radical theories . . . advanced by enthusiastic young instructors . . . [which] are likely to have a poor effect upon Freshmen" (AAUP 1916, 135). These instructors, they went on, "seek publicity by discussion of various public topics in a manner which is likely to arouse class prejudice and fallacious conclusions" (AAUP 1916, 138). Their doctrines, moreover, were "wholly at variance with those of the founder of the Wharton School." The charges became more inflated as they focused on Nearing himself. He was said to have talked "wildly and in a manner wholly inconsistent with Mr. Wharton's well-known views," his "intemperate, persistent and astonishing expressions of untested theories, and . . . [his] unrestrained condemnations of institutions and rules which form the basis of civilized society, passed the most generous bounds of freedom of speech allowed by any institution" (AAUP 1916, 139).

Ross's case precipitated the founding of the AAUP; Nearing's was one of the first cases investigated by the fledgling organization. In neither instance did formal protest by colleagues manage to keep the professor in his job. Both cases starkly posed the problem of knowledge and power. How protect faculty from the wrath of those upon whom they necessarily depended for financial support?

The AAUP sought to answer that question in at least three ways: by defining the faculty as self-regulating, independent "appointees" (akin to judges in a federal court); by insisting on the knowledge-producing mission of the university itself; and by clarifying the role of its trustees. Since, according to the "Declaration," it is faculty who are trained to produce knowledge—whether as researchers, teachers, or technical experts—it is they who *embody* the function of the university and so warrant the protection of academic freedom.

> A university is a great and indispensable organ of the higher life of a civilized community, in the work of which the trustees hold an essential and highly honorable place, but in which the faculties hold an independent place, with quite equal responsibilities—and in relation to purely scientific and educational questions, the primary responsibility. (AAUP 1915, 27)

If the function of the university is critical thinking, it is the job of trustees to protect it. The "Declaration" compares proprietary institutions (the old model), whose purpose is "not to advance knowledge . . . but rather to subsidize the promotion of the opinions of persons, usually not of the scholar's calling, who provide the funds for their maintenance," with colleges and universities (the modern kind) "not strictly bound . . . to a propagandist duty." These latter are devoted to the public interest, to advancing the common good. They constitute a public trust and so the "trustees are trustees for the public," whether the university is supported by state funds or by private endowment (AAUP 1915, 22). The trustees' job from this perspective was all-important according to the "1915 Declaration of Principles," for it involved guaranteeing the upkeep of the university and the autonomy of the faculty—this was a matter not of exercising private proprietorship but of fulfilling a "public trust"; it was a commitment to securing the common good through the advancement of knowledge. "Trustees of . . . universities and colleges have no moral right to bind the reason or the conscience of any professor" (AAUP 1915, 23). Indeed they must use their power to insulate free inquiry from powerful interests that might corrupt it. Being "trustees for the public" does not mean directly reflecting public opinion, since it is likely to be a set of "hasty and unconsidered impulses" (AAUP 1915, 32) based on orthodoxy or ignorance. Rather it is the protection of the faculty from outside meddling that is the calling of the trustees; only in this way will knowledge be advanced and society improved. Protection means that trustees must defer to faculty on substantive matters, for they have no competence to judge them. Boards that violate this precept by "exercising an arbitrary power of dismissal" are "barbarous" since they fail to understand "the full implications of the distinction between private proprietorship and a public trust" (AAUP 1915, 24). The public trust is that of keeping the "indispensable organ" alive, providing for its physical and financial upkeep, while allowing the faculty to breathe freely so that society may progress. This was the "essential nature of a university": it was "a place dedicated to openness of mind" (AAUP 1915, 38–39). Here the AAUP founders offer a model for university governance that makes protection of academic freedom a moral, indeed almost a physical, obligation of any board of trustees.

> In all . . . domains of knowledge, the first condition of progress is complete and unlimited freedom to pursue inquiry and publish its results. Such freedom is the breath in the nostrils of all scientific activity. (AAUP 1915, 28)

The biological analogy continues with faculty's teaching function—one which reproduces not orthodoxy but the propensity for new thinking in the next generation. Students, the authors insist, must be provided not "ready-made conclusions"; they must be trained "to think for themselves" (AAUP 1915, 34). Even as the anxieties of some of the founding fathers get articulated in the "Declaration"—the need, for example, to treat with great care "immature students," who may be unready to form opinions of their own—the document returns repeatedly to the instructor's "duty" to "give to any students old enough to be in college a genuine intellectual awakening" (AAUP 1915, 35)—an awakening that depends on the student's confidence in the intellectual integrity of the teacher.[1]

> It is clear, however, that this confidence will be impaired if there is suspicion on the part of the student that the teacher is not expressing himself fully or frankly, or that college and university teachers in general are a repressed and intimidated class who dare not speak with that candor and courage which youth always demands in those whom it is to esteem. . . . There must be in the mind of the teacher no mental reservation. He must give the student the best of what he has and what he is. (AAUP 1915, 28)

Of course, the freedom being claimed for faculty entailed "correlative obligations." As researchers, teachers, and expert consultants they must be trained and credentialed according to the rules of their disciplines; without such training their "science" would have no legitimacy. But the articulation and enforcement of professional standards must be left in the hands of the professionals. "It is, in any case, unsuitable to the dignity of a great profession that the initial responsibility for the maintenance of its professional standards should not be in the hands of its own members. It follows that university teachers must be prepared to assume this responsibility for themselves" (AAUP 1915, 34).

The theory of academic freedom goes even further, insisting not only on the moral principle of nonintervention by trustees in faculty work but also on the incompetence of these people to judge the value of the work produced. Academic freedom thus demands extraordinary restraint from those used to exercising power based on judgments they themselves make and outcomes they project and pay for. So it ought not to be surprising that the principle is often ineffective in eliciting that restraint in practice. The long history of AAUP investigations as well as a number of historical studies provide ample documentation of this point (Schrecker 1986). We might say then that the theory of academic freedom as it was articulated by Progressives continues to be useful and important because it addresses, although it does not resolve, a tension at the heart of the modern university: that between corporate power and intellectual inquiry, between instrumental knowledge production and open-ended inquiry.

DISCIPLINARY POLITICS

The principle of academic freedom was not, as critics sometimes describe it, an endorsement of the idea that in the university anything goes. The call for faculty autonomy rested on the guarantee of quality provided by disciplinary bodies whose role is to establish and implement norms and standards and so to certify their members' professional competence. Disciplinary associations were depicted as uncorrupted by the play of interests that shaped the world outside the academy, even if the scholars they licensed dealt, as Dewey put it, with "face-to-face problems of life, not with problems of technical theory." Dewey wrote about "an organized society of truth-seekers," by which he meant the newly created disciplinary associations of his day, those intercollegiate bodies that set standards of inquiry and assessed the validity (the apparent scientific quality or truthfulness) of the ideas offered by their members. In return for fulfilling one's responsibilities to the discipline, one received protection from outside intervention. It was, wrote Arthur Lovejoy in the 1937 edition of the *Encyclopedia of the Social Sciences*, "qualified bodies of his own profession" that protected an individual scholar from interference by "political or ecclesiastical authority, or from the administrative officials of the institution in which he is employed" (Lovejoy 1937, 384). Glenn Morrow, in the 1968 edition of the *International Encyclopedia of the Social Sciences*, echoed his forebears:

> Even after prolonged examination and testing, the claim [to truth] can be accorded only a high degree of probability; and its status is never immune to later criticism. These conditions imply a community of scholars and scientists cooperating with one another through mutual criticism and selecting and recruiting new members through disciplined and systematic training. These very requirements tended to produce such a community, animated by a professional spirit and resentful of any attempts by incompetent outside authorities to control its activities or judge its results. (Morrow 1968, 5–6)

Indeed, disciplinary authorization was meant to defend those whose work was unavoidably controversial against charges of partisanship and from political retribution. If their colleagues attested to the soundness of their methods and the plausibility of their interpretations, these faculty could be represented not as interested parties but as objective seekers after truth.

Yet, as is well known to all of us, disciplinary communities are hierarchical with a power dynamic of their own. If the community certifies the competence of its members and protects them from external meddling, it also establishes methods of inquiry ("disciplined and systematic training"), standards of judgment ("selecting and recruiting new members"), and behavioral norms ("cooperating through mutual criticism"). Those who write the history of disciplines and those of us who have broken new ground in our fields know that discipline and disciple can be synonyms as well as antonyms and that punishment is not always the alternative to discipline, but often its regulatory tool. The devastating review, the charges of incomplete research, mockery by one's elders can bring an end to a promising academic career, especially one that engages in a critique of disciplinary premises. These are not external interventions by the incompetent into the workings of the academy; they are internal conflicts, involving not public morality or conventional social belief, but disciplinary *politics*. And, of course, even the line drawn between disciplinary politics and those of the "outside world" is not a clear one, since as Dewey and his colleagues recognized a century ago, research in the human sciences especially is often inspired by contemporary concerns with inevitable political ramifications.

Those of us historians who challenged prevailing views in the name of disciplinary redefinition well remember the kind of opposition we faced when we asked who got to count as a historian, what got to count as history, and how those determinations were made. The critique—and it was a critique in the technical philosophical sense of the term: an interrogation of founding premises, an illumination of methodological and interpretive blind spots—aimed at the very grounds on which the field was based and at the notion that there could be a single prototype of a disciplinary subject. A woman historian was not just a historian with female genitals, but someone who might bring different perspectives to her work. How did those perspectives affect the idea of an appropriate historical inquiry? Women's history was not just another topic, a minor theme in the exalted stories of nations and their leaders, it was for many of us an inquiry into the founding assumptions of so-called mainstream history. (African American history, postcolonial history, queer history offered similar interrogations.) The reply was often furious and it wielded the weapons of the strong in a defense of scholarship against corruption by politics. They were professionals, we were politicizing history by exposing the ways in which standards of inclusion effectively discriminated on the basis of gender or race. They were defending the terrain of disinterested history; we were substituting ideology for scholarly rigor. Reviewing a book on nineteenth-century French women, Norman Hampson dismissed it as "uterine history" and Lawrence Stone, offering his ten commandments to historians of women, warned of the dangers of "distorting evidence" to "support modern feminist ideology"—as if the meaning of evidence were unequivocal and otherwise presented no problems about the position, point of view, and interpretations of historians (Hampson 1982, 18; Stone 1985, 21–27; Scott 1996). Accusations from feminists of male bias were greeted as political and ideological; the men's rejection of women's history was taken as a defense of the integrity of the field.

Poststructuralism met an even more vehement refusal, the intensity of which differed according to discipline. Lawrence Stone (erstwhile champion of History) denounced Michel Foucault as a failed or *faux* historian.

Some literary critics (and many others, of course) used Paul de Man's early Nazi writings to call the entire "linguistic turn" into question. The charges of nihilism and moral relativism, of destruction (a play on Jacques Derrida's deconstruction) and irrelevance portrayed the struggle in Manichean terms. The guardians of orthodoxy were defending mastery and excellence against those who, they claimed, were directly or indirectly bringing political considerations into a hitherto purely objective arena. Hence, John Searle:

> The biggest single consequence of the rejection of the Western Rationalistic Tradition is that it makes possible an abandonment of traditional standards of objectivity, truth, and rationality, and opens the way for an educational agenda, one of whose primary purposes is to achieve social and political transformation. (Searle 1992, 72)

In 1985, as these struggles were unfolding, a report of the AAUP's Committee A warned that orthodoxy might endanger academic freedom, in effect acknowledging the existence of power dynamics internal to disciplinary communities. The report came in response to an inquiry from Stanford Law School professor Paul Brest about a comment by Paul Carrington, then dean of the Duke Law School. Carrington had written that those who identified with "critical legal studies" disqualified themselves from any law school faculty appointment. The report rejected Carrington's statement, maintaining that belief in the governing principles of a discipline ought not to be a condition of employment:

> In many instances a show of disrespect for a discipline is, at the very same time, an expression of dissent from the prevailing doctrines of that discipline. There is more than a sonant connection between respectfulness and respectability; there is no wide gap between respectability and ideological conventionalism. Thus, while a litmus test of belief in the worth of a subject as a minimum qualification for appointment to a position where one is expected to teach it or teach about it may seem modest in the abstract, on reflection it may prove to be very mistaken; it may end by barring those most likely to have remade the field. . . . It is not merely that the long history of academic freedom teaches that charges of irreverence can readily serve as covers to objections to unorthodoxy; rather, it is that it is all but impossible to extenuate the one without abetting the other. (AAUP 1986)

The internal/external, thought/action contrast, which makes power and politics the activity of threatening outsiders, has on the one hand, been taken as the necessary condition for faculty and university autonomy, yet—as the AAUP statement makes clear—it also masks the challenge posed by the legitimating disciplinary authority to the free exercise of critical thought. Disciplinary communities provide the consensus necessary to justify academic freedom as a special freedom for faculty. But the inseparable other side of this regulatory and enabling authority is that it can suppress innovative thinking in the name of defending immutable standards. Paradoxically, the very institutions that are meant to legitimize faculty autonomy can also function to undermine it.

ACADEMIC RESPONSIBILITY

There is another area of tension that academic freedom addresses but does not resolve. Like the first two issues I have discussed, it is also the source of controversy and adjudication that never ends. This is the notion of academic responsibility. Conceived as the correlative of academic freedom ("there are no rights without corresponding duties," reads the "1915 Declaration of Principles" [AAUP 1915, 33]), it was in fact an attempt to bring into being in the very person of the professor the boundary between knowledge and power, thought and action, truth and politics upon which the principle of academic freedom rested. Academic responsibility referred to the deportment of a faculty member, his performance as an academic subject; it was no longer attached explicitly to the motivation for truth-seeking (that was taken to be a freely performed activity, not the fulfillment of a responsibility). Responsibility somehow meant a commitment to keeping thought and politics distinct, or at least to maintaining the appearance of such a distinction and that in two ways: in the manner or style of one's academic conduct and in the spatial separation between the world of ideas and the world at large.

The early attempts to separate knowledge and power appealed to the idea of objectivity. The closer scholars could come to it, the more legitimate their work would be, the more the inside could be protected from the outside. The problem, of course, was that—as Dewey and the AAUP founders well knew—work in the human sciences could never claim the objective status of pure science. So, one way of keeping the taint of politics away from scholarship was to displace the problem onto the *manner* in which ideas were articulated.

In the heat of public controversies about the undeniably political ideas of Progressive social scientists, the founders of the AAUP suggested that a faculty member's demeanor could affect the reception of his work. Thus Dewey noted in 1902 (and the AAUP founders again in 1915), that the deportment of critical scholars could make all the difference. Indeed, they went further, maintaining that academic responsibility demanded that professors set forth their views in "a scholar's spirit," "with dignity, courtesy, and temperateness of language" (AAUP 1915, 33). "It is the manner of conveying the truth," Dewey insisted, that can provoke censure or toleration. (The example he chose is telling for its acknowledgment of the political import of a scholar's ideas and of the challenge they might pose to conventional wisdom.)

> One might, for example, be scientifically convinced of the transitional character of the existing capitalistic control of industrial affairs and its reflected influences upon political life; one might be convinced that many and grave evils and injustices are incident to it, and yet never raise the question of academic freedom. . . . He might go at the problem in such an objective, historic, and constructive manner as not to excite the prejudices or inflame the passions even of those who thoroughly disagreed with him. On the other hand, views at the bottom exactly the same can be stated in such a way as to rasp the feelings of everyone exercising the capitalistic function. What will stand or fall upon its own scientific merits, if presented as a case of objective social evolution, is mixed up with all sorts of extraneous and passion-inflaming factors when set forth as the outcome of the conscious and aggressive selfishness of a class. As a result of such influences the problem of academic freedom becomes to a very large extent a personal matter. (Dewey [1902] 1976, 59)

In the classroom, the teacher must be patient, considerate, wise, even as he challenges convention and sparks new thought. Outside the classroom, he is "under a peculiar obligation to avoid hasty or unverified or exaggerated statements and to refrain from intemperate or sensational modes of expression," even as he exercises "the political rights vouchsafed to every citizen" (AAUP 1915, 37). Recognizing the difficulties of laying down rules for personal conduct ("such rules are likely to be innocuous truisms"), Dewey proceeds, Polonius-like, nonetheless: loyalty to truth, the courage of one's convictions, respect in the face of controversy are positive traits; conceit, "bumptiousness," "lack of reverence for the things that mean much to humanity," and a "craving for public notoriety" are negative (Dewey [1902] 1976, 60). The aim was not to compromise one's beliefs in order to win public approval, but rather to embody something of the "scientific" auspices of ideas in one's very demeanor ("objective, historic, constructive," dispassionate, calm).

The notion that personal style might mitigate the impact of one's ideas was, of course, futile. As the case of Scott Nearing (discussed earlier) suggests, radical substance and radical style were often read as interchangeable, the one implying the other. In the statements I cited from the Wharton School alumni, it is hard to distinguish between "intemperate," "wildly," "astonishing," and "unrestrained" on the one side, and "untested theories" and "fallacious conclusions" on the other. Was Nearing let go because he questioned "the institutions and rules which form the basis of civilized society," or because he lacked the restraint associated with objectivity? Weren't his ideas proof enough that he did not have the appropriate demeanor? When the trustees came to justify firing Nearing, they were more careful about distinguishing between freedom of expression ("there is not and never will be the slightest wish on the part of the board or of a single of one the trustees to restrict the broadest latitude of opinions, research, and discussion" [AAUP, 1916, 146]) and style ("when individual opinions of members of the teaching staff are expressed in a proper manner, upon proper occasions, and with proper respect for the dignity of their relationship to the university . . . such opinions and utterances are welcomed as indicative of progressive growth—no matter how divergent they may be from current or general beliefs" [AAUP, 1916, 146]). "Proper" is invoked as something entirely self-evident ("proper manner," "proper occasions," "proper respect"), though, of course, its meaning is completely obscure. Or, at least, it assumes a shared understanding of what constitutes propriety: commitment to a set of norms that set boundaries both for gentlemanly decorum and gentlemanly ideas, the one being the measure of the other. According to this notion of propriety, it does not seem possible that Nearing's manner, however dispassionate, could have offset the objections to his ideas.

Recent controversies about teachers of Middle Eastern studies are only the latest example of the fact that those who disagree with the content of one's teaching often hear it as intemperate, dangerous, and wild, even if the demeanor of the teacher is careful and courteous. It is not easy to separate the contents of the teaching from judgments about the character of the scholar. Still, the emphasis on good manners has never been dropped entirely in AAUP documents and elsewhere in the academy. It stands in the much-cited

"1940 Statement of Principles on Academic Freedom and Tenure"—in effect a "constitution" for academia. And it has had something of a resurgence these days in administrators' pleas for "civility" and in tests for "collegiality" that, despite AAUP warnings about the discriminatory impact such tests can have, are included in standards for tenure at some universities (AAUP [1940] 2001). The idea that academic deportment ought not to seem political or, better, that the political resonances of academic work can be made acceptable by one's "civility" is still there to be drawn on. As such it constitutes a check on the notion that academic freedom is about the unqualified autonomy of scholars in their writing and teaching, or at least it poses a serious challenge to that idea.

The second area of academic responsibility is about the spatial separation of activity, captured in the distinction between legitimate scholarly work and "extramural" expression, between acceptable classroom discourse and opinions offered outside that protected space that are not necessarily related to a faculty member's expertise. Was there a responsibility to behave in a certain "academic" manner even when one was exercising one's rights as a citizen? Did the special right of academic freedom entail limits on the public right of free speech? Surely outrageous opinions uttered to the public could redound negatively to the university, imperiling academic freedom within its walls by tarring with the brush of politics the professor's scholarly reputation (and so the university's neutral standing). The 1915 "Declaration" went back and forth. On the one hand, "academic teachers are under a peculiar obligation to avoid hasty or unverified or exaggerated statements, and to refrain from intemperate or sensational modes of expression." On the other hand, they should not have "their freedom of speech, outside the university, . . . limited to questions falling within their own specialities." Nor should they be "prohibited from lending their active support to organized movements which they believe to be in the public interest." "It is neither possible nor desirable to deprive a college professor of the political rights vouchsafed to every citizen" (AAUP 1915, 37).

But what of cases of extramural utterance that "raise grave doubts concerning [a faculty member's] fitness for his position?" Should these be treated as a matter of individual conscience or submitted to collective institutional judgment? The question was the subject of much discussion in the drafting of the 1940 "Statement"—a joint endeavor of AAUP, representing faculty, and the Association of American Colleges (AAC), representing administrators. The result was a compromise. Paragraph C of the document addressed the issue, but it was followed by an interpretive footnote—so vexed was the problem. The paragraph took the language of the 1915 "Declaration": the faculty member's "special position in the community imposes special obligations." "He should at all times be accurate, should exercise appropriate restraint, should show respect for the opinions of others, and [this was an addition that imposed a new obligation and suggested that faculty autonomy and university autonomy might be at odds] should make every effort to indicate that he is not an institutional spokesman" (AAUP [1940] 2001, 36). The interpretive note actually muddied the issue while exposing the basted seams of compromise. It granted the right of administrators to file charges in an appropriate manner against a faculty member whom they considered to have violated the "admonitions" of paragraph C, but cautioned that teachers were also citizens and "should be accorded the freedom of citizens."

What this said was that "academic responsibility," as a standard for faculty deportment off campus, could not provide an entirely effective barrier between knowledge and politics. Academic freedom has come to mean the absolute right of a faculty member to "the freedom of citizens" off campus, but restrictions on those rights of expression in the classroom. That the matter has not, however, been resolved is indicated by the fact that the vast number of cases investigated by AAUP involve the relationship between a faculty member's extramural speech and his or her fitness as a scholar and teacher. A series of cases illustrates this point.

The first case actually occasioned a debate among AAUP leaders about the value of invoking "academic responsibility" as a test of professorial merit. It concerned an assistant professor of biology at the University of Illinois in 1963 who wrote a letter to the editor of the student newspaper that so outraged public opinion that he was dismissed by the president. Leo Koch's letter was about sex. In response to an article by two students complaining about the ritualized nature of relations between men and women on campus, Koch counseled greater freedom. Arguing that the students treated the issue too narrowly, he diagnosed a "serious social malaise . . . caused . . . by the hypocritical and downright inhumane moral standards engendered by a Christian code of ethics which was already decrepit in the days of Queen Victoria" (AAUP 1963, 26). The cure was to end the psychological inhibition of healthy needs by condoning sexual intercourse "among those sufficiently mature to engage in it without social consequences [i.e., by using modern contraceptives and with good medical advice] and without violating their own codes of morality and ethics." The response, as one can imagine, was explosive. It was led by the Rev. Ira Latimer, a member of the University of Illinois' Dad's Association who (following the double standard of the day) wrote to parents of *women* students. He called Koch's letter "an audacious attempt to subvert the religious and moral foundations of America" and identified it as the "standard operating procedure of the Communist conspiracy" (AAUP 1963, 27). Letters of protest poured in to university administrative offices. Following the recommendations of the executive committee of the College of Liberal Arts and Sciences, the president decided that "Professor Koch's published letter constitutes a breach of academic responsibility so serious as to justify his being relieved of his University duties." He went on: "The views expressed are offensive and repugnant, contrary to commonly accepted standards of morality and their public espousal may be interpreted as encouragement of immoral behavior. It is clear that Mr. Koch's conduct has been prejudicial to the best interests of the university" (AAUP 1963, 28). Here was a statement that called for condemnation if one took critical thinking to be the mission of the university and if the free speech rights of citizens were to be respected. There was never evidence presented that either Koch (a botanist) uttered these views in his classroom or that he was unfit to teach his subject. Indeed, his colleagues on the faculty senate committee on academic freedom concluded that at most his letter deserved a reprimand. The AAUP investigating committee agreed, concluding that there were administrative violations both procedural and principled, and it called upon the board of trustees to resist public pressure, to "take a broader view of the function of the university and the value of academic freedom. . . . to recognize [the university's] maturity, its ability to absorb a few gadflies and its need for uninhibited freedom of discussion" (AAUP 1963, 34).

The investigating committee went on at some length about the utility of the notion of academic responsibility, arguing, in effect, that in cases of extramural utterance an individual faculty member's rights as a citizen could not be limited by such a vague and ambiguous term. Citing a passage from John Stuart Mill's *On Liberty*, they maintained that "any serious application of the standard would tend to eliminate or discourage any colorful or forceful utterance. More likely . . . the standard would be reserved as a sanction only for the expression of unorthodox opinion" (AAUP 1963, 37). These comments gave rise to heated debate among the members of Committee A (which receives and acts on these investigatory reports) and to the publication, along with the report, of two statements on "Academic Responsibility," one the majority view, the other, a dissent. While not disagreeing with the investigators' conclusion that Professor Koch had been denied due process and while conceding that "academic responsibility is admittedly very difficult to define," the majority nonetheless insisted that academic responsibility was a standard worth enforcing because "we can hardly expect academic freedom to endure unless it is matched by academic responsibility" (AAUP 1963, 40). The notion might, of course, be abused, but this was not grounds for denying its importance. "The remedy is, instead, insistence on proper procedural safeguards, a highly significant role for the faculty, . . . and a vigilant oversight by this Association" (AAUP 1963, 41). The dissenters were not convinced. They insisted that the majority had misinterpreted the "1940 Statement," which on the question of speech outside the classroom, was unambiguous: "By law, in the expression of his opinions, the teacher is no less free than other citizens" (AAUP 1963, 42). The only legitimate ground for dismissal was—historically and in the present—"demonstrated unfitness to teach."

> To speak of "academic responsibility" as a standard or test for dismissal because a teacher has expressed an unpopular opinion without anchoring it to unmistakable particulars is to waver on a floating bog of semantics. (AAUP 1963, 43)

A special standard of academic responsibility, the dissenters continued, not only treated teachers differently from other citizens, but it opened

> a Pandora's box of all the coercive and compulsive crusades of sectarian, political, and economic pressure groups together with consequent attempts at dismissal by administrators who are unable to resist the public pressure engendered by such groups whose causes often contain more heat than light. (AAUP 1963, 43)

Oberlin College English professor Warren Taylor, the author of the dissent, undoubtedly had the previous decade's experience in mind. During the McCarthy period, many faculty were fired, some for having admitted to membership in the Communist Party, some for simply having been accused of such membership, some for having declined to name names, and others for having taken the Fifth Amendment (Schrecker 1986). "Academic responsibility" was directly or indirectly used as a justification for these firings.

Sometimes the need to protect the university from legislative intervention was the reason, sometimes the refusal of the professor to come clean with his colleagues inside the university was the issue, sometimes it was that communism was by definition antithetical to free thought. Thus the American Committee for Cultural Freedom (the group of Cold War intellectuals founded in 1951) argued that "a member of the Communist Party has transgressed the canons of academic responsibility, has engaged his intellect to servility, and is therefore professionally disqualified from performing his functions as a teacher" (Lasch 1969, 83). This logic substituted for any need to provide concrete evidence of scholarly or pedagogic unfitness. And it ruled out the possibility that, for some faculty at least, communism was more about developing a critical theory of society than it was about offering unquestioned obeisance to the Soviet state.

Most often, as Warren Taylor had predicted, academic responsibility was invoked when administrators or trustees were unable to resist public pressure to punish a professor whose off-campus speech had offended their sensibilities. In these cases, the responsibility was not to think freely (not to exemplify the function of the university), but to protect the public reputation of the university (by refraining from the expression of critical ideas). The AAUP investigators found themselves time and again arguing against administrative judgments "in applying what are necessarily somewhat imprecise standards for the limits of propriety of extramural controversy" (AAUP 1971, 398). In most of these instances, in fact, faculty committees (and AAUP investigators) made a case for a professor whose extramural speech was deemed outrageous based not on the content or style of that speech, but on the fairness (according to AAUP recommendations) of procedures followed in judging the individual and, usually more importantly, on the quality of his or her professional standing as a scholar and teacher. In this they carefully restricted "academic responsibility" to the fulfillment of teaching and disciplinary requirements, thereby reinforcing the distinction between knowledge production and politics as forms of activity, not as personal qualities that separated professors from ordinary people. That they did not usually prevail is an indication, I think, of the difficulty of maintaining the distinction in practice.

The case of Angela Davis provides another illustration of the way in which "academic responsibility" could be used. When Davis was not renewed as a lecturer in philosophy at the University of California, Los Angeles in 1970 because of her membership in the Communist Party and because in public speeches she attacked police as "pigs" and maintained that academic freedom was an "'empty concept' if divorced from freedom of political action or if 'exploited' to maintain such views as the genetic inferiority of black people" (AAUP 1971, 391), her colleagues argued that nothing in her lectures or classroom behavior indicated dereliction of duty.[2] Students talked about her courses as rigorous and open-minded; they were not expected to parrot her conclusions, which were, in any case, offered as tentative interpretations. If her off-campus rhetoric was inflated, inaccurate, and even "distasteful and reprehensible," it had not spilled over into her research and teaching. One of the few regents who opposed her firing noted that "in this day and age when the decibel level of political debate . . . has reached the heights it has, it is unrealistic and disingenuous to demand as a condition of employment that the professor address political rallies in the muted cadences of scholarly exchanges. Professors are products of their times even as the rest of us" (AAUP 1971, 417). Absent here was the idea that "academic responsibility" extended beyond one's purely academic responsibilities. Although the style and manner of one's performance still counted (Davis was said to be as calm in the classroom as she was outrageous in public), it did so only within the walls of academe. Though this was the dissenting opinion of a regent in the Davis case, it came increasingly to characterize the restriction of the notion of academic responsibility to things academic. There was indeed a separation between knowledge and politics, but an academic could participate in both as long as she distinguished between her roles as a scholar and a citizen. Academic freedom was meant to guarantee this separation in theory, difficult as it might be to maintain in practice.

But what if a professor's political engagement led to revelations about the quality of his scholarship? This is what happened in the case of Ward Churchill at the University of Colorado. Churchill's reference to the September 11, 2001, World Trade Center victims as "little Eichmanns" who deserved their fate infuriated the regents of the university. In response to demands from the regents and the governor that he be fired immediately, the administration of the university (following AAUP procedures) asked a faculty committee to examine his professional competence. The inquiry into his work produced information about "research misconduct" considered so damning that neither the committee nor the AAUP felt they could come to his rescue. It was certainly true, his colleagues conceded, that there would have been no examination of his scholarly opus if the political charges had not been made, yet given the questionable nature of his academic credentials and the extensive criticism that came from within his own field of American Indian studies, it was extremely difficult to make a strong bid for his retention.

Although the Churchill and Davis cases differed on the question of the scholarly integrity and teaching performance of the professors, both were fired and for the same reasons: their extramural speech incurred the wrath of outside groups whose power influenced the decisions of university administrators. These were cases that revealed the weakness of the notion that a full separation was in fact possible between thought and action, scholarship and politics. Academic freedom was easily compromised by a notion of academic responsibility that could be extended to include the responsibility to protect the university from exactly those forces that Dewey and his colleagues in 1915 and Warren Taylor and his fellow dissenters in 1963 warned would compromise its mission of free and critical inquiry.

BLURRED BOUNDARIES

In 1970, in the context of the heated politics of the Vietnam War, the AAUP issued a statement on "academic responsibility" that, while recognizing how politics had become part of campus life, insisted on what had by then become the classic distinction between the scholar and the citizen. "Because academic freedom has traditionally included the instructor's full freedom as a citizen, most faculty members face no insoluble conflicts between the claims of politics, social action, and conscience, on the one hand, and the claims and expectations of their students, colleagues, and institutions on the other" (AAUP [1970] 2001, 136). As the subsequent years of political and epistemological turmoil (identity politics, culture wars and science wars, linguistic and cultural turns, structuralism and poststructuralism) would reveal, however, what is missing in those sharp distinctions between outside/inside, power/knowledge, action/thought, politics/truth is, ironically, the idea that one's sense of responsibility as a citizen could legitimately affect one's scholarship. Ironically, because among the members of AAUP were many who, like the founding Progressive fathers, were motivated by concerns about the direction of society, the organization of the economy, and the conduct of politics to undertake the research and teaching that earned them scholarly distinction. As in the attempt to mask with good manners the political implications of academic research, so the consignment of politics to "extramural" speech, while it offered an important way of defending a professor's rights as a citizen, left aside the more difficult question of how and whether contemporary concerns (the stuff of political contests) might legitimately and explicitly be addressed by scholars in their capacity as teachers and researchers.

Where is the line between polemical advocacy and critical scholarship in work that rereads the history of democracy as a story of the exclusion of differences based on ethnicity, gender, and race? It may be relatively simple to decide that a teacher of women's studies who requires that students share her outrage at all things "patriarchal" is unwisely polemical in her pedagogy, or that a chemistry professor's use of class time to denounce the war in Iraq is inappropriate, but the tougher questions involve scholarly interpretations — what might be called the point of view that necessarily informs research, writing, and teaching in the humanities and social sciences. In a recent book, the literary scholar and academic administrator Stanley Fish has cautioned academics to "save the world on your own time," urging us to teach the facts or the texts in our chosen fields without taking a position on them (Fish 2008). Fish adheres to the idea that politics and scholarship are entirely separable entities. But the separation between them is easier in theory than in practice, since taking positions — on the quality of evidence used to support interpretations, on the reliability of certain methods of investigation, on the premises of the writers of texts and textbooks, on the ethical issues — is part of the scholar's job, part of what makes her a compelling and inspiring teacher. Moreover, those positions are not neutrally arrived at by, say, balancing all sides until an objective view emerges; rather they are the result of some kind of deeply held political or ethical commitment on the part of the professor. The tension between professorial commitments and academic responsibility is an ongoing one that the principle of academic freedom is meant to adjudicate.

In recent years, the blurring of the lines between politics and scholarship, the acknowledgment that there is some connection, has opened the way for full-fledged political assaults on university teachers: from the Israel lobby on Middle Eastern studies courses that address the ethics of the occupation and the rights of Palestinians or that are presented by professors whose loyalty to current Israeli policy is in question; from evangelical Christians on evolution in the biology curriculum or on classes that question their views of sexual morality; from organized student groups — Right and Left — who find themselves made "uncomfortable" by readings assigned in courses; from right-wing trustees and alumni who feel that "public tax dollars should not be used to promote political, religious, ideological or cultural beliefs or values as truth when such values are in conflict with the values of American citizenship and the teaching of Western Civilization" (Arizona State Legislature 2008). Despite the valiant efforts of some administrators to resist the pressure, these groups have had an impact (a "chilling effect") on the organization of the curriculum, on the hiring and firing of faculty, and on the kinds of speakers and conferences permitted on campuses.

When administrators do resist the pressure, it is in the name of academic freedom—the right, indeed the necessity, of autonomy for a self-regulating faculty—and this is a demonstration of the continuing value of the concept, whatever its inherent tensions and limitations. In pointing out the ongoing tensions that the principle of academic freedom mediates, I do not mean to call its utility into question. On the contrary, it seems to me that it is precisely because the tensions evident a century ago continue to trouble the relationships among faculty, administrators, and boards of trustees; because the value of critical thinking is regularly under siege in the disciplines, the universities, and the nation; and because the tensions I have been describing are not susceptible to final resolution, that we need this principle in our ongoing struggle to preserve that which is best about universities and university education—the commitment to free and unfettered inquiry as an ideal that we reach for, even as its attainment never seems quite complete.

NOTES

This essay is a revised version of my essays in *Social Research* 76, no. 2, Free Inquiry at Risk: Universities in Dangerous Times, Part I (Summer 2009): 451–480, and *Academic Freedom in Conflict*, ed. James L. Turk (Toronto: Lorimer 2014).

1. Here the "Declaration" reads like a conversation among the authors, with the majority conceding some points to more conservative colleagues, while returning again and again to the main point—the need for absolute freedom in the classroom.

2. Note that this took place before Davis was indicted in the jailbreak attempt of George Jackson.

REFERENCES

American Association of University Professors. 1915. "General Report of the Committee on Academic Freedom and Academic Tenure." *Bulletin of the AAUP* 1, part 1 (December): 20–43.

American Association of University Professors. 1916. "Report Concerning the University of Pennsylvania." *Bulletin of the AAUP* 2:3, 127–177.

American Association of University Professors. (1940) 2001. "1940 Statement of Principles on Academic Freedom and Tenure." In *Policy Documents and Reports*, 9th ed., 3–10. Washington, D.C.: AAUP.

American Association of University Professors. 1963. "Academic Freedom and Tenure: the University of Illinois." *AAUP Bulletin* 49:1, 25–43.

American Association of University Professors. (1970) 2001. "A Statement of the Association's Council: Freedom and Responsibility." In *Policy Documents and Reports*, 9th ed., 135–36. Washington, D.C.: AAUP.

American Association of University Professors. 1971. "Reports on Academic Freedom and Tenure: The University of California at Los Angeles." *AAUP Bulletin* 57:3, 382–420.

American Association of University Professors. 1986. "Response to an Inquiry by Professor Paul Brest," in "Report of Committee A for 1985–86." *Academe* 72 (September): 13a, 19a. Cited again (1988) in *Academe* 74 (September/October): 55.

Arizona State Legislature. Senate Proposed Legislation. Spring 2008. www.azleg.gov.

Certeau, Michel de. 1986. "History: Science and Fiction." In *Heterologies: Discourse on the Other*. Trans. Brian Massumi. Minneapolis: University of Minnesota Press.

Dewey, John. (1902) 1976. "Academic Freedom." In *John Dewey: The Middle Works, 1899–1942*, ed. Jo Ann Boydston, 53–66. Carbondale: Southern Illinois University Press.

Donoghue, Frank. 2008. *The Last Professors: The Corporate University and the Fate of the Humanities*. New York: Fordham University Press.

Fish, Stanley, 2008. *Save the World on Your Own Time*. New York: Oxford University Press.

Hampson, Norman. 1982 "The Big Store." *London Review of Books*, January 21–February 3, 18.

Lasch, Christopher. 1969. *The Agony of the American Left*. New York: Knopf.

Lovejoy, Arthur O. 1937. "Academic Freedom." In *Encyclopedia of the Social Sciences*, ed. E. R. A. Seligman, 1:384–87. New York: Macmillan.

Metzger, Walter. 1955. "The Age of the University." In *The Development of Academic Freedom in the United States*, ed. Richard Hofstadter and Walter Metzger. New York: Columbia University Press.

Morrow, Glenn. 1968. "Academic Freedom." In *International Encyclopedia of the Social Sciences*, ed. David L. Sills, 1:4–9. New York: Macmillan/Free Press.

Schrecker, Ellen. 1986. *No Ivory Tower: McCarthyism and the Universities*. New York: Oxford University Press.

Scott, Joan W. 1996. "Academic Freedom as an Ethical Practice." In *The Future of Academic Freedom*, ed. Louis Menand, 163–180. Chicago: University of Chicago Press.

Searle, John. 1992. "Rationality and Realism: What Is at Stake?" *Daedalus* 122 (Fall): 55–84.

Stone, Lawrence. 1985. "Only Women." *New York Review of Books*, April 11, 21–27.

6

OBSCURANTISM AND ACADEMIC FREEDOM

JON ELSTER

INTRODUCTION

T HE MOST COMMONLY cited threat to academic freedom takes the
form of formal, vertical pressures. Congress, government agencies,
university trustees, deans, and departmental chairs possess a large
repertory of subtle and unsubtle means to dissuade speech and writing they
do not like. They can, for instance, withhold funding or impose sanctions of
various kinds. Organizations and associations in civil society may also bring
pressure to bear on scholars, perhaps most frequently by the indirect method
of lobbying those in a position to impose formal sanctions. In this essay, I
shall discuss the threats to academic freedom that arise from more informal,
horizontal mechanisms. Specifically, I shall argue that the pervasive practices
of what I shall call *hard* and *soft obscurantism* undermine the spirit of free
inquiry, notably in the humanities and the social sciences. The format is that
of a polemical essay, rather than of a fully documented scholarly article. I
offer more sustained analyses elsewhere (Elster 2000, 2007, 2009, 2011).

The idea of freedom on which I rely here is not the freedom to write or
to say what one thinks, but the *freedom to think*. This is obviously a nebulous
idea; some would say hopelessly so. I shall not attempt to define it, but appeal
to our intuitive notions of a free inquiry or a "free spirit." As observed by Felix
Frankfurter, cited by Cole, Cole, and Weiss (this volume), "It matters little
whether intervention occurs avowedly or through action that inevitably tends

to check the ardor and fearlessness of scholars, qualities at once so fragile and so indispensable for fruitful academic labor." Although Frankfurter referred to vertical intervention by the government, the "ardor and fearlessness" of scholars can also be checked by horizontal peer intervention.

Freedom to think is undermined by psychological as well as by sociological mechanisms. Moreover, the freedom is undermined, paradoxically, by what may be either excessive politeness or lack of public-spiritedness on the part of free spirits. If more scholars were willing to expose nonsense for what it is, fewer students and teachers would waste their lives. In many cases, society as a whole would also benefit. The soft obscurantist theory of the "refrigerator mother" caused parents of autistic children to feel deep, unfounded guilt. The hard obscurantist theories of mathematical finance wreaked havoc with the world economy.

I shall proceed as follows. In section 2 I discuss the well-known phenomenon of soft obscurantism, illustrated by Alan Sokal's hoax. In section 3 I consider the more recent phenomenon of hard obscurantism, well understood since Keynes but made prominent by the financial crisis from 2007 onward. In section 4 I discuss the sociological and psychological mechanisms that may explain the emergence and persistence of these pathologies. I conclude by discussing what, if anything, can be done to counteract them.

SOFT OBSCURANTISM

The idea of soft obscurantism has been studied by scholars under the heading of "bullshit." Within philosophy, *bullshitology* has in fact emerged as a minor subdiscipline. The seminal paper was written by Harry Frankfurt in 1988, republished as Frankfurt (2005); see also Cohen (2002) and Gjelsvik (2006). By and large, however, these writers focus on the conceptual analysis of the phenomenon, mostly without naming names. I shall name some. Because of limitations of space, my treatment will be heavily selective. I shall not discuss, for instance, the absurdities of psychoanalysis or of the structural interpretation of myth (stipulating the existence of "mythemes"). Concerning the latter, however, I cannot resist the temptation to recount what the current holder of the chair of anthropology at the Collège de France, previously held by Claude Lévi-Strauss, told me when I asked whether his predecessor had formed a school in the interpretation of myths. "No," he said, "only Lévi-Strauss could do what he did." *When intersubjectivity is discarded, subjectivity reigns.*

Let me tell another personal story. Some time in the 1980s, before Frank-furt's publication, I received a phone call from Amos Tversky, who was at the time on the standing committee at Stanford that evaluates all tenure proposals before they go to the president. He asked me, "The Department of Romance Languages wants to hire Michel Serres. Where is he on the bullshit scale?" I answered, "Not as good as Foucault [i.e., more bullshitty], but better [i.e., less bullshitty] than Derrida." Stanford hired Serres. Although in France he lists himself as a philosopher, at Stanford he was appointed by a literature depart-ment. This seems appropriate.

At the time, Foucault had been teaching at Berkeley. I assumed that Stan-ford, too, wanted a famous French intellectual on their faculty. It was and is a striking fact that the appointment of intellectually substandard scholars is not reserved to second-tier or third-tier schools. Harvard appointed Homi Bhabha, Yale hired Paul de Man, New York University appointed Arjun Appa-durai, and my own university appointed a Derrida scholar whom for reasons of local politeness I shall not name. As these names suggest, the main refer-ences of soft obscurantism in the American humanities have been postmod-ern "French theory" and "subaltern" or "postcolonial" theory from the Indian subcontinent. Why first-tier universities appoint third-tier scholars to presti-gious chairs remains a mystery.

I shall not try to argue for my negative evaluation of these scholars. One cannot argue *with* them, since an almost defining feature of their writings is that they assert or gesture rather than argue. As Sokal learned, when met with argued objections they respond by ridicule or insinuation ("le pauvre Sokal," said Derrida). Moreover, scholars outside their charmed circle do not need to be persuaded of their nullity. I cannot imagine anyone saying that postmod-ernism is "70 percent good, 30 percent bad," as the Chinese are currently saying about Mao.

I shall, however, try to characterize some of their writings. Perhaps the main flaws are to be found in their *functionalism* and in their reliance on *analogies*.

One of the canonical books of soft obscurantism, Foucault's *Surveiller et punir*, relies heavily on what one might call "the functionalism of actorless intentions," as in this passage:

> But perhaps one should reverse the problem and ask oneself *what is served* by the failure of the prison: *what is the use* of these different phenomena that are continually being criticized; the *maintenance* of delinquency, the *encouragement*

of recidivism, the *transformation* of the occasional offender into a habitual delinquent, the organization of a closed milieu of delinquency. Perhaps one should
look for what is hidden beneath the apparent cynicism of the penal institution,
which, after *purging* the convicts by means of their sentence, continues to *follow*
them by a whole series of "brandings" (a surveillance that was once de jure and
which is today de facto; the police record that has taken the place of the convict's
passport) and which thus pursues as a "delinquent" someone who has acquitted
himself of his punishment as an offender? Can we not see here a consequence
rather than a contradiction? If so, one would be forced to suppose that the prison,
and no doubt punishment in general, is not *intended to eliminate* offences, but
rather to *distinguish them, to distribute them, to use them*; that it is not so much
that *they render docile* those who are liable to transgress the law, but that *they
tend to assimilate* the transgression of the laws in a general tactics of subjection.
Penality would then appear to be a way of *handling* illegalities, of *laying down*
the limits of tolerance, of *giving free* rein to some, of *putting* pressure on others,
of *excluding* a particular section, of *making another useful*, of *neutralizing* certain
individuals and of *profiting* from others. (Foucault 1977, 272; my italics)

This use of verb or verbal nouns without a grammatical subject is an
unmistakable indicator of obscurantism.

Foucault's analysis is embedded in a seamless, paranoid vision of society as
wholly shaped by an omnipresent and intangible *"dispositif"* or "apparatus":

What I'm trying to pick out with this term [*dispositif*] is, firstly, a thoroughly heterogeneous ensemble consisting of discourses, institutions, architectural forms,
regulatory decisions, laws, administrative measures, scientific statements, philosophical, moral and philanthropic propositions—in short, the said as much as
the unsaid. Such are the elements of the apparatus. The apparatus itself is the
system of relations that one can establish between these elements. I understand
by the term "apparatus" [*dispositif*] a sort of—shall we say—formation which
has as its major *function* at a given historical moment that of responding to
an urgent need. The apparatus thus has a dominant strategic *function*. This
may have been, for example, the assimilation of a floating population found to
be burdensome for an essentially mercantilist economy: there was a strategic
imperative acting here as the matrix for an apparatus which gradually undertook the control or subjection of madness, sexual illness and neurosis. (Foucault
1980, 195; my italics)

As I know from teaching in France and participating in French intellectual life, the *dispositif* is a key that opens all doors and preempts the need for empirical investigation. In that respect, it is similar to Bourdieu's concept of "habitus," which is essentially a modern version of the dormitive virtue of opium. The existence of a habitus is proved by the behavior it is supposed to explain.

Another canonical text, Edward Said's analysis of *Mansfield Park* and colonialism, relies on analogy. Consider his comments on Austen's description of Sir Thomas Bertram's reaction to the chaos and frivolity he finds upon coming back from the West Indies:

> The force of this paragraph is unmistakable. . . . It is an early Protestant eliminating all traces of frivolous behavior. There is nothing in Mansfield Park that would contradict us, however, were we to assume that Sir Thomas does exactly the same things—on a larger scale—in his Antigua "plantations." Whatever was wrong there . . . Sir Thomas was able to fix, thereby maintaining his control over his colonial domain. More clearly than elsewhere in her fiction, *Austen here synchronizes domestic with international authority, making it plain* that the values associated with such higher things as ordination, law, and propriety must be grounded firmly in actual rule over and possession of territory. She *sees clearly* that to hold and rule Mansfield Park is to hold and rule an imperial estate in *close, not to say inevitable association* with it. (Said 1993, 104; my italics)

True, there is nothing in the work to contradict this interpretation. Nor is there anything that supports it. It is absurd to argue, as Said does, that a reading that is not explicitly contradicted by the text can ipso facto be imputed to the author as a "clear" expression of her intentions. The interpretation is based on an analogy between Antigua and Mansfield Park that exists only in Said's mind.

The repertoire of soft obscurantism also includes the following:

"Arguments" from etymology. Fraser (1993, 142) asserts, for instance, that the masculine character of politics is revealed in the etymological connection between "public" and "pubic."

Unsubstantiated claims that "it is no accident that . . . ."

Rhetorical questions that insinuate without asserting (see the passage from Foucault 1977 quoted earlier).

Statements invoking the Stalinist notion of objective complicity: "Don't you see that what you say will harm the Left?" Gambetta and Origgi (2013, 12) cites an example.

Puns, as when Derrida in a debate with John Searle famously referred to him as S.A.R.L., *société anonyme de responsabilité limitée* (limited liability company).

For most of my intended readers, these comments will sound like kicking in an open door. I turn, therefore, to more controversial and more interesting matters.

HARD OBSCURANTISM

There have been many attempts to explain human behavior using quantitative models. I shall consider two: rational-choice theory (including game theory) and statistical data analysis. With regard to the first, I can claim some firsthand competence. With regard to the second, I rely on authorities.

Before I state the grounds for my skepticism of rational-choice theory, let me emphasize that for some purposes it is highly valuable. In my opinion, the development of rational-choice theory as a conceptual tool for understanding human action and interaction has been the greatest achievement of the social sciences to date. Before Schelling (1960), for instance, we had no idea that it could be rational to burn one's ships or bridges. The theory is, moreover, an indispensable policy tool for changing behavior, for the simple reason that people often respond to incentives in predictable ways. (The idea that they *always* do can lead to disasters, as the American policy in Vietnam amply proved.) What I deny is that the theory has a privileged status as an *explanatory* tool.

To achieve explanatory success, a theory should, minimally, satisfy two criteria: it should have determinate implications for behavior, and the implied behavior should be what we actually observe. Rational-choice theory often fails on both counts. The theory may be indeterminate, and people may be irrational. In what was perhaps the first sustained criticism of the theory, Keynes emphasized *indeterminacy*, notably because of the pervasive presence of uncertainty. His criticism applied especially to cases in which agents have to form expectations about the behavior of other agents or about the development of the economy in the long run. In the wake of the current economic crisis, this objection has returned to the forefront. Between Keynes and the current crisis, the main objections to the theory were based on pervasive *irrational* behavior. Experimental psychology and behavioral economics have uncovered many mechanisms that cause people to deviate in predictable ways from what rational-choice theory prescribes and predicts.

Disregarding some technical (and important) sources of indeterminacy, the most basic one is embarrassingly simple: how can one impute to the social agents the capacity to make the calculations *in real time* that occupy many pages of mathematical appendices in the leading journals of economics and political science and that can be acquired only through years of professional training? Here are some frequently made answers to this question, with my rejoinders:

1. We should accept a theory if it produces correct predictions, even if we do not understand how it does so (quantum mechanics). *Rejoinder*: the social sciences produce very few correct predictions, except regarding the short-term impact of small changes in economic variables.
2. Even though agents are incapable of intentional maximizing in complex situations, natural or social selection will eliminate nonmaximizers. *Rejoinder*: this is mere hand-waving. No explicit model exists.
3. Individual errors will cancel each other in the aggregate. *Rejoinder*: there is no reason to think that errors are symmetrically distributed around the correct answer.
4. An expert billiard player whose experience helps him figure out the angles would be utterly incapable of solving the relevant equations; yet he acts *as if* he could. *Rejoinder*: nobody can be an expert in all the situations where economists apply rational-choice theory. Development of expertise in any field is said to require 10,000 hours of practice.

For the varieties and pervasive presence of human irrationality, I refer to Kahneman (2011), usefully supplemented by Ainslie (1992). The mechanisms of *loss aversion* and of *hyperbolic time discounting* that they uncovered are extensively documented and flat-out irreconcilable with the postulates of rationality. Less systematic studies have documented the importance of *emotions*. These findings do not prevent thousands of economists and political scientists all over the world from continuing to rely on rational-choice theory as if its foundations had not been fatally undermined.

Many purported rational-choice explanations turn out, on closer inspection, to be nothing but "just-so" stories. They do not provide a causal account of how the *explanandum was* produced, but of how it *might have been* produced. Economists in particular seem to delight in the invention of rational-choice stories of behaviors such as revenge, addiction, participation in collective action, suicide bombing, and the like. Although these stories are not intrinsically flawed, they are often contrived, sometimes bordering on the ridiculous (e.g., Wintrobe 2006).

With regard to data analysis, I cannot make claims to firsthand competence. I rely mainly on the work of David Freedman, an acknowledged master of pure and applied statistics. He carried out detailed analyses of six articles published in leading academic journals: four from *American Political Science Review*, one from *Quarterly Journal of Economics*, and one from *American Sociological Review* (Freedman 2005). One of them was named "best article of the year" by the journal in which it appeared. The number of mistakes and confusions that he finds—some of them so elementary that even I could understand them—is staggering.

Freedman demonstrated the many pitfalls, fallacies, and temptations that arise in regression analysis as it is routinely carried out, and concluded as follows:

> A crude four-point scale may be useful:
>
> 1. Regression usually works, although it is (like anything else) imperfect and may sometimes go wrong.
> 2. Regression sometimes works in the hands of skillful practitioners, but it isn't suitable for routine use.
> 3. Regression might work, but it hasn't yet.
> 4. Regression can't work.
>
> Textbooks, courtroom testimony, and newspaper interviews seem to put regression into category 1. Category 4 seems too pessimistic. My own view is bracketed by categories 2 and 3, although good examples are quite hard to find. (Freedman 2010, 46)

When I have presented my objections to data analysis to various audiences, my critics have usually located themselves at point (1) of this scale.

Freedman's catalogue of responses to this criticism is also worth citing. It is a caricature, but a good one.

We know all that. Nothing is perfect. Linearity has to be a good first approximation. Log linearity has to be a good first approximation. The assumptions are
reasonable. The assumptions don't matter. The assumptions are conservative.
You can't prove the assumptions are wrong. The biases will cancel. We can
model the biases. We're only doing what everybody else does. Now we use
more sophisticated techniques. If we don't do it, someone else will. What would
you do? The decision maker has to be better off with us than without us. We
all have mental models, not using a model is still a model. The models aren't
totally useless. You have to do the best you can with the data. You have to make
assumptions in order to make progress. You have to give the models the benefit
of the doubt. Where's the harm? (Freedman 2010, 212)

The models do in fact cause harm. Consider the impact of Chicago-style
economics on legislation concerning the death penalty and gun control. In
one summary, "In 1975, Isaac Ehrlich's analysis of national time-series data
led him to claim that each execution saved eight lives. Solicitor General
Robert Bork cited Ehrlich's work to the Supreme Court a year later, and
the Court, while claiming not to have relied on the empirical evidence,
ended the death penalty moratorium when it upheld various capital punishment statutes in *Gregg v. Georgia* and related cases" (Donohue and Wolfers
2005, 792). Although Ehrlich's work was discredited, a new wave of studies claimed to have found similar effects. Commenting on an analysis that
challenged this conclusion, Ehrlich said, "If variations like unemployment,
income inequality, likelihood of apprehension and willingness to use the
death penalty are accounted for, the death penalty shows a significant deter-
ring effect" (*New York Times*, September 22, 2000). In sobering contrast,
Achen (2002, 446) warns that "A statistical specification with more than
three explanatory variables is meaningless." There are just too many ways to
fiddle with the numbers.

Similar remarks apply to the claim by John Lott (2000)—cited by John
Ashcroft as attorney general in the George W. Bush administration—that
the right to carry concealed handguns saves lives. Commenting on his work,
Hashem Dezhbakhs (cited after Donohue and Wolfers 2005, 845) writes: "The
academic survival of a flawed study may not be of much consequence. But,
unfortunately, the ill-effects of a bad policy, influenced by flawed research,
may hurt generations." In other words, we can tolerate waste, but we should
not accept harm.

The main problems with the routine use of regression analyses and similar techniques are *data mining* and *curve fitting*. By choosing appropriate independent variables and appropriate ways of operationalizing both the dependent and the independent variables, it is always possible to "explain" variations in the independent variable to a desirable level of significance. The result is junk science. Although it is possible to take precautions against this temptation, by estimating the model against half the data and then testing it against the other half, this is not standard or mandatory practice in the social sciences. Alternatively, one could post the hypothesis on the Internet before exploring it, to eliminate the scope for fiddling. To my knowledge, this is virtually never done. Why don't scholars want to be honest?

Many of the "large-N" analyses that dominate comparative politics are doomed from their inception. When scholars compile lists of civil wars to determine their triggers or compare countries to determine the link between political organization and economic growth, they are trying to do something that cannot be done. The complexity of any given case, the heterogeneity of different cases, and the problem of reliable data collection combine to create an insurmountable obstacle to statistical analysis. To understand *one* civil war may take a lifetime and require huge "shoe-leather" investments. The idea that one can understand *many* by the mechanical creation and analysis of large data sets is chimerical. The editor of a major journal of development economics told me that he sees one of his main functions as keeping large-N studies out of the journal. Journals that publish large-N studies of civil wars are less restrained.

MECHANISMS

The pathologies of soft and hard obscurantism are not marginal phenomena. In some countries, in some universities, and in some departments, they have a dominant status. In France and in Argentina, psychoanalysis is *the* main form of psychology. In France, the current success of Bruno Latour and Alain Badiou testifies to the dominance of soft obscurantism, in addition to the continuing influence of the slightly less absurd (although more easily imitable) writings of Bourdieu and Foucault. In the United States, some universities seem to specialize in soft obscurantism. Duke University is (or at least was) an example. A former editor of history books at Duke University Press quit his job because too many of the submitted manuscripts were about our *memory* of the past (a favorite postmodern topic) rather than about the past itself. In the United States, departments of literature and anthropology are, with honorable exceptions, dominated by soft obscurantists. In economic departments everywhere and in political science in the Anglo-Saxon world, hard obscurantism sets the tone. A younger colleague in a political science department complained to me that all his good articles were turned down by the leading journals, whereas his bad articles—those that conformed to the norms of hard obscurantism—were accepted.

These facts—I firmly believe they *are* facts—call for an explanation. How do large academic communities get locked into practices that are sterile, wasteful, and sometimes harmful? I cannot offer testable answers to this question, only speculations, some perhaps more robust than others. They should be supplemented by the study of the notoriously corrupt Italian academic system in Gambetta and Origgi (2013), by the acute analyses of French academic pathologies in Tagliatesta (2005), and by studies of incompetence in other areas (e.g., Dixon 1976; McMaster 1997).

I take it for granted that the aim of science is to explain and that all explanation is causal explanation (Elster 2007). When we believe we have found the cause of a phenomenon, there occurs a mental click of satisfaction. Other mental operations can also trigger clicks. There is the click of observing a *similarity* between the phenomenon and another one, the click of observing that the phenomenon has *consequences that benefit* someone or something, and the click of observing that some other phenomenon *could have been* the cause of the phenomenon we are studying. Because all these observations satisfy our deep-seated need to find order, patterns, and meanings in the universe, *they trigger a click that is easily mistaken for the real thing*, the click of explanation. (This is especially likely to happen to those who have never been exposed to the real thing.) I offer this not as an established truth, but as a hypothesis that might explain the grip that analogies, functional explanations, and just-so stories have on the mind.

There is some evidence to support these suggestions. The brain seems to have a built-in tendency to seek and find order and patterns in the universe even when there are none (Ramachandran and Blakeslee 1999, 136ff.; Shermer 2011, chap. 4). It also seems to prefer explanations that impute events—especially negative events—to agency rather than to an accident (Shermer 2011, chap. 5). In agrarian societies, high prices of grain are never seen as due to a bad harvest but to hoarding by speculators (Kaplan 1982).

Foucauldian theories are nurtured by this tendency. They are also nurtured by a natural tendency to explain phenomena in terms of their consequences rather than their causes: "A ready recourse to unwarranted functional or con-sequence explanation has long been observed in young children, and has been thought to be increasingly restrained in us as our acquisition of causal mechanical ideas and knowledge proceeds. However, recent research sug-gests that the inclination to these explanations is never truly overcome but instead *remains a default mode among adults*. . . . If the inclination is indeed so deep-seated and persistent, it becomes all the more important to recognize and resist it" (Vayda and Walters 2011, 15; my italics). *Social science should study bias, not instantiate it.*

In the case of hard obscurantism, notably among economists, one may add the temptation to believe that social science could one day become a real science on an analogy with physics. Although there is no reason to believe that "the unreasonable effectiveness of mathematics in the natural sciences" (Wigner 1960) has a parallel in the social sciences, the mere use of (moder-ately complex) mathematics in economic modeling may create or sustain an illusion to that effect.

I find it hard to believe, however, that these psychological mechanisms could, by themselves, account for the emergence of obscurantism. It seems more plausible that they could sustain and reinforce it once it is in place. The same is true of the various sociological mechanisms I shall discuss shortly. I confess, in other words, my inability to explain, however conjecturally, the *emergence* of obscurantism. This is not an unusual case in the social sciences. I believe, for instance, that we have some understanding of the operation of social norms once they are in place, but that their emergence is not well understood. In situations with multiple equilibria—one good, one bad for instance—we may be unable to predict which will emerge but understand the equilibrium behavior quite well. Nor do social scientists have much to say about strategies for modifying or abolishing harmful norms or changing bad equilibria. In the next section I discuss what, if anything, can be done to abolish obscurantism.

One obscurantism-sustaining mechanism is *mind binding*, an idea con-ceived on analogy with the Chinese practice of foot binding, which persisted as a bad equilibrium for centuries (Mackie 1996). Given that no parents would let their son marry a woman who did not have her feet bound, it was in the interest of the parents of girls to adhere to the practice. Although crippling and horribly painful, the practice was sustained by the fact that no family had an incentive to deviate unilaterally. My observation of the American academic situation strongly suggests to me that departments of economics and, increasingly, political science are caught in a bad equilibrium. The mind binding to which they subject their students is due, at least in part, to the perceived need to produce marriageable—hirable—candidates. A department that reduced the course load in game theory and increased the course requirements in economic or political history would have difficulties placing their students in first-tier universities.

A second mechanism arises through pluralistic ignorance. This idea dates from 1837, when Hans Christian Andersen published his tale "The Emperor's New Clothes." It was given a more theoretical formulation three years later, in the second volume of Tocqueville's *Democracy in America*, and then rediscovered in the early twentieth century. In an extreme case, pluralistic ignorance obtains when no member of a community believes a certain proposition or espouses a certain value, but each believes that everybody else holds the belief or the value. For a game-theoretic example, we may imagine a case of collective action in which all participants have Assurance Game preferences, but each believes that all others have Prisoner's Dilemma preferences. In the more common case, pluralistic ignorance obtains when only a few members hold the belief or the value in question, but most of them believe that most others do.

In the game-theoretic example, when people act on their false beliefs about the preferences of others, the observed actions will confirm their beliefs. Each will make the non-cooperative choice as his best response to the non-cooperative behavior that his false belief makes him expect from others. They are trapped in a bad equilibrium. In the case of economic and statistical models, this situation would obtain if each scholar, although secretly worried about the procedures, kept quiet because of the perception that his colleagues are firmly convinced of their validity. There are several mechanisms that might be at work here. From my own experience I know very well how a scholar's confidence in his own judgment can be undermined by the fact that the majority thinks differently. *How could all these people, who are certainly smarter than I am, be so wrong?* Also, even with unshakable self-confidence, a scholar might worry that speaking up might cause ostracism and career obstacles.

A third mechanism derives from the use of citation rankings to allocate funds to universities or to departments. Although many writers have commented on the perverse and pathological features of this system, they have not, to my knowledge, noted its obscurantist-sustaining effects. Once a group of obscurantist scholars in a given field has reached a critical mass, the number of within-group citations can be used to argue for funds and positions that will further cement their grip on the discipline in question.

Fourth, obscurantism is sustained by informal norms of the academic community that prevent frank criticism. In Norway, where I have criticized soft and hard obscurantism on a number of occasions, I have been regularly accused of being arrogant (and sometimes of being ignorant) and of not recognizing "the value of value pluralism." The fear of being the target of such accusations, together with the uncomfortable situation of charging colleagues whom one meets on a regular basis with doing substandard research, is probably an important reason why obscurantism continues to thrive. In this essay, I am to some extent guilty of such misplaced politeness, by failing to name my colleague at Columbia and my former colleague at the Collège de France. Interested readers can easily identify them, however. ·

Finally, obscurantism is sustained by the self-interest of nonobscurantist scholars. To be effective, an attack on obscurantism has to be well documented and well argued. Mere diatribes are pointless and probably counterproductive. (Sokal's hoax was effective, but cannot be repeated.) Yet scholars have a greater personal interest in achieving positive results than in exposing the flaws of others, not only because of the reward system of science, but also because the achievement of positive results is intrinsically more satisfying. On grounds of self-interest, therefore, many scholars will hesitate to take time off from their main work and hope that someone else will do the cleaning up. The stage is set for another bad equilibrium, with the difference that if all scholars have selfish preferences, there *is* no good equilibrium.

WHAT IS TO BE DONE?

If the situation is as bad as I think it is, what can be done to improve it? My basic answer is "nothing." The forces that resist change are too powerful. Yet it may be worthwhile to ask whether the five sociological mechanisms I discussed in the previous section could provide some hope.

Foot binding was abolished when a group of families got together and made a collective and public pledge to refrain from binding the feet of their daughters and to forbid their sons from marrying a woman with bound feet. This leap was possible only because the situation was perceived as a bad—indeed, horrible—equilibrium. It is doubtful, to put it mildly, whether members of the economics and political science professions perceive their situation to be that of a bad equilibrium. Self-satisfaction rather than self-doubt seems to be the rule.

As we know, pluralistic ignorance can be lifted when someone observes that the emperor has no clothes. It is possible that a similar effect could be produced in the economics profession if a prestigious insider affirmed loud and clear that the discipline as a whole is a degenerating research program. Nobody so far has done so. Ariel Rubinstein is perhaps the one who has come closest, but not in a systematic fashion. If prestigious insiders with doubts spoke up, younger members of the profession would probably feel freer to carve out their own path of research. I do not think, however, that the whole obscurantist network would unravel. The number of hard-headed and self-confident practitioners is simply too large.

There is an apparently simple remedy for the pathologies of citation counts: stop using them and instead evaluate scholars by *reading* their work. To induce competent scholars to take on this task, one would have to grant them some leave from teaching and administrative duties. Although I believe this measure could be effective in some cases, a fundamental question remains: Who would choose the evaluators? How could one prevent obscurantists from being assessed by other obscurantists?

The force of informal norms and of self-interest can be overcome only by public-spiritedness. Brian Barry (2002) was a paradigm of a scholar who was both unbothered by norms of politeness (when they were irrelevant) and willing to perform a public service by demolishing, line by line, argument by argument, obscurantist multicultural writings. One can cite, in the same vein, David Freedman (2005, 2010), Robyn Dawes (1994), and Alan Sokal (1996). Their practice suggests a rousing call to conscientious scholars: "Liberate your students!"

REFERENCES

Achen, C. 2002. "Towards a New Political Methodology." *Annual Review of Political Science* 5: 423–50.

Ainslie, G. 1992. *Picoeconomics*. Cambridge: Cambridge University Press.

Barry, B. 2002. *Culture & Equality*. Cambridge, Mass.: Harvard University Press.

Cohen, G. A. 2002. "Deeper into Bullshit." In *Contours of Agency: Essays on Themes from Harry Frankfurt*, ed. S. Buss and L. Overton. Cambridge, Mass.: MIT Press.

Dawes, R. 1994. *House of Cards*. New York: Free Press.

Dixon, N. 1976. *The Psychology of Military Incompetence*. London: Futura.

Donohue, J., and J. Wolfers. 2005. "Uses and Abuses of Empirical Evidence in the Death Penalty Debate." *Stanford Law Review* 58: 791–846.

Elster, J. 2000. "Rational-Choice History: A Case of Excessive Ambition?" *American Political Science Review* 94: 685–95.

——. 2007. *Explaining Social Behavior*. Cambridge: Cambridge University Press.

——. 2009. "Excessive Ambitions." *Capitalism and Society* 4: 1–30.

——. 2011. "Hard and Soft Obscurantism in the Humanities and Social Sciences." *Diogenes* 58: 159–70.

Foucault, M. 1977. *Discipline and Punish*. New York: Vintage.

——. 1980. "The Confession of the Flesh." In *Power/Knowledge Selected Interviews and Other Writings*, ed. Colin Gordon. London: Harvester.

Frankfurt, H. 2005. *On Bullshit*. Princeton, N.J.: Princeton University Press.

Fraser, N. 1993. "Rethinking the Public Sphere." In *Habermas and the Public Sphere*, ed. C. Calhoun. Cambridge, Mass.: MIT Press.

Freedman, D. 2005. *Statistical Models*. Cambridge: Cambridge University Press.

——. 2010. *Statistical Models and Causal Inference: A Dialogue with the Social Sciences*. Cambridge: Cambridge University Press.

Gambetta, D., and G. Origgi. 2013. "The LL Game: The Curious Preference for Low Quality and Its Norms." *Politics, Philosophy & Economics* 12: 3–23.

Gjelsvik, O. 2006. "Bullshit Illuminated." In *Understanding Choice, Explaining Behaviour*, ed. J. Elster, O. Gjelsvik, A. Hylland, and K.O Moene. Oslo: Oslo Academic.

Kahneman, D. 2011. *Thinking, Fast and Slow*. New York: Farrar, Straus and Giroux.

Kaplan, S. 1982. "The Famine Plot Persuasion in Eighteenth-Century France." *Transactions of the American Philosophical Society* 72 (3): 1–79.

Lott, J. 2000. *More Guns, Less Crime*. Chicago: University of Chicago Press

Mackie, G. 1996. "Ending Footbinding and Infibulation: A Convention Account." *American Sociological Review* 61: 999–1017.

McMaster, H. R. 1997. *Dereliction of Duty*. New York: Harper.

Ramachandran, V. S., and S. Blakeslee. 1999. *Phantoms in the Brain*. New York: William Morrow.

Said, E. 1993. "Jane Austen and Empire." In *Raymond Williams: Critical Perspectives*, ed. T. Eagleton. Boston: Northeastern University Press.

Schelling, T. 1960. *Strategy and Conflict*. Cambridge, Mass.: Harvard University Press.

Shermer, M. 2011. *The Believing Brain*. New York: Times Books.

Sokal, A. 1996. "Transgressing the Boundaries: Towards a Transformative Hermeneutics of Quantum Gravity." *Social Text* 46/47: 217–52.

Tagliatesta, F. 2005. *Instructions aux académiques*. Rouen: Christophe Chomant.

Vayda, A., and B. Walters. 2011. Introduction to *Causal Explanation for Social Scientists* Lanham, Md.: Altamira.

Wigner, E. 1960. "The Unreasonable Effectiveness of Mathematics in the Natural Sciences." *Communications on Pure and Applied Mathematics* 13: 1–14.

Wintrobe, R. 2006. *Rational Extremism*. Cambridge: Cambridge University Press.

7

WHAT'S SO SPECIAL ABOUT ACADEMIC FREEDOM?

MICHELE MOODY-ADAMS

INTRODUCTION: THE UNIVERSITY AS "INTELLECTUAL EXPERIMENT STATION"

N THE AUTUMN of 1999, Princeton University's appointment of Peter Singer to a chair in bioethics generated protest from national disability-rights groups and critics of abortion, as well as from a small but vocal group of Princeton undergraduates and alumni. Singer had long been the subject of controversy for claiming that the lives of some severely disabled people are not worth living, and therefore that it can be justifiable to euthanize them. A different kind of controversy emerged when an influential member of Princeton's board of trustees publicly linked Singer's views on euthanasia of severely disabled infants to Nazism, and declared that he would make no further contributions to the university until Singer's appointment was rescinded—even though he had initially voted, as a trustee, in favor of the appointment.[1]

Ultimately, the Princeton board refused to rescind the appointment, insisting it would not apply "any ideological litmus test to the appointment of distinguished scholars and teachers" and "unequivocally and unanimously" reasserting its commitment to academic freedom.[2] The board thus affirmed the notion that in order to further the university's defining purposes— of producing knowledge, preserving traditions of inquiry and argument, educating undergraduates, and training scholars and researchers in the disciplines—academics and the institutions in which they work must be protected from demands to conform to convictions and orthodoxies external to the academic enterprise. To the question "What's so special about academic freedom?" Princeton's trustees answered that it is essential to the proper functioning of the university.

In virtue of its role in the university, moreover, academic freedom is indispensable to the creation of goods essential to modern society at large: the extension of basic knowledge; the growth of translational research; and the education of students who are capable of participating constructively in political life and responding creatively to social diversity and global economic complexity. In the "1915 Declaration of Principles" that became the charter for the American Association of University Professors (AAUP), philosopher Arthur Lovejoy and economist Edwin Seligman emphasized the connection between academic freedom and human achievement. Academic freedom, they argued, is necessary to protect the university as "an intellectual experiment station, where new ideas may germinate and where their fruit, though still distasteful to the community as a whole, may be allowed to ripen," and they urged that the self-regulating university is essential to the realization of fundamental human goods.[3] Lovejoy and Seligman thus understood that academic freedom is a good that any stable political society will rationally choose to protect.[4]

Yet if academic freedom is really a fundamental social good, why do some critics remain resistant to, and even fearful of, the very idea of academic freedom? Contemporary challenges to academic freedom have four main sources. First, academics have become complacent about explaining and defending academic freedom in the public arena, often assuming that what justifies academic freedom is too obvious to need restating and that challenges to particular claims of academic freedom can only be politically motivated attacks on the academy. But while unsympathetic critics do sometimes dominate public discussion of academic freedom, the dearth of careful reflection on the topic can leave even sympathetic critics confused about what constitutes a legitimate exercise of academic freedom.[5] In late 2011, for example, when New York University professor Andrew Ross expressed solidarity with students in the "Occupy Wall Street" movement by calling for mass defaults on student loans, a critic accused Ross of "academic malpractice" for urging action that she urged (not unreasonably) could actually harm the students and called (I believe unjustifiably) for the university to "silence" him on the issue of student debt.[6] Ross responded by linking the criticism to "neo-McCarthyist" attacks on the academy and suggested the author just did not appreciate the "niceties of academic freedom."[7] But the reply would have been more effective had it spelled out these "niceties" and articulated plausible grounds for protecting an instructor who makes controversial public pronouncements from university reprisals. In the absence of such a reply, any appeal to academic freedom can suggest professional arrogance and intellectual arbitrariness.

Second, though few academics will ever have such prominence as Singer or Ross, most nonetheless have extensive influence and authority in the classroom. Even the simplest exercise of academic freedom by the most junior instructor can have a profound effect on students at a formative stage in their intellectual lives. Many commentators appreciate how seriously most academics take the responsibilities that come with this authority. But even a sympathetic critic may wonder whether a self-regulating academy can respond effectively and fairly to credible allegations of professorial misconduct. It does not inspire confidence to learn of an episode involving an instructor at a midwestern university who supplemented his human sexuality course with a live "demonstration" of female sexual response.[8] Attendance at the demonstration was apparently optional. But might some students have felt subtle pressure to attend an event described as "valuable" by the professor?[9] It was eventually revealed that the event was hastily arranged. But can a demonstration involving human subjects conform to reasonable regulations on research involving human subjects when the decision to allow it is made in haste?[10] The course was ultimately eliminated from the university's curriculum. But the episode raises serious concern that the autonomy granted to professional academics in virtue of academic freedom means that student complaints about possible misuses of that freedom will be taken seriously only when alleged misconduct generates public uproar.[11]

But third, the protections bound up with academic freedom include a robust right to exclude certain kinds of disagreement. A biology professor who lectures on evolution cannot be required to give equal time to creationism, and a World War II historian cannot be forced to give equal time to Holocaust denials. Yet even if we support these choices, we may still wonder about the grounds of the authority to exclude creationism or Holocaust denials from certain academic contexts. How can we show that these exclusions are not intellectually arbitrary or politically suspect? Still further, why do the rights of citizens to express their differences about "the facts of the matter" not carry the same weight in academic contexts as they do in nonacademic contexts? Are the principles that define academic freedom really so different from those practices that define freedom of speech?

I will argue that freedom of speech and academic freedom must, indeed, be justified on very different grounds. Yet the two kinds of freedom raise similar questions about how to distinguish offensive expression that deserves protection from harmful expression that might not. This challenge generates a fourth important questioning of academic freedom. Even those who defend academic freedom may wonder how far the bounds of tolerance must extend. Critics of Singer's views on euthanasia or of Ross's call for student loan defaults are not unreasonable to be concerned about other goods that must be weighed in the balance, and possibly sacrificed, in order to protect academic freedom. There can be serious conflicts, for instance, between Singer's view that some lives are not worth living and the commitment to the equal worth of persons that is fundamental to democratic institutions. Even a sympathetic critic can reasonably ask why a democratic society should protect the freedom to defend views that appear to conflict with basic democratic values.

Academic freedom thus underwrites policies and practices that, as Jonathan R. Cole has urged, are "designed to be unsettling."[12] My account addresses the concerns that lead to criticisms of these policies and practices in order to show that the benefits of protecting academic freedom outweigh its potential dangers. Section 1 discusses the basic elements of academic freedom to inform the consideration, addressed in section 2, of how to determine when academic freedom has actually been abused. I show in section 3 that the practices of exclusion that are central to academic freedom must be understood as the defining practices of a professional guild, and I consider the conditions under which it is reasonable to invest public trust in the authority of the guild. Section 4 offers a detailed account of the legitimate exercise of academic freedom; and in section 5, I explore one of the social goods that academic freedom underwrites: the opportunity for inquiry that enhances one's capacity to respond constructively to human diversity. The paper concludes, in section 6, by showing that contemporary attacks on academic freedom endanger a precious social good on the strength of a mistaken and impoverished view of human possibility.

THE FUNDAMENTAL ELEMENTS
OF ACADEMIC FREEDOM

In affirming the value of academic freedom, we defend a notion that marks the convergence of three historical developments: (1) the evolution of the idea of faculty self-governance that emerged in medieval English universities; (2) the ascendancy of the nineteenth-century German concept of *Lehrfreiheit*, which emphasized the role of research in university life; and (3) the modernizing impulses of early twentieth-century America that encouraged the professionalization of scholarly activity.[13] In the "1915 Declaration of Principles" on which the AAUP was founded, Arthur Lovejoy and Edwin Seligman articulated the emerging consensus about what academic freedom should achieve:

> The proper fulfillment of the work of the professoriate requires that our universities shall be so free that no fair-minded person shall find any excuse for even a suspicion that the utterances of university teachers are shaped or restricted by the judgment, not of professional scholars, but of inexpert and possibly not wholly disinterested persons outside of their ranks.[14]

The "1915 Declaration" has been superseded in some respects by other AAUP documents, most notably by the "1940 Statement of Principles on Academic Freedom and Tenure" and various supplements from later decades.[15] Yet Lovejoy and Seligman's founding idea, that the university must be "an inviolable refuge" from the "tyranny" of public opinion, helped to determine the legal outcomes, institutional structures, and cultural conventions that define academic freedom in America, and thus their stance continues to shape debate about the nature and justification of that freedom.

Over time, the founding principle gave rise to a basic norm of academic practice according to which persons, groups, and institutions constituting "the academy" may justly expect society to protect them in the exercise of a robust right of self-regulation. That robust right is actually a *set* of rights through which professional academics may dictate, within reasonable limits, the terms of their work: (1) the right to determine the fundamental content of research and publication; (2) the right to make important decisions about the content and terms of teaching; and (3) the right to "speak or write as citizens

. . . free from institutional censorship or discipline."[16] Implicit in all three of these rights of self-regulation is the notion of a right to determine content. As I show in section 5, the right to determine content is essentially a right of nonneutrality, comprising (1) a right to exclude, (2) a right to advocate, and (3) a right to risk offending one's audience.

Taking the broadest view, the academic freedom rights of individuals are inextricably linked to the processes through which academics become accredited professionals.[17] Stanley Fish's provocative claim that academic freedom originated, and indeed continues, as a "guild practice" is thus an apt analysis of the processes by which academic freedom came into existence in America.[18] The AAUP has cautioned that the guild must set limits on the reasonable exercise of academic freedom and that the secure enjoyment of its rights and privileges demands professional commitment to those limits on the part of every academic. In particular, research must conform to disciplinary standards of argument and inquiry; teaching must respect the freedom of students to learn; and extramural expression must be carefully distinguished from official university positions. To be sure, academic freedom rights are secure only when guild practices are underwritten by certain enabling conditions, in particular by material resources sufficient to run a college or university, and by social conventions and legal structures that protect faculty governance and, especially, permanent or continuous tenure.[19] But when the material resources and legal structures are in place and there is confidence in the academy's principles and policies, professional academics are granted a degree of autonomy enjoyed by few nonacademic professionals.

At the start of the twenty-first century, however, confidence in the academy's practices is at an especially low point. Many critics argue that far from being a defense against the coercive force of *external* orthodoxies, academic freedom more often insulates the academy's *internal* orthodoxies from critical scrutiny. Academic orthodoxies, they continue, are unjustifiably hostile to many ideas and assumptions that should at least be contemplated as part of a proper education. Some of the most influential charges of this kind originate in the work of twentieth-century political conservatives in America. Perhaps the best known example is William F. Buckley's *God and Man at Yale*, which challenges what Buckley deemed the overwhelming "secularism" and "collectivism" of his alma mater.[20] But no political ideology has a monopoly on challenges to academic freedom. Less than twenty years after the publication of *God and Man at Yale* feminist thinkers and ethnic studies scholars, who would mostly have rejected Buckley's politics, challenged the guild structures that underwrite academic freedom on the basis of their tendency to exclude new kinds of scholarship from the university or at a minimum to hinder their reception.

Over the last two decades, critics have been increasingly likely to charge that academic freedom is too often a license for overtly *coercive* activity in the classroom. These critics claim that many faculty members are allowed to actively silence students who disagree with prevailing academic orthodoxies. They also charge that departments and institutions design curricula that ignore the diversity of moral and political conceptions in their student constituencies, thereby creating courses that are either barely indistinguishable from indoctrination or that involve concerted efforts to offend rather than to enlighten. The charge of insensitivity to diversity is most often made with regard to religious convictions, but the academy has also been criticized for marginalizing or deriding conservative political views that may be underrepresented among the faculty.

Recent challenges to academic freedom have also involved a fundamental change in proposed remedies to presumed offenses. Especially noteworthy are efforts to subject all substantive academic decision making to regulation by state and federal legislation.[21] Such measures could license direct government intervention in decisions about hiring and firing, promotion and tenure, and standards for determining the limits of acceptable academic expression in teaching, research, and public debate. This intervention would obviously produce profound changes in the functioning of colleges and universities.[22] Academics who hope to protect academic freedom must therefore confront the question of whether a self-regulating academy can and will respond appropriately when academic freedom may have been abused. To that end, we must also address the more basic question of how to determine when some policy or practice really constitutes an abuse of academic freedom in the first place.

HOW CAN WE DETERMINE WHEN ACADEMIC FREEDOM HAS ACTUALLY BEEN ABUSED?

Public mistrust of academic freedom, and academic self-regulation in the broadest sense, is often based on fundamental misunderstandings of the academic enterprise. Most academics believe a good education will encourage students to contemplate at least some ideas and practices that they not only find unfamiliar but that they might initially resist or even find offensive. Such encounters may well be crucial to the development of critical intelligence. Yet vocal critics charge that academic presentations of ideas and beliefs students resist or find offensive are too often indistinguishable from indoctrination or "thought control." Some critics even seem to believe that the very fact of discomfort and feelings of offense constitutes proof the encounter that caused those feelings is academically illegitimate.

But the legitimacy of an educational experience cannot be determined by how controversial or unsettling the ideas might seem to the public. As I argue more fully in section 5, the educational legitimacy of an academic encounter is a function of the extent to which the ideas and practices under consideration are connected to recognized disciplinary standards, along with how reasonably the instructor has balanced the risks and benefits of possible offense. For instance, discussing nonvoluntary euthanasia of disabled infants can be a reasonable exercise of academic freedom in a college course on bioethics, even if the idea unsettles or offends students in the course. The philosophical community accepts that discussions of euthanasia invite sophisticated critical reflection on the nature of personhood and the moral weight of human suffering, and if the instructor presents such material in a manner that leaves students free to question and dissent, its presentation can be a fully legitimate and justifiable exercise of academic freedom.[23]

Why, then, do vocal critics of academic freedom continue to argue that offense or discomfort might be a measure of academic inappropriateness? Part of the difficulty is the inevitable asymmetry between the instructor's academic freedom and the students' freedom to disagree with what the instructor presents. It is sometimes suggested that the student who disagrees deserves "equal time" in the classroom—or something close to equal time—to articulate the full measure of her disagreement. But academic freedom is not an extension of free speech rights. As Louis Menand has argued, although the content of what is protected by academic freedom frequently overlaps with the content of what is protected by the laws and conventions protecting free speech, the two freedoms have profoundly different conceptual origins and are rooted in quite different purposes and goals.[24] Freedom of speech protects the equal rights of citizens to express their convictions in private exchanges and in many written and oral contexts in the "public square," subject to the proviso that the exercise of the right is compatible with an equal opportunity for others to exercise the right. But academic freedom protects the rights of the accredited scholar to (respectfully) limit the expression of dissent in academic contexts. Students must be free to learn, free to speak about what they learn, and free to disagree with their instructors in appropriate ways and contexts. But there is neither a moral nor a legal imperative to extend the full range of rights and privileges of academic freedom to all who may want it.

Academic freedom, especially as it concerns the classroom, is sometimes discussed in the same context as the notion of "a fair and balanced forum" for the discussion of conflicting opinions. But as I show in section 4, one of the central academic freedom rights is the instructor's right to exclude certain ideas, points of view, or methods of argument from a course on the basis of expert judgment. In this regard, the expertise and authority of professional academics is analogous to the expertise and authority of other professionals, such as medical doctors. Just as it is unreasonable to demand that medical patients should be able to write their own prescriptions and determine their own treatment, it is not reasonable to demand that the content of the curriculum be determined by reference to what students want to discuss. As Supreme Court Justice David Souter wrote in the concurring opinion in *Regents of Univ. of Wisconsin v. Southworth*, a case about the use of student fees on college and university campuses, "Some fraction of students' tuition payments may be used for course offerings that are ideologically offensive to some students, and for paying professors who say things in the university forum that are ideologically offensive to some particular students."[25] A responsible instructor will provide opportunities for reasonable expression of student disagreement with course material, and responsible institutions will devise fair and effective means for responding to credible concerns about possible abuses of academic freedom. But when students register for classes, they implicitly consent to be exposed to at least some ideas and concepts that may trouble or offend them and also to be less free to express disagreement than they would be in a public, nonacademic context.

This shows that there can be fundamental tensions between important liberal democratic values—in this case, the value attached to free speech rights—and many of the values embodied in defensible academic practice. Of course, there are also important connections between some central aims of liberal democracy and certain exercises of academic freedom, as I will show in section 6. But the fact remains that democratic values and the values of academic life are sometimes in conflict. Defenders of academic freedom have sometimes been unwilling to acknowledge these conflicts, because it may seem to concede too much to the academy's critics. Yet the potential for conflict between the values of academic life and democratic values that underwrite the protection of free speech is unmistakable. Stanley Fish reminds us that when academic historians deny that the work of Holocaust deniers is serious history, the deniers will predictably (and plausibly) complain that academic intolerance shuts them out of the life of the academy. But as Fish rightly argues, this intolerance can be defended, because the principles that justify academic freedom in higher education are not rooted in democratic values but in the authority of the disciplines in which academics are trained and accredited.[26]

AUTHORITY, EXCLUSION, AND THE VIRTUES OF ACADEMIC PRACTICE

Practices of exclusion play a fundamental role in the structures that underwrite academic freedom. Communities of academic inquiry are constituted by exclusionary practices governing membership, and standards of argument and inquiry evolve as shared understandings that are internal to these exclusive "communities of the competent."[27] These shared understandings involve the notion that some ways of arguing, and some points of view, are simply not worthy of recognition within the community of inquiry. A responsible academic is thus *by definition* committed to certain orthodoxies—in particular, to the orthodoxies that define communities of competent inquirers and underwrite standards for inquiry carried out in those communities. Judith Jarvis Thomson has convincingly defended this feature of academic disciplines, particularly as it shapes the practice of faculty selection.[28] Stanley Fish notes further that in addition to governing faculty selection, practices of exclusion are fundamental to determining the content of the curriculum and the nature and function of various forums for scholarly research.[29] Indeed, he insists that "inclusion" is not "an attainable goal" in the university, and that

> it is not even a worthy one, for to attain it would be to legitimize all points of view and directions of inquiry and thereby to default on the responsibility of the university to produce knowledge and to refine judgment. The debate is never between the inclusive university and a university marked by exclusions; the debate is always between competing structures of exclusion.[30]

But can we not reasonably ask whether some structures of exclusion are more defensible than others? Fish sometimes writes as though all the exclusionary practices of the academy are merely manifestations of interest-group "politics" and even what appear to be thoughtful exclusionary practices are never more than "politics":

> The assertion of interest is always what's going on even when, and especially when, interest wraps itself in high-sounding abstractions. This is not an indictment of anyone, certainly not an indictment of anyone for having forsaken principles for politics; politics is all there is, and it's a good thing too. Principles and abstractions don't exist except as the rhetorical accompaniments of practices in search of good public relations.[31]

Yet there is one context in which Fish claims to find nonarbitrary uses of the academy's exclusionary practices. In his account of the resistance of academic history to Holocaust deniers, for example, he vehemently rejects the idea that this resistance is just a "naked exercise of power":

> Shutting Holocaust deniers out would be a naked exercise of power if it were arbitrary, if there were nothing behind it except the desire wholly to own the franchise and prevent anyone else from claiming a part of it. But standing behind the exclusion of deniers is the massive record of rigorous research by superbly credentialed men and women whose conclusions have met every reasonable test put to them.[32]

Standing behind the actions of the historians who exclude Holocaust deniers, then, is not just "politics" but the eminently reasonable authority of the "guild."[33]

Fish rightly traces the legitimacy of academic freedom to the guild authority of the academy. But, like many contemporary academics, he fails to acknowledge that what is under attack in most challenges to academic freedom is precisely the academy's *claim* to authority—its claim to be engaged in the rightful, nonarbitrary exercise of intellectual power and influence in classrooms, in research, and in the public forum. Bernard Williams once observed that some disciplinary authority is in greater danger of attack than others, most obviously in the humanities and social sciences.[34] Yet attacks on academic freedom in the humanities and social sciences endanger all the disciplines. Challenges to academic freedom in the sciences have so far mainly affected elementary and secondary schools on such topics as evolution and climate change. But these challenges should be taken as a sign that even in the university, the authority of science could someday be subject to broad popular challenge. The responsibility to defend academic freedom therefore must be shared across the disciplines, and an appropriate defense must articulate the circumstances under which academics, in general, *rightfully* exercise control over the functions of the university.[35] Both the influence and the authority of academics will be in jeopardy unless academics themselves become more rigorous in defending the grounds of academic freedom. But is it really possible to provide a compelling counterweight to unsympathetic critics who treat the academy's claims to authority as the mere monopoly of an arrogant and self-righteous professional guild? I believe that a compelling reply must start from an idea that informed the 1915 founding of the AAUP: the idea that academic freedom must be seen as *a public trust*, rooted in the belief that those to whom its rights and privileges are granted can be safely accorded a wide-ranging freedom to regulate themselves.[36] This idea gets very little attention even in some of the most thoughtful contemporary treatments of academic freedom. Yet even in ostensibly private institutions, and quite obviously in public institutions, practices such as tenure are underwritten by legal customs and cultural conventions that depend for their continuance on public trust. It is thus essential to consider what might be the basis of that public trust.

Bernard Williams's account, in *Truth and Truthfulness*, of how to think about the problem of authority in the academy offers a helpful start.[37] Following Williams, I contend that public trust in the academy and its disciplines depends upon the public's confidence that accredited academics can be counted on to embody certain virtues. By "virtues," here, I mean intellectual virtues: habits of mind and practice that are conducive to excellence in an intellectual discipline. One of the most important of the relevant virtues is what I call seriousness, by which I mean the agent's readiness to engage in careful inquiry and to translate the outcomes of that inquiry into responsible teaching, research, and (in some cases) extramural pronouncements. Because serious inquiry is ideally disinterested inquiry that aims at truth, the protection of public trust in the academy also requires two additional virtues under the umbrella of what Williams calls "truthfulness"—particularly the virtues of sincerity and accuracy.[38] By "sincerity," here, Williams means "a disposition to make sure that one's assertion expresses what one actually believes," and I think he is right to assume that this disposition is a central component of scholarly trustworthiness.[39] Taken together, the virtues of seriousness, accuracy, and sincerity can provide a foundation of the trustworthiness capable of grounding the authority of the academy and its disciplines.

Fish seems to recognize that intellectual virtues (like seriousness, sincerity, and accuracy) can ultimately distinguish the attitudes and practices of academic historians who reject Holocaust deniers from interest-group politics.[40] But he fails to explore the possibility that possessing and displaying those virtues is what makes it reasonable for society to trust in the nonarbitrariness of excluding Holocaust deniers from ordinary academic life. Academic freedom is secure and the self-regulated academy operates properly only when it is reasonable for the public to believe that academic practice embodies recognizable intellectual virtues.

UNDERSTANDING AND RESPONSIBLY APPLYING THE RIGHT OF NONNEUTRALITY

Yet it can be difficult, in practice, to know precisely how to provide the assurance on which public trust depends. As I noted at the outset, the right to determine content that is a central right of academic freedom is a right of nonneutrality, understood as a set of more specific rights (1) to exclude, (2) to advocate, and (3) to risk giving offense. The challenge is to combine seriousness, sincerity, and accuracy with the robust exercise of the right of nonneutrality. But how is it possible to effectively combine a commitment to accuracy, for instance, with exercise of a robust right to exclude certain claims from the realm of academic discourse? More generally, is there any compelling answer to the charge that academic life has become an extended exercise in shielding academic orthodoxies from critical scrutiny?

But consider the academic historian who insists that Holocaust denials are not serious history. Surely we can say this stance is justifiable if it conforms to reasonable principles, and we can say what makes the relevant principles reasonable. What constitutes a reasonable principle will follow, in large measure, from disciplinary expertise—which, properly exercised, can be the source of sincere and discerning judgment. The most fundamental principle of reasonableness, here, is that it must be possible to establish clear connections between the relevant exclusions and the disciplinary expertise from which the exclusions flow. That is, any decision to exclude must either have a clear relation to standards of argument and inquiry sanctioned by the discipline (or disciplines) in which a course is rooted or must embody standards that can be convincingly shown more reasonable than current disciplinary practices. In this context, "compelling" means susceptible of articulation to knowledgeable colleagues and secondarily (though no less seriously) to students and other concerned stakeholders. Thus one might demonstrate the relevant academic virtues by being willing to explain the link between particular curricular decisions and relevant disciplinary standards.

Intellectually virtuous and responsible uses of the right to exclude will tend to be intellectually "conservative," most often deferring to disciplinary standards (or working hard to say why it is not necessary to do so). This conservatism will be especially pronounced in the natural sciences, where, as Thomas Kuhn has argued, "mature" communities of inquiry exercise extraordinary control not only over modes of argument and inquiry but also over the problem-defining processes that shape research activity and, ultimately, the teaching that presupposes it.[41] By virtue of the subject matter, standards of exclusion that shape problem-defining processes in the social sciences and the humanities are far less insulated from the concerns of everyday life and hence less tightly controlled by the relevant communities of inquiry. But even in the social sciences and the humanities, it is an unavoidable fact that some "orthodoxies" cannot be relinquished without destroying the fabric of the communities of inquiry that constitute the disciplines. If protecting such orthodoxies serves to exclude Holocaust deniers, astrologists, and would-be inventors of perpetual motion machines, this is surely a price worth paying.

"Outsiders" are not the only ones constrained by such orthodoxies. They sometimes constrain the scholar's ability to mount constructive criticism to a discipline from within communities of inquiry. I have certainly worried about the intellectually conservative tendencies of my own discipline of philosophy, particularly in its initial hostility to the feminist thinkers and critical race theorists who have influenced some of my own work in the discipline. Yet such hostility generates an unavoidable irony of academic life: structures that might impede the entry of feminists or critical race theorists into the philosophical profession, for instance, ultimately protect their rights and privileges as philosophers, when (and if) they make their way into the academy. To be sure, defenders of academic orthodoxies tend to respond slowly even to the most plausible challenges to their authority. But instructors can prevent unduly coercive consequences of this tendency in the classroom if they respectfully articulate the reasons for exclusions and, where possible, provide possibilities for students to opt out of unsettling demands.

Academic freedom is not exhausted by the right to exclude, however. If teaching and research are to have valuable content, the right of academic nonneutrality must include a right to positive advocacy. It is impossible to teach, for instance, unless one advocates *something*. Still further, some forms of advocacy that are most fundamental to pedagogical practice may actually be the most controversial of all. For instance, merely by walking into most university classrooms as an instructor, one advocates for the value of inquiry rooted in reason, something that may not be valued by everyone on the other side of the lectern. Further, a statement on a course syllabus announcing that plagiarism will not be tolerated is an advocacy of academic integrity—a stance that far too many of our students will reject. Still further, when certain *kinds* of people enter a university classroom as teachers—say, members of social groups that produce relatively few academics or few academics in particular disciplines—their very presence in the classroom endorses their status as authorities, even if some students (and some colleagues) resist their presence. Those who say that advocacy "has no place" in the classroom, then, simply fail to appreciate the extent to which controversial messages can be embodied in the very act of entering a classroom. A general right to engage in advocacy in a course is thus the second right that defines pedagogically appropriate nonneutrality.

When forms of advocacy must go beyond this kind of expressive conduct, say, to the mention of examples or positions with politically controversial content, the exercise of the advocacy right is (as before) justified only when governed by plausible principles. Here, the main governing principle once again requires that the instructor be able to establish clear and strong connections between the controversial example or position and the subject matter of the course, competencies and habits of mind appropriate to the course, or success elsewhere in the university. Moreover, as in the case of the right to exclude, responsible and intellectually virtuous uses of the right to advocate must be rooted not only in the *fact* of such connections but in the instructor's ability and willingness to articulate them.

Given the moral and political content of so many basic pedagogical decisions—particularly in courses directly concerned with moral and political ideas—the right to advocate must sometimes extend to positions with substantive political or moral content. A philosophy professor asked to defend the inclusion of King's "Letter from Birmingham Jail" in a discussion of civil disobedience can plausibly argue that King's role in the American civil rights movement—and his subsequent influence on philosophical theories of civil disobedience—gives the "Letter" a special place in the canon of ethical reflection. But this seemingly simple, and eminently plausible, pedagogical choice may trouble the student who has been taught that King was a dangerous and politically subversive force. The instructor must be ready to show that the choice is likely to produce a deeper understanding of course subject matter or further the development of relevant skills and that it draws on understandings shared by the relevant community of competent inquirers. Again, a careful instructor will, whenever possible, allow reasonable dissent in class discussions and assignments.

The third and final right of academic nonneutrality—what I call the right to risk offense—follows quite naturally from the right to advocacy. But how does one combine a commitment to seriousness and care in the conduct of inquiry with the exercise of the right to risk offense? As before, there are conditions dictating the reasonable exercise of this right, and a responsible use of academic freedom always requires an instructor to consider these conditions with great care. In this case, there are four governing principles to observe. The first general principle is that one must aim for "truth in advertising." That is, a responsible instructor will take every appropriate opportunity (a course syllabus, the first day of class, informal discussions with students) to be explicit about the main assumptions shaping the class, as well as about potentially controversial methods or claims important to the class. The second governing principle prescribes care in choosing potentially offensive materials. This means that the responsible exercise of the right presupposes efforts to reflect in advance on which materials or claims might prove upsetting or offensive and to consider carefully the emotional and intellectual strengths and limitations of the intended audience. The third principle promotes demands that the instructor make every effort to present potentially offensive or upsetting material that respects the conditions of civility and respect in the classroom and in the institution as a whole. Indeed, in ignoring regulations governing human subjects and insufficiently explaining why an event he deemed "valuable" could also be optional, the instructor who offered an optional live "demonstration" of female sexual response gave insufficient attention to these conditions of civility and respect for his students and for the institution. The fourth governing principle demands that the instructor consider carefully whether the potential pedagogical benefits of expressing the potentially offensive idea or argument can genuinely outweigh any of the three most likely kinds of risks: (1) risks for the well-being of individual students, (2) risks for classroom relations between students who disagree, and (3) risks for classroom relations between students, as a whole, and the instructor.

These four principles governing the right to risk (and give) offense sometimes require an instructor to consider self-censorship—at least with regard to certain very controversial topics expressed or discussed in certain contexts. This is the point, of course, of my analysis of the human sexual response case. But it must be observed, first, that self-censorship is not intrinsically a bad thing; a disposition to thoughtful self-censorship has long been recognized as a fundamental support of a civil society. A broad commitment to civility in certain academic contexts might have as much value for our students as a dogged insistence on exercising the right to offend at every turn. Second, I am not urging that civility should trump the deep and engaged exploration of difficult ideas in appropriate forums. Rather, as I have urged, the reasonable and responsible exercise of the right to offend must be attentive to the strengths and limitations of its audience. An undergraduate classroom does not provide the same kind of audience as a graduate seminar, and even a graduate seminar may not contain as sophisticated and discerning an audience as a professional association conference or the readership of a scholarly journal.

But perhaps most important, I also maintain that when principled constraints and relevant considerations have been weighed in the balance with what the subject matter demands, the responsible instructor should be prepared to carry the exercise of academic freedom as far as course material requires. Academic nonneutrality is sometimes a duty as much as a right; moreover, the virtue of sincerity should make an instructor ready to meet the demands of nonneutrality even if a course must then include some ideas and arguments that a student finds offensive. Those who are prepared to exercise academic freedom in this way must be prepared for unsettling results. I have had a disgruntled student storm out of an ethics class during a discussion of readings that challenged his beliefs about the moral status of homosexuality; in another setting, class discussion of Singer's views on euthanasia brought a student to tears on realizing the implications of those views for a sibling born with spina bifida. The responsible exercise of academic freedom thus requires the instructor to prepare intellectually respectful and emotionally sensitive ways to respond to student disagreement or distress. Such preparation is a central component of what it means to demonstrate respect for our students' freedom to learn. But although the exercise of rights of nonneutrality and exclusion sometimes will have intellectually distressing or emotionally poignant results for those we teach, having the courage of one's sincere scholarly convictions is the only means of adequately acknowledging the truth that nonneutrality is both a right and a duty of academic freedom.

WHY LEARNING TO UNDERSTAND THE "UNFAMILIAR" DOES NOT COUNT AS "INDOCTRINATION"

But how can it be reasonable to expect the (nonacademic) public to defend this robust nonneutrality if courses taught in accordance with it and research and public comment relying on it may conflict with some of their deeply held personal beliefs or with certain public values on which political stability depends? The answer crucially depends on the fact that the institutional contexts of reflection protected by academic freedom have the potential to further important public purposes. Of course, the opportunity to extend basic knowledge and enlarge translational research is important in this regard, as are the disciplines that provide this opportunity. But so, too, is the opportunity for students and scholars to have serious engagement with the moral and cultural diversity that characterizes contemporary life. This opportunity is particularly important for democratic societies. The political stability of democratic institutions may well depend upon citizen appreciation of diversity in belief; indeed sustained and careful engagement with the nature and sources of moral and cultural diversity seems to be essential preparation for responsible democratic citizenship. Institutions of higher education are uniquely prepared to encourage this kind of engagement, and the disciplines that are central to this task—literature, language study, religious studies, anthropology, sociology, history, government, and philosophy, for instance—can play an important role in helping to promote political stability, even when they do not directly aim at it. The relevant disciplines can be valuable supports of liberal democracy, even though their governing principles may have little to do with the fundamental aims of democracy.

I have argued that academic nonneutrality can be justifiably embodied in classroom practices that sometimes offend their participant audiences.

Consider the "freshman reading projects" first adopted by many American colleges and universities in the late 1990s and that continue at many institutions to this day. These programs were meant to create a common intellectual experience for incoming students before they encountered a diverse and increasingly bewildering array of academic choices and possibilities across a broad array of disciplines. But the reading projects also have sometimes been regarded as vehicles for introducing students to difficult or unfamiliar ideas and cultures, particularly in response to world events or influential cultural movements. The introductory common intellectual experience, proponents argue, encourages the kind of open-mindedness that helps to prepare new students for the intellectual, social, and cultural challenges of the full undergraduate experience. In the summer of 2002, for instance, a reading project at the University of North Carolina at Chapel Hill required incoming students to read and discuss a book about the Koran as part of a campus-wide response to the tragic events of September 11, 2001.[42]

Like many such efforts, the Chapel Hill program quickly became a lightning rod for critics of the academy. The North Carolina chapter of the American Civil Liberties Union wondered whether the project would allow professors to "proselytize" and thus violate the separation of church and state that is required at a public university.[43] Some conservative Christian groups contended the project was an attempt at "forced Islamic indoctrination" and filed a federal lawsuit against the university.[44] The general secretary of the AAUP responded by characterizing the critics' challenges as evidence of "growing threats to academic freedom that can occur in times of economic and political turmoil" and traced the threats to fear of the university's capacity for "going to the source of the ideas that threaten us."[45] When the courts eventually denied all requests for an injunction to stop the project, the chief counsel for the plaintiffs charged that "post-September 11 . . . the academic police are falling all over themselves to uphold Islam in a favorable light" and dismissed the decision to allow the project to continue as "a political correctness ruling."[46]

Yet how could the mere idea of reading a book about the Koran involve an abuse of academic freedom? A particular faculty member's attempt to put the idea into practice might overstep the bounds of academic propriety. But the critics of the Chapel Hill project were reacting not to the implementation but to the very idea of requiring students to read a book about the Koran. Further, why should simply being asked to read a book about the Koran seem to violate the First Amendment protection of freedom of religion? This charge makes sense only if we assume that coming to understand an unfamiliar religion or way of life through critical reflection on its tenets might be the same thing as coming to believe in those tenets. But of course, understanding and approving are two very different phenomena. I might understand why a hungry child steals food despite my disapproval of the act of theft. Charges that the Chapel Hill program was a project of indoctrination thus rest on a fundamental confusion.

Yet, ironically, these charges embody a conception of moral understanding that is potentially more compelling than the unreflective moral relativism that is far too common both outside and inside the academy. What critics of freshman book projects have realized is that it is possible for an "outsider" to develop a genuine understanding of even the most unfamiliar moral view, even if that view initially seems entirely alien or even repugnant. The book projects' critics appreciate that such a stance is accessible only to the outsider who comes to understand the unfamiliar view "from the inside" and that an important aim of the projects under attack is to encourage just this kind of understanding. The critics recognize that "controversial" books chosen for freshman reading programs with the aim of encouraging the understanding of diversity have the potential to make various unfamiliar "others" more perspicuous to outsiders.

But what happens when one comes to understand an unfamiliar view or way of life? One result is that practices of which one does not approve or which one even vehemently condemns come to be understood as an alternative means of expressing concern for some of the "familiar" things one actually values.[47] A critic of polygamous societies, for instance, might come to view such societies as very good at caring for children.[48] The attempt to produce just such an understanding—an understanding of how a way of life of which one is generally critical might embody at least some admirable values—is central, in my view, to any effort to take moral and cultural diversity seriously. When such efforts succeed, they enhance one's appreciation of the fact that serious moral disagreement with a way of life need not keep one from finding morally admirable dimensions of the practices one resists. But it is precisely this tendency of sustained moral engagement with unfamiliar, alien, or even "repugnant" moral ideas—its tendency to make those ideas seem familiar or even no longer repugnant—that generates the most vehement criticisms of the book projects in question. Some of the criticisms may be rooted primarily in a simple fear of "threatening" ideas. But the more fundamental fear informing many protests is that as a consequence of the reading, the objects of the critics' animus may no longer seem threatening enough.

Yet these critics fail to appreciate that even for a college freshman, there is a fundamental difference between understanding an unfamiliar moral view—even from the inside—and being actively committed to the values entailed by that view. That is, there is a fundamental difference between understanding and approving, and in virtue of this difference, being put in a position to understand an unfamiliar view is not the same thing as being indoctrinated into it. If there were no difference between understanding and approving, it would be impossible for any serious scholar of another way of life ever to avoid indoctrination and conversion. Of course, some people who contemplate an unfamiliar conception or an alien way of life will make the "evaluative leap" from understanding to approval. But most of the time that evaluative leap is possible only because the person making the leap was already prepared to make it. The relevant preparation typically includes lengthy patterns of experience with a way of life and a long history of exposure to local social meanings that are seldom accessible to the neophyte. Indeed, in general, what we call conversion experiences are usually the culmination of processes that began long before the "experience" itself.

To be sure, some critics who recognize the difference between understanding and approving may remain troubled by instruction that encourages understanding of unfamiliar views. These may realize that understanding an unfamiliar moral view can produce sympathy with that view and that such sympathy can be corrosive of orthodoxies that demand internal intolerance of dissent. Because participating in a mandatory first-year project is not entirely akin to taking an ordinary class (even a "required" class), universities should try to provide those who accept such orthodoxies with intellectual space to express disagreement with the project if this can be done without encouraging active intolerance.

INTELLECTUAL DIVERSITY AND ACADEMIC FREEDOM IN CONTEMPORARY ACADEMIC LIFE

I submit that most students will not object to considering the diversity of convictions that is so central to contemporary life. But even if there are more dissenters than I imagine likely, their resistance should not stop colleges and universities from promoting understanding of diversity. A cross-disciplinary reading project for incoming students can provide a valuable initiation into academic life. Further, when the consideration of diversity grows out of inquiry within an academic discipline, it is an invitation to deepen one's moral education and social understanding in subtle and complex ways. John Stuart Mill reminds us in chapter 2 of *On Liberty* not only that none of us is infallible but also that we are sometimes most aware of our fallibility when we are confronted with ideas with which we disagree.[49] Even if we are right in some particular instance, Mill continues, the quality of the arguments we offer to support our views can be strengthened by serious engagement with opposing positions. This is why providing opportunities to encounter a diversity of convictions can be a means of promoting scholarly excellence in the university.[50]

Determining how best to preserve diversity of convictions in the university without endangering the university's proper functioning has become a vexing problem for American higher education. Some observers charge that, at present, colleges and universities lack appropriate "scholarly balance" and that this reflects an unacceptable dearth of contemporary academics with conservative religious and political convictions.[51] Of course, nonacademic commitments sometimes shape a scholar's academic interests and pursuits. Yet political labels are coarse and often misleading indicators of an individual's habits of mind that tell us very little about the complex intellectual choices one might make over the course of an academic career. A "conservative" Catholic might be convinced by Pope John Paul II, writing in the encyclical *Evangelium Vitae*, that respect for the dignity of human life demands limiting or even abolishing the death penalty and preserving a robust social welfare system that responds to human needs. A political "liberal" might hold an uncompromising conception of personal responsibility, challenging a view held by many conservatives according to which we cannot hold someone like Thomas Jefferson responsible for moral wrongs of slavery that "simply conformed" to the conventions of Jefferson's time. The intellectual commitments of reflective people of any political alignment will be realized in complex and often unpredictably subtle ways.

Thus, while it is important to have a broad range of scholarly perspectives and interests in the academy, the facile identification of political affiliation and intellectual commitments rests on a fundamentally mistaken and deeply impoverished view of human possibility. Still further, diversity—of any kind— is just one of *many* values that can have a role in shaping academic life, and as thoughtful commentators remind us, it must not be allowed to trump the fundamentally important value of academic excellence. We must not allow any pursuit of "scholarly balance," whatever its political or religious origins, to substitute intellectually arbitrary processes of interest-group politics for the sincere and discerning judgment of competent academic inquirers. Robust protections for academic freedom ensure the quality of that judgment; they also preserve institutions in which intellectual experimentation can reliably produce knowledge, encourage critical inquiry and argument, and prepare young people to become responsible citizens. Academic freedom is thus a precious social good, and however unsettling or unpopular some instance of its exercise might be, we cannot afford to dismantle the structures that protect it.

NOTES

1. Debra Galant, "Peter Singer Settles in, and Princeton Looks Deeper," *New York Times*, March 5, 2000.

   The Board member was Steve Forbes, also a former candidate for the American presidency.

2. "Trustees Reaffirm Commitment to Academic Freedom," *Princeton Weekly Bulletin*, 89, no. 6 (October 18, 1999).

3. American Association of University Professors, "1915 Declaration of Principles," in *Policy Documents and Reports* (Washington, D.C.: American Association of University Professors, 2006), 10: 297.

4. An especially compelling recent statement of this view appears in Jonathan R. Cole, "Academic Freedom Under Fire," *Daedalus* 135 (2005): 2.

5. Cole rightly insists that the tenured faculty of great universities and other academic leaders must respond to critics to show that "a threat to academic freedom poses a threat as well to the welfare and prosperity of the nation." Cole, "Academic Freedom Under Fire," 5–6.

6. The details of this exchange appear in an online blog published by the *Chronicle of Higher Education*. See Diane Auer Jones, "Academic Freedom or Educational Malpractice?," *Chronicle of Higher Education* (blog), December 1, 2011, http://chronicle.com/blogs/brainstorm/academic-freedom-or-educational-malpractice/41815; and Andrew Ross, "Andrew Ross Responds," *Chronicle of Higher Education* (blog), December 5, 2011, http://chronicle.com/blogs/brainstorm/dr-andrew-ross-responds/41861.

7. Ross, "Andrew Ross Responds."

8. This episode is detailed in a series of articles that appeared in the *Chicago Tribune* in spring 2011: Jodi Cohen and Lisa Black, "Live Sex Toy Demonstration Held on Northwestern Campus," *Chicago Tribune*, March 3, 2011; Cohen and Black, "NU President 'Troubled' by Sex Toy Demonstration on Campus," *Chicago Tribune*, March 3, 2011; Cohen, "Northwestern Cancels Human Sexuality Class," *Chicago Tribune*, May 9, 2011.

9. In a prepared statement, the professor described the event as valuable because it offered "examples and extensions of concepts students learn about in traditional academic ways." Cohen and Black, "Live Sex Toy Demonstration Held on Northwestern Campus."

10. The professor responsible for the course was quoted describing the demonstration as "unplanned": it was the result of "a quick decision to allow it." See Staff Report, "NU Professor Issues New Statement on Sex Controversy," *Chicago Tribune*, March 5, 2011. This account also revealed that the episode involved a device that looked like "a machine-powered saw with a phallic object instead of a blade." Might the episode therefore have (unintentionally) encouraged violence against women? If so, this surely provides another reason to reject the instructor's claims that the episode was an entirely reasonable, if challenging, exercise of academic freedom.

11. According to the authors of the "1915 Declaration of Principles," "the classroom utterances" of college and university teachers "ought always to be considered as privileged communications"; they are often "designed to provoke opposition or arouse debate" and can thus be the subject of "garbled," "unauthorized," and "misleading" publication. Though rarely discussed explicitly, this assumption seems implicit in the conception of academic freedom held by many academics. Yet what might the idea of classroom utterances as "privileged communications" mean for faculty accountability?

12. Cole, "Academic Freedom Under Fire," 13.

13. Thomas Haskell, "Justifying the Rights of Academic Freedom in the Era of 'Power/ Knowledge,'" in *The Future of Academic Freedom* (Chicago: University of Chicago Press, 1996), 43–90. See also Robert K. Poch, "Academic Freedom in American Higher Education: Rights, Responsibilities and Limitations," *ASHE-ERIC Higher Education Report No. 4* (Washington, D.C.: George Washington University School of Education and Human Development), 3–8; and William Van Alstyne, "Academic Freedom and the First Amendment in the Supreme Court of the United States: An Unhurried Historical Review," *Law and Contemporary Problems* 79 (1990): 79–154.

14. "1915 Declaration of Principles," 294. See also Haskell, "Justifying the Rights of Academic Freedom," 58–59.

15. AAUP, "1940 Statement of Principles on Academic Freedom and Tenure with 1970 Interpretive Comments," in *Policy Documents and Reports* (Washington, D.C.: AAUP, 2006), 3–11.

16. Ibid.

17. This means that in contrast to the individual rights of free speech protected by the Constitution, academic freedom rights are actually professional rights. Robert Post has rightly rejected the effort to treat them as akin to individual constitutionally protected rights. See Post, "The Structure of Academic Freedom," in *Academic Freedom After September 11* (New York: Zone, 2006), 61–106. It is important that unlike the academic freedom of individuals, *institutional* academic freedom has been determined primarily by the courts. A series of twentieth-century Supreme Court cases about loyalty oaths and subversive speech define institutional academic freedom in terms of the rights of universities to decide faculty appointments and tenure, curriculum,

pedagogy, and student admissions. See Van Alstyne, "Academic Freedom and the First Amendment in the Supreme Court of the United States."

18. Stanley Fish, "Academic Freedom: When Sauce for the Goose Isn't Sauce for the Gander," *Chronicle of Higher Education*, November 26, 1999.

19. Academic freedom rights have very little substance without tenure.

20. William F. Buckley, *God and Man at Yale: The Superstitions of Academic Freedom*, 50th anniversary ed. (Washington, D.C.: Regnery, 1986).

21. See the measures put forward in the SAF "Academic Bill of Rights," www.students-foracademicfreedom.org/documents/1925/abor.html.

22. For AAUP replies concerning longer-term implications of the proposal, see "Academic Bill of Rights & Intellectual Diversity," www.aaup.org/our-work/government-relations/GRarchive/ABOR; and "The Academic Bill of Rights," www.aaup.org/issues/academic-bill-rights.

23. Though his critics were not mollified, Singer insisted that his undergraduate classroom was always an open forum for discussion and debate. See *Princeton Alumni Weekly*, January 26, 2000.

24. Louis Menand, "The Limits of Academic Freedom," in *The Future of Academic Freedom*," ed. Louis Menand (Chicago: University of Chicago Press, 1996), 6–7.

25. *Regents of Univ. of Wisconsin v. Southworth*, 529 US 217 (2000).

26. Stanley Fish, "Holocaust Denial and Academic Freedom," *Valparaiso University Law Review* 35, no. 3 (2001): 499.

27. Haskell cites Francis Abbott, a member of the "Metaphysical Club" from which American pragmatism emerged, as the author of the phrase "community of the competent." Haskell, "Justifying the Rights of Academic Freedom," 84.

28. Judith Jarvis Thomson, "Ideology and Faculty Selection," *Law and Contemporary Problems* 53 (1990): 155–76.

29. Stanley Fish, "Sauce for the Goose," in *The Trouble with Principle* (Cambridge: Harvard University Press, 2011), 34–45.

30. Ibid., 44.

31. Ibid., 45.

32. Fish, "Holocaust Denial and Academic Freedom," 6.

33. Ibid.

34. Bernard Williams, *Truth and Truthfulness* (Princeton: Princeton University Press, 2002), 2–4.

35. See also, Cole, "Academic Freedom Under Fire."

36. The authors of the "1915 Declaration of Principles" viewed the notion of a public trust as central to the university, although they focused primarily on the public trust "reposed in the governing boards" (even of private institutions). They argued that college and university trustees have no right to "bind the reason or conscience" of any professor or to treat their relation to professors as one of private employer to private employees, because even a private institution is not a board's "private proprietorship" (293–94). My claim is that the authority of the professoriate must be more explicitly linked to the upholding of a public trust.

37. Williams, "The Problem," 12.
38. Williams, "The Problem," 11–12; "Sincerity: Lying and Other Styles of Deceit," 5; "Accuracy: A Sense of Reality," 6.
39. Williams, 96–100. In a provocative challenge to Williams's long-standing views about the differences between science and other forms of inquiry, Richard Rorty considers the possibility of a "psycho-historical" account that would rely on the notion that people drawn to science are just more likely to possess certain "moral virtues" than others, including "incorruptibility," patience, reasonableness, and a preference for persuasion over force. Rorty insists, however, that these are moral and not intellectual virtues. See "Is Natural Science a Natural Kind?," in *Objectivity, Relativism and Truth* (Cambridge: Cambridge University Press, 1991), 61–62.
40. Fish, "Academic Freedom and Holocaust Denial," 7.
41. Thomas Kuhn, *The Structure of Scientific Revolutions*, 2d ed. (Chicago: University of Chicago Press, 1970), 164–65; Michele Moody-Adams, *Fieldwork in Familiar Places: Morality, Culture and Philosophy* (Cambridge: Harvard University Press, 1997), 134–135.
42. Richard Morgan, "Three Freshmen Sue U. of North Carolina Over Assigned Reading About Koran," *New York Times*, July 26, 2002.
43. Richard Morgan, "Beach-Blanket Bookworms," *New York Times*, July 19, 2002.
44. Kate Zernike, "Talk, and Debate, on Koran as Chapel Hill Classes Open," *New York Times*, August 20, 2002.
45. Mary Burgan, "Academic Freedom in a World of Moral Crises," *Chronicle of Higher Education*, September 6, 2002.
46. Zernike, "Talk, and Debate, on Koran as Chapel Hill Classes Open,"
47. Moody-Adams, *Fieldwork in Familiar Places*, 57–58.
48. Moody-Adams, *Fieldwork in Familiar Places*, 58–60.
49. John Stuart Mill, *On Liberty* (London, 1869).
50. Fish believes that intellectual diversity is "not an academic value." See his "Intellectual Diversity: the Trojan Horse of a Dark Design," *Chronicle of Higher Education*, February 13, 2004. But if exposure to different opinions does, as Mill says, better enable us to recognize our mistakes, intellectual diversity is clearly one intellectual value among others.
51. There is a range of views on the causes and consequences of the current distribution of political and religious convictions in the academy. A brief but helpful survey of the issues is contained in John Tierney, "The Left Leaning Tower," *New York Times*, July 22, 2011.

8

ACADEMIC FREEDOM AND THE CONSTITUTION

ROBERT POST

I N MODERN AMERICAN usage, the concept of academic freedom can refer either to the set of institutional principles by which universities should ideally be governed, or it can refer to the standards by which universities and their personnel receive constitutional protection.[1] In this chapter I shall discuss academic freedom understood as a concept of constitutional law.

For the past fifty years, the First Amendment has been interpreted to generate protections for academic freedom. The Supreme Court has proclaimed that academic freedom is a "special concern of the First Amendment, which does not tolerate laws that cast a pall of orthodoxy over the classroom."[2] But the doctrine of academic freedom stands in a state of shocking disarray and incoherence. One eminent commentator has remarked that "there has been no adequate analysis of what academic freedom the Constitution protects or of why it protects it. Lacking definition or guiding principle, the doctrine floats in the law, picking up decisions as a hull does barnacles."[3]

The constitutional doctrine of academic freedom is incoherent because courts lack an adequate theory of why the Constitution should protect academic freedom. The Supreme Court believes that academic freedom should be protected because the First Amendment demands that the "marketplace of ideas" must be safeguarded. It has announced that "the classroom is peculiarly the 'marketplace of ideas.' The Nation's future depends upon leaders trained through wide exposure to that robust exchange of ideas which discovers truth 'out of a multitude of tongues, (rather) than through any kind of authoritative selection.'"[4]

In this chapter I shall argue that this theory of constitutional protection for academic freedom is fundamentally unsound, and I shall advance what I regard as a more defensible account of why the Constitution might protect academic freedom. The theory I advance should strip barnacles from the hull of the great ship of academic freedom, resolving many of the puzzles that presently paralyze its progress and usefulness.

■ ■ ▦ ■

Today we are likely to find unexceptionable, perhaps even banal, Karl Jasper's claim that "the university is the corporate realization of man's basic determination to know. Its most immediate aim is to discover what there is to be known and what becomes of us through knowledge."[5] Almost every modern university includes in its mission statement the purpose of striving "to create knowledge."[6] The modern university is indeed defined in terms of "the preservation, advancement, and dissemination" of knowledge.[7]

This concept of the university did not always exist in the United States. During the major part of the nineteenth century, the objective of most American colleges was to instruct young men in received truths, both spiritual and material. It is only when American scholars became infected with the German ideal of *Wissenschaft*, with the idea of systematizing and expanding knowledge, that American universities began to transform their mission. It is a moment of great historical significance when Daniel Coit Gilman could in 1885 address the assembled officers, students, and friends of the Johns Hopkins University to assert, with confidence and at length, that the "functions" of the university "may be stated as the acquisition, conservation, refinement and distribution of knowledge. . . . It is the business of a university to advance knowledge."[8]

The professional concept of academic freedom, as distinct from the constitutional concept of academic freedom, emerged in the United States at roughly the same time and in response to this transformation of the purpose of higher education.[9] Writing during this moment of transition, John Dewey could with characteristic lucidity observe the emerging relationship between the new concept of the university and the new idea of academic freedom:

> In discussing the questions summed up in the phrase academic freedom, it is necessary to make a distinction between the university proper and those teaching bodies, called by whatever name, whose primary business is to inculcate

a fixed set of ideas and facts. The former aims to discover and communicate truth and to make its recipients better judges of truth and more effective in applying it to the affairs of life. The latter have as their aim the perpetuation of a certain way of looking at things current among a given body of persons. Their purpose is to disciple rather than to discipline. . . . The problem of freedom of inquiry and instruction clearly assumes different forms in these two types of institutions.[10]

Real universities *discipline*, institutions without academic freedom merely disciple.

Dewey's distinction quite accurately captures the professional ideal of academic freedom of research and publication,[11] which was first systematically set forth in the 1915 *Declaration of Principles on Academic Freedom and Academic Tenure*, published by the newly formed American Association of University Professors (AAUP), of which John Dewey was then president.[12] The *Declaration* justifies academic freedom of research and publication on the ground that universities cannot fulfill their purpose, which is "to promote inquiry and advance the sum of human knowledge,"[13] unless they award faculty "complete and unlimited freedom to pursue inquiry and publish its results. Such freedom is the breath in the nostrils of all scientific activity."[14]

The freedom protected by the *Declaration* is at root *disciplinary* in nature. The *Declaration* explicitly repudiates the position "that academic freedom implies that individual teachers should be exempt from all restraints as to the matter or manner of their utterances, either within or without the university."[15] Instead it announces that academic freedom implies that the "liberty of the scholar within the university to set forth his conclusions, be they what they may, is conditioned by their being conclusions gained by a scholar's method and held in a scholar's spirit; that is to say, they must be the fruits of competent and patient and sincere inquiry."[16] The *Declaration* conceives academic freedom as the freedom to pursue the "scholar's profession"[17] according to the standards of that profession.[18]

Academic freedom, the *Declaration* precisely notes, upholds "not the absolute freedom of utterance of the individual scholar, but the absolute freedom of thought, of inquiry, of discussion and of teaching, of the academic profession."[19] Disciplinary norms of the profession link the university to the achievement of its mission to produce knowledge. Universities produce knowledge because they give scholars the freedom to pursue the disciplinary practices that produce the kind of expert knowledge we demand of universities.

This view of academic freedom implies that it must depend upon a *double* recognition: that knowledge cannot be advanced "in the absence of free inquiry" and that "the right question to ask about a teacher is whether he is competent."[20] Only competent faculty can advance knowledge. Universities assess competence by using the standards of the scholarly profession. And they assess the competence of faculty all the time: whenever they hire, promote, tenure, or award grants to professors. Universities invoke the doubled structure of academic freedom whenever they honor the need for critical freedom while simultaneously making the judgments of quality required to advance knowledge.[21]

This doubled structure differentiates academic freedom from the larger genus of "intellectual freedom." All persons are entitled to intellectual freedom, but only academics are entitled to academic freedom. Intellectual freedom does not presume the responsibility of competence, but academic freedom does. Intellectual freedom is not bound to any specific institution, like a university, but academic freedom is. Like intellectual freedom, however, academic freedom presupposes the necessity and importance of critical inquiry.

■ ■ ■ ■

The theory of the marketplace of ideas, which the court believes generates the constitutional concept of academic freedom, is radically incompatible with the doubled structure of academic freedom. The theory of the marketplace of ideas was first articulated by Justice Holmes in his justly famous dissent in *Abrams v. United States*:[22]

> But when men have realized that time has upset many fighting faiths, they may come to believe even more than they believe the very foundations of their own conduct that the ultimate good desired is better reached by free trade in ideas — that the best test of truth is the power of the thought to get itself accepted in the competition of the market, and that truth is the only ground upon which their wishes safely can be carried out. That at any rate is the theory of our Constitution. It is an experiment, as all life is an experiment.[23]

The U.S. Supreme Court has since and frequently proclaimed that "it is the purpose of the First Amendment to preserve an uninhibited marketplace of ideas in which truth will ultimately prevail."[24] There is a general belief in constitutional circles that the point of First Amendment doctrine is to "advance knowledge and the search for truth by fostering a free marketplace of ideas and an 'uninhibited, robust, wide-open debate on public issues.'"[25] Indeed, "the most influential argument supporting the constitutional commitment to freedom of speech is the contention that speech is valuable because it leads to the discovery of truth."[26]

The premise of the marketplace of ideas is that truth will emerge from the clash of conflicting opinions. The theory of the marketplace of ideas therefore deploys First Amendment doctrine to prevent the state from interfering in the free flow of public discussion. It permits the regulation of speech only when the state can meet a strict "requirement of viewpoint neutrality."[27] Courts pursuing the ideal of the marketplace of ideas apply "the most exacting scrutiny to regulations that suppress, disadvantage, or impose differential burdens upon speech because of its content."[28]

A doctrinal structure of this nature is in fundamental tension with the forms of disciplinary knowledge that underlie academic freedom of research and publication. The point of the professional ideal of academic freedom is to ensure that universities are organized to advance their mission of producing expert, disciplinary knowledge. But if, as the theory of the marketplace of ideas holds, "the First Amendment recognizes no such thing as a 'false' idea,"[29] then it cannot sustain, or even tolerate, the disciplinary practices necessary to sustain the truth claims to which the ideal of expert knowledge aspires.[30]

Not only is the theory of the marketplace of ideas incompatible with ordinary judgments that universities must continuously make to identify and promote "competence," it is also incompatible with the forms of social order our society ordinarily uses to produce professional knowledge. Expert knowledge is produced by disciplines, and as the *Oxford English Dictionary* reminds us, disciplinarity refers to "the training of scholars or subordinates to proper and orderly action by instructing and exercising them." Disciplines are not organized according to market or even democratic principles.

For example, disciplines commonly use professional journals to serve as gatekeepers for the recognition and distribution of knowledge. Journals could not perform this function if they were required to operate according to the theory of the marketplace of ideas. If disciplinary journals were forced by constitutional doctrine to accept all manuscripts on a first-come, first-served basis, or if they were constitutionally prohibited from engaging in the content discrimination required to distinguish good from poor submissions, they could no longer serve as disciplinary gatekeepers for the recognition and distribution of knowledge. If a marketplace of ideas model were to be imposed upon *Nature* or the *American Economic Review* or *The Lancet*, such publications would very rapidly lose their capacity to authoritatively register what we do and do not know about the world.[31]

I do not mean to deny that scholars in the arts, humanities, and sciences sometimes possess powerful personal charisma. My point is rather that the creation of disciplinary knowledge—the kind of knowledge that justifies modern universities and therefore also the professional ideal of academic freedom—requires the maintenance of *disciplinary* authority.[32] Disciplinary authority rests on forms of discrimination incompatible with the marketplace of ideas. It is simply a confusion to believe the marketplace of ideas can generate doctrine remotely compatible with modern university practices. If the constitutional concept of academic freedom is to be justified, therefore, it cannot be by the theory of the marketplace of ideas. Instead we need a constitutional rationale that can validate simultaneous commitments to critical freedom *and* to rigorous disciplinary standards of judgment.[33]

Universities cannot fulfill their social function unless they are authorized to evaluate scholarly speech based upon its content and professional quality.[34] No doubt if the *New York Times* were to editorialize that the moon is made of green cheese, the First Amendment, deploying the concept of the marketplace of ideas, would prohibit government from imposing any sanction. Yet no astronomy department could survive if it were constitutionally prohibited from denying tenure to young scholars who were similarly convinced. It is no wonder that the constitutional doctrine of academic freedom lies in shambles: it is justified by a theory that is incompatible with the mission of the modern university.

■ ■ ■ ■

How, then, might we justify a constitutional law of academic freedom? The more one knows about the organizing logic of First Amendment jurisprudence, the more difficult the question becomes.

This chapter is not the venue in which to defend the point, but I have elsewhere argued in detail that the fundamental purpose of the First Amendment is to protect a communicative process of democratic legitimation.[35]

It is essential that our state maintain its democratic legitimacy—that "we the people" continue to believe that our government represents us, that it speaks for us, and that it is answerable to us. As a matter of constitutional design, we accomplish this goal by ensuring that government is responsive to public opinion and that the state is precluded from interfering with persons who wish to participate in the formation of public opinion.

If we denominate as "public discourse" the communicative practices deemed necessary for public opinion formation, the First Amendment prohibits viewpoint and content discrimination within public discourse in order to guarantee to each person the unfettered possibility of altering the content of public opinion. Democratic legitimation is egalitarian, because it values equally each person's effort to shape public opinion. Discrimination between persons based upon the content of their speech is inconsistent with this equality. To the extent that the state excludes a person from public discourse, it denies the potential of democratic legitimation to that person.

Although law must frequently distinguish true from false factual statements, expressions of expert knowledge in public discourse tend to be constitutionally characterized as statements of opinion. The first Amendment holds that opinions cannot be penalized as false. Statements "that describe present or past conditions capable of being known through sense impressions"[36] are classified as factual, whereas statements in which a speaker "is expressing a subjective view, an interpretation, a theory, conjecture, or surmise"[37] tend to be classified as opinion, which is protected from state regulation.

This tendency is no accident, for First Amendment doctrine presupposes that democratic legitimation is maximized whenever participation in public discourse is protected from state control. First Amendment doctrine thus displays a pronounced inclination to characterize assertions of expert knowledge within public discourse as statements of opinion and in this way to protect a marketplace of ideas within public discourse.

The egalitarian premises built into the foundations of First Amendment doctrine undermine the disciplinary authority necessary for the maintenance of expert knowledge. Whereas law has no difficulty holding accountable for malpractice a lawyer who gives bad advice to a client outside of public discourse, a lawyer who offers the same advice to the gullible public tends to be immunized from legal regulation. Because scholarship is often addressed to the public, the question of how to reconcile First Amendment doctrine with university judgments of competence is quite perplexing.

A solution to this dilemma emerges if we carefully consider the concept of democratic legitimation. Because "contemporary Western societies are in one sense or another ruled by knowledge and expertise,"[38] a state that can freely manipulate the production and distribution of disciplinary knowledge can set the terms of its own legitimacy. By fiat it can make the dangers of climate change inevitable or illusory, or it can make the harms of smoking obvious or speculative. By controlling knowledge, it can make a mockery of the aspiration to democratic self-governance.

The insight is common in the twentieth century.[39] No less a democrat than John Dewey affirms that "opinions and beliefs concerning the public presuppose effective and organized inquiry" and that "genuine public policy cannot be generated unless it be informed by knowledge, and this knowledge does not exist except when there is systematic, thorough, and well-equipped search and record."[40] Claude Lefort concisely summarizes the insight when he distinguishes democratic from totalitarian regimes on the ground that in the latter "a condensation takes place between the sphere of power, the sphere of law and the sphere of knowledge. Knowledge of the ultimate goals of society and of the norms which regulate social practices becomes the property of power, and at the same time power itself claims to be the organ of discourse which articulates the real as such."[41]

This line of analysis suggests that within the constitutional value of democratic legitimation lies implied a second constitutional value, which I shall call "democratic competence." Democratic competence refers to the cognitive empowerment of those who participate within public discourse. In this chapter I shall focus on the aspects of democratic competence that concern the production and distribution of expert knowledge, which it is the business of universities to generate and publish. Only on the basis of expert knowledge can we know whether nicotine is in fact harmful, or whether climate change is indeed probable and caused by human factors.

Although democratic legitimation requires democratic competence, democratic legitimation rests upon a doctrinal structure that is inconsistent with the maintenance of democratic competence. Democratic legitimation requires that the speech of all persons be treated with toleration and equality. By contrast, democratic competence requires legal support for disciplinary authority capable of distinguishing good ideas from bad ones.

In circumstances of direct conflict, the value of democratic legitimation should prevail over that of democratic competence. Democratic legitimation underwrites the general legitimacy of the government and is therefore a necessary prerequisite for any and all government action. Nevertheless, because many communications lie outside the domain of public discourse where democratic legitimation holds sway, there remain many opportunities for courts to implement the value of democratic competence.

A simple illustration of the difficulty may be found in a recent Nebraska statute that requires doctors who are treating women seeking an abortion to disperse false information to their patients.[42] Communications between doctors and patients in the course of medical treatment are not within public discourse; they are not attempts to participate in the formation of public opinion. Thus the state can freely regulate physician speech in order to uphold professional standards. A doctor sued for malpractice will not have a First Amendment defense; he will not be able to claim, with Justice Holmes, that his advice was "an experiment, as all life is an experiment." The doctrinal principles appropriate to democratic legitimation do not apply to physician–patient communications.

Yet if the state were to require doctors to communicate false information to patients, the independent value of democratic competence may be implicated. We can thus glimpse the influence of democratic competence when we find a federal district court easily concluding that the First Amendment rights of physicians were violated by the Nebraska statute, because it would compel them "to give untruthful, misleading and irrelevant information to patients."[43] The Nebraska statute runs afoul of the distinct constitutional value of democratic competence. It corrupts the communication of expert knowledge to the population.[44]

If we ask how the district court is able to determine that the information required to be communicated by the Nebraska statute is in fact false, the answer must be that the court hears and credits expert medical testimony. This point has quite radical implications. It suggests that the protection of democratic competence extends independent constitutional status to professional disciplinary practices that produce expert knowledge. Democratic competence would have no meaning if the state could freely manipulate these knowledge practices, which exemplify disciplinarity.

■　■　■　■

We are now in a position to postulate how academic freedom might become an independent, freestanding constitutional concept. The value of democratic competence, already visible in many aspects of contemporary First Amendment jurisprudence,[45] attributes constitutional status to the creation and distribution of expert knowledge. Universities are unique institutions in this regard. Although knowledge is widely produced by many contemporary organizations, ranging from pharmaceutical companies to think tanks, only universities define, reproduce, and constitute the disciplinary standards by which expert knowledge is recognized and validated. That is why virtually all contemporary sites of knowledge production employ personnel trained in universities.

The value of democratic competence should lie at the core of the constitutional concept of academic freedom. As a constitutional principle, academic freedom must preserve the integrity of disciplinary practices from unrestrained political control.[46] This is consistent with the professional ideal of academic freedom,[47] which essentially claims that the scholarly profession should be self-regulating. Decisions about disciplinary competence cannot be made on the basis of public opinion or on the basis of the personal views of those who happen to provide the funds that support universities.

Conceiving constitutional academic freedom in this way solves many of the doctrinal puzzles that presently render the constitutional law of academic freedom all but incoherent. In the remainder of this chapter, I discuss three such puzzles.

DOES CONSTITUTIONAL ACADEMIC FREEDOM APPLY TO PROFESSORS OR TO INSTITUTIONS?

Courts[48] and commentators[49] have noticed a potential conflict between individual and institutional concepts of academic freedom. The question is whether individual professors hold constitutional rights of academic freedom, or whether these rights are instead held by universities as institutions. The conflict between the two perspectives comes into view if a professor, alleging a violation of academic freedom, sues a university for the denial of tenure. A university might well defend the suit on the ground of its own academic freedom to determine the quality of its faculty. A great deal of ink has been spilled over the question of whether rights of constitutional academic freedom attach to individuals or to universities.

The tension between individual and institutional academic freedom can be reconciled if we appreciate that constitutional protections for academic freedom of research and publication serve the distinct value of democratic competence. This value encompasses *both* the ongoing health of universities as institutions that promote the growth of knowledge *and* the capacity of individual scholars to inquire and to disseminate the results of their inquiry.

Universities promote the growth of new knowledge when they support scholars who apply and improve the professional scholarly standards that define knowledge in particular disciplines. That is why American university administrators, despite their formal legal control over university governance, nevertheless typically and properly defer heavily to the peer judgments of faculty when making decisions about how to govern university affairs, especially in evaluating faculty competence.

If administrators were instead to defer to "the prevailing opinions and sentiments of the community in which they dwell" and thus override professional standards in the name of "this multitudinous tyrannical opinion,"[50] universities as institutions would cease to serve the constitutional value of democratic competence. They would become, in the words of the *Declaration*, "essentially proprietary institutions" that do not "accept the principles of freedom of inquiry, of opinion, and of teaching; . . . Their purpose [would not be] to advance knowledge by the unrestricted research and unfettered discussion of impartial investigators, but rather to subsidize the promotion of opinions held by the persons, usually not of the scholar's calling, who provide the funds for their maintenance."[51] It is "manifestly important," the *Declaration* asserts, that such institutions "not be permitted to sail under false colors."[52]

From a constitutional point of view, therefore, academic freedom has nothing to do with the autonomy of institutions that happen to include the name "university" in their titles. It applies only to institutions that actually protect the application of professional scholarly standards to advance knowledge.[53] Academic freedom does not entail deference to university administrators "who have expertise in education."[54] It instead entails deference to the professional scholarly standards by which knowledge is created. If a professor sues a university for a violation of academic freedom for its refusal to award him tenure, the right question for a court to decide is neither the individual rights of the professor nor the institutional prerogatives of the university. It is instead whether the tenure decision is made on the basis of the proper disciplinary standards.

In deciding this question it is entirely appropriate for courts to conclude that "when judges are asked to review the substance of a genuinely academic decision . . . they should show great respect for the faculty's professional judgment. Plainly, they may not override it unless it is such a substantial departure from accepted academic norms as to demonstrate that the person or committee responsible did not actually exercise professional judgment."[55]

The justification for this deference is that courts are not well equipped to second-guess the exercise of the professional scholarly standards that advance the constitutional value of democratic competence in the context of university scholarship. Courts are properly concerned that "judges should not be ersatz deans and educators."[56] Nothing in the concept of academic freedom, however, justifies deference when universities make executive decisions that do not purport to reflect professional standards.[57]

This suggests that the supposed tension between the institutional and individual accounts of academic freedom is based upon a misunderstanding. The constitutional value of academic freedom depends upon the exercise of professional standards, which inhere neither in institutions as such nor in individual professors as such. In the context of academic freedom, courts should ask how to fashion doctrine that best protects the "freedom of thought, of inquiry . . . of the academic profession."[58]

This can be a complicated question, because administrative decisions often purport to express professional standards. It is important, however, not to confuse the question of when deference is appropriate with the question of whether academic freedom inheres in institutions or in individuals.[59]

DOES ACADEMIC FREEDOM APPLY ONLY TO MATTERS OF PUBLIC CONCERN?

The most controversial recent decision involving academic freedom has been *Urofsky v. Gilmore*,[60] decided en banc by the Fourth Circuit in 2000. The case concerns a challenge to a Virginia statute providing that state employees, including university professors, cannot "access, download, print or store any information infrastructure files or servers having sexually explicit content," unless such access is approved in writing by an "agency head."[61]

Gilmore realizes that the statute, because it restricts the research of faculty, is inconsistent with academic freedom conceived as "a professional norm,"[62] but it concludes that "the Supreme Court, to the extent it has constitutionalized a right of academic freedom at all, appears to have recognized only an institutional right of self-governance in academic affairs" rather than "a First Amendment right of academic freedom that belongs to the professor as an individual."[63] *Gilmore* does not seem to realize that if the Supreme Court had articulated a constitutional right of academic freedom that attaches to universities, the only possible constitutional value at stake is that of democratic competence, which must apply equally to the need for individual professors to pursue their professional research free from government interference.[64]

Gilmore is explicit that "because the Act does not infringe the constitutional rights of public employees in general, it also does not violate the rights of professors."[65] *Gilmore* uses Supreme Court precedents like *Pickering v. Board of Education,*[66] *Connick v. Myers,*[67] and *Waters v. Churchill*[68] to analyze the constitutional rights of public employees. These decisions hold that the First Amendment does not protect the speech of state employees unless their speech involves "a matter of public concern."[69]

Gilmore is unusual because it frankly acknowledges that the "public concern" test of the *Pickering–Connick–Churchill* line of cases refers to general First Amendment rights that apply to all public employees and hence that have no particular relevance to the specific value of academic freedom. But courts generally have not recognized this, and they have used the "public concern" test to assess whether state regulations infringe academic freedom.[70] This represents a rather deep misunderstanding of the nature of academic freedom of research and publication.[71]

The *Pickering–Connick–Churchill* line of cases rests on the premise that in a democracy the implementation of government decisions frequently requires the creation of organizations. If a democratic state wishes to create a social security system, it must establish a social security administration; if it wishes to provide a welfare system, it must establish a social service bureaucracy. State organizations are purposive; they exist to achieve the ends for which they are created. Within such organizations the state must manage its employees, including their speech, in ways designed to fulfill organizational objectives. That is why the speech of soldiers can be regulated as is necessary to secure the national defense, or the speech of lawyers within a courtroom can be regulated as is necessary to secure justice.[72] "The state has interests as an employer in regulating the speech of its employees that differ significantly from those it possesses in connection with the regulation of the speech of the citizenry in general."[73]

When an employee speaks about a matter of "public concern," she is attempting to participate in public discourse "as a citizen."[74] The state must therefore "balance between the interests of the [employee], as a citizen, in commenting upon matters of public concern and the interest of the State, as an employer, in promoting the efficiency of the public services it performs through its employees."[75] The instrumental logic of an organization must somehow be reconciled with the egalitarian structure of public discourse. The *Pickering–Connick–Churchill* line of cases is about how this reconciliation should be effected.

The management of faculty at public universities must also be reconciled with the faculty's participation in public discourse as citizens. Within the organizational domain of the university, the speech of faculty is typically regulated as is necessary to achieve the purposes of higher education.[76] Faculty can be required to teach at certain hours on certain days about certain subjects. Their speech can be sanctioned if it is inconsistent with the educational mission of a university—if it is abusive or harassing or violates professional confidences. But because faculty may also wish to participate in public discourse as citizens, the value of democratic legitimation requires that their speech about matters of "public concern" should receive independent constitutional protection, in the same manner as would the public speech of any government employee.

Courts that use the "public concern" test to measure the scope of academic freedom fail to recognize that academic freedom of research and publication does not concern the freedom of faculty to speak in public "as citizens." Academic freedom triggers First Amendment coverage not because of the value of democratic legitimation, which protects the right of all citizens equally to participate in the formation of public opinion, but because of the value of democratic competence, which concerns the creation and distribution of knowledge. University faculty are uniquely situated with respect to the value of democratic competence, which is why academic freedom does not apply equally to all government employees.

Because the criterion of "public concern" turns on the application of the value of democratic legitimation, it has nothing to do with the value of democratic competence that underlies constitutional protections for academic freedom. Constitutional questions of academic freedom arise whenever the freedom of the scholarly profession to engage in research and publication is potentially compromised. It makes no difference whether a scholar wishes to publish about a matter of public concern, like American foreign policy, or about Hittite inscriptions, which may not constitute a matter of public concern debated by citizens in public discourse. Constitutional protections for academic freedom exist to ensure the effective creation and distribution of expert knowledge at universities.

If the "public concern" test of the *Pickering–Connick–Churchill* line of cases is relevant to any aspect of academic freedom, it is to the component of academic freedom that the *Declaration* called "freedom of extramural utterance and action."[77] This aspect of professional academic freedom refers to the freedom to "speak or write as citizens"[78] rather than as experts. An example of freedom of extramural expression might be an astronomer who wishes to write in public about NAFTA[79] or a computer scientist who wishes to speak out about the war in Afghanistan.[80] When faculty engage in such speech, they attempt to influence public opinion so as to make it responsive to their views. They do not speak as experts conveying knowledge but as citizens participating in public debate.

Experts have for years debated whether freedom of extramural speech should be considered an aspect of professional academic freedom. The difficulty is that extramural speech is by hypothesis unrelated to the special training and expertise of faculty.[81] From a constitutional point of view, however, freedom of extramural expression raises the same question of democratic legitimation as that which arises whenever government seeks to suppress the participation of its employees in public discourse. The "public concern" test of the *Pickering–Connick–Churchill* line of cases is an effort to identify and resolve this question. This is a quite different question than that of academic freedom of research and publication, which turns on the constitutional value of democratic competence rather than that of democratic legitimation.

WHO IS SPEAKING—WHEN CAN PROFESSORS ASSERT THE PROTECTIONS OF ACADEMIC FREEDOM?

If the "public concern" test of the *Pickering–Connick–Churchill* line of cases is frequently invoked by lower courts attempting to wrestle with thorny questions of constitutional academic freedom, so also is another decision of the Supreme Court—*Hazelwood School Dist. v. Kuhlmeier.*[82] In *Hazelwood* the court held that a secondary school was authorized to restrict or compel speech as necessary in order to fulfill its chosen curriculum. In the context of higher education, *Hazelwood* is typically invoked whenever a professor claims that a university has interfered with his freedom in the classroom. A good example is *Bishop v. Aronov*,[83] in which a university professor was instructed to refrain from interjecting his religious beliefs or preferences during instructional time periods.

Citing *Kuhlmeier*, the court in *Aronov* held that "as a place of schooling with a teaching mission, we consider the University's authority to reasonably control the content of its curriculum, particularly that content imparted during class time. Tangential to the authority over its curriculum, there lies some authority over the conduct of teachers in and out of the classroom that significantly bears on the curriculum or that gives the appearance of endorsement by the university."[84] *Aronov* felt driven to the conclusion that "though we are mindful of the invaluable role academic freedom plays in our public schools, particularly at the post-secondary level, we do not find support to conclude that academic freedom is an independent First Amendment right."[85]

Most apparently at issue in *Aronov* was the component of academic freedom that the *Declaration* identifies as freedom of teaching.[86] Freedom of teaching is an exceedingly complex and ill-defined topic, for it must be reconciled not only with the capacity of faculty departments and universities to design and implement curricular requirements,[87] but also with the academic freedom of students. If there is an argument for constitutionalizing freedom of teaching, it must be of the kind sketched by Frankfurter in his famous concurrence in *Wieman v. Updegraff*:

> That our democracy ultimately rests on public opinion is a platitude of speech but not a commonplace in action. Public opinion is the ultimate reliance of our society only if it be disciplined and responsible. It can be disciplined and responsible only if habits of open-mindedness and of critical inquiry are acquired in the formative years of our citizens. The process of education has naturally enough been the basis of hope for the perdurance of our democracy on the part of all our great leaders, from Thomas Jefferson onwards.
>
> To regard teachers—in our entire educational system, from the primary grades to the university—as the priests of our democracy is therefore not to indulge in hyperbole. It is the special task of teachers to foster those habits of open-mindedness and critical inquiry which alone make for responsible citizens, who, in turn, make possible an enlightened and effective public opinion. Teachers must fulfill their function by precept and practice, by the very atmosphere which they generate; they must be exemplars of open-mindedness and free inquiry. They cannot carry out their noble task if the conditions for the

practice of a responsible and critical mind are denied to them. They must have the freedom of responsible inquiry, by thought and action, into the meaning of social and economic ideas, into the checkered history of social and economic dogma. They must be free to sift evanescent doctrine, qualified by time and circumstance, from that restless, enduring process of extending the bounds of understanding and wisdom, to assure which the freedoms of thought, of speech, of inquiry, of worship are guaranteed by the Constitution of the United States against infraction by national or State government.[88]

In this passage, Frankfurter advances the argument that democracy can succeed only if persons are educated to become competent democratic citizens. The forms of pedagogy necessary for what we may call "democratic education"[89] should thus be invested with constitutional value.[90]

I do not in this chapter address the thorny subject of freedom of teaching.[91] I focus instead on classroom regulations that affect academic freedom of research and publication. This freedom includes the right to disseminate the results of research to laypersons, including and most especially to students in the classroom. Freedom of research and publication is implicated in the classroom not merely because classrooms are a primary medium for the transmission of scholarly expertise to the public, but also because classrooms are the only medium through which the next generation of scholars can be produced.

Freedom of research does not in this sense seem to have been at issue in *Aronov*, because in that case the professor was teaching a class in "exercise physiology" and the classroom remarks for which he was disciplined concerned how "God came to earth in the form of Jesus Christ and he has something to tell us about life which is crucial to success and happiness."[92] It is difficult to construe these remarks as a report of scholarly expertise. At most they were an effort to motivate and engage students in the classroom. Such an effort would exemplify freedom of teaching rather than freedom of research and publication.

A university must be free to regulate the incompetent communication of research within the classroom. But a university cannot regulate the communication of research within the classroom on the ground that it disapproves of the message that is conveyed. Such a purpose would be, as Dewey observed at the outset of the last century, to perpetuate "a certain way of looking at things current among a given body of persons. . . . To disciple rather than to discipline."[93] The effort to disciple the communication of research, inside or outside the classroom, ought to be regarded as inconsistent with the constitutional value of democratic competence.

Several years ago the court rendered a decision that potentially takes a long step toward entrenching a constitutional vision of universities that disciple rather than discipline. In *Garcetti v. Ceballos*,[94] the court held "that when public employees make statements pursuant to their official duties, the employees are not speaking as citizens for First Amendment purposes, and the Constitution does not insulate their communications from employer discipline."[95] In the secondary school context, *Garcetti* has been interpreted to deny all academic freedom in the classroom, because a "school system does not 'regulate' teachers' speech as much as it *hires* that speech. Expression is a teacher's stock in trade, the commodity she sells to her employer in exchange for a salary."[96] In the context of public universities, courts are beginning to interpret *Garcetti* to mean that "in order for a public employee to raise a successful First Amendment claim, he must have spoken in his capacity as a private citizen and not as an employee."[97] This conclusion essentially implies that universities are proprietary institutions that hire faculty in order to speak for them.

Aware that this holding would have drastic implications for academic freedom of research, *Garcetti* itself notes that "there is some argument that expression related to academic scholarship or classroom instruction implicates additional constitutional interests that are not fully accounted for by this Court's customary employee-speech jurisprudence," and it concludes that "we need not, and for that reason do not, decide whether the analysis we conduct today would apply in the same manner to a case involving speech related to scholarship or teaching."[98]

It is precisely to avoid the logic implicit of *Garcetti* that the drafters of the *Declaration* insisted that faculty "are the appointees, but not in any proper sense the employees," of universities.[99]

> Once appointed, the scholar has professional functions to perform in which the appointing authorities have neither competency nor moral right to intervene. The responsibility of the university teacher is primarily to the public itself, and to his judgment of his own profession; and, while, with respect to certain external conditions of his vocation, he accepts a responsibility to the authorities of the institution in which he serves, in the essentials of his professional activity his

duty is to the wider public to which the institution itself is morally amenable. So far as the university teacher's independence of thought and utterance is concerned—though not in other regards—the relationship of professor to trustees may be compared to that between judges of the federal courts and the executive who appoints them. University teachers should be understood to be, with respect to the conclusions reached and expressed by them, no more subject to the control of the trustees, than are the judges subject to the control of the president, with respect to their decisions; while of course, for the same reason, trustees are no more to be held responsible for, or to be presumed to agree with, the opinions or utterances of professors, than the president can be assumed to approve of the legal reasonings of the courts.[100]

Translated into contemporary constitutional terms, the argument of the *Declaration* is that faculty serve the "public" insofar as they serve the public function of identifying and discovering knowledge. It is this function that triggers the constitutional value of democratic competence. Were faculty to be merely the employees of a university, as *Garcetti* conceptualizes employees, they would be responsible in their "official duties" for promulgating the opinions of the governors (or underwriters) of the university. They could then no longer serve the function of identifying and advancing knowledge, because in modern society the creation of knowledge is inseparably connected to the application of professional, disciplinary standards.

Were that consequence to obtain, our nation would have lost an invaluable resource, one that has propelled us to the forefront of the world stage. In today's information age, intellectual stagnation implies economic and military death. Much depends, therefore, on the extent to which the court appreciates the full weight that rides on the casual reservation that it advanced in *Garcetti*. The implications of *Garcetti* are especially foreboding in a world in which universities are increasingly desperate for funding and perhaps even willing to sell the academic freedom of their faculty in order to secure a stable financial future.

NOTES

1. Walter P. Metzger, "Profession and Constitution: Two Definitions of Academic Freedom in America," *Texas Law Review* 66 (1988): 1265.
2. Keyishian v. Board of Regents, 385 U.S. 589, 603 (1967).
3. J. Peter Byrne, "Academic Freedom: A 'Special Concern of the First Amendment,'" *Yale Law Journal* 99 (1989): 253.

4. *Keyishian*, 385 U.S. See Rosenberger v. Rectors and Visitors of the University of Virginia, 515 U.S. 819, 831 (1995); Healy v. James, 408 U.S. 169, 180 (1972); Dambrot v. Cent. Mich. Univ., 55 F.3d 1177, 1188 (6th Cir. 1995) ("the purpose of the free-speech clause . . . is to protect the market in ideas, broadly understood as the public expression of ideas, narratives, concepts, imagery, opinions—scientific, political, or aesthetic—to an audience whom the speaker seeks to inform, edify, or entertain."); Thomas Gibbs Gee, "Enemies or Allies? In Defense of Judges," *Texas Law Review* 66 (1988): 1617 (referring to "academic freedom and to the all but indistinguishable first amendment right of free speech.").

5. Karl Jaspers, *The Idea of the University*, trans. H. A. T. Reiche and H. F. Vanderschmidt (Boston: Beacon, 1959), 2.

6. "What Is Harvard's Mission Statement?," Harvard University, www.harvard.edu/faqs/mission-statement. For a good survey, see R. George Wright, "The Emergence of First Amendment Academic Freedom," *Nebraska Law Review* 85 (2007): 793.

7. David Madsen, "Review Essay: The American University in a Changing Society: Three Views," *American Journal of Education* 91, 356–65 (1983): 361. See Harry D. Gideonse, "Changing Issues of Academic Freedom," *Proceedings of the American Philosophical Society* 94 (1950): 92 ("The function of a university is the discovery and the dissemination of the truth in all branches of learning.").

8. D. C. Gilman, *The Benefits Which Society Derives from Universities: An Address* (1885). Gilman's view should be contrasted with John Henry Newman's assertion in 1852 that the *"essence"* of a university was to be a place *"of teaching* universal *knowledge,"* which for Newman implied that the purpose of a university was "the diffusion and extension of knowledge rather than the advancement. If its object were scientific and philosophical discovery, I do not see why a University should have students." John Henry Newman, *The Idea of a University*, ed. Frank M. Turner (New Haven, Conn.: Yale University Press, 1996), 3.

9. Arthur Twining Hadley, the president of Yale, noted in 1903 that "in Germany the increase of academic freedom is to a surprisingly large measure the result of public interest in modern science and public demand for competent and trained technical experts." Arthur Twining Hadley, "Academic Freedom in Theory and Practice," *Atlantic Monthly* 91 (1903): 341.

10. John Dewey, "Academic Freedom," *Educational Review* 23 (1902): 1–14. "The university function is the truth-function. At one time it may be more concerned with the tradition or transmission of truth, and at another time with its discovery. Both functions are necessary, and neither can ever be entirely absent" (3). For an example of how academic freedom would appear under the more traditional concept of education, see Kay v. Board of Higher Education of City of New York, 18 N.Y.S. 2d 821, 829 (N.Y. Sup. Ct 1940), upholding dismissal of Bertrand Russell from the College of the City of New York because "this court . . . will not tolerate academic freedom being used as a cloak to promote the popularization in the minds of adolescents of acts forbidden by the penal Law. . . . Academic freedom does not mean academic license. It is the freedom to do good and not to teach evil. . . . Academic freedom cannot teach that

. . . adultery is attractive and good for the community. There are norms and criteria of truth which have been recognized by the founding fathers."

11. There are four components to the professional idea of academic freedom: freedom of research and publication; freedom of teaching; freedom of extracurricular speech; freedom of intramural speech. See Matthew Finkin and Robert Post, *For the Common Good: Principles of American Academic Freedom* (New Haven, Conn.: Yale University Press, 2009). In this chapter I discuss academic freedom *only* as it pertains to freedom of research and publication.

12. The "Declaration" is reprinted in American Association of University Professors, *Policy Documents and Reports*, 9th ed. (Washington, D.C.: AAUP, 2001), 291–301 (hereafter referred to as *AAUP Documents*). Its major authors included Edwin R. A. Seligman and Arthur O. Lovejoy. See Walter P. Metzger, "The 1940 Statement of Principles on Academic Freedom and Tenure," *Law and Contemporary Problems* 3 (1990): 12–13. The concept of academic freedom advanced in the "Declaration" was later incorporated in the canonical "1940 Statement of Principles on Academic Freedom and Tenure," *AAUP Documents*, 3–11. The "1940 Statement" has been endorsed by more than 180 educational organizations and has become "the general norm of academic practice in the United States." William W. Van Alstyne, "Academic Freedom and the First Amendment in the Supreme Court of the United States: An Unhurried Historical Review," *Law and Contemporary Problems* 53 (Summer 1990): 79. See Browzin v. Catholic Univ. of Am., 527 F.2d 843, 848 & n. 8 (D.C. Cir. 1075), "[The 1940 Statement] represent[s] widely shared norms within the academic community, having achieved acceptance by organizations which represent teachers as well as organizations which represent college administrators and governing boards."

13. "Declaration," 295.

14. Ibid.

15. Ibid., 300.

16. Ibid., 298. On the relationship between academic freedom and a theory of knowledge, see John R. Searle, "Two Concepts of Academic Freedom," in *The Concept of Academic Freedom*, ed. Edmund L. Pincoffs (Austin, Tex.: University of Texas Press, 1975), 88–89, 92.

17. "Declaration," 298, 31–45.

18. For a discussion, see Finkin and Post, *For the Common Good*, 31–45.

19. "Declaration," 294. Hence the conclusion of Thomas Haskell: "Historically speaking, the heart and soul of academic freedom lie not in free speech but in professional autonomy and collegial self-governance. Academic freedom came into being as a defense of the disciplinary community (or, more exactly, the university conceived as an ensemble of such communities)." Thomas L. Haskell, "Justifying the Rights of Academic Freedom in the Era of "Power/Knowledge," in *The Future of Academic Freedom*, ed. Louis Menand (Chicago: University of Chicago Press, 1996), 54.

20. Robert M. Hutchins, "The Meaning and Significance of Academic Freedom," *Annals of the American Academy of Political and Social Science* 300 (July 1955): 72–73.

21. On the paradoxes that underlie this doubled stance, see Finkin and Post, *For the Common Good*, 38–41.
22. Abrams v. United States, 250 U.S. 616 (1919).
23. *Abrams*, 250 U.S. 630 (Holmes, J., dissenting).
24. Red Lion Broad. v. FCC, 395 U.S. 367, 390 (1969).
25. Gloria Franke, "The Right of Publicity vs. The First Amendment: Will One Test Ever Capture the Starring Role?," *Southern California Law Review* 79 (2006): 958. See S. Brannon Latimer, "Can Felon Disenfranchisement Survive Under Modern Conceptions of Voting Rights?: Political Philosophy, State Interests, and Scholarly Scorn," *Southern Methodist University Law Review* 59 (2006): 1862 (A central purpose of the First Amendment is that of "'advancing knowledge' and 'truth' in the 'marketplace of ideas.'")
26. William P. Marshall, "In Defense of the Search for Truth as a First Amendment Justification," *Georgia Law Review* 30 (1995): 1.
27. *Rosenberger*, 515 U.S. 819 at 834 (1995).
28. Turner Broad. Sys., Inc. v. FCC, 512 U.S. 622, 642 (1994).
29. Hustler Magazine v. Falwell, 485 U.S. 46, 51 (1988).
30. See, e.g., the opinions in the court's recent decision in United States v. Alvarez, 567 U.S. 11–210 (2012), in which the court ruled that Congress could not impose criminal sanctions on false claims to have won a Congressional Medal of Honor. Even the dissent, which would have allowed such sanctions, was moved to remark:

> There are broad areas in which any attempt by the state to penalize purportedly false speech would present a grave and unacceptable danger of suppressing truthful speech. Laws restricting false statements about philosophy, religion, history, the social sciences, the arts, and other matters of public concern would present such a threat. The point is not that there is no such thing as truth or falsity in these areas or that the truth is always impossible to ascertain, but rather that it is perilous to permit the state to be the arbiter of truth.
>
> Even where there is a wide scholarly consensus concerning a particular matter, the truth is served by allowing that consensus to be challenged without fear of reprisal. Today's accepted wisdom sometimes turns out to be mistaken. And in these contexts, "even a false statement may be deemed to make a valuable contribution to public debate, since it brings about 'the clearer perception and livelier impression of truth, produced by its collision with error.'" . . .
>
> Allowing the state to proscribe false statements in these areas also opens the door for the state to use its power for political ends. Statements about history illustrate this point. If some false statements about historical events may be banned, how certain must it be that a statement is false before the ban may be upheld? And who should make that calculation? While our cases prohibiting viewpoint discrimination would fetter the state's power to some degree, . . . the potential for abuse of power in these areas is simply too great.

In stark contrast to hypothetical laws prohibiting false statements about history, science, and similar matters, the Stolen Valor Act presents no risk at all that valuable speech will be suppressed. (Alito, J., dissenting)

Justice Alito's opinion was joined by Justices Scalia and Thomas. Concurring, Justice Breyer, joined by Justice Kagan, asserted:

As the dissent points out, "there are broad areas in which any attempt by the state to penalize purportedly false speech would present a grave and unacceptable danger of suppressing truthful speech." . . . Laws restricting false statements about philosophy, religion, history, the social sciences, the arts, and the like raise such concerns, and in many contexts have called for strict scrutiny. But this case does not involve such a law. The dangers of suppressing valuable ideas are lower where, as here, the regulations concern false statements about easily verifiable facts that do not concern such subject matter. Such false factual statements are less likely than are true factual statements to make a valuable contribution to the marketplace of ideas. (Breyer, J., concurring)

31. "The institutional structure of scholarly journals serves to reinforce disciplinary hierarchies: at the lowest level, the evaluator, reader, or reviewer is implicitly considered to be qualified to make judgments about a contribution at a level above that of the contributor himself. From there the hierarchy extends to the editorship, and the selection processes for filling the intervening positions evidently reinforce the hierarchizing and orthodoxy of the discipline in question." Wolfram W. Swoboda, "Disciplines and Interdisciplinarity: A Historical Perspective," in *Interdisciplinarity in Higher Education*, ed. Joseph J. Kockelmans (University Park: Pennsylvania State University Press, 1979), 78–99. See Ellen Messer-Davidow, "Book Review," *Signs*, 17, no. 3 (Spring 1992): 676–688: "Gatekeepers, by virtue of their position as evaluators (editors of journals, referees of manuscripts, reviewers of grant proposals), decide which work will be presented in public forums and which will languish in obscurity. Upon cumulative decisions of this kind depend the professional and epistemological selections—who gets tenured and promoted, which knowledges are advanced and disseminated—that constitute a disciplinary repertoire" (679).

32. For a discussion of this difference, see Robert Post, "Debating Disciplinarity," *Critical Inquiry* 35, (2009): 749.

33. Perhaps Charles Sanders Peirce said it best:

Some persons fancy that bias and counter-bias are favorable to the extraction of truth—that hot and partisan debate is the way to investigate. This is the theory of our atrocious legal procedure. But Logic puts its heel upon this suggestion. It irrefragably demonstrates that knowledge can only be furthered by the real desire for it, and that the methods of obstinacy, of authority, and every mode of trying to reach a foregone conclusion, are absolutely of no value. These things are proved. The reader is at liberty to think so or not as long as the proof is not set forth, or as long as he refrains from examining it. Just so, he can preserve, if he likes, his freedom of opinion in regard to the propositions of geometry; only, in that case, if he takes a fancy to read Euclid, he will do well to skip whatever he finds with A, B, C, etc., for, if he reads attentively that disagreeable matter, the freedom of his opinion about geometry may unhappily be lost forever.

Charles Sanders Peirce, *Collected Papers*, ed. Charles Hartshorne, Paul Weiss, and Arthur Burks (Cambridge, Mass.: Harvard University Press, 1931–1958), 2:635.

34. "Academic freedom is not a doctrine to insulate a teacher from evaluation by the institution that employs him." Carley v. Arizona Board of Regents, 737 P.2d 1099, 1103 (Aria. App. 1987).

35. Robert Post, *Democracy, Expertise, Academic Freedom: A First Amendment Jurisprudence for the Modern State* (New Haven, Conn.: Yale University Press, 2012); Robert Post, *Citizens Divided: Campaign Finance Reform and the Constitution* (Cambridge, Mass.: Harvard University Press, 2014).

36. Ollman v. Evans, 750 F.2d 970, 978 (D.C. Cir. 1984) (en banc), *cert. denied*, 471 U.S. 1127 (1985).

37. Haynes v. Alfred A. Knopf, 8 F.3d 1222, 1227 (7th Cir. 1993). See Gray v. St. Martin's Press, Inc., 221 F.3d 243, 248 (1st Cir. 2000), *cert. denied*, 531 U.S. 1075 (2001).

38. Karen Knorr Cetina, *Epistemic Cultures: How The Sciences Make Knowledge* (1999), 5. Nikolas Rose and Peter Miller, "Political Power Beyond the State: Problematics of Government," *British Journal of Social Psychology* 43 (1992): 175 ("Knowledge is . . . central to [the] activities of government and to the very formation of its objects, for government is a domain of cognition, calculation, experimentation and evaluation.").

39. See, e.g., George Orwell, *The Collected Essays, Journalism, and Letters of George Orwell: As I Please, 1943–1945*, ed. Sonia Orwell and Ian Angus (New York: Harcourt, 2000), 3:87–89: "The really frightening thing about totalitarianism is not that it commits 'atrocities' but that it attacks the concept of objective truth; it claims to control the past as well as the future."

40. John Dewey, *The Public and Its Problems* (New York: Holt, 1927), 177–79. "Unless there are methods . . . what passes as public opinion will be 'opinion' in its derogatory sense rather than truly public, no matter how widespread the opinion is" (177).

41. Claude Lefort, *Democracy and Political Theory*, trans. David Macey (Cambridge, UK: Polity, 1988), 15.

42. Planned Parenthood v. Heineman, 724 F.Supp.2nd 1025 (D. Neb.2010).

43. Ibid. at 1048.

44. Similarly, the constitutional value of democratic competence is implicated whenever the state attempts to prevent the communication of true expert knowledge outside of public discourse. See Post, *Democracy, Expertise, and Academic Freedom*, 47–53.

45. Post, *Democracy, Expertise, and Academic Freedom*, 34.

46. In American constitutional law, constitutional rights generally apply only against state action. Professional ideals of academic freedom are not so restricted.

47. I stress once again that in this chapter I am analyzing only academic freedom of research and publication, and not the other three dimensions of academic freedom. See note 11.

48. Regents of University of Michigan v. Ewing, 474 U.S. 214, 226 n.12 (1985). (Academic freedom thrives not only on the independent and uninhibited exchange of ideas among teachers and students. See *Keyishian*, 385 U.S. at 603; Sweezy v. New Hampshire, 354 U.S. 234, 250 (1957) (opinion of Warren, C. J.), but also, and somewhat inconsistently, on autonomous decision making by the academy itself, see Regents of the University of California v. Bakke, 438 U.S. 265, 312 (1978) (opinion of Powell, J.); *Sweezy*, 354 U.S. at 263 (Frankfurter, J., concurring in result.); Dow Chemical Co. v. Allen, 672 F.2d 1262, 1275 (7th Cir. 1982) ("Case law considering the standard to be applied where the issue is academic freedom of the university to be free of governmental interference, as opposed to academic freedom of the individual teacher to be free of restraints from the university administration, is surprisingly sparse."); Piarowski v. Illinois Community College District 525, 759 F.2d 625, 629 (7th Cir. 1985) ("Though many decisions describe 'academic freedom' as an aspect of the freedom of speech that is protected against governmental abridgment by the First Amendment, . . . the term is equivocal. It is used to denote both the freedom of the academy to pursue its ends without interference from the government (the sense in which it used, for example, in Justice Powell's opinion in Regents of the University of California v. Bakke, 438 U.S. 265, 312 (1978), or in our recent decision in EEOC v. University of Notre Dame Du Lac, 715 F.2d 331, 335–36 (7th Cir.1983)), and the freedom of the individual teacher (or in some versions–indeed in most cases–the student) to pursue his ends without interference from the academy; and these two freedoms are in conflict, as in this case."); Keen v. Penson, 970 F.2d 252, 257 (7th Cir. 1992) ("As this case reveals, the assertion of academic freedom of a professor can conflict with the academic freedom of the university to make decisions affecting that professor."); Cooper v. Ross, 472 F. Supp 802,813 (D.C. Ark. 1979) ("The present case is particularly difficult because it involves a fundamental tension between the academic freedom of the individual teacher to be free of restraints from the university administration, and the academic freedom of the university to be free of government, including judicial, interference.").

49. Byrne, "Academic Freedom: A 'Special Concern of the First Amendment,'" 3; J. Peter Byrne, "The Threat to Constitutional Academic Freedom," *Journal of College & University Law* 31 (2004): 79; David M. Rabban, "Functional Analysis of 'Individual' and 'Institutional' Academic Freedom Under the First Amendment," *Law and Contemporary Problems* 53 (Summer 1990): 227–302; Richard H. Hiers, "Institutional Academic Freedom vs. Faculty Academic Freedom in Public Colleges and Universities," *Journal of College & University Law* 35 (2002): 31; Richard H. Hiers, "Institutional Academic Freedom or Autonomy Grounded Upon the First Amendment: A Jurisprudential Mirage," *Hamline Law Review* 1 (2007): 30; Elizabeth Mertz, "The Burden of Proof and Academic Freedom: Protection for Institution or Individual?," *Northwestern University Law Review* 82 (1988): 292; Frederick Schauer, "Is There a Right to Academic Freedom?," *University of Colorado Law Review* 77 (2006): 907; Matthew Finkin, "On 'Institutional' Academic Freedom," *Texas Law Review* 61 (1983): 817; Michael A. Olivas,

"Reflections on Professorial Academic Freedom: Second Thoughts on the Third 'Essential Freedom,'" *Stanford Law Review* 45 (1993): 1835; Rachel Fugate, "Choppy Waters Are Forecast for Academic Free Speech," *Florida State University Law Review* 26 (1998): 187; Mark G. Yudof, "Three Faces of Academic Freedom," *Loyola Law Review* 32 (1987): 853–57; Alan K. Chen, "Bureaucracy and Distrust: Germaneness and the Paradoxes of Academic Freedom Doctrine," *University of Colorado Law Review* 77 (2006): 955.

50. Charles W. Eliot, "Academic Freedom," *Science* 26 (July 5, 1907): 1–2.

51. "Declaration," 293.

52. Ibid.

53. As Kant observes, "The university would have a certain autonomy (since only scholars can pass judgment on scholars as such)." Immanuel Kant, *The Conflict of the Faculties*, trans. J. Gregor (New York: Abaris, 1979), 23.

54. Carley v. Arizona Board of Regents, 737 P.2d 1099,1102 (Ariz. App. 1987).

55. *Regents of the University of Michigan v. Ewing*, 474 U.S. 214, 225 (1985). See Board of Curators, Univ. of Mo. v. Horowitz, 435 U.S. 78, 90–92 (1978); ibid. at 96 n.6 (Powell, J., concurring); Clark v. Whiting, 607 F.2d 634 (4th Cir. 1979); Brown v. George Washington Univ., 802 A.2d 382, 385 (D.C. 2002).

56. Bishop v. Aronov, 92 F.2d 1066, 1075 (11th Cir. 1991).

57. See, e.g., Judith Areen, "Government as Educator: A New Understanding of First Amendment Protection of Academic Freedom and Governance," *Georgetown Law Journal* 97 (2009): 945, 994–99.

58. "Declaration," 294.

59. For a discussion of when judicial deference may or may not be appropriate when reviewing institutional decision making, see Robert Post, "Between Management and Governance: The History and Theory of the Public Forum," *UCLA Law Review* 34 (1987): 1713.

60. Urofsky v. Gilmore, 216 F.3d 401 (4th Cir. 2000).

61. Ibid. at 404.

62. Ibid. at 411.

63. Ibid. at 412. "The Court has focused its discussions of academic freedom solely on issues of institutional autonomy" (at 415).

64. The court also failed to realize that the Virginia statute was in fact a regulation of the university itself. See Byrne, supra note 49, at 112. *Gilmore* should be compared to Henley v. Wise, 303 F.Supp. 62, 66 (D.C. Ind. 1969), which struck down an Indiana statute criminalizing the possession of obscene material without intent to sell, lend, or give away, in part because the statute "intruded" into "the right of scholars to do research and advance the state of man's knowledge."

65. *Gilmore*, 216 F.3d at 415.

66. Pickering v. Board of Education, 319 U.S. 563 (1968).

67. Connick v. Myers, 461 U.S. 138 (1983).

68. Waters v. Churchill, 511 U.S. 661 (1994).

69. *Connick*, 461 U.S. at 146–47.

70. Hardy v. Jefferson Community College, 260 F.3d 671 (6th Cir. 2001); Jeffries v. Harleston, 52 F.3d 9 (2nd Cir. 1995); Hong v. Grant, 516 F.Supp.2d 1158 (C.D. CA. 2007); Blum v. Schlegel, 18 F.3d 1005 (2nd Cir. 1994); Bonnell v. Lorenzo, 241 F.3d 800 (6th

Cir. 2001); Dambrot v. Central Michigan University, 55 F.3d 1177 (6th Cir. 1995); Scallet v. Rosenblum, 911 F.Supp. 999, 1009–14 (W.D. Va. 1996); Trejo v. Shoben, 319 F.3d 878 (7th Cir. 2003); Rubin v. Ikenberry, 933 F.Supp. 1425 (C.D. Ill. 1996); Silva v. University of New Hampshire, 888 F. Supp. 293 (D.N.H. 1994); Robert J. Tepper, "Speak No Evil: Academic Freedom and the Application of *Garcetti v. Ceballos* to the Public University Faculty," *Catholic University Law Review* 59 (2009): 129; Ailsa W. Chang, "Resuscitating the Constitutional 'Theory' of Academic Freedom: A Search for a Standard Beyond Pickering and Connick," *Stanford Law Review* 53 (2001): 915; Chris Hoofnagle, "Matters of Public Concern and the Public University Professor," *Journal of College and University Law* 27 (2001): 669; Edgar Dyer, "Collegiality's Potential Chill Over Faculty Speech: Demonstrating the Need for a Refined Version of Pickering and Connick for Public Higher Education," *Education Law Reporter* 119 (1997): 309; Richard H. Hiers, "Academic Freedom in Public Colleges and Universities: O Say, Does That Star-Spangled First Amendment Banner Yet Wave?," *Wayne Law Review* 40 (1993): 1; Jennifer Elrod, "Academics, Public Employee Speech, and the Public University," *Buffalo Public Interest Law Journal* 22 (2003–2004): 1.

71. See Areen, "Government as Educator," 975–76.

72. The logic of this and the following paragraph is developed in detail in Post, supra note 59.

73. *Pickering*, 391 U.S. at 568.

74. *Connick*, 461 U.S. at 142.

75. Ibid. Immanuel Kant early on identified this tension. In "An Answer to the Question: 'What is Enlightenment?'" he observes:

> The public use of man's reason must always be free. . . . the private use of reason may quite often be very narrowly restricted. . . . By the public use of one's own reason I mean that use which anyone may make of it as a man of learning addressing the entire reading public. What term the private use of reason is that which a person may make of it in a particular civil post or office with which he is entrusted.
>
> Now in some affairs which affect the interests of the commonwealth, we require a certain mechanism whereby some members of the commonwealth must behave purely passively, so that they may, by an artificial common agreement, be employed by the government for public ends. . . . It is, of course, impermissible to argue in such cases; obedience is imperative. But in so far as this or that individual who acts as part of the machine also considers himself as a member of a complete commonwealth or even of cosmopolitan society, and thence as a man of learning who may through his writings address a public in the truest sense of the word, he may indeed argue without harming the affairs in which he is employed for some of the time in a passive capacity. Thus it would be very harmful if an officer receiving an order from his superiors were to quibble openly, while on duty, about the appropriateness or usefulness of the order in question. He must simply obey. But he cannot reasonably be banned from making observations as a man of learning on the errors in the military service, and from submitting these to his public for judgement.

Immanuel Kant, *Political Writings*, ed. Hans Reiss, trans. H. B. Nisbet (New York: Cambridge University Press, 1991), 55–56.

76. Yudof, "Three Faces of Academic Freedom," 838–40; Robert Post, "Racist Speech, Democracy, and the First Amendment," *William and Mary Law Review* 32 (1990): 317–25.
77. See note 11.
78. "1940 Statement," quoted in note 12.
79. See, in this regard, the remarks of Harvard President Abbott Lawrence Lowell:

> The right of a professor to express his views without restraint on matters lying outside the sphere of his professorship is not a question of academic freedom in its true sense, but of the personal liberty of the citizen. It has nothing to do with liberty of research and instruction in the subject for which the professor occupies the chair that makes him a member of the university. The fact that a man fills a chair of astronomy, for example, confers on him no special knowledge of, and no peculiar right to speak upon, the protective tariff. His right to speak about a subject on which he is not an authority is simply the right of any other man, and the question is simply whether the university or college by employing him as a professor acquires a right to restrict his freedom as a citizen

> Quoted in Henry Aaron Yeomans, *Abbott Lawrence Lowell, 1856–1943* (Cambridge, Mass.: Harvard University Press, 1948), 310.

80. Consider the case of Sami Al-Arian, a computer science professor, who was disciplined for statements concerning terrorism in the Middle East after September 11, 2001. See Joe Humphrey, "Professors Condemn Al-Arian's Firing," *Tampa Tribune*, June 15, 2003. For the AAUP investigative report on the Al-Arian case, see *Academe* 89, no. 3 (2003): 59.
81. For a discussion, see Finkin and Post, *For the Common Good*; William W. van Alstyne, "The Specific Theory of Academic Freedom and the General Issue of Civil Liberties," *Annals of the American Academy of Political and Social Science* 404 (1972): 140–156, 146.

> The phrase "academic freedom," in the context "the academic freedom of a faculty member of an institution of higher learning" refers to a set of vocational liberties: to teach, to investigate, to do research, and to publish on any subject as a matter of professional interest, without vocational jeopardy or threat of other sanction, save only upon adequate demonstration of an inexcusable breach of professional ethics in the exercise of any of them. Specifically, that which sets academic freedom apart as a distinct freedom is its vocational claim of special and limited accountability in respect to all academically related pursuits of the teacher-scholar: an accountability not to any institutional or societal standard of economic benefit, acceptable interest, right thinking, or socially constructive theory, but solely to a fiduciary standard of professional integrity. To condition the employment or personal freedom of the teacher-scholar upon the institutional or society approval of his academic investigations or utterances, or to quality either even by the immediate aspect of his professional endeavors upon the economic

well-being or good will of the very institution which employs him, is to abridge his academic freedom. The maintenance of academic freedom contemplates an accountability in respect to academic investigations and utterances solely in respect of their professional integrity, a matter usually determined by reference to professional ethical standards of truthful disclosure and reasonable care.

Van Alstyne explicitly contrasts academic freedom to the civil liberties protected by extramural speech: "The legitimate claims of personal autonomy possessed equally by all persons, wholly without reference to academic freedom, frame a distinct and separate set of limitations upon the just power of an institution to use its leverage of control" (146). At the time of the "1940 Statement," before the demise of the rights/privilege distinction, First Amendment doctrine did not extend the civil liberty to participate in public discourse to government employees.

82. Hazelwood School Dist. v. Kuhlmeier, 484 U.S. 260 (1988). "The most commonly applied tests are variations of one sort or another of what we have called the Hazelwood test and the Pickering-Connick-Garcetti or PCG test." R. George Wright, "The Emergence of First Amendment Academic Freedom," *Nebraska Law Review* 85 (2007): 816. See Axson-Flynn v. Johnson, 356 F.3d 1277 (10th Cir. 2004); Scallet v. Rosenblum, 911 F. Supp. 999, 1010 (W.D. Va. 1996).

83. Bishop v. Aronov, 926 F.2d 1066 (11th Cir. 1991).

84. Ibid. at 1074.

85. Ibid. at 1075.

86. See note 11.

87. For a discussion of this tension, see Piggee v. Carl Sandburg College, 464 F.3d 667, 670–71 (7th Cir. 2006).

88. Wieman v. Updegraff, 344 U.S. 183, 196–98 (1952) (Frankfurter, J., concurring).

89. Amy Gutmann, *Democratic Education* (Princeton, N.J.: Princeton University Press, 1987). See Benjamin R. Barber, *An Aristocracy of Everyone: The Politics of Education and the Future of America* (New York: Ballantine, 1992), 15: "In democracies, education is the indispensable concomitant of citizenship."

90. Court decisions have sometimes analyzed student rights in primary and secondary schools on the assumption that the constitutional purpose of public education is to produce democratically competent students, and they have sometimes analyzed such rights on the assumption that the constitutional purpose of public education is to reproduce existing cultural values. Compare Tinker v. Des Moines School District, 393 U.S. 503 (1969) with Bethel v. School Dist. No. 403 v. Frazer, 478 U.S. 675 (1986). For a discussion, see Post, supra note 76, at 317–25.

91. Nor do I address academic freedom to engage in so-called "intramural speech," which concerns matters of internal university governance. See Areen, "Government as Educator," 975–76.

92. *Aronov*, 926 F.2d at 1068.

93. Dewey, "Academic Freedom."

94. Garcetti v. Ceballos, 547 U.S. 410 (2006).

95. Ibid., 421.
96. Mayer v. Monroe County Community School Corp., 474 F.3d 477, 479 (7th Cir. 2007). Yudof observes that "unless an abridgement of speech lies in every exercise of governmental authority to speak through individuals—and how else might abstract entities called governments speak?—it is difficult to countenance the view that government control of its own professional speakers violates the historically developed concepts of freedom of expression." Yudof, "Three Faces of Academic Freedom," 839.
97. Renken v. Gregory, 541 F.3d 769, 773 (7th Cir. 2008). See, e.g., Isenalumhe v. McDuffie, F.Supp.2d, 2010 WL 986580 (E.D.N.Y.); Sadid v. Idaho State University, 6th Jud. Dist. Idaho, No. CV-2008–3942-OC, December 18, 2009. But see Kerr v. Hurd, 694 F.Supp.2d 817, 843–44 (S.D. Ohio 2010). See also Savage v. Gee, F.Supp.2d, 2010 WL 2301174 (S.D. Ohio 2010); Tepper, "Speak No Evil," supra note 70.
98. Garcetti, 547 U.S. at 425.
99. "Declaration," 295.
100. Ibid. See "Matthew Finkin, Intramural Speech, Academic Freedom, and the First Amendment," Texas Law Review 66 (1988): 1337–38, esp. 1323.

9

IRB LICENSING

PHILIP HAMBURGER

T HE LICENSING OF speech or the press is widely assumed to be an obsolete problem.[1] Back in the dimly lit past, the Inquisition and the Star Chamber licensed the press and thereby suppressed much scientific and political inquiry. By contrast, in the enlightened present, such licensing apparently is no longer a significant threat.

The licensing of speech and the press, however, has returned on a wider scale than anything imagined by the Inquisition or the Star Chamber. In response to anxieties about the academic study of human beings, Health and Human Services (HHS) has led the federal government in imposing licensing of speech and the press on "human-subjects research." The government carries out this licensing through institutional review boards—what are known as "IRBs." Although not familiar to the general public, these boards exist at all universities and most other research institutions, and they license and suppress much talking, reading, analyzing, printing, and publishing.

As it happens, the government also relies on IRBs in more specialized ways—for example, to review new drug and device trials under the auspices of the Food and Drug and Administration (FDA). The specialized use of IRBs under FDA regulations, however, is not at issue here. Instead, this essay concerns the use of IRBs under the laws and regulations that generally govern human-subjects research—what for convenience are here called the "IRB laws."[2]

These laws are unconstitutional on many grounds, but the central problem is that they impose licensing of speech and the press. Indeed, the IRB laws are the most widespread and systematic assault on the freedom of speech and the press in the nation's history.[3]

LICENSING

The First Amendment's speech clauses prohibit nothing as clearly or emphatically as licensing. But licensing no longer occupies a prominent place in academic theory or judicial doctrine. It therefore is essential to begin by understanding licensing and why the prohibition of it is so fundamental.

WHAT IS LICENSING OF SPEECH OR THE PRESS?

Licensing is a requirement that one get permission. Thus, when the First Amendment prohibits Congress from licensing speech or the press, it bars Congress from requiring one to get permission for speaking or publishing.

This licensing of speech and the press is very different from a driver's license. Before driving, you need a license. Imagine, however, the same for speaking or publishing—that you needed permission from government to be qualified to speak or publish. This would be bad enough and clearly would be unconstitutional, but licensing of speech and the press usually goes further. Imagine that you also needed permission each time you spoke or published. At least, after you get a driver's license, you can drive where you please. Suppose, however, that you needed prior permission not merely initially, but every time you talked to someone or published an article. You would need permission to begin a conversation, to ask each question, and to publish the answer.

SOCRATES AND GALILEO

Nothing better illustrates the distinctive character of licensing than the different treatment of the two greatest victims of suppression. The one was punished after the fact; the other was licensed.

Socrates spent his life testing a hypothesis stated by the oracle at Delphi. The oracle declared that no one was wiser than Socrates. But rather than accept this as true, Socrates set about to prove it wrong by questioning his contemporaries. His efforts were a sort of empirical inquiry, to test an hypothesis about himself and, by extension, human nature.

Socrates, in other words, used his interlocutors as "human subjects." As he understood, questions that cut deep necessarily cause discomfort, and the deeper the question, the greater the discomfort. The advantage is that, by causing internal distress and external shame, such inquiries can force a person to reevaluate herself and, indeed, can educate an entire society. Socrates therefore went out of his way to show up the intellectual and moral failings of his subjects.

On account of his inquiries, Socrates was punished by the demos. Had he put the questions to himself, he would have been left alone. But he posed his questions to others—to his human subjects—and he thereby seemed to call into doubt the gods of the city. In modern terms, he questioned national pieties. Socrates therefore was prosecuted before a jury and condemned to drink hemlock.

But he at least was punished only after the fact, not beforehand. He was not asked to get a license, to get permission, before asking questions. And his student Plato was able to publish the resulting dialogues without getting permission. Although Socrates probably would have much to say about the licensing of speech and press, he himself did not experience it.

In contrast, Galileo was subjected to licensing. Whereas Socrates was able to ask questions and share his views before being censored, Galileo needed to get permission before publication. After Galileo developed proof that the Earth revolved around the sun, Cardinal Bellarmine warned Galileo that his work was unsuitable for publication. But of course Galileo wanted to publish. And he knew that he first needed a license. So in 1632 he quietly obtained a license from a cleric who did not know of the prior warning. Although Galileo thereby got past the licensing system, the Inquisition was not amused. It could not proceed against him for failing to get a license, but it imprisoned him for failing to make adequate disclosure to the licenser.

This method of control, licensing, was what inspired eighteenth-century Americans to seek constitutional protection for the freedom of speech and the press. Of course, Americans were familiar with after-the-fact punishments, whether those experienced by Socrates or more recent victims. But licensing—the prior permission required by the Inquisition and the Star Chamber—seemed more dangerous. Therefore, when Americans in the First Amendment guaranteed the freedom of speech and the press, they most clearly and emphatically secured a freedom from licensing.[4]

AN INVARIABLY DANGEROUS METHOD

Licensing is a consistently dangerous method of controlling speech or the press. It therefore is consistently forbidden.

It is commonly assumed that licensing is not distinctively worrisome. Certainly, in some instances, after-the-fact constraints can be just as dangerous as licensing. But that is not the point. The special danger from licensing is that it is invariably dangerous.

Most after-the-fact constraints on the freedom of speech or the press are not particularly troubling. Indeed, many such constraints are valuable and lawful, as evident from tort, contract, and copyright law. In contrast, licensing is always a dangerous method of controlling speech and the press. Traditionally, therefore, at least as to verbal expression (the expression done through words), licensing was flatly unconstitutional.[5]

Licensing is consistently dangerous for several reasons. First, it is a means of wholesale suppression. The government ordinarily must enforce laws against speech in retail fashion, proving the danger of each publication, one by one, in a complex court proceeding. In its licensing, however, the government generally bars publications until they get permission, and it thereby suppresses them wholesale, without individual proceedings and other due process in court. Second, licensing in any sphere of speech is profoundly overbroad and disproportionate. In order to prevent harm in some instances, it imposes prior review in all instances, and it thereby suppresses or at least chills much entirely innocent speech. Most seriously, third, licensing requires individuals to get permission from the government before they speak or publish—as if they had no authority on their own to share information and ideas. Licensing in this manner forces the people to be submissive about their words. It makes them acknowledge the government's sovereignty over the very means by which they hold the government to account, and it thereby inverts the relationship of individuals to their government.

Being an inherently dangerous method of control, licensing is forbidden without regard to content. The Supreme Court's doctrine on content discrimination and political speech has led many scholars to assume that the First Amendment protects speech only on the basis of its content. And this makes sense for modes of control, such as injunctions or after-the-fact constraints, that are not inherently dangerous. But licensing is a predictably dangerous method of controlling speech, and because the method is so dangerous, the content of the licensed speech becomes less important. For centuries, therefore, it has been recognized that, quite apart from content, licensing as a method of controlling speech is prohibited.

The last time this sort of censorship flourished in common-law jurisdictions was in the seventeenth century. Back then, if you wrote a book, you needed a license or permission before you could print or publish. Just as the Inquisition imposed this licensing in Italy, the Star Chamber required it in England. Even if you merely wanted to speak, you might need a license—as when acting companies in Shakespeare's time needed a license before they could recite plays on stage.[6]

Such is the censorship that has come back to life. It usually is assumed that licensing came to an end when Parliament abandoned it in 1695 and especially when the First Amendment barred it in 1791. During the past four decades, however, it has returned. As a result, many individuals again need permission for the mere use of language.

THE STRUCTURE OF IRB LICENSING

The government imposes the contemporary licensing system through an elaborate administrative hierarchy, structured in four levels. At each stage, the IRB laws revive seventeenth-century licensing of speech and the press.

THE GOVERNMENT

At the top of the hierarchy is the federal government, especially HHS. The government worries that research on human beings will harm them, and it therefore relies on IRBs, as overseen by HHS, to license such research.

Rather than directly carry out the licensing, the government requires universities and other research institutions to do it. In a free society, it is difficult for government itself to impose licensing of speech and the press. This is why the Star Chamber long ago required universities to impose its licensing and why, again today, the federal government makes the universities implement its newer version of the licensing.

Like prior governments that imposed licensing, the federal government assumes it is acting on elevated, even benevolent principles, and it sets out its principles for the licensing in a document known as *The Belmont Report*. The government then provides more detailed standards for the licensing in a regulation known as the "Common Rule"—so called because many government departments or agencies have adopted it. The government also authorizes individual IRBs to add their own, local requirements. The result is a federal baseline for the licensing, and federal authorization for more severe local standards, which vary from IRB to IRB, at their discretion.

The government forces universities and other research institutions to impose IRBs in three ways—most prominently through conditions on research grants. The government, primarily HHS, requires all research funds for individuals to run through universities or other research institutions, thus giving the government an institutional means of control. In order for a professor to get HHS research funds, his university first must assure HHS that all human-subjects research at the institution will comply with the principles of *The Belmont Report* (or some equivalent document), including the underlying principle that all human-subjects research requires a prior license.[7] The university also must assure the government that it will impose the licensing of federally funded research in compliance with the standards of the Common Rule.

HHS and the other agencies, however, are interested in regulating not merely federally funded research but all human-subjects research, and they therefore use their conditions to impose the licensing on all such research regardless of its source of funding. They do this most generally by requiring each institution receiving federal research funding to commit that "all of its activities related to human subjects research, regardless of the source of support," will be guided by the *Belmont* or equivalent principles.[8] In addition, the agencies invite the institutions to commit themselves to apply the Common Rule to all human-subjects research done by their personnel—that is, not only to federally funded human-subjects research but also to other human-subjects research. Although this commitment is said to be voluntary, it has not always been so in practice, and most institutions assume they are obliged to impose IRB licensing for all human-subjects research, whatever the source of funding.

The federal government also relies on state negligence law. The government, beginning in the 1970s, understood that if it used its conditions to make the licensing pervasive, it could eventually establish the licensing as the standard of care for research. In other words, it used its unconstitutional conditions to inculcate the understanding that a research institution would be violating its duty of care if it failed to impose the licensing. Institutions therefore feel obliged not merely by federal pressures, but more concretely by state tort law, to apply the licensing to all research conducted by their personnel, even when the research is not federally funded. As a result, state negligence law, or at least the fear of it, has these days become the primary force behind the licensing.

To top it off, many states add a third mode of coercion. They adopt statutes requiring the use of IRBs. These statutes vary, and some are sweeping. For example, some impose IRBs not merely on the personnel of research institutions but on the general public.[9]

One way or another, the licensing comes with the force of law. Federal law sets the standards for the licensing and uses conditions to establish an initial layer of coercion. Then state tort doctrine and specialized statutes add more direct coercion.

THE UNIVERSITIES

At the next level of the hierarchy are universities and other research institutions. They uniformly comply with the government's demands.

Most basically, they establish IRBs and require all faculty and students to comply with the IRB licensing. They also typically hire staff to help enforce the licensing—for example, to help track down violators. Recently, many universities have even established entire administrative branches, headed by vice presidents of research, to give force to IRB demands.

Having established IRBs and their associated bureaucracies, how do universities induce faculty and students to submit? Some universities euphemistically threaten "serious consequences"; others speak more bluntly of dismissal or expulsion. Either way, universities rarely have to resort to such measures, as IRBs rely on their own power to enforce the licensing.

IRBs

The IRBs consist of faculty, administrators, and at least one community member, all of whom are to be chosen for their "sensitivity to . . . community attitudes."[10] Like the Inquisition, they act in secret, and they welcome anonymous denunciations. Like the Inquisition, moreover, they combine all legal functions: they regulate and license speech, they accuse violators, and they judge and punish them. And to protect their secrecy and discretion, they allow no appeals. In short, they provide the very opposite of due process and separation of powers.

The most common activity of IRBs is to license speech and the press, both in the getting of information and the sharing of it. When a faculty member or student seeks to do research on human subjects, she must prepare a research proposal and submit it to the IRB at her institution. The IRB then will review the proposal and follow one of several options: it will permit her work, deny permission, or most typically deny permission until she agrees to make changes—changes that usually limit her acquisition or sharing of information.

In particular, the IRB can interfere with her use of words. It can forbid her from talking to human subjects, reading about them, observing and taking notes about them, or publishing about them. It can do this even if she merely wants to interview government officials, distribute social science surveys, or read public records (such as court documents and public census data). The IRB also can directly modify her research: it can rewrite her questions, adjust her academic method, or otherwise alter her inquiry. And of course the IRB can limit what she may publish. The Inquisition inked over or rewrote passages in book manuscripts, and IRBs similarly limit what academics publish in their articles and books.

Almost always, IRBs direct how one can initiate conversation or otherwise interact with other people. They do this through their regulation of "informed consent," which sounds innocuously like medical informed consent but which actually is an additional layer of licensing. Indeed, IRBs usually insert their limits on speech and publication in the informed consent documents, thus presenting their coercive censorship as if it were simply a matter of getting consent.

An IRB will at best give a scholar a Hobson's choice. He must promise not to learn the identity of the persons from whom or about whom he gets information. Or he must promise not to publish the identity of such persons. And this is merely the formal choice. The IRB often will skew the choice toward limiting the acquisition of information where it does not fully trust the researcher to refrain from revealing what he knows—the point being that what a researcher does not know, he cannot publish. Even more pervasively, IRBs often delay approval or hold out the threat of delay to get scholars to self-censor, this being part of what the Supreme Court calls a "chilling effect."

The suppression of speech and the press by IRBs even goes far beyond what is conventionally understood as licensing of speech and the press. For example, IRBs often require the destruction of data. When scholars publish, they have a moral and academic duty to preserve their data—so that the accuracy of their conclusions can be tested. When scholars do not preserve and share their data, one might reasonably suspect fraud. Nonetheless, IRBs require scholars to disaggregate and otherwise destroy their data—whether by requiring that "identifiers" be separated from other information or by requiring scholars to destroy all of their data, usually after three years. Either way, such destruction means that many studies can never be challenged for fraud or even merely for misunderstanding the data.

As if this were not enough, some IRBs order scholars and students to stop analyzing data—as when the University of Michigan warns that without IRB permission, "no identifiable data may be . . . analyzed."[11] In other words, IRBs not only license the acquisition and publication of information; they not only require the destruction of knowledge; they also bar thinking. Even the Inquisition did not do this.

INDIVIDUALS

At the bottom of the system are the scholars and students who hope to learn and publish. One might be forgiven for forgetting them, for they really are at the bottom of the pile.

They face two layers of licensing. First, already in the course of their inquiries, researchers must get permission before talking, writing, distributing printed materials, or even merely reading. Second, at the same time that they get permission for talking, etc., in their inquiries, they also must get permission for what they ultimately will publish.

Faculty and students face devastating punishments for nonconformity— most pervasively because if an individual fails to comply, his IRB will identify him as "uncooperative" and will review his future work with greater severity. Thus, the greatest weapon for getting researchers to submit to the licensing is the power of IRBs to deny researchers permission for their later inquiry and publication. In other words, the licensing serves a double function. The current licensing is the means of dictating what can be said and published and what cannot. At the same time, the threat of future licensing is the means of enforcing the current licensing.

If a scholar begins inquiry or prepares a paper for publication without permission, the IRB can tell him to stop. If he submits such a paper to a journal, the IRB can demand that he withdraw it.[12] Indeed, IRBs increasingly compare faculty publications with IRB records to ferret out which scholars failed to get permission. IRBs even can declare a scholar unfit to do any future research, and they sometimes cooperate to suppress scholarship or harass scholars into quitting.[13]

Faculty and students therefore often retreat from inquiry and publication that might annoy their IRB. As a result, entire areas of scholarship have declined, and much important inquiry is never even begun, let alone published.

This is a standard complaint among scholars. For example, a distinguished scholar of journalism, Margaret Blanchard, abandoned her work on contemporary topics. She explains: "I am . . . leaving the contemporary period behind. It is much safer in the nineteenth century." Only living persons are "human subjects," and therefore "you do not have to worry about the IRB when you work in the nineteenth century." Blanchard adds: "I have seen students alter research projects to avoid IRB contact. I have seen some give up projects because of the red tape involved. I have heard words such as 'thought control' used far too often." She concludes: "A better formula for stultifying research is beyond contemplation."[14]

Academics even are afraid to complain openly about the licensing. They privately mutter about IRBs, but they are too fearful to speak up, lest their IRB limit their future work. A journalist who wrote about IRBs found that "everyone" he talked to (except one whose case was already public) "requested anonymity." The faculty members wanted anonymity because they were "afraid of their IRB," and "the IRB members all requested anonymity" because they were "afraid of the federal regulators."[15] The licensing system thus stifles not only academic inquiry and publication but also complaints about its suppression of speech.

Such is the modern licensing system—all four layers of it. As in past, the government demands licensing; the universities do the government's bidding; the licensers deny permission to speak or publish; individuals suffer. The seventeenth century has come back to life.

THE UNCONSTITUTIONALITY OF THE IRB LAWS

In imposing licensing of speech and the press, the IRB laws—the statutes and regulations on human-subjects research—revert to the past in a way that has contemporary significance. They return to the sort of control developed by the Inquisition and the Star Chamber, and they thereby clearly are unconstitutional.

The constitutional point rests on both federal and state law. At the federal level, the First Amendment provides that "Congress shall make no law . . . abridging the freedom of speech, or of the press." This clause, moreover, is understood, under the Fourteenth Amendment, to limit the states. Last but not least, state constitutions contain their own speech and press clauses. Although the argument here is framed in terms of the First Amendment, the reasoning obviously also extends to the state guarantees.

FORCE OF LAW

To begin with, the licensing system is imposed by force of law. Although the system sometimes is excused as voluntary, government force is apparent in three ways.

First, the federal government requires the use of IRBs as a condition of its research grants. This mode of coercion raises complex constitutional issues; yet even under current doctrine the conditions are clearly unconstitutional. The conditions apply not only to federally funded research but also, at most universities, to privately funded research. In other words, the government leverages its grants to a relatively small number of professors so as to control the speech of all professors and students, and this shows that the conditions are profoundly disproportionate and not at all germane. Indeed, licensing of speech by its nature is disproportionate, for in order to prevent harm in some instances, it imposes prior review in all instances, and it thereby inevitably suppresses and chills much speech that is harmless. Thus, even as to federally funded research, the IRB licensing is always disproportionate and is an unconstitutional condition.[16]

Second, as already noted, state negligence law is understood to require the use of IRBs as part of a university's duty of care. Although the federal government initially relied on its conditions to impose the licensing, it increasingly has shifted weight to negligence law. By the beginning of the twenty-first century, negligence law was enough to get universities to impose IRBs on all of their personnel, whatever the source of funding. It even was enough to get universities to impose IRBs in conformity with the standards of the Common Rule and federal guidance. Thus, although some universities opt out of the conditions requiring application of the Common Rule to non–federally funded research, these universities, in response to negligence law, usually apply the Common Rule to all human-subjects research.

The third layer of coercion comes from the state statutes that directly require IRBs. Some of these statutes come into play only in the absence of federal law, but this does not weaken the point. If ever the federal conditions and state negligence law were insufficient, the state statutes would remove any doubt about the government force.

DIRECT LICENSING OF SPEECH

The central constitutional question is whether the IRB laws license speech. It often is assumed that because the regulations refer to "research," they concern conduct, but in fact they directly focus on speech.

Incidentally, even if the IRB laws were regulations of conduct, they still would be unconstitutional, for they single out academics and academic inquiry for utterly repressive licensing. This is not the place to parse the constitutional doctrine on expressive conduct; but if flag burning, porn movies, and nude dancing are constitutionally protected, so too is academic research and its publication. There is no need to go down this road, however, for the IRB laws directly license speech in two ways.

WHAT MUST GET A LICENSE

First, when specifying *what* must get a license, the IRB laws focus on speech. The laws begin by requiring licensing for human-subjects research, but they then define this in terms of publication. For example, the Common Rule defines a "human subject" as "a living individual about whom an investigator . . . conducting research obtains (1st) Data through intervention or interaction with the individual, or (2nd) Identifiable private information."[17] The laws thus define a human subject in terms of "data" and "information" and thereby focus not on harm, but on the acquisition and sharing of knowledge.

Going even further in this direction, the Common Rule defines "research" as a "systematic investigation" designed to produce "generalizable knowledge."[18] In the scientific model of research, researchers develop generalizable statements or theories, and these are expected to be published, so they can be tested by other scholars. Following this model, the Common Rule defines research as an attempt to produce generalizable knowledge, and it thereby requires individuals to submit to the licensing when they seek the sort of knowledge that is publishable.

That this is what the Common Rule does is acknowledged by IRBs. They widely assume they must license not just any research, but that which the researcher "plans to publish" or which is "publishable." For example, the University of Michigan IRBs state that "publication" is an "indicator" of "generalizable knowledge."[19]

The focus on publication is confirmed by the perverse results. Even when an academic engages in dangerous physical interactions, she needs no permission as long as she is not aiming for "generalizable knowledge"—the sort of knowledge that academics consider publishable. But when she pursues entirely harmless activities, she needs permission if she is aiming for what might be publishable. Thus, not only on the formal surface of the regulations, but also in reality, the guiding principle as to what must get a license is publication rather than harm.

In the biomedical sciences, for example, academic doctors do not need permission if their efforts are narrowly to cure their patients, for however dangerous their conduct, it aims merely at particularized knowledge. But the same doctors must get permission as soon as it becomes apparent that they may acquire "generalizable knowledge," that which may be publishable. Of course, this is exactly the sort of knowledge that has the potential to be applicable to other patients and that therefore needs to be published, so other doctors can test it and improve their treatment of their patients. Under the IRB laws, however, this potential for publication triggers the licensing and suppression.

Similarly, in the humanities and social sciences—for example, in English and politics departments—faculty and students can read, write, and publish about their human subjects without permission, while they seek only particularized knowledge—for example, when writing up their family's genealogy. But when they seek generalizations and thus publishable conclusions, they must get permission. Thus, what is evident from the definitions in the IRB laws is confirmed by the bizarre results: the laws require licensing not for harmful activity, but rather for attempts to develop publishable knowledge.

HOW IRBs MUST CONDUCT THE LICENSING

The second way the IRB laws focus directly on speech is in dictating how IRBs must conduct the licensing. The laws require IRBs to review research for its risks, including the risks from what researchers say or publish.

Under the IRB laws (most directly, the Common Rule), IRBs must review and suppress speech already at the inquiry stage when researchers ask questions, distribute printed questionnaires, or otherwise communicate with people. IRBs also must review and suppress what they anticipate researchers will say or publish at the next stage, when researchers will present papers, publish articles, or otherwise share their results. The laws thus directly ask IRBs to license speech in both the acquisition and the sharing of information. Even the Inquisition and the Star Chamber licensed words only at the dissemination stage, not in the preceding inquiry.

In defense of IRBs, it sometimes is said that they do not overtly stop much research, but usually only limit what researchers say and publish. But that is exactly the problem. Under the IRB laws, IRBs mostly control various forms of speech, whether talking, writing, printing, or publishing.

The IRB laws thus directly require licensing of speech and the press. They do this, first, in defining what must get a license and, second, in dictating how IRBs should do the licensing. On both grounds, the IRB laws are unconstitutional.

OTHER FIRST AMENDMENT VIOLATIONS

Although the central constitutional difficulty is licensing, the IRB laws present a smorgasbord of First Amendment violations. Indeed, the IRB laws infringe almost every free speech doctrine.[20]

For starters, the IRB laws penalize academic speech and publication, and they thus engage in content discrimination. The IRB laws also engage in viewpoint discrimination, for they single out the direct study of human beings, in particular the scientific empirical method. That this is viewpoint discrimination becomes especially clear when one considers how empiricism has repeatedly challenged moral and political verities. So emphatic is the targeting of empiricism that many scholars have shifted to theoretical work. Mere theory often is less effectual than empirical study, but it at least avoids the censors.

The IRB laws also run into trouble under the overbreadth doctrine, for when they impose licensing, they inevitably authorize the review and suppression of vast amounts of talking and publication that will never be harmful. The laws allegedly aim at harm, but they suppress the harm by generally subjecting human-subjects research to licensing, and they thereby are grossly overbroad.

The IRB laws, moreover, impose standards that are unconstitutionally vague. The regulations require IRBs to weigh the "risks" and "benefits" of research, including the risks and benefits of publication. In its guidance, HHS acknowledges that these "determinations of risk and benefit" are "subjective." Rather than worry about the vagueness, however, HHS embraces it as an opportunity. It openly asks IRBs to take into account "prevailing community standards"—what Socrates would recognize as the arbitrary and repressive demands of the demos.[21]

Government agencies even require IRBs to prevent many of the constitutionally protected benefits of free speech. The National Science Foundation, for example, expects IRBs to suppress inquiry and publication where it would lead to "legal harm," "financial harm," "moral harm," social "stigma," mental "upset," or even mere "worry."[22] These, however, can be among the advantages of research and its publication. For example, I used to study the Ku Klux Klan. Although I worked on the Klan out of intellectual curiosity, and although most of the Klan members I studied were already dead, I would not have been overly dismayed if my research had caused some of them legal and financial harm, or if it had caused them social stigma and worry. Some "risks" are benefits.

In getting IRBs to prevent these risks, HHS and the National Science Foundation impose a sort of Victorian prudishness. Little nowadays is not openly discussed, but HHS cautions IRBs: "Stress and feelings of guilt or embarrassment may arise simply from thinking or talking about one's own behavior or attitudes on sensitive topics such as drug use, sexual preferences, selfishness, and violence."[23] In other words, when scholars study addiction, desire, or other aspects of human nature, IRBs should use their censorship to protect individuals from academic questions that might cause them discomfort. And this is about the use of words to acquire information; the censorship is even more stringent when it gets to what scholars can publish. Although the First Amendment (as recognized in *Cohen v. California*) protects the freedom to offend, the IRB laws stifle entirely civil discussions of serious matters.

The IRB laws thus brazenly violate one First Amendment doctrine after another. This should not be a surprise, for the licensing of speech lends itself to other First Amendment problems. Licensing, however, is the preeminent constitutional problem. Although details of the First Amendment's freedom of speech and press are disputed, nothing is more clear than that the amendment barred licensing of speech or the press. Such licensing traditionally was understood to be the epitome of tyranny, and as evident from the IRB laws it remains a profound danger.

NEWSPAPER REVIEW BOARDS

To understand the unconstitutionality of the IRB laws, just imagine an NRB, that is, a newspaper review board. Imagine that the government used conditions and regulations to require not universities but newspapers to establish review boards. Imagine, moreover, that a journalist had to get permission from an NRB before beginning any investigation designed to produce publishable knowledge.

Of course, publishable knowledge is different for journalists than for academics. Accordingly, whereas the IRB laws focus on "generalizable knowledge," the NRB laws would focus on "particularlizable knowledge." All the same, the NRBs would license investigations designed to produce publishable knowledge.

A journalist thus would need permission before beginning any investigation—even before merely reading, observing, talking, or interviewing—if her goal were to get publishable information. When examining her acquisition of information, the NRB would weigh the "benefits" and "risks" of her research, including the risks arising from publication. To limit the risks, it could rewrite her questions, and it certainly would dictate how she could converse or interact with other people, lest she ask insensitive, stressful, or embarrassing questions. As for her sharing of information, the NRB would prevent her from publishing the names of persons who might suffer financial, reputational, or emotional harm, including mere anxiety, as a result of publication. It even would bar her from sharing information with other journalists, unless she got further permission. Last but not least, it would require the de-identification and other destruction of her information, so that her files could not be used later by other journalists.

All of this licensing is outrageously unconstitutional. It is unconstitutional regardless of whether it is required directly or by condition. And if it is unconstitutional for journalists, it also is unconstitutional for academics and students.

ALLEGED JUSTIFICATIONS

Notwithstanding the constitutional difficulties, IRB licensing is commonly said to be warranted by the doctrines of the Supreme Court. Accordingly, it is time to turn to the most concrete of these doctrinal justifications, to see if they really can sustain the licensing.

LICENSING OF CONDUCT?

Although it has been seen that the IRB laws focus on speech, especially publication, there still may be a lingering concern that research is conduct and that the licensing therefore is justifiable. The First Amendment undoubtedly leaves room for the licensing of conduct, even much expressive conduct, and on such grounds perhaps the IRB laws are lawful.

This line of reasoning, however, fails to distinguish between popular perceptions of the targeted conduct and the legal definition of what is suppressed. Certainly, some research includes conduct, and at least some such conduct has the potential to be harmful. Yet the IRB laws define "research" in terms of an attempt to publish rather than in terms of conduct, and they require IRBs to limit what can be published. Therefore, notwithstanding that IRBs do stop some harmful conduct, it is difficult to justify the IRB laws as regulations of harmful conduct. Of course, the government could license harmful conduct, including that done in research, if it adopted laws that focused on this danger, but that is not what the government has done.

The concern about conduct, moreover, fails to distinguish between the licensing of expressive conduct and the licensing of words said in a range of conduct. Although it is unconstitutional for the law to require licensing of words in general, it also is unlawful for the law to impose such a constraint in a narrow range of circumstances. In this instance, the IRB laws directly require licensing of the speech done in connection with the academic conduct known as "research." Although the licensing of words is thus confined to what is said and published in pursuit of this conduct, it remains licensing of words. In fact, the linkage to the conduct merely serves to ensure that the law discriminates against the unpopular activity of an unpopular group. Far from justifying the licensing, this focus of the licensing suggests an additional reason why it is unconstitutional.

Ultimately, the government should never be able to mask its licensing of words by tying the words to conduct. For example, although a state can license driving, and can bar the use of phones while driving, it cannot license speaking while driving, nor can it license driving on the basis of what will be said while driving, for this would be licensing of speech.[24] If the government could get away with such excuses, it could always get cover for licensing words. In fact, the sixteenth- and seventeenth-century English licensing laws illustrate this danger, for rather than impose licensing on words in general, they imposed licensing on printing—that is, on conduct in the use of a new technology. But the licensers were meant to focus on the words that would be printed, and the English licensing laws thus were a perfect example of what the First Amendment prohibited when it barred the licensing of words. To be sure, a flat anti-masking rule could not be sustained for injunctions, after-the-fact constraints, or nonverbal expression. The licensing of words, however, has long been strictly forbidden, and as evident from the licensing of printing and now of research, the constitutional freedom would be utterly enfeebled if the government could justify licensing simply by focusing it on words used within a range of conduct or on conduct involving words.

LICENSING OF A PRECURSOR TO PUBLICATION?

In a variation of the conduct justification, it sometimes is said that when IRBs license research, they suppress only a precursor to publication, not publication itself. On this reasoning, the licensing is not unconstitutional.

The First Amendment, however, does not bar licensing only for formal publication. So narrow a reading of the amendment would give less protection to speech than to the press, and would protect publication while allowing the government to suppress the manuscript words that lead up to publication. In fact, English licensing regulations originally licensed the production of manuscripts, and when (as already noted) they eventually kept pace with technology, they focused on printing rather than publication. Other licensing regulations, moreover, controlled speaking on stage and even preaching. It thus becomes apparent that when the First Amendment barred licensing, it protected all sorts of words, whether spoken, written, printed, or published.

Nonetheless, the IRB licensing controls the words of researchers at all stages of their work, in research, publication, and beyond. It begins by controlling what academics say, write, or print in the course of their research; it then controls what they say when formally presenting or publishing the research; it concludes by barring their transfer of their data. Therefore, even if the First Amendment made a fetish of publication, what gets licensed by IRBs is no mere precursor.

The precursor excuse looks especially feeble when one recognizes that much research consists of nothing more than talking, writing, or distributing printed materials. For example, much epidemiological research consists of interviewing; much medical research consists of taking notes; much sociological research consists of sending out printed questionnaires. It therefore is highly misleading to talk about research as a precursor to speech or publication. Already when IRBs license the acquisition of knowledge, they very often are dealing with mere talking, writing, printing, and publishing.

Even when research consists of more than mere speech, its status as a precursor to publication leads to a very different conclusion than may be assumed. In licensing research (including the research that involves conduct), IRBs mostly limit the acquisition and dissemination of information. In limiting the acquisition of information, moreover, IRBs are mainly concerned about the harm from its dissemination. In other words, IRBs restrict the getting of knowledge chiefly in order to limit the sharing of the knowledge. It will be recalled that what a scholar cannot learn, he cannot publish. The licensing of research is thus the most effective way of controlling its publication.

On several grounds, therefore, the precursor argument obscures the realities. Most basically, it simply is mistaken to assume that speaking, writing, printing, and publishing occur only when scholars disseminate their knowledge in articles and books. All of these things, and the licensing of them, occur already in the acquisition of knowledge.

SCIENTIFIC RATHER THAN POLITICAL SPEECH?

Another justification of the IRB laws rests on the political speech doctrine. On the assumption that the First Amendment centrally protects political speech—even perhaps only political opinion—it is supposed that the amendment does not fully protect the scientific or academic speech licensed by IRBs. Scientific and academic speech, however, is foundational.

The inquiry done by scientists and other academics has long been a central illustration of the importance of freedom of speech and the press. Even before the Athenians forced Socrates to drink hemlock, they condemned Anaxagoras for speculating about the physical character of the sun and the moon. Two millennia later, Galileo revealed not only the arrangement of the heavens but also, much closer to Earth, the danger of licensing scientific or other academic publication. The earthly importance of his work was recognized by John Milton in his famous 1644 tract, *Areopagitica, A Speech for the Liberty of Unlicensed Printing*. Milton recalled that he had visited Galileo in prison and had learned how the licensing had stifled scientific development in Italy.

Ever since, Galileo's ordeal has been understood as the preeminent illustration of the dangers from licensing.

Early Americans recognized the value of protecting the full range of knowledge from licensing. When the Continental Congress in 1774 explained "the importance of the liberty of the press," it began by observing the liberty's significance for "the advancement of truth, science, morality, and arts in general."[25] An American poem on the freedom praised the breadth of the protected knowledge, including "philosophic goods," "works of wit," "schemes of art," and other "learning." Of course, the freedom also had political advantages against "lawless pow[e]r." Yet its value was not limited to politics. As summarized in the poem, it was both the *"Nurse of Arts* and *Freedom's Fence."*[26]

In fact, scientific speech—in both inquiry and publication, and in both the hard sciences and the social sciences—is the foundation of modern society. By continually challenging accepted truths, it lays the basis for the society's wealth, its progressive character, and its politics. In Galileo's era, the view that the world circled around the sun seemed to turn the universe upside down, thus elevating human beings and their world and overturning the authority that had seemed to run from God and the church to kings. Today, science similarly threatens accepted assumptions in one field after another, including education, the environment, and medicine—as evident from debates about evolution, climate change, and various drugs.

In short, already in ancient Athens, even more so in seventeenth-century Europe, and especially in contemporary America, political debate rests on scientific debate. Nor should this be a surprise. If politics is to depend on realities rather than illusions, it must arise from accurate foundations. Licensing therefore is at least as dangerous when focused on scientific or academic speech as when aimed at political speech.

COMPELLING GOVERNMENT INTERESTS

A final doctrinal justification of the IRB laws rests on claims about compelling government interests. According to the Supreme Court, the freedom of speech is not absolute, and a constraint on speech can be justified by a sufficiently strong government interest.

Undoubtedly, there is a government interest in preventing harms, including those arising from research. But this does not settle the matter, as it has been seen that the IRB laws focus not so much on harm as on speech—indeed, on the full range of talking, reading, writing, printing, and publishing. The constitutional inquiry therefore cannot rest with the generic question of whether there is a compelling government interest in preventing research harms. Instead, the inquiry must concentrate on whether there is a government interest that justifies using the licensing of speech as a means of preventing research harms.

The question of whether there really is a compelling government interest here must await this essay's discussion of harms; but even if there were such an interest, it is improbable that it could justify the licensing. Although a compelling government interest can justify after-the-fact penalties, and even can justify the licensing of moving pictures and other expressive conduct, the Supreme Court has never upheld the licensing of words on such grounds. Nor should it. Licensing is a distinctively dangerous method of controlling words, and it therefore was flatly forbidden.

Put more gently, it is difficult to discern how the government can have a compelling interest in the licensing of speech. Government always has a range of options for addressing harms, and thus even if it has a compelling government interest in regulating research harms, this does not mean it has such an interest in relying on a singularly unconstitutional and ill-fitting method of regulation. A compelling government interest can justify much, but not a law that is most dangerous and least narrowly tailored.

Evidently, the doctrinal justifications for IRB laws are very weak, and this can be confirmed by returning to the notion of newspaper review boards. In justifying their licensing of journalistic research, NRBs would claim to be licensing mere conduct and, indeed, a mere precursor to speech; they further would claim to be licensing only empirical speech and publication, not political opinion; they even would claim a compelling government interest in preventing harm. Such justifications, however, would be of no avail. Any law establishing NRB licensing would clearly be unconstitutional, and what is sauce for the NRB goose is sauce for the IRB gander.

HOW THE GOVERNMENT BECAME INVOLVED IN CENSORSHIP

Although the constitutional logic against the IRB laws is fairly straightforward, there may remain a sense of incredulity. Is it really possible that the government of the United States has adopted the method of controlling speech and the press employed by the Inquisition and the Star Chamber? At first blush this seems unlikely. Why would the government have done this? Indeed, why would HHS—the department devoted to health—have taken the lead in imposing such licensing? And how could the licensing have succeeded in the face of the First Amendment? The improbability of the censorship begs an explanation.

HHS AND THE MEDICALIZATION OF SPEECH HARMS

An initial hint can be found in the role of HHS. On the face of the matter, it is odd that HHS has led the imposition of the licensing, for much of the licensed research has nothing to do with health. Upon closer inspection, however, it is no coincidence.

An underlying factor was the growing tendency to take a medical view of speech harms. Only a narrow range of harms are legally significant, and this confined conception of harm is essential for a broad vision of free speech. Medically, however, any harm, no matter how slight or ephemeral, can be considered significant, and this medical attitude found support in the mid-twentieth century in what now is HHS (then the Department of Health, Education, and Welfare).[27] This department thus began to assume that even minor harms from words and inquiry were dangerous in ways that required its solicitude.

Allied with this broad medical vision of harm was a recognition that the scientific understanding of research rests on publication. From the scientific perspective, the goal of research is to develop a theory or statement of general application—the generality being what makes it publishable and what allows it to be tested. HHS therefore had good reason to understand research in terms of "generalizable" or publishable knowledge. Accordingly, when it began to worry about harms in research, including speech harms in research, it assumed it had to focus its regulations on attempts to produce the sort of knowledge that could be generalized or published.

This anxiety about medical harms in research led to licensing because HHS aimed not merely to punish harms, but to prevent them. Most regulation merely punishes harm after it occurs. HHS, however, wanted to prevent what it considered harm, and it therefore turned to licensing to intervene before any harm took place.

On these foundations, already in the 1950s and 1960s, HHS imposed an early version of its licensing of speech on the research it funded. Already then there were expectations that all research, even privately funded research, should be licensed. But it was not until the next decade that an unprecedented crisis made this possible.

The Public Health Service, which was part of HHS, had for decades been studying latent syphilis among black men at Tuskegee. Although initially the study was not necessarily harmful, the Public Health Service did not tell the men about penicillin when it became available after World War II. The drug would have helped at least some of them, but the service apparently wanted to preserve its opportunity to study untreated men. The Public Health Service's callous behavior became public in 1972, and the exposure of Tuskegee and the government's other medical misadventures should have prompted caution about expanding government power over research. The federal health establishment, however, responded in a way that Sigmund Freud would have recognized.

Rather than accept that government medical research was distinctively risky, the government declared that all human-subjects research was risky and that it therefore needed to be licensed. Through this projection, the government simultaneously deflected criticism and extended its licensing from federally funded research to privately funded research. The department that had been most responsible for risky medical research thus came to oversee a vast swath of academic inquiry.

Far from being a conspiracy, this was merely a natural response to the circumstances. HHS already understood research in terms of publication and already saw speech harms in research as a medical problem that required licensing. It therefore did not blanch at licensing the full range of "human-subjects research," regardless of whether the research involved physical interactions or mere talk, and regardless of whether it was biological, medical, sociological, political, legal, religious, or literary. No longer a private matter among consenting adults, speech and publication in research had become what medically minded officials considered a health threat, and on this basis it seemed squarely within HHS's mission.

THE SUPREME COURT

Unfortunately, the role of the federal government in licensing speech does not stop with HHS and the other complicit agencies. Even more fundamentally, it is necessary to consider the doctrines of the Supreme Court.

Although the First Amendment's core protection for speech was an unqualified bar against the licensing of words, the Supreme Court, during the twentieth century, focused on the amendment's protection against a wider range of threats. There is much to be said for taking a broad view of the freedom of speech, but the court protected the periphery in a manner that weakened the core freedom from licensing.

Of particular concern, the Supreme Court sometimes defended its expansive vision of freedom of speech by generalizing about the threats to this freedom as if there were nothing special about the central danger from licensing. Reenforcing this suggestion of equivalence, the court loosely distinguished between "postpublication restraints" and "prepublication restraints," thus blurring the distinction between licensing and injunctions. The court, moreover, sometimes suggested that it made little difference whether restraints came before or after publication. The court even spoke loosely about a freedom of expression, as if the licensing of merely verbal speech could be evaluated in the same way as the licensing of moving pictures and expressive conduct.

This lumping together served a purpose, for it justified the Supreme Court's expansive vision of freedom of speech, but it probably was not necessary for this end, and it certainly has come with a cost. The reality is that most injunctions, most after-the-fact constraints, and most limits on expressive conduct are lawful. Accordingly, when the court spoke generally about a freedom in these matters, it did not mean a freedom for all expressive conduct or from all injunctions and all after-the-fact constraints, and it therefore had to develop doctrines explaining the limits of the freedom. For example, it developed doctrines about content discrimination, political speech, expressive conduct, and compelling government interests. None of these doctrines were necessary for understanding the licensing of words, but all of them were essential for sorting out when there would be protection for expressive conduct or against injunctions and after-the-fact constraints.

Although these doctrines were designed to police the boundaries of the freedom enjoyed at the edges, they were stated so broadly that they cut back on the core freedom from licensing. The doctrines seemed to suggest that licensing—even licensing of merely verbal speech—could be constitutional if it did not focus on political speech, if it did not discriminate on the basis of content, or if it served a compelling government interest. Of course, some of the Supreme Court's more sober opinions pointed toward other conclusions, but its primary doctrines, when stated abstractly, practically invited the government to license speech.

The court undergirded its doctrines limiting speech by intoning that the freedom of speech is not absolute. This certainly is true as to injunctions, after-the-fact constraints, and expressive conduct. But the licensing of words is invariably dangerous, and the First Amendment therefore centrally and without qualification barred the licensing of words. Thus, although it makes sense to say that freedom of speech is not absolute at the periphery of the freedom, it is profoundly misleading to reach such a conclusion about the core freedom from licensing. Indeed, the doctrines that suggested as much have cut a gaping hole in the center of the First Amendment, for they have left room for the government to justify itself in doing what the amendment most clearly forbade.

CONSEQUENCES

This is not the place to examine in detail how the Supreme Court's speech doctrines have legitimized the licensing of speech and the press. But it is revealing to examine the effects of at least one such doctrine—the overgeneralization that the freedom of speech is subject to compelling government interests and thus is not absolute.

After the Supreme Court repeatedly said that the freedom of speech was not absolute and that speech rights were subject to compelling government interests, HHS and other government agencies felt fully justified in imposing the IRB licensing. For example, a consultant to the government defended the licensing by reciting that "the First Amendment is not an absolute bar to prior restraint."[28] Similarly, a key government commission reported that the government could regulate research methods "in order to protect interests in health, order and safety."[29]

The implications of such doctrines became painfully apparent when Ithiel de Sola Pool—a distinguished political theorist—protested against the licensing. During the drafting of the current regulations in 1980, he complained that, notwithstanding the experience with McCarthyism, IRB licensing would be "a more fundamental attack, because it would institutionalize a system of censorship over what is at the very heart of free speech, namely, inquiry into political, economic, and social matters, which has always been precisely the thing that people could do at will, without asking anyone."[30] The regulators, however, confronted Pool with the Supreme Court's doctrine that the freedom of speech is not absolute. Pool therefore felt obliged to retreat to the "balancing" approach and pathetically had to concede, "we all understand that freedom of speech is not absolute."[31] The advocates of the licensing then triumphantly told him that the court's doctrine "require[d] an argument as to why the impermissible impact on speech is not justified by legitimate state interests."[32] Judicial doctrine seemed to justify the licensing, and for decades after Pool's defeat, no academic (let alone any academic institution) questioned the constitutionality of the IRB laws.

The path toward licensing was paved with the best of intentions. HHS aimed to protect the public from harm, and the Supreme Court hoped to secure a broad freedom of speech. But the medical vision of harm included speech harms that are not legally cognizable, and the judicial doctrine defining the periphery of free speech was stated so broadly that it cut into the core freedom from licensing. Licensing thus became plausible.

THE HARMS

A final question concerns not the law, but the underlying harms. Although the First Amendment flatly barred licensing, the harms from human-subjects research have seemed to legitimize the licensing, both legally and morally. This essay therefore must close by examining the harms. What are they?

HARMS CAUSED BY HUMAN-SUBJECTS RESEARCH

In theory, the IRB laws are necessary to protect "human subjects" from harm arising in research. Certainly, what is done in the course of research can cause injury. But is it true that human-subjects research is distinctively harmful? And if not, how can the fear of harm justify the licensing?

When discussing the harms arising from human-subjects research, many apologists for IRBs cite the injuries arising in FDA drug trials. As already noted, however, the IRB laws—the laws that generally impose licensing on human-subjects research—are different from the FDA regulations, even though the latter also make use of IRBs. The harms resulting from FDA drug trials thus occur under their own regulatory scheme, and they consequently are not revealing about any need for the laws under consideration here.

Apologists also frequently cite the notorious mid-twentieth-century studies, such as the Tuskegee syphilis study, the Willowbrook hepatitis research, and the Army radiation experiments. These famous cases, however, do not show the danger of human-subjects research in general. Instead, they illustrate something more specific: the danger of government medical research.

These studies involved research by government medical personnel on patients who either were wards of government or were otherwise dependent on government. In such circumstances, medical personnel are not apt to feel constrained by the market or by negligence law. On the contrary, being government agents engaged in the pursuit of the public good, they tend to feel profoundly empowered. It therefore is unsurprising that government medical research (especially when done on wards of government or other dependent persons) has repeatedly led to abuses. But there is no reason to attribute the dangers of government medical research to other human-subjects research.

Indeed, there is no scientifically serious empirical evidence that, overall, human-subjects research is particularly dangerous. Of course, some research projects do cause injuries. Yet there is no scientifically serious empirical evidence that, overall, anything is more harmful when done in research than when done in other circumstances. Nor is there any such evidence that, overall, anything done with intent to learn generalizable knowledge, or done with intent to publish, is more harmful than when done for other purposes. Nor is there any such evidence that any of these things are more dangerous when done by academics than when done by others.

In fact, the article most frequently cited to show the harmfulness of human-subjects research turns out to be unreliable. Henry Beecher's 1966 article in the *New England Journal of Medicine* famously describes twenty-two studies that involved unethical human-subjects research. But his article suppresses the identities of the researchers who conducted these studies, as well as the relevant citations, apparently because Beecher considered the researchers to be his human subjects.[33]

This suppression of evidence allowed Beecher to get away with sloppy research. The citations to the studies examined by Beecher have recently come to light, and the suppressed information reveals that Beecher represented his evidence in a self-serving manner. In fact, of the twenty-two studies, three were not American research projects and were thus irrelevant for understanding the dangers of American research. Of the remaining nineteen, at least fourteen apparently included patients in government institutions. The fourteen studies, moreover, were probably carried out by researchers with ties to the government. (Many of them probably were government employees or at least were funded by the government.) Thus, Beecher's evidence does not show the danger of human-subjects research in general but instead confirms the danger of mixing the government with medical research. In particular, it shows the danger of research done by government or government-funded medical personnel on persons within the control of government.[34]

Many commentators concede that IRBs should not be applied to the social sciences, but insist that IRBs are necessary for regulating biomedical research because it involves dangerous physical interactions. Once again, however, there is no evidence that physical interactions are more dangerous when done in academic or other publishable research, even in biomedical research, than when done in other circumstances, such as a doctor's office, a football field, or a comfortable bed. On the contrary, physical interactions probably are slightly safer in research than elsewhere.

Even if physical interactions really were more injurious in academic research than in other circumstances, there would be many ways of regulating the harm without licensing speech. If the goal is generally to regulate injurious conduct, there already are applicable laws, such as negligence. If the goal is to regulate specific types of physical interactions, the government can easily adopt additional laws directed at these acts. The government therefore has no need to impose unconstitutional licensing of speech.

HARMS CAUSED BY THE LICENSING OF SPEECH

If one is genuinely worried about harm, one needs to consider not only the harm from human-subjects research but also the harm from suppressing knowledge. This is what systematically hurts and even kills people.

IRBs annually censor thousands of research proposals. The exact number of proposals that come before IRBs under the IRB laws is difficult to discern, for IRB records are secret, and they do not typically differentiate the proposals that come under the human-subjects research regulations from those that arise under FDA regulations. Nonetheless, the proposals reviewed every year clearly run into the tens of thousands, and by some estimates well over 100,000. In addition, an uncertain but large number of projects are never begun or are abandoned because of the IRB laws, this being the "chilling effect." One way or another, the IRB laws lead to widespread abandonment, alteration, and other suppression of research.

At least some of what get suppressed might otherwise have had profound effects in saving and improving lives. Imagine that each year a single transformative project gets suppressed on account of the censorship. Even if only one such project is lost, the consequences for human life are sobering. If one adds up the costs over decades, it is difficult to avoid the conclusion that IRBs cause far more harm than they ever could prevent. The cost of IRBs therefore must be measured in the lives of people across the globe who have been deprived of the benefits of research.

The lethal effects came to light in 2006 in Michigan. When catheters are introduced near the heart in intensive care units, they often cause fatal bloodstream infections. Some researchers from Johns Hopkins therefore attempted an experiment in Michigan hospitals to test whether the infections could be reduced by instituting simple checklists—requiring, for example, that the doctors wash their hands before inserting the catheter.[35]

The checklist approach has since been made famous by Atul Gwande, and it was very successful. According to the *New York Times*: "Within three months, the rate of bloodstream infections from these I.V. lines fell by two-thirds. . . . Over 18 months, the program saved more than 1,500 lives and nearly $200 million."[36] The benefits of publishing the study were even greater, for every year, in the United States alone, there were perhaps 80,000 catheter-related bloodstream infections, resulting in up to 28,000 deaths, with annual costs of over $2 billion.[37] The study thus clearly has saved many lives, not to mention the money.

But the key point here is the role of the IRB licensing. The researchers dutifully got IRB permission before they began their research, but after the study was well underway, HHS concluded that the IRB had not met HHS's licensing standards. To be precise, the IRB should have required the researchers to consider not only the patients but also the doctors as human subjects. Under the logic of the IRB laws, HHS was right, but under such a requirement, the researchers probably would not have been able to do their study. On account of the IRB's failure to comply with HHS's standards for licensing, HHS ordered the Johns Hopkins doctors to shut down the ongoing research. Fortunately, however, HHS acted too late to stop the research altogether or to prevent its publication.

The Michigan case therefore is revealing. By escaping the licensing, it shows how much might have been lost if the IRB had done its job under the IRB laws. The suppression in this one case alone would have cost more than ten thousand lives every year.

Nonetheless, it is difficult to do a body count. Although the Michigan case reveals the scale of the losses that can occur in even a single case, how can one measure the full range of lives not saved or improved as a result of the suppression? Where research is not completed, where it is completed only in censored form, or where it is otherwise suppressed, one cannot determine what benefits might have ensued. The overall losses to life and limb, however, are extensive. They evidently extend to thousands, even tens of thousands or more, each year. Put graphically, the annual losses greatly exceed the combined costs imposed by many mass murderers. Of course, IRBs do not physically stab individuals, but they strangulate the inquiry and publication that would have kept untold thousands alive.

The harm done by the licensing obviously is especially extensive in biomedical research. As already noted, apologists for IRBs often take the fallback position that even if IRBs are unnecessary in the social sciences, they are essential for the biomedical sciences. This is puzzling, however, for medicine is precisely where IRBs have the highest death toll. The suppression of words is harmful in all areas of inquiry—for example, both in political science and in pathology—but the harms are most clear where the interference with inquiry and publication leaves numerous patients to die.

In fact, the harm caused by the licensing of biomedical research is much greater than the harm it prevents. Most biomedical research on human subjects examines only a limited number of persons in order to explore theories designed to help much larger numbers in the general public. Thus, almost inevitably, the harms prevented by IRBs are relatively small compared with the harms they cause. In addition, biomedical research tends to become the foundation for yet more such research, which then benefits even larger numbers. Consequently, whereas the harms prevented by IRBs expand only arithmetically, the harms caused by them tend to expand exponentially.

In a society based on freedom of inquiry and publication, the IRB licensing is literally deadening. It has reduced many scholars to misery. It has ruined much scholarship. It has impeded graduate education. It has stifled whole areas of learning. And it has obstructed the advancement of knowledge, with increasingly lethal results.

POLITICAL HARMS

Of course, the licensing is harmful in ways that go beyond the deaths and other immediate costs, for the licensing has political consequences. It already has been noted that licensing inverts the relationship of individuals to government. At a more practical level, how can the people have well-informed opinions about their government's policies, if the government censors almost all direct study of persons affected by its policies?

Consider, for example, the health-care regulations issued by HHS. This executive department exercises the full range of government powers: It legislates regulations; it enforces them; it adjudicates disputes under them. Because HHS and other government departments exercise so much power with so little formal accountability, the freedom of speech has become ever more important—far more so than when laws were made merely by Congress. The freedom of speech, however, is now subject to licensing under HHS regulations.

In fact, by means of the IRB laws, HHS stifles a sort of inquiry that once was a major source of information about health care and its delivery. Academic studies of human subjects traditionally were uncensored, and through their radical critique of government, these studies did much to shape the establishment of government health services. Now, however, the very government department that imposes health-care regulations also imposes licensing on much of the academic study of health care. It thereby profoundly limits the studies that draw information at a personal level from doctors, nurses, administrators, patients, and their families. Such studies are essential for judging any health-care policy, but they have been largely stultified, for they cannot be begun, let alone published, without IRB permission.

HHS is confident that its data allows it to make good judgments about how to regulate health care. But HHS licenses and thereby discourages, alters, or otherwise suppresses much of the independent academic research that directly studies human beings and their experiences with health care. The result is a calamity for both HHS and the public. HHS regulates the public and is judged by the public on a scientific record that HHS has largely crushed under its censorship.

The licensing even bars academics and students from interviewing most persons in government, let alone publishing the interviews, without first getting IRB permission. To be sure, there is a "public official" exemption, but the government interprets it very narrowly to include, at most, only elected officials and heads of agencies.[38] As a result, almost all public officials or employees (including those from whom one might learn what actually is happening in agencies) are protected from inquiry. And even officials in exempted research are protected, for although such research is exempt from the Common Rule, it remains subject to IRB licensing to ensure its compliance with the ethical principles of *The Belmont Report* and any additional local rules.[39] As explained by the National Science Foundation, even "when the subjects are public officials or candidates for public office," IRBs should ensure "respect for respondents to guard their privacy."[40]

To understand the political implications, consider that all HHS officials are thus protected by the licensing. So too are all members of IRBs. An academic or student therefore typically cannot interview such officials or members for academic purposes without first submitting to the censorship, which is designed to protect the interviewees from embarrassment and other ordinary consequences of speech. As a result, empirical academic critiques of HHS decisionmaking, and even of IRB licensing, are profoundly difficult—often practically impossible.

In these circumstances, what does it mean to say that Americans live in a free society? The government aims to act responsibly on the best information it can get, and the people try to evaluate their government on the basis of the information available to them. But the government systematically suppresses the very sort of academic inquiry and publication that could illuminate central political questions and that could shed light on the persons who exercise power.

EVEN DEEPER HARMS

Alarming as the political costs are, the harms go even further, for they threaten the very nature and success of modern society. Francis Bacon long ago envisioned the progressive amelioration of the human condition, and indeed modern life has come to center on human beings and their material comforts. This vision of life, however, rests on empirical experimentation about human beings, and therefore when licensing threatens such experimentation, it imperils the nature and prosperity of modern society.

Intellectual inquiry always will cause discomfort among dominant forces in a society, whether egalitarian or hierarchical. Socrates studied human nature in a way that seemed to challenge the deities of the city, and for this the demos condemned him to death. Galileo studied the nature of the universe in a way that seemed to offend the dignity of God, and for this the hierarchy imprisoned him. In our society, the dignity of God is left by the wayside. But the dignity of human beings has been elevated, and to offend this is to incur the wrath of the demos—at least, that is, the populist wrath of those who claim to speak for the people.

In other words, academic inquiry continues to inspire anxiety, and this anxiety continues to prompt the desire to suppress. What has changed is merely the object of concern. Whereas anxiety about God's dignity inspired the Inquisition to suppress the study of the heavens, anxiety about human dignity inspires HHS to suppress the study of human beings.

Life itself is a sort of experiment, in which we learn from experience, and modern society is a sort of experiment in living. Such a society depends for its prosperity and very nature on empirical studies of human beings, perhaps especially inquiries that test and challenge our most basic assumptions. This can be unnerving, but what is even more worrisome is that the government of the United States now responds with licensing of speech and the press.

CONCLUSION

Although much has changed since the seventeenth century, much is the same. In the seventeenth century, the Inquisition and the Star Chamber licensed the press. Now IRBs license both speech and the press. Licensing is back, this time even more intrusively than in the past.

Fortunately, no amount of censorship can obscure the truth about the censorship. The licensing imposed under the IRB laws is utterly unconstitutional. If a newspaper review board for journalists would be unconstitutional, so is an institutional review board for faculty and students. In fact, it is difficult to find a more systematic and widespread violation of the freedom of speech and the press in American history.

The First Amendment recognizes that America is an experiment in freedom and that this depends on the freedom of speech and the press. The amendment therefore establishes this freedom as a constitutional right, and on this foundation Americans can resist the current licensing. Socrates died for his freedom. Galileo went to prison for his freedom. All that Americans need is a judge who is willing to enforce the Constitution.

NOTES

1. The author is grateful to the Martin and Selma Rosen Research Fund for research support.
2. For the statutory authority, see 42 U.S.C. §289(a) (2010). For the HHS regulations adopting the Common Rule, see 45 C.F.R. pt. 46 (2009). In addition, there is a plethora of interpretation and guidance. For further details of the argument against the IRB laws, and for citations, see Philip Hamburger, "Getting Permission," *Northwestern University Law Review* 101 (2007): 405; Philip Hamburger, "The New Censorship: Institutional Review Boards," *Supreme Court Review* 2004 (2005): 271.

3. Equally serious and more political is the suppression of churches and other tax-free organizations under I.R.C. §501(c)(3), but the suppression under the IRB laws is more far-reaching and systematic. Similarly, McCarthyism was more overtly political, but the IRB licensing is much more pervasive and methodical, and its consequences are far more lethal.

4. For the way in which Americans understood the extent of their freedom from after-the-fact constraints, see Philip Hamburger, "Natural Rights, Natural Law, and American Constitutions," *Yale Law Journal* 102 (1993), 907.

5. The word "verbal" is used here to signify not merely oral expression, but all expression through words, including what in effect are words, such as numbers and symbols in mathematical and computer languages. Of course, the traditional bar against licensing was unqualified only as to civilian constraints, not as to licensing in the military or in the provision of government services, such as the U.S. Postal Service.

6. The licensing of speech in plays was revived for a while in eighteenth-century England after 1737.

7. In theory a university can commit to other principles, if approved by the government, but there is no evidence that any other principles have ever received government approval.

8. Federalwide Assurance (FWA) for the Protection of Human Subjects, OMB No. 0990–0278 (approved for use through June 30, 2014).

9. See, e.g., Code of Virginia, §32.1–162.19 (1979),

10. 45 C.F.R. §46.107(a).

11. "Activities Subject to the HRPP (July 2011)," *Operations Manual*, part 4, section 4, University of Michigan, Human Research Protection Program, Office of the Vice President for Research, www.hrpp.umich.edu/om/Part4.html.

12. This has happened at at least three schools: the University of Illinois, George Washington University, and the University of Pittsburgh. Philip Hamburger, "The New Censorship," 303.

13. For example, after a member of one of the University of Michigan IRBs wrote a secret memorandum denouncing Professor Guyer, the memo was acquired by the University of Washington, which then used it against Guyer's coauthor, Professor Loftus. The University of Washington prevented her from pursuing their research and publication, which led to her departure for the University of California, Irvine. Carol Tavris, "The Cost of Courage," in *Do Justice and Let the Sky Fall: Elizabeth F. Loftus and Her Contributions to Science, Law, and Academic Freedom*, ed. Maryanne Garry and Harlene Hayne (Mahwah, N.J.: Erlbaum, 2007), 207.

14. Comments of Margaret Blanchard in "Should All Disciplines Be Subject to the Common Rule?," *Academe* 88 (May–June 2002): 62–69, 68.

15. Cary Nelson, "Can E.T. Phone Home? The Brave New World of University Surveillance," *Academe* 89 (September–October 2003): 30–35, 35. The exception was David Wright, whose case had become notorious. Ibid.

16. More generally, the consent to the conditions cannot justify them. The Constitution is a legal limit imposed by the people as a whole. The federal government therefore can

go beyond this limit only with the consent of the people as a body, not merely with the consent of the states, private institutions, or private individuals. The First Amendment, for example, is a legal limit on government adopted by the people, and as a result, no amount of private consent can give the government the power that the people, in the amendment, denied to it. Put simply, private contract cannot enlarge federal power.

Nor can the consent to the IRB conditions preclude the possibility of federal force, for even with consent, there always can be force in the inducement or in the implementation. The conditions imposing IRBs allow the government to go to court to recover its funding from institutions that fail to comply with the conditions, and the conditions thereby are backed by the force of law. For further details of these arguments, see Philip Hamburger, "Unconstitutional Conditions: The Irrelevance of Consent," *Virginia Law Review* 98 (2012): 479.

17. 45 C.F.R. §102(f).

18. 45 C.F.R. §102(d). Indeed, the government requires institutions to acknowledge that "generalizable knowledge" means what is "expressed." The government asks institutions to commit to "the ethical principles" stated in *The Belmont Report*, which explains that "the term 'research' designates an activity designed to test an hypothesis, permit conclusions to be drawn, and thereby to develop or contribute to generalizable knowledge (expressed, for example, in theories, principles, and statements of relationships)." In thus echoing the words of the Common Rule, the government and the institutions recognize that the rule requires licensing of attempts to develop or contribute to knowledge "expressed" in theories or statements. Terms of the "Federalwide Assurance for the Protection of Human Subjects," §1, U.S. Department of Health and Human Services, www.hhs.gov/ohrp/assurances/assurances/filasurt.html.

19. "Activities Subject to the HRPP (July 2011)," *Operations Manual*, part 4, section 4.C, table 4, University of Michigan, Human Research Protection Program, Office of the Vice President for Research, www.hrpp.umich.edu/om/Part4.html.

20. Of course, the First Amendment is not the only problem, for the IRB laws and IRBs also violate many of the Bill of Right's procedural guarantees, including the guarantee of due process of law.

21. *Institutional Review Board Guidebook*, chapter 3, part A, U.S. Department of Health and Human Services, Office of Human Research Protections, www.hhs.gov/ohrp/archive/irb/irb_chapter3.html.

22. "Frequently Asked Questions and Vignettes," National Science Foundation, Division of Institution and Award Support, www.nsf.gov/bfa/dias/policy/hsfaqs.jsp.

23. U.S. Department of Health and Human Services, Office of Human Research Protections, "Institutional Review Board Guidebook, Chapter III, Part A."

24. The point here only concerns the licensing of words, and there thus are no implications for after-the-fact penalties, such as those on using a phone while driving.

25. "A Letter to the Inhabitants of the Province of Quebec (1774)," *A Decent Respect to the Opinions of Mankind: Congressional State Papers 1774–1776*, ed. James H. Hutson (Washington, D.C.: Library of Congress, 1975), 63.

26. "On the Freedom of the Press," *(Philadelphia) Independent Gazetteer*, January 4, 1783. In focusing on the freedom from licensing, the poem compared the freedom of the press to an unlicensed tavern and complained about inquisitors.

27. Of course, this expansion of ideas of harm was not only medical, but its other foundations, most profoundly its theological foundations, need not be recounted here. For the sake of simplicity, and to recognize the continuity of federal research policy, the Department of Health, Education, and Welfare is referred to here as "HHS."

28. Robert Levine, *Ethics and Regulation of Clinical Research*, 2d ed. (New Haven, Conn.: Yale University Press, 1988), 388 (citing Lawrence Tribe).

29. National Commission for the Protection of Human Subjects of Biomedical and Behavioral Research, *Report and Recommendations: Ethical Principles and Guidelines for the Protection of Human Subjects of Research*: (1978), 78–79.

30. Transcripts of Proceedings, President's Commission for the Study of Ethical Problems in Medicine and Biomedical and Behavioral Research, 243, July 12, 1980, box 37, Special Collections, National Reference Center for Bioethics Literature, Georgetown University.

31. Letter from Ithiel de Sola Pool to Morris Abrams and Alexander M. Capron, July 29, 1980, President's Commission for the Study of Ethical Problems in Medicine and Biomedical and Behavioral Research, box 3, Special Collections, National Reference Center for Bioethics Literature, Georgetown University.

32. Letter from Alexander M. Capron to Ithiel de Sola Pool, August 13, 1980, President's Commission for the Study of Ethical Problems in Medicine and Biomedical and Behavioral Research, box 3, Special Collections, National Reference Center for Bioethics Literature, Georgetown University.

33. Henry K. Beecher, "Ethics and Clinical Research," *New England Journal of Medicine* 274 (1966): 1354. The role of Beecher's study in justifying the licensing raises interesting questions about research ethics. Beecher suppressed the identities of his human subjects to protect them from embarrassment and other harm, but he thereby hid the real import of his data, prevented other scholars from testing his conclusions, and provided a false foundation for the imposition of licensing on nongovernmental research. It therefore is necessary to reconsider what constitutes unethical research. Although medical ethicists tend to assume that ethical dangers come mainly from publishing information, there may be even more serious dangers from suppressing information, such as the self-suppression in Beecher's case or the government suppression that was based on Beecher's work. Indeed, when one considers how Beecher's suppression of information justified the government's suppression of research and its publication, his work appears to be among the most damaging in American medical history.

34. See Philip Hamburger, "Getting Permission," *Northwestern University Law Review* 101 (2007): 455–56.

35. Peter Pronovost et al., "An Intervention to Decrease Catheter-related Bloodstream Infections in the ICU," *New England Journal of Medicine* 355 (2006): 2725.

36. Atul Gawande, "A Lifesaving Checklist," *New York Times*, December 20, 2007.

37. Pronovost et al., "An Intervention to Decrease Catheter-related Bloodstream Infections in the ICU."

38. The Common Rule exempts research "involving the use of educational tests (cognitive, diagnostic, aptitude, achievement), survey procedures, interview procedures, or observation of public behavior that is not exempt under paragraph (b)(2) of this section," if "the human subjects are elected or appointed public officials or candidates for public office." 45 C.F.R. §46.101(b)(3). Nonetheless, there is good reason to believe that the Office of Human Research Protections (OHRP) has interpreted "public officials" to mean only public figures. Even the reforms proposed by the Secretary's Advisory Committee on Human Research Protections (SACHRP) seem to take only a slightly softer version of this, apparently distinguishing between heads of agencies and lesser officials. According to SACHRP, OHRP's "guidance should include examples of 'public officials.' In particular, the guidance should include examples that OHRP has provided in the past, such as university faculty, public school teachers, and police officers in general are not considered to be elected or appointed public officials, whereas mayors, governors, school superintendents, school board members, and police chiefs are considered to be elected or appointed public officials." U.S. Department of Health and Human Services, Office of Human Research Protections, Secretary's Advisory Committee on Human Research Protections, "SACHRP Letter to HHS Secretary, September 18, 2008," www.hhs.gov/ohrp/sachrp/sachrpletter091808.html. In fact, some IRBs have not exempted the study of even major figures, such as Ronald Reagan or federal judges.

39. OHRP "recommends that institutions adopt clear procedures under which the IRB (or some authority other than the investigator) determines whether proposed research is exempt from the human subjects regulations." U.S. Department of Health and Human Services, Office of Human Research Protections, "Guidance on Written IRB Procedures," §D(1), www.hhs.gov/ohrp/policy/irbgd107.html. For practical purposes, this means a determination by the IRB. The exemptions in the Common Rule apply only to its policies, and thus, as the government makes clear in its Federalwide Assurance, "All of the Institution's human subjects research activities, regardless of whether the research is subject to the . . . Common Rule . . . , will be guided by a statement of principles," almost always *The Belmont Report*. U.S. Department of Health and Human Services, Terms of the Federalwide Assurance for the Protection of Human Subjects, §1, www.hhs.gov/ohrp/assurances/assurances/filasurt.html.

40. The NSF states: "When the subjects are public officials or candidates for public office, the research is exempt even when identifiers are included or disclosure might be harmful. However, all research should be bound by professional ethics and respect for respondents to guard their privacy whether or not the research is exempt (unless the participants understand that their information may be made public and permission is granted)." "Frequently Asked Questions and Vignettes," National Science Foundation, Division of Institution and Award Support, www.nsf.gov/bfa/dias/policy/hsfaqs.jsp. This sometimes is repeated in turn by universities and their IRBs. See, e.g., "Committees on Human Research, Behavioral Module," University of Vermont, http://www.uvm.edu/irb/education/supplemental001%20keep%20temp%20Donna%20checking/behavorialmodule001.htm; Classroom Research Conducted by Students, 9, at George Mason University, College of Education and Human Development, cehd.gmu.edu/assets.

10

TO FOLLOW THE ARGUMENT WHERE IT LEADS

An Antiquarian View of the Aim of Academic Freedom at the University of Chicago

RICHARD A. SHWEDER

W HAT IS ACADEMIC freedom for?[1] And how is it doing these days at the University of Chicago, which proudly thinks of itself as a Socratic, free-thinking, and contentious institution, and where I have been a member of the faculty for over four decades? If the values and norms associated with academic freedom are fragile (as history has shown) yet central to the intellectual life of any great university (which is a proposition I endorse and therefore will leave to other skeptics to contest) from which threats, external and internal, must it be protected?

With respect to the first question, two constitutional conservatives, both of them famous for their advocacy of judicial restraint, have given about as cogent an answer as one is going to get. The first is United States Supreme Court Justice Felix Frankfurter, whose answer appeared in a 1957 opinion opposing a government-led subversive activities inquiry into the content of a lecture at the University of New Hampshire delivered by the Marxist economist Paul Sweezy.[2] Frankfurter's answer, in sum and in paraphrase, was that the constitutional structure of our way of life protects the ardor and fearlessness of scholars to follow the argument where it leads. That is what academic freedom is for—to make it possible for scholars who are dedicated to the life of the mind to follow the argument where it leads, unfettered of received wisdom and popular views of political correctness and regardless of the practical, social or moral implications of their conclusions. Instead of putting Socrates on trial, in a free society we welcome him (or perhaps exile him) to the halls of the academy. For reasons I hope will become more obvious later I will dub Justice Frankfurter's conception the old-fashioned or antiquarian view of academic freedom.

The second voice affirming that antiquarian view is that of Justice Frankfurter's former law clerk Alexander Bickel, who, many years later, while living the disputatious life of a free academic as a constitutional legal scholar at Yale Law School, gave a similar answer to the question "What is academic freedom for?" Bickel addressed the question in a chapter in which he assessed the various threats to academic freedom he managed to perceive in "the furor [student protests] of the campuses in the late 1960s." Of far greater importance than his particular animus toward the protestors (and toward his colleagues who lent them support) is Bickel's general conception of the duties and responsibilities of institutions of higher learning and of the scholars and intellectuals who occupy them. "Knowledge and insight, like art," he argued, "are the products of independent minds following each its own bent, and are not often to be attained otherwise. In universities, professionals of many disciplines can follow lines of inquiry determined by themselves, individually and collectively, and dictated by no one else, on grounds either ideological or practical. While not all universities or colleges pretend to be such places, and other institutions like research institutes can be, only in a university can inquiry and teaching constitute one creative whole,[3] so that the knowledge and insight of the scholar and the methods by which he gained them are shared with the student; so that the student may be the scholar's company, nourishing him, giving as well as taking, in a word, collaborating. To this end, teachers must be free to teach, as free in their teaching as in their scholarship, and the enterprise—with its twin freedoms of inquiry and of teaching—must be judged by professional criteria and none other."[4] Among the many threats Bickel perceived to academic freedom were the demands of committed activists in the late 1960s as they tried to enlist institutions of higher learning in the project of solving immediate social problems or attaining immediate social ends conceived of as moral imperatives.[5]

In sum and in paraphrase, Bickel's answer to the question was this. What is academic freedom for? Its purpose is to protect "the autonomy of independent minds and the method of reason" against pressures, impulses and temptations of various kinds, whether ideological, moral, or practical. In short, Bickel argued, genuine academics, those who are true to the obligations of their role as intellectuals, researchers, and scholars at academically free universities, are duty bound by their professional status to defend the ideal of "thought without action."[6] And they should be morally committed to a principle of intellectual neutrality that has the following practical consequences. It fosters critical reason and dispassionate analysis. It encourages deliberative (even if disputatious) intellectual engagement with others. Academics, if they practice their trade in good faith and are true to their academic mission, will not only apply the method of reason to deepen their knowledge of the world but in their role as academics, will exercise self-restraint in the face of popular, lucrative, politically expedient, heartfelt, or even righteous calls for collective social and political action.[7]

THE PROFESSOR VERSUS
THE ATTORNEY GENERAL

Bickel's mentor Justice Felix Frankfurter said as much in that 1957 subversive activities case pitting the economist Paul Sweezy against the attorney general of the state of New Hampshire.[8] Sweezy, an outspoken Marxist, had been ordered by the courts in the state of New Hampshire to testify in a 1954 legislative hearing (run by the attorney general) investigating subversive political activity in New Hampshire. After some initial resistance he agreed to show up for the hearing. The attorney general, acting in his legislatively appointed role as inquirer into subversive activities, asked Professor Sweezy a long series of questions, most of which Sweezy answered. But when asked "What was the subject of your lecture [on March 22, 1954]?" and "Didn't you tell the class at the University of New Hampshire on Monday, March 22, 1954, that socialism was inevitable in this country?," the professor balked and refused, both on principle and as a matter of academic conscience, to be responsive. He was then held in contempt and sanctioned for his silence by the state of New Hampshire. His case and his conscience ended up in the Supreme Court of the United States.

Notably, although the legal dispute between Paul Sweezy and the state of New Hampshire had the potential to become consequential with respect to the place of academic freedom within our constitutional tradition, the four most liberal justices on the court at that time (Justices Warren, Brennan, Douglas, and Black) assumed a conservative legal posture favoring judicial restraint. While in their joint decision they expressed views acknowledging an undeniable constitutional right to liberties in the area of academic freedom and political expression, they ultimately reversed the state of New Hampshire's contempt verdict by basing their legal judgment on narrow procedural due process grounds (the reliance of the state legislature on the attorney general of the state functioning as its sole information gatherer with too much discretion and overly broad and unlimited inquisitorial powers) that had nothing to do directly with the Constitution's protections, if any, of academic freedom. At least in this case, the liberals on the Supreme Court declined to be First Amendment judicial activists and found a way to avoid grounding their judgment on the constitutional academic freedom questions thrown their way.[9]

Of greater interest was the concurring opinion written by Justice Felix Frankfurter (which was supported by Justice Harlan). This form of government interrogation and intrusion into the internal affairs of the university was just too much (and too deep in its implications for a free society) for the two of them to stomach. They formulated their revulsion (in part) in these terms:

> Insights into the mysteries of nature are born of hypothesis and speculation. The more so is this true in the pursuit of understanding in the groping endeavors of what are called the social sciences, the concern of which is man and society. The problems that are the respective preoccupations of anthropology, economics, law, psychology, sociology, and related areas of scholarship are merely departmentalized dealing . . . with interpenetrating aspects of holistic perplexities.
>
> For society's good—if understanding be an essential need of society—inquiries into these problems, speculations about them, stimulation in others of reflection upon them, must be left as unfettered as possible. Political power must abstain from intrusion into this activity of freedom, pursued in the interest of wise government and the people's well-being, except for reasons that are exigent and obviously compelling.
>
> These pages need not be burdened with proof, based on the testimony of a cloud of impressive witnesses, of the dependence of a free society on free universities. This means the exclusion of governmental intervention in the intellectual life of a university. It matters little whether such intervention occurs avowedly or through action that inevitably tends to check the ardor and fearlessness of scholars, qualities at once so fragile and so indispensable for fruitful academic labor. One need only refer to the address of T. H. Huxley at the opening of Johns Hopkins University, the Annual Reports of President A. Lawrence Lowell

of Harvard, the Reports of the University Grants Committee in Great Britain, as illustrative items in a vast body of literature. Suffice it to quote the latest expression on this subject. It is also perhaps the most poignant because its plea on behalf of continuing the free spirit of the open universities of South Africa has gone unheeded.

> "In a university knowledge is its own end, not merely a means to an end. A university ceases to be true to its own nature if it becomes the tool of Church or State or any sectional interest.[10] A university is characterized by the spirit of free inquiry, its ideal being the ideal of Socrates — 'to follow the argument where it leads.' This implies the right to examine, question, modify or reject traditional ideas and beliefs. Dogma and hypothesis are incompatible, and the concept of an immutable doctrine is repugnant . . ."

Echoes of Frankfurter's view of the dependence of a free society on academic freedom at universities can be found in two relatively recent Supreme Court decisions both written by justices associated with the politically conservative wing of the court, namely Sandra Day O'Connor and John Roberts. Writing the majority decision in a 2007 affirmative action case in which the court disallowed race-based assignment plans in primary and secondary schools in Seattle, Washington (*Parents Involved in Community Schools v. Seattle School District No. 1 et al.*, 551 U.S. 701 [2007]), Chief Justice Roberts invoked a key sentence and feature of reasoning in Justice O'Connor's 2003 majority ruling in *Grutter v. Bollinger* (the affirmative action decision allowing the University of Michigan Law School to continue with its affirmative action admissions policy [539 U.S. 306 (2003)]) so as to distinguish that earlier University of Michigan case from the Seattle case at hand. Roberts pointed out that in upholding the admissions plan at the University of Michigan Law School "this Court relied upon considerations unique to institutions of higher education, noting that in the light of 'the expansive freedoms of speech and thought associated with the university environment, universities occupy a special niche in our constitutional tradition'" (539 U.S. at 329). Justice Frankfurter's 1957 response to a government-appointed investigator asking questions about the content of university lectures suggests that Frankfurter too believed there are "expansive freedoms of speech and thought" uniquely associated with the university environment, which even an advocate of judicial restraint such as himself acting in his capacity as a justice of the Supreme Court should be concerned to defend.

Although the question of whether the Constitution does in fact provide a strong foundation for the defense of academic freedom may be far less settled than Justices O'Connor and Roberts opine, it is noteworthy (and should be heartening for academics) that the chief justice of the Supreme Court is a champion of academic freedom, at least at institutions of higher learning. It is noteworthy too that academic freedom per se is never explicitly mentioned in the Constitution. And it is far from heartening (for academics) that the answer to the crucial question—does the implicit structure of the Constitution project a penumbra sufficiently spacious to accommodate a special niche for institutions of higher learning?—is still elusive and shadowy in debates among constitutional scholars. Nevertheless and regardless of whether (or not) "the expansive freedoms of speech and thought associated with the university environment" are in fact protected by the Constitution, those who live in the halls of the academy might well value and defend those liberties simply by reference to the virtues associated with their calling.[11]

ON BEING TRUE TO ONE'S NATURE VERSUS PRETENDING TO BE SUCH A PLACE

I have begun this essay with a discussion of Frankfurter's and Bickel's conceptions of academic freedom: as those conditions (legal, customary, institutional) that empower scholars to freely and fearlessly follow the argument where it leads. I have done this because for someone with neo-antiquarian sensibilities,[12] Frankfurter's and Bickel's ancient Socratic view about freedom of thought as the ultimate end of the academic life has a familiar and resonant ring that summarizes very well the ideals of the University of Chicago, which I have long viewed as occupying a special niche because the University of Chicago is (or was, that is the question) a neo-antiquarian institution. And also because Frankfurter's and Bickel's words draw our attention to a contrast between a discourse from out of the dawn of the great American university and an increasingly commonplace contemporary discourse I associate with its twilight.[13] It is that contrast that is the focus of the remainder of this essay, with special reference to changes at the institution of higher learning with which I am most in love, to which I am most dedicated, and with which I am most familiar.

On October 9, 2009, the University of Chicago held, and celebrated, its 500th convocation.[14] The event unfolded ceremoniously in our Rockefeller

Chapel, a building that by design and mandate is the tallest on campus and also the architectural symbol of a tradition of free and critical inquiry that was explicitly honored on that day. Less than two weeks later, on the Upper West Side of Manhattan, the president of the University of Chicago, Robert Zimmer, explicated and defended that tradition of free inquiry, this time to participants in the Columbia University Heyman Humanities Center Conference addressing the question "What Is Academic Freedom For?"[15] I was one of the participants in the conference, and as a professor at the University of Chicago and a member of the sizable audience who heard the lecture, Bob Zimmer's talk and the ideals it expressed inspired me and made me feel proud.[16] I found myself thinking about the university news coverage I had read about the uplifting ideals feted twelve days earlier in Rockefeller Chapel.[17]

There is a story about Rockefeller Chapel that circulates around Hyde Park and dates from the years of Robert Maynard Hutchins, who became president of the University of Chicago in 1929 at the startling age of 30 years old and remained president for a very long time. Many members of the graduate faculty thought it was far too long, and viewed President Hutchins as a somewhat autocratic administrator who was insufficiently respectful of the role and scope of faculty governance. Nevertheless, for a variety of good reasons (some directly related to his defense of the freedoms of speech and thought at universities in the United States) Hutchins remains legendary in the annals of academic history. Rockefeller Chapel used to be open twenty-four hours a day. The notorious (famous and infamous) Hutchins ordered the building closed at night. When asked why, he remarked with characteristic wit, "Unfortunately, more souls have been conceived in Rockefeller Chapel than have been saved there." Inspired by Felix Frankfurter, Alexander Bickel, and the idea of a University of Chicago true to its ideals as articulated by its current president, I am going to engage in a kind of reflection on the saving of academic souls, in the hope that if we can save enough souls by making some progress figuring out what academic freedom is really for, perhaps Bob Zimmer will consider ordering Rockefeller Chapel open again at night.

That our academic soul needs to be saved (or at least re-ignited) may or may not seem obvious to the reader. Being in the business of conceiving souls is probably more fun than being in the business of trying to save them. In this brief reflection on intellectual life at a university where provocation has long been thought to be a virtue, my aim is to stimulate a lively and upbeat conversation about matters of concern while avoiding the hazard of merely adducing a list of complaints or projecting an earnest sense of gloom and doom. Nevertheless I do think there is a need to worry from time to time about our academic souls and about the aggregate and cumulative effect of the many small compromises of the Socratic ideal that are characteristic of the contemporary American university; and this is true even at proud institutions such as the University of Chicago and Columbia University, which define themselves as among the very greatest free and intellectually playful environments in the world.[18]

One might, for example, begin the process of resuscitation by juxtaposing and critically pondering the following two official University of Chicago discourses, the first an example of a discourse from out of the dawn of the great American university, and the second an example of the discourse which, as noted, I associate with its twilight.

This straightforward example of the first type of discourse is from the University of Chicago Articles of Incorporation, Bylaws, and Statutes (p. 44).[19] Simply put: "The basic policies of the University of Chicago include complete freedom of research and the unrestricted dissemination of information."

An example of the second discourse comes from an official communication from the University of Chicago Social and Behavioral Science Institutional Review Board to the faculty sponsor of a personally funded research project (dated September 2005): "We regret to inform you that IRB approval for your research Protocol has expired. Please note that research related activities (including interaction with human subjects, data collection, and/or data analysis) may not continue or be initiated until the IRB has approved the continuation of this research."[20]

Incoherencies in the practice of academic freedom and gratuitous restraints on inquiry of that type (originating in this instance within the walls of the academy and voluntarily overextending the reach of restrictions tied to federal research grants to researchers who do not have or seek such funds) are just one sign of the twilight. There are many others, although I hasten to add that in our disputatious academic communities not everyone agrees about what is the dawn and what is the twilight.[21]

Consider, for example, this principle, taken from a famous 1972 official University of Chicago report on academic appointments (the so-called Shils report) written by a faculty committee chaired by the sociologist Edward Shils and expressing a certain view of the core values of an academic community, including the exclusive focus on free thinking and scholarly achievement as a condition of membership: "There must be no consideration of sex, ethnic or national characteristics, or political or religious beliefs or affiliations in any decision regarding appointment, promotion, or reappointment at any level of the academic staff."[22]

Today on many college campuses that principle is viewed as an impediment to moral progress, or as old-fashioned, or as controversial, and it has been set aside or ignored. Yet I suspect some of the faculty members on the committee that prepared that report (which included world-renowned scholars of Asian, African, and European descent) might reasonably have argued that the principle is resonant with the legacy of academic freedom; and that we should feel proud, not embarrassed, to defend it and to act on it for the sake of the triumph of character over color, of the intellectually free individual over the ethnic (stereo) type.

Or how about this comment by a former president of the University of Chicago, Edward Levi, delivered to the University of Chicago's citizens board in 1967?[23] Embracing something like a view expressed by Edward Shils that the primary aim of a great university is "improving the stock of ordered knowledge and rational judgment"—that is what academic freedom is for—the then president of the University of Chicago told the citizen's board that it is not the role of the university to serve the community in which it is embedded or to directly respond to the needs of the broader world of politics and commerce or to be popular with the general public. Noting that we live in a time when "rational discussion itself is suspect," when "our society is fascinated with the manipulative techniques of persuasion, coercion, and power," and a time when "the sense of injustice, which all must prize, is subject to manipulation," he told the citizens board that first and foremost "the university conceives of itself as dedicated to the power of the intellect. Its commitment is to the way of reason." As noted earlier Robert Maynard Hutchins looms large in the self-consciousness of University of Chicago presidents, and President Levi went on to note that the University of Chicago stands "as Robert Hutchins said, in perpetual agreement with Cardinal Newman that the object of a university is intellectual and not moral." One wonders how much agreement such views would garner among faculties and administrators at Chicago today.

It seems noteworthy in that regard that Edward Levi was also the first member of the faculty of the University of Chicago to occupy the newly created post of provost in 1962, and his appointment more than fifty years ago was officially celebrated by current and former university administrators and others on September 21, 2012.[24] There is a certain irony in this celebration of his life and work, for in recent decades the antiquarian vision of the mission of the University of Chicago articulated by Edward Levi has truly become something of an antique and has more or less been renounced by our administrative leaders and even many members of the faculty. Quite recently, on June 13, 2012, on the occasion of the 511th convocation of the university, in an address titled "The Life of the Mind and Social Action" delivered to the graduating class of the college and their guests, the convocation speaker, the sociologist Stephen Raudenbush, essentially (and with no discernible tears in his eyes) observed that at the University of Chicago Edward Levi's vision of the mission of the university was more or less dead.[25]

Professor Raudenbush is a brilliant, prominent, socially concerned, and affable member of the faculty. In his convocation address he accurately characterized Levi's general view this way: that the University of Chicago, if it is to remain true to itself, has a singular purpose, in particular, "It exists to increase the intellectual understanding and powers of mankind." There is another way to put this: Edward Levi believed that whatever the unintended consequences (benefits or costs) of a University of Chicago education (and there are costs as well as benefits), those outcomes are not part of our mission statement. As Levi explained, the University of Chicago "does not exist to train the many technicians needed for our society, nor to develop inventions important for industry." Those and other quotes framed the Raudenbush convocation address, which sounded a bit like a funeral oration for the Levi conception of the raison d'être for the existence of the University of Chicago.

With reference to Edward Levi's remark that "The University of Chicago . . . does not exist to increase the earning power of its students," the speaker offered this reply: "As an aside to the parents gathered here today, I am not sure the University told you this four years ago!" As an aside of my own, one certainly hopes they did. And although I am confident that in his heart of hearts Steve Raudenbush hopes so as well, his lighthearted, facetious remark (and his convocation speech in general) did put me in an ironic frame of mind. It made me wonder whether the university has reached that point in its abandonment of the Levi vision where students and faculty should now expect the annual Aims of Education speaker to proudly declare that "one of the main purposes of the University of Chicago is to increase the earning power of our students" or expect our admissions officers to be on the lookout for academically qualified students who are likely to respond to that message with applause?.

Stephen Raudenbush, who has made major contributions to the quantitative analysis of school outcomes and whose own scholarship and research is in the applied area of school reform, the sociology of education, and explanations for the educational achievement gap between racial and ethnic groups, then posed the following question: Given the University of Chicago's historical commitment to something like Edward Levi's vision of the mission of the university how are we to explain the fact that, for example, the university now manages four charter school campuses on the South Side of Chicago and runs a large applied research consortium that evaluates policy options for the Chicago Public Schools? (How indeed are we to explain this shift in academic norms? Again as an aside, individual members of the faculty have always been at liberty to conduct research in school settings or even to hire themselves out as paid or unpaid consultants to the city of Chicago, as long as their consulting business was on the side, not the business of the institution per se or one that carried the weight or imprimatur of the University of Chicago, and was not a central part of a faculty member's calling within the halls of the academy. With the abandonment of the Levi vision this seems to have changed.)

Professor Raudenbush went on to praise the new developments, the spirit of social problem solving, and the blurring of the boundaries between the role of the academic and the role of the morally motivated social activist now increasingly embraced by administrators and trustees at the University of Chicago. Speaking to a graduating class of the college he essentially argued, *pace* Bickel, Frankfurter, Levi (and Socrates), that the ardor and fearlessness of scholars to follow the argument where it leads and the robustness of the tradition of free thinking within university environments are NOT best protected by separating thought from well-intended social action. Such is the contemporary state of intellectual play at the University of Chicago, which makes the recent celebration of the work and life of Edward Levi quite ironical.[26]

ACADEMIC FREEDOM'S SACRED TEXT: THE KALVEN COMMITTEE REPORT

Writing as a neo-antiquarian the document that makes me feel most proud to be a professor at the University of Chicago is a short and influential official policy statement about the institution's conception of academic freedom. It is locally known as the Kalven committee report ("Report on the University's Role in Social and Political Action").[27] It is not surprising that Robert

Zimmer, the current president of the university, focused his discussion of the ideals of academic freedom at the University of Chicago on the principles in that report or that both of us treated it as a document of interest in preparing our essays for this volume. The document identifies two fundamental and interconnected qualities of academically free institutions, namely the autonomy of voice of members of the community and institutional neutrality. The Kalven report has been influential enough to have been the basis for three highly visible refusals of the University of Chicago to engage in social and political action, with regard to the Vietnam War, in the face of calls to divest endowment funds from companies doing business in South Africa during the era of apartheid, and more recently with respect to calls to divest from companies doing business in Darfur during a period of violent conflict in the Sudan.

The Kalven committee report was written in 1967 by a faculty committee that included the historian John Hope Franklin, the Nobel Prize economist George Stigler, and faculty from all the academic divisions in the university. The committee was chaired by Harry Kalven Jr., who was at the time a professor in our Law School. Kalven was a Socratic eminence and a brilliant stylist who wrote a seminal book called A Worthy Tradition: Freedom of Speech in America, a book I recommend to all readers of this essay.

The Kalven committee report describes a fundamental aim of the University of Chicago as follows: "A university faithful to its mission will provide enduring challenges to social values, policies, practices, and institutions. By design and by effect, it is the institution which creates discontent with the existing social arrangements and proposes new ones. In brief, a good university, like Socrates, will be upsetting."

In the service of that mission (and of that worthy tradition) the report, quite crucially, points to two sacred (and closely linked) University of Chicago principles, two fundamentalisms for Highbrows: "institutional neutrality" and "faculty and student autonomy." The university as an institution is cautioned against taking any collective or institutional stance on the social and political issues of the day, in part because there is no intellectually defensible process "by which it can reach a collective position without inhibiting the full freedom of dissent on which it thrives." In other words, the university as an institution refrains from social, political, and moral posturing out of respect for the autonomy of its faculty and students, and especially out of respect for those individuals in a disputatious academic community who may embrace an unpopular or politically incorrect point of view.

My former provost, Geoffrey Stone, who I am sure was quite proud to be for some years the Harry Kalven, Jr., Distinguished Service Professor in our Law School (a title well suited to a legal scholar of the First Amendment) and who must be equally proud to now be the Edward H. Levi Distinguished Service Professor in our Law School, invoked the Kalven committee report (and the principles of faculty and student autonomy and institutional neutrality) to defend the University of Chicago's Darfur decision. He offered that defense despite the fact that as a student he had strong feelings, as did I, during the time of student unrest on college campuses in the late 1960s, about the importance of getting our universities to condemn the war in Vietnam. Geof Stone described the Darfur decision in the following terms: "What the Kalven Report forbids . . . are decisions of the University designed expressly or symbolically to proclaim 'right' moral, political, or social positions . . . Lawyers know all about slippery slopes. If the University divests from Darfur, then others will surely insist that the University must divest from corporations that manufacture cigarettes, perform abortions, sell arms to Israel, and pollute the environment. Of course, there are degrees of right and wrong and degrees of evil. But it is not the role of the University to take positions on such questions. Indeed, the University should no more divest on the basis of these sorts of issues than it should prohibit students and faculty from speaking freely on campus in support of tobacco subsidies, the moral legitimacy of murdering abortionists, the right of Palestinians to destroy Israel, or even the morality of genocide."

Geof Stone goes on to conclude his reflection (which appeared on the "University of Chicago Law School Faculty Blog" on February 9, 2007, http://uchicagolaw.typepad.com/faculty/2007/02/darfur_and_the_.html) by noting: "The role of the University is not to 'decide' such questions, but to create and nurture an environment in which we may freely and openly debate them, without fearing that the University has already resolved them on our behalf." He might just as well have said (in effect, by means of his provocative and indignation-arousing examples, he did say): "In brief a good university, like Socrates, will be upsetting." Yet right here and now while quoting my former provost, I do wonder: How many members of the faculties of the great universities of the United States (including the University of Chicago) would actively (or even passively) support an institutional environment that protected such debates and conversations?

There is of course much more to be said about autonomy of voice and institutional neutrality. I do research in a Hindu temple town in India. Some years ago, I invited a friend and scholar from that temple community to visit my temple community, the University of Chicago. It was his first trip abroad, so he came to the United States quite fresh. I invited him to attend my section of a social science core course. He noticed things we take for granted. He noticed that, as I walked into the classroom, the students did not stand up and show their respect for my status. He noticed that males and females were sitting together. He noticed that I encouraged the expression of opinions from my students. All those things went against his notion of what the practice of classroom teaching is about.

Such observations by an "outsider" helped me recognize a fundamental message of the organization of the classroom in our intellectual community. The message has much to do with the autonomy of voice. We participate in the community as individuals, not as social categories. We try to detach our evaluation of the ideas that are voiced from the social identity of the person who voiced them.[28]

There are many ways to lose your voice or to have it taken from you. Laryngitis is the least of them. I can recall losing my voice twice in recent decades, both at academic conferences. On the first occasion, one of the main speakers at the conference declined to participate in roundtable discussion with the males in the room on the grounds that her only interest in men was as sexual objects. Her gesture may seem outdated today; nevertheless, at the time, it was an astonishing and wickedly witty way of telling a story about the loss of voice. On the second occasion, a speaker denounced the musical West Side Story on the grounds that it had been produced by "successful white males" who, she argued, had no authority to represent the Puerto Rican–American experience. When it was pointed out by a wounded female fan of the show that West Side Story was a variation on Romeo and Juliet, a play created by a successful white male who was neither Italian nor a citizen of Verona, the speaker denounced William Shakespeare as a racist.

"Racist" is an epithet that along with a small and highly disparaging set of other stigmatizing and argument-ending accusations (such as sexist, anti-Semite, homophobic, socialist, self-hating Jew, neocolonialist, and, increasingly, neoliberal and libertarian) have all too often been showstoppers on the stage of academic freedom; out of a fear of the reputational effects of being so labeled, such epithets have at the very least inhibited many academic souls from assumption-questioning dialogue and the forthright expression of critical judgments about matters of consequence.

I think there is a message about the authority of voice to be drawn from these examples, and it is this: the authority of a voice has a lot to do with what is said and very little to do with who says it (or even, arguably, their motives for saying it). In other words, you do not have to be a Westerner or a male to articulate a Western or masculine perspective, and most Westerners and most males are not very good at it, anyhow. Authoritative voices ought to have authority not because of their census category or social identity, but because what they say either has in the past or currently binds you to a reality. Indeed, "insiders" are not necessarily the best ones to speak about themselves. That is why some of the best books about social life in the United States have been written by "outsiders" from Asia, Africa, and Europe. It was an observation by a friend from India that got me to realize that in a truly academically free university you never have to sacrifice your ardor, your fearlessness, or the autonomy of your voice.

The academic freedom ideals—autonomy of voice and institutional neutrality—defined by Harry Kalven, John Hope Franklin, George Stigler, and others are extraordinarily difficult to uphold and defend. There are many powerful forces in our contemporary society (both inside and outside the academy) that threaten the principles of student and faculty autonomy and institutional neutrality at the increasingly timid, cowed, and compromised universities and colleges of America; and I do not just have in mind the Patriot Act or attempts to control what is done at Middle Eastern area centers.

Those who love Kalven's report in principle do not always love it in practice; for example, when they want the university (or the office of the president or the office of the provost) to take a collective stance in support of their own favorite social or political cause, or to officially celebrate their own cultural or activist heroes, or to censure the expression of opinions or attitudes they find objectionable or offensive. The principle of institutional neutrality (which, it is useful to remind oneself, is upheld for the sake of protecting the autonomy of thought of faculty and students) makes manifest the antiquarian conception of academic freedom. Reiterating Geof Stone's interpretation, the principle forbids "decisions of the University designed expressly or symbolically to proclaim 'right' moral, political, or social positions."

Although the relevant scope of the definition of the institutional or collective entity "the university" might not be fully transparent, the concept of a "decision of the university" expressly or symbolically proclaiming "right" moral, political, or social positions presumably includes endorsements by the board of trustees, by administrators speaking on behalf of the university or by faculty speaking on behalf of their division, school, department, center, institute, or program. It would presumably offend the principles of the Kalven committee report if the faculty of the Department of Economics voted to have their department endorse a particular candidate for president of the United States; or if the provost of the university, speaking in his capacity as provost, sent a message to faculty, students, and staff advocating a particular stance on *Roe v. Wade*. Yet the principle of institutional neutrality seems less principled when it is put to very selective use, defending academic freedom by defying the demands of activists to condemn the war in Vietnam or to divest from South Africa during the era of apartheid, yet having no such defiant conviction when it comes to symbolically proclaiming the "right" moral, political, or social position by entering into a well-funded partnership with the Chicago public schools and placing one's imprimatur as an institution (in contrast to ones name as an individual faculty member) on some particular educational policy goal. Or when the office of the provost declares publicly in a noble and principled way that the university administration does not comment on (or take an official position with respect to) the sometimes provocative, upsetting, or unsettling views expressed in private or in public by individual members of the faculty, yet then less openly makes it clear to other administrative officials that the expressed views of individual faculty members upon which it does not comment (but which, precisely because such expressed views are provocative, annoying or upsetting, may create concerns among administrators and faculty about their unbidden negative reputational effects for the institution) are not only unwelcome but that the faculty member should in some way be censured, for example, by suggesting or encouraging the chair of his or her department to take steps to criticize or marginalize the faculty member, for example, by removing him or her from highly visible departmental responsibilities (such as chairing a student admissions committee).[29]

Other more or less debatable violations of institutional neutrality and faculty and student autonomy do occur, and they sometimes do so without much comment or even recognition—for example, when the University of Chicago administration all of a sudden, and completely out of character, sets aside several days around the time of Martin Luther King Jr.'s birthday to commend a hero and to celebrate his civil rights activities and officially encourages all members of the university community to attend (the issue turning not on whether there are plenty of citizens of the United States who were inspired by Dr. King and eager to honor him—I myself participated in the March on Washington in the summer of 1963—but rather whether it is the role of an academically free contentious university committed to debate and criticism and institutional neutrality on social, political, and moral issues to have its administrative officers promote this form of piety for any social, political, or moral figure). Or when the dean or the faculty of a university department, school, or program refuses to rent their lecture hall to a student organization because he, she, or they (the dean or the faculty of that program) loathe the views of an invited speaker or fear the consequences of international attention to his or her presence in their academic space; or when officials of the university disregard the notions of institutional neutrality and student autonomy and step across the line (wherever that line might be) between sensibly maintaining the civility and respect for persons presupposed by any robust free speech/free thought environment (enforcing a prohibition on shouting down speakers for example) and dubiously imposing a "heckler's veto" by playing to the gallery and sanctioning students or student organizations because they dramatically said something or did something (often in the form of parody or hyperbole or burlesque) that is politically incorrect or deeply offensive to the beliefs and values of other outspoken students.

In the 1960s a University of Chicago student organization invited the then head of the American Nazi party to speak on campus. They did this shortly after administrators at Northwestern University cancelled a similar invitation to that campus. They wanted to dramatize the idea of no-topics-barred open debate at the University of Chicago. The very idea that the head of the American Nazi party received an invitation to speak at the University of Chicago seemed vile and was so deeply offensive to some members of the faculty, including some very famous and prominent Jewish scholars such as Leo Strauss, that they wrote a letter to the then dean of the college, urging him to cancel the invitation. He declined to do so, while standing firmly in defense of the right of the students to invite and debate whomsoever on any topic they wanted. The event went forward, apparently without disruption, and everyone had a conversation about the nature and limits of academic freedom. I have no way of knowing whether the lecture/conversation and questioning and discussion that may have ensued added to the "stock of ordered knowledge and rational judgment." Those who protested the event were confident that the chance of that happening was zero.

Fast forward to today. Imagine that the members of a free speech student organization on campus read Geof Stone's blog (mentioned previously), where he notes that among the topics open for debate and protected by the academic freedom principles set forth in the Kalven committee report are the moral legitimacy of murdering abortionists, the right of Palestinians to destroy Israel, and the morality of genocide. Imagine the student organization then organizes a series of three lectures and invites to campus strong advocates for each of those positions, thereby inciting the faculty members of this or that department or program (the Committee on Jewish Studies or the Center for Gender Studies, for example) to issue an official statement denouncing the event and anyone who believes that Israel has no right to exist and should be destroyed or that there is ever a moral justification for violence against abortionists, and calling on the University of Chicago administration to cancel the talks. Who has behaved inappropriately here (in the sense of violating the principles of the Kalven committee report), the students or the faculty of the Committee on Jewish Studies and the Center for Gender Studies? And how should the provost, president, and board of trustees of the university respond, given their principled commitment to institutional neutrality (whatever their own moral or political views) in the cases of the Vietnam War, South African apartheid, and the violent conflict in Darfur?

No doubt some controversial social, political, and moral issues cannot be avoided by institutions of higher learning or kept off their radar screen. But is that any less true of the corporate investment decisions of the university than it is of decisions about faculty recruitment or student admissions? When the University of Chicago and its deans place strict limits on new faculty appointments (or even freeze new appointment lines in some departments) yet at the same time create a special fund effectively enabling the unlimited recruitment of faculty from a targeted and small set of particular minority groups (and only those minority groups), in some sense they take the step that Geof Stone (in his defense of the decision not to divest from Darfur) suggests is forbidden: the institution decides a controversial question (the moral status of what one side views as "reverse discrimination" and the other as "benign discrimination" or "viewpoint diversity" aka "affirmative action") on behalf of its disputatious faculty and students, declaring what is the right-minded and moral thing to do, while increasing the risk that its institutional action will inhibit the full freedom of debate and dissent on which the institution thrives.

To make matters worse it invites a cynical response from those in the academic community who care about following the argument where it leads and "increasing the stock of ordered knowledge and rational judgment." Having circumvented the process of robust debate, the decision is taken without a rigorous assessment of the actual impact of the affirmative action hiring policy on viewpoint diversity on campus. Not surprisingly, given the particular social justice agenda actually being pursued (out of moral concern over, for example, the legacy of the practice of slavery in the United States), the preferential hiring is implemented incompletely with respect to the logic of genuine viewpoint diversity (a brilliant scholar from an "untouchable" or "scheduled" caste in India would not qualify no matter how different or fascinating that person's viewpoint or life experiences). Instead of encouraging the ardor and fearlessness of scholars to follow the argument where it leads, the policy is embraced by the institution in such a way that it quickly becomes politically incorrect (or it is viewed as ethically callous) to even point to the neutral appointment principle articulated in other official university policy documents. To wit, and as noted earlier, that "there must be no consideration of sex, ethnic or national characteristics, or political or religious beliefs or affiliations in any decision regarding appointment, promotion, or reappointment at any level of the academic staff." Despite the admonitions and cautions inherited from Edward Levi and Robert Hutchins, in this instance the mission of the university appears to have become primarily moral and probably not sufficiently intellectual.

And not everyone loves the Kalven committee report, even in principle. For example, one finds some members of one's own academic community arguing (as do some politicians in Washington and bureaucrats in the once revealingly named Office of Compliance—now renamed the Office of Human Research Protections) that conducting research at a place like the University of Chicago is a kind of indulgence (or a favor) and certainly not a fundamental right. In fact there are many in the academy these days who believe that any student or faculty member who talks to human beings as part of his or her research in fact *should* be required to have his or her project approved in advance by an institutional licensing board (the so-called institutional review board), in part to guarantee (especially in the social sciences and humanities, but also in some forms of biomedical research) that no one asks questions that are too upsetting to some.[30]

IS FACULTY GOVERNANCE A THREAT
TO ACADEMIC FREEDOM?

It may well be a measure of the fragility of academic freedom that it can be threatened on many fronts. In 1957 Justice Frankfurter recognized that academic freedom (the ardor and fearlessness of scholars) is both fragile and indispensable for fruitful academic labor and needs to be protected from *government intervention* in the intellectual life of the university. In 1967 the Kalven committee recognized that academic freedom (the ardor and fearlessness of scholars) is both fragile and indispensable for fruitful intellectual labor and needs to be protected from *institutional or administrative intervention* in the intellectual life of a university. Recently there has been a new development at the University of Chicago in which the administration (the president, provost, and all the deans, with the support of some members of the faculty) has argued that academic freedom is fragile and indispensable for fruitful academic labor and needs to be protected from *faculty intervention* in the intellectual life of the university.

That last threat to academic freedom, whether real or imagined, needs to be examined in more detail. So does the solution offered by those who fear the threat. Their proposed remedy for the threat being that at the University of Chicago, faculty ruling bodies should have jurisdiction and decision-making powers (a vote) only over the educational and teaching activities of the university; and that the administration and ultimately the board of trustees (typically but not necessarily in nonbinding consultation with individual faculty or faculty ruling bodies) should have jurisdiction and decision-making powers over the research activities of the university (including decisions about the creation of research centers and research institutes and the development of new directions of inquiry).

There is little doubt that from an ultimate corporation point of view the board of trustees has final authority over what happens at the university and probably has the legal authority, if the trustees were so inclined, to close down the current departments and end all student admissions, teaching, and degree granting at the University of Chicago and to turn the institution into a research institute of applied microbiology, translational medicine, brain science, molecular engineering, economics, public policy and school reform. Yet it should be pointed out as well that it is the delegation of authority over the intellectual life of the institution to the faculty and the understandings, values, and norms that insulate the faculty from top-down management of intellectual life that characterize the academic culture of the great universities of our land.

On the surface at least it may seem ironic to try to preserve the academic freedom of the faculty by restricting their role in decision making about the evolution of the intellectual life of the university. Recall Alexander Bickel's observation (discussed previously) that "only in a university can inquiry and teaching constitute one creative whole." At the University of Chicago these days the administrative leaders of the university appear to be intent on splitting those functions apart. And the faculty itself (at least those who pay attention to debates about faculty governance)[31] are themselves split apart over how to interpret the meaning of a key faculty governance statute in the articles of incorporation of the University of Chicago that establishes or at least articulates a framework for its academic way of life.

During the 2012 academic year the Council of the University Senate (the most centralized faculty ruling body at the university) appointed a faculty committee to examine the jurisdiction and division of powers of the faculty versus the administration in matters of governance; and to examine as well the extent to which (and the topics about which) that most centralized faculty ruling body (the Council of the University Senate) might legitimately exercise authority over the decisions of other more local faculty ruling bodies and their deans. The president of the University of Chicago, Robert Zimmer, who supported the council decision to appoint a faculty committee to examine jurisdictional issues, then appointed a second faculty committee to examine the same questions. In a letter to the council (dated January 23, 2012) he explained that the appointment of the second faculty committee was motivated by a concern "that no Ruling Body or office of the University has the prerogative to define its own jurisdiction in a unilateral way given the distribution of authority under the Statutes."

Special attention was given by the faculty members on both committees to the history and meaning of a particular statute in the articles of incorporation, bylaws, and statutes of the University of Chicago, and its application to decision making about the creation of research institutes and research centers and the development of new research directions. The reports of those faculty committees were made available to all members of the faculty.

Those two reports are impressive and astonishing not just because of the seriousness, thoroughness, and intelligence with which the issues are addressed but also because they arrive at such different and consequential conclusions, revealing not only a potential conflict and unfortunate divide in faculty understandings of the formal aspects of university governance, but also the challenges and complexities of governing in such a way that academic freedom actually flourishes in a university environment. I myself came away from reading the two reports hoping (perhaps against hope) that the issue is not forced and does not get settled one way or the other as a matter of principle; and hoping as well that the administration and the faculty carry on mucking through together, as we have in the past, doing whatever seems to best honor our academic freedom traditions with respect to any case at hand. A letter to the provost cosigned by all the deans of the university, who in this instance are uncharacteristically and surprisingly uniform in their judgment—namely that teaching and inquiry are separable functions at the University of Chicago and only the former is within the domain of faculty governance—was also part of the record made available to the faculty.[32]

The key statute, whose meaning is contested, is statute 12 of the University of Chicago Articles of Incorporation, Bylaws, and Statutes, which defines "The Organization and Powers of the University Senate and the Ruling Bodies." It states (12.1): "All advisory, legislative, and administrative powers in the University concerning its *educational work*, except those vested in the President by the Board of Trustees shall be exercised by, or be under the authority of, the Ruling Bodes specified in article 12" (italics added). "Local ruling bodies" (for example, the social science faculty) are then given authority and jurisdiction over educational work of local (divisional, college) concern and the Council of the University Senate (an elected faculty body representing the entire university faculty) is given authority and jurisdiction over educational work of relevance to the whole university. Nothing is said about which parts of "the educational work" of the university are of sufficient relevance to the university as a whole to become matters for consideration by the Council of the University Senate.

The most basic question faced by the two faculty committees, however, was this one: Does the phrase "educational work" encompass "the twin freedoms of inquiry and of teaching" that Alexander Bickel argued constitute one creative whole at great universities (a view supported by some members of the University of Chicago faculty); or, as the university administration and other faculty members who support the administration's point of view have argued, does that statute severely limit the authority of faculty ruling bodies to decision making about "educational work" narrowly construed, namely teaching and course work and requirements for degrees?

Why would the president, the provost, and all the deans of the University of Chicago want to split the inquiry function from the teaching function when it comes to faculty governance? What problems do university administrators see in the idea of faculty ruling bodies having jurisdiction over the research activities of the university, including decisions about the creation of research centers and research institutes or the development of new directions of inquiry? It is all too easy to be cynical about the administration's stance on this question, positing, as some faculty do, that this is all about those who want to follow the money where it leads (typically to the practical and applied policy agendas favored by wealthy patrons, members of the board of trustees, well-endowed foundations, and social problem-solving government agencies) not wanting to lose control over their fund-raising capacities and not wanting to be constrained by skeptical scholars. It is all too easy as well to simply support the administrative stance on this question, positing, as some faculty do, that the market for funding (for example, in energy, health, brain science, school reform, economic development) is a good measure of where academic research agendas ought to go and that too many of those intellectual (and financial) benefits will not be pursued and sufficiently realized if disputatious (or change-resistant) faculty ruling bodies living in an ideologically divided ivory tower are permitted to have a vote or veto over the evolution of the realms of inquiry on campus.

Given the particular circumstances that originally gave rise to this debate, the perception by the university administration that academic freedom at the University of Chicago needs to be protected from faculty interference in the intellectual life of the university is not entirely hallucinatory. It appears to have been a response to the disgruntlement of significant numbers of faculty who organized a protest against the creation of a particular high-profile (and prospectively well-endowed) research institute named after the economist Milton Friedman. The research institute (which was eventually named the Becker Friedman Institute for Research in Economics) was approved by the administration and went forward without the vote of any faculty ruling body, on the grounds that research centers and institutes are not part of the "educational work" of the university.

In that instance (one that received national attention) it is not hard to see how the organized disgruntlement might have been seen by the administration (and those faculty involved in the project) as a threat to the core academic values of the university. At the time, I myself, who was not involved in the project, saw it that way.

Milton Friedman was a distinguished former member of the University of Chicago faculty, a Nobel laureate, and a contentious and influential voice of the Chicago School of Economics who in some ways exemplified the against-the-current and provocative character of the university in his times. Shortly after he died in 2006 (which was shortly before the meltdown of the U.S. financial system) there was a nationwide outpouring of affection from his supporters and a desire among some members of the University of Chicago community (especially in the Department of Economics and the Business School) to capitalize on and memorialize his legacy. Within a very short amount of time rumors circulated on campus recounting optimistic, or perhaps even grandiose, estimates of fund-raising possibilities ($100 million has already been pledged, one heard; and $200 million was said to be easily within reach). Soon there followed a proposal from the Department of Economics and the dean of the social sciences to create a research institute bearing Milton Friedman's name, which was supported by the president and provost of the university, presented or "aired" at a meeting of the Council of the University Senate (the most centralized faculty ruling body), and approved by the board of trustees, all without a vote by any faculty ruling body.

There was no outpouring of affection however from Milton Friedman's detractors on the faculty or from faculty critics of the Chicago School of Economics. Instead there was a petition campaign opposing the plan and expressing a range of concerns about the corporatization of the University of Chicago and the erosion of faculty governance and control over the direction of research currents.[33] Ultimately the petition was signed by well over one hundred members of the faculty (many of them from the social sciences and humanities).

I thought the petition campaign was un-collegial and inconsistent with our academic freedom traditions, as I noted in a personal communication responding to an e-mail from a colleague who was quite critical of the creation of a Milton Friedman Institute for Economic Research on the University of Chicago campus. The discipline of economics is often described as "the dismal science" even by economists (although the provenance of the label is typically traced to the nineteenth-century historian Thomas Carlyle).

Given the nature of viewpoint diversity in the academy there are faculty members at the University of Chicago (and in the humanities and social sciences more widely) who experience the ideas and intellectual agenda of the Chicago School of Economics not only as dismal but also as imperial, offensive, and perhaps even a kind of pollution or desecration of the life of the mind. Expressing my thoughts about the proposed institute and the petition campaign opposing it I responded as follows:

I have a somewhat different view of the Milton Friedman Institute. It seems to me the nature, implications and value of the institutions and logic of capitalism, free markets, private choice and contractual exchange are amongst the core issues that ought to be examined and debated in the academy—and within the academy one ought to expect and encourage the full range of voices along the spectrum from "Gemeinschaft" to "Gesellschaft."[34] Our department of economics tries to push the logic of "Gesellschaft" very far—that is their ideological commitment (and in a sense their claim to fame) but it is a voice that has to be taken seriously, engaged and where appropriate critiqued. Likewise for the voices of "Gemeinschaft." You have been a major critic but as you well know the debates of relevance here have been going on for a long time and have stretched from Voltaire and Adam Smith to Tonnies, Simmel, Weber, Sahlins and Friedman; and, at least in my view, at a great university all those types of voices should be active and vital. I don't think we would be the great Social Science Division of the University of Chicago without both the sacred and the profane, without the Depts. of Anthropology and Economics, and I think both departments bring great prestige to our institution. Indeed one hopes for more direct debate and critical engagement across those potential divides. There are central academic freedom issues at stake in this case and the spirit of our disputatious intellectual community has been diminished a bit I think by what amounts to a viewpoint based protest against the voice of "Gesellschaft" within the academy. Moreover I do not see anything wrong with naming a building or institute after a former and influential member of our faculty (I find it more appealing than naming it after benefactors) and the Institute is not an administrative decision to promote some new area of scholarship or research for the sake of funding (although it seems to me this has been done in some other areas—and it troubles me) but rather as an extension of existing faculty projects and interests and a measure of their success and achievements . . . Among the concerns I do have are (1) making sure that the new institute does not administratively function like the Hoover Institute—that is to say that is remains under normal University of Chicago academic governance procedures and is not semi-autonomous from an administrative point of view; and (2) getting our Dean and everyone else to worry about the problem of resource imbalances within the Division. More positively I think we should treat this development as an opportunity for broader engagement between anthropologists, economists, philosophers and others about those central issues concerning the market mentality that you have written about so brilliantly.

My colleague, as I recall, thought I was naive to imagine fearless scholars on either side of that divide talking to one another at all or that the faculty could count on administrative leaders to maintain a balance in resources and viewpoints across the faculties in the social science division. While I would like to believe the jury is out on those judgments,[35] the creation of research institutes and centers has exposed a weakness in the structure of the university's governance. To the extent such institutes and centers are merely institutional mechanisms for the extension and development of particular lines of inquiry by independent scholarly minds working alone or collectively at intellectually freewheeling universities they are unquestionably in need of protection or insulation from the prospects of a hostile vote that might emerge from the very fact of viewpoint diversity on college campuses. Providing that protection is what academic freedom is for.

Unfortunately those research centers and research institutes also tend to become academic fiefdoms and financial resource centers, which not only satisfy the interests (and egos) of individual faculty members but also tend to weaken decision making within departments and reduce the likelihood that those who hold different viewpoints will have the opportunity to engage one another in debate.[36] In the worst-case scenario they become a device by which individual faculty members in collaboration with administrators (who are always concerned to do their best on the fund-raising front) leverage the funds available to research institutes and research centers to influence faculty hiring in academic departments and hence exercise a not so subtle form of top-down control over the future research agenda of the institution. If and when the process moves in that direction, the insistence on a vote by faculty ruling bodies when new institutes and centers are proposed becomes more understandable, as does the skittishness that has surfaced over the perception of undue influence.

But that is not the only reason to be cautious about ceding research or inquiry to administrative control (research or inquiry being an academic function that, Bickel-like, some members of the faculty continue to define as central to the "educational work" of the university, which also includes teaching). The evolution of the regulations that currently require all research- ers who study human beings to produce a research protocol for prior review and licensing by an institutional review board is caution enough about the fragility of the norms that protect academic freedom. While there certainly may be risks to letting faculty ruling bodies intervene in the intellectual life of the university, there are hazards as well to placing the research function in the hands of administrators, who are not necessarily as fearless as Edward Levi in protecting the core mission of a Socratic academic life, or as free as Robert Hutchins (who administered the university in an era when private educational institutions were less regulated because less dependent on the federal purse) to resist the practical demands, pressures, or recommendations of funding agencies, risk-management advisors, efficiency experts, legal offi- cers, benefactors, social activists, journalists, or politicians.

IS ADMINISTRATIVE GOVERNANCE A THREAT TO ACADEMIC FREEDOM?

The federal regulatory scheme specifically requiring institutional review board (IRB) oversight of federally funded research at American universities and colleges (the Department of Health and Human Services 45 CFR 46 rules and definitions, also known as the "Common Rule") was initiated by an act of Congress in 1974 and is currently enforced by the Office for Human Research Protections (the OHRP). The original act of Congress was moti- vated by concerns over perceived ethical violations in biomedical research conducted by the Public Health Service;[37] and its aim was to make sure that all federally sponsored research is ethically sound. University researchers who elect to apply for federal funding support make that choice knowing that their freedom of inquiry (for example, to talk to other human beings as a means of gaining knowledge or to analyze evidence) and expressive liberties (to write, to publish, to lecture about their research) will be restricted and controlled by the regulatory system known as the IRB. Within the terms of those federal regulations, research that is not federally funded is *not* mandated for Com- mon Rule or IRB regulation. Alternatively stated, within the terms of the 45

CRF 46 regulations the scope and depth of OHRP enforcement is limited to federally funded projects; and it is legally possible for academic research institutions to shield and protect privately funded, personally funded, and unfunded projects from the reach of the IRB surveillance and research licensing process (and its various definitions, rules, and regulations), while at the same time assuring by other means that all research with human subjects will be guided by professional ethical standards. For example, with respect to student research in the social sciences and humanities that is not federally funded and involves interactions with human beings, the university could decide that thesis proposal hearings are a natural and sufficient context for the discussion and application of ethical research standards. For example, with respect to research that is not federally funded, the university faculty in each of the disciplines could decide for itself what types of research are exempt from ethical licensing processes (for example, without prejudging the outcome of local decisions, yes to observations conducted in public places; yes to journalistic interviews conducted with adults; no to clinical medical trials) and leave it up to the researchers themselves to decide whether they are exempt, with no requirement of formal approval of the exemption.

Proposals of that sort have been put forward by committees of the American Association of University Professors (AAUP) who have expressed concern about the evolution of the IRB system and its implications for academic freedom (see the references cited in note 30). Almost no university, including the free-thinking University of Chicago, has taken an interest in limiting the application of the IRB regulatory system to federally funded research; indeed, almost all research universities, including the free-thinking University of Chicago, now run an elaborate research licensing system in which permission must be sought to even ask an adult a series of questions or publish the results of that conversation. A neo-antiquarian might well judge that to be both surprising and disturbing, especially in the light of the expectation (held by Justices Frankfurter, Roberts, and O'Connor, as previously discussed) of the "expansive freedoms of speech and thought associated with the university environment." Surprising because that tradition of academic freedom, as explicated in the Kalven committee report, holds that a university is a place where the life of the mind of individual scholars is granted very high degrees of autonomy. This implies that proposed restraints on faculty and student research and other suggestions for regulating, monitoring, controlling, or constricting scholarship that are not mandated by law should be viewed with a very skeptical eye ("except for reasons that are exigent and obviously compel-ling," as Justice Frankfurter put it in *Sweezy v. The State of New Hampshire*). One might ask: Why were such regulations not generally resisted within the academic community rather than uncritically embraced and voluntarily and quickly (over) generalized?

That lack of a resistance to external regulations that are legally avoidable seems especially disturbing if one comes to view the nearly four decades of IRB "mission creep" as a kind of death of academic freedom by a thousand cuts. It is possible to view it that way, the more so because as a result of a slow but inexorable process of implementation and efficiency management we have now reached a point in the academy where prior review and research licensing by an administratively appointed committee has come to seem nor-mal (or at least irresistible) to the many scholars who are now routinely told by their own university administrators that they must seek permission to engage in research at all.

There may be times when academic freedom is threatened by the interfer-ence of the faculty in the intellectual life of the university. In this instance, however, the voluntary and discretionary extension of the Department of Health and Human Services (DHHS) regulations to all university research-ers (regardless of their funding source or whether the scholarship is funded at all) has been the result of decades of decision making by well-meaning university administrators who thought they were protecting the university— its flow of external funding, its ability to attract members of the public to participate in medical experiments, its capacity to defend itself against law-suits. With the best of intentions a system of regulation has been put in place that belies the discourse of the dawn ("The basic policies of the University of Chicago include complete freedom of research and the unrestricted dis-semination of information"). This has happened without the benefit of open and robust debate about its implications for academic values and research performance or its effects on the ardor and fearlessness of scholars (faculty and students).[38] Notably the annual monitoring and prior review of research, this issuing of commands to refrain from research and data analysis and to cease and desist from the dissemination of information has evolved without a vote by any faculty ruling body. Indeed, the fact that there is no federally mandated legal requirement to universalize the 45 CFR 46 regulations (or any of its sub-parts) beyond federally funded projects has pretty much been a well-kept secret among academic administrators, most of whom have done very little to educate their faculty in this regard or to bring the matter forward for deliberation. Perhaps in 1974, when the whole system of prior review was first put in place, a proposal to generalize IRB review to all inquiries involving human subjects at the University of Chicago (rather than limit it to individual researchers applying for federal grants) would not have survived an open debate in a faculty ruling body. Today, at least for some faculty, the IRB licensing process (even if intrusive, irritating, and time consuming) has come to seem almost normal. For others the review and permission granting is valued as the safekeeping instrument of a beneficent campaign designed to protect the vulnerable. It is not unimaginable that if a vote on a proposal to universalize IRB regulations were taken today the threat to academic freedom might well come from the faculty itself.

The IRB at the University of Chicago is probably my most faithful correspondent. This is because despite the commitment of the University of Chicago (as expressed in the Kalven committee report) to the intellectual autonomy of students and faculty, student scholars are required by the university administration to designate a faculty member as the signatory principal investigator who is legally and ethically responsible for the student's research project. In response to one of the innumerable cease and desist orders I have received over the years telling me (and the student) to stop all inquiry, data analysis, writing, and information dissemination (the communication typically arrives when a student has failed to apply for an annual renewal of his or her research permission) I composed the following e-mail seeking the advice of three free-thinking, open-minded, and dedicated members of the University of Chicago faculty, who also happen to be university administrators: the president, the provost and the associate provost for what is called "research administration."

I am sending you this e-mail to seek your counsel and get your reactions to a disclaimer I have composed, which I am contemplating attaching to the next non-federally funded student research IRB protocol application on which my name appears as "the signatory P.I."

I have heard Bob[Zimmer] speak powerfully and eloquently about University of Chicago style academic freedom; and as an institution we do not hesitate to proudly point to some inspiring events in our history in that regard (President Hutchins' testimony before the Illinois Seditious Activities Investigation Committee, the "Kalven Committee Report," etc.). Nevertheless over the past forty

years or so we have not been particularly vigilant in noticing and countering
the erosion of those academic freedom values in the face of the Federal Institutional Review Board/Protection of Human Subjects movement—and by "we"
here I include the faculty, the administration and our legal office. An instructive
history of the protection of human subjects movement and its implications for
academic freedom and social science research can be found in the recent book
by the historian Zachary Schrag titled *Ethical Imperialism: Institutional Review
Boards and the Social Sciences, 1965–2009* (Johns Hopkins University Press).

From my point of view, however, the problem is immediate. A recent
exchange of e-mails with our Social Science IRB was enlightening in that it
reactivated in me a long-standing matter of conscience and alerted me to the
fact that I can no longer proceed with business as usual when it comes to the
presumptions now built into our Institutional Review Board procedures, definitions and required declarations with regard to the responsibilities of University
of Chicago faculty to their students, and with regard to the academic research
and writing enterprise more generally, particularly with respect to non-federally
funded research projects in the social sciences. Thus I am sending you this
e-mail. I would welcome your reactions to the following disclaimer, which I am
contemplating attaching to the next non-federally funded or unfunded student
research IRB application on which my name appears as the signatory P.I.

The disclaimer reads as follows:

This student project has my approval. Given that the University of Chicago
administration has decided to go beyond the requirements of federal law and
insist that all non-federally funded or even unfunded research with human
beings in the social sciences must be reviewed by an I.R.B. and has mandated
the formality of listing a faculty member as the P.I. on student research projects
it should be understood that I am guided in my relationships with my students
and with the University of Chicago administration by certain principles set forth
in the University of Chicago Articles of Incorporation, Bylaws, and Statutes
and in the "Kalven Committee Report." As articulated in those two documents
"The basic policies of the University of Chicago include complete freedom of
research and the unrestricted dissemination of information" and provide a guarantee of "autonomy" to both students and faculty "in the discovery, improvement and dissemination of knowledge." At the very least what emerges from
those principles is a robust presumption in favor of academic freedom and one
that strongly inclines to the view that any general requirement calling for administrative prior review and a system of permit granting for all research is in conflict

with those principles. I approve this student project but do not voluntarily agree to renounce the academic freedom principles mentioned above, if that is what the I.R.B. process is asking me to do.

Why am I contemplating this move at this point? One reason is because last week the Social Science IRB sent me its standard expiration notice, in this instance concerning an unfunded student research project on which my name appears as the principal investigator. My name currently appears as a formality on many student research projects. It appears because the University has for some reason mandated that student researchers (for example those working on a Master's thesis in the Divisional Master's Program or those working on a PhD in a graduate program in the social sciences) cannot submit an application on their own, despite our commitment to student autonomy "in the discovery, improvement and dissemination of knowledge." Typically students ask their main research advisor to play the part of "signatory P.I."; and I advise a fair number of students in the social sciences, on projects that typically involve talking to other human beings or observing behavior in settings to which the researcher has access. Hence when one of those IRB protocols for a student research project expires I receive a notification.

This is what the standard IRB expiration notice in the social sciences states: "IRB approval for your research protocol has expired. Please note that the University requires active IRB approval for all research activities involving human subjects, including participant recruitment, data collection, and analysis/write-up of data containing or linked to identifying information about individuals (including, e.g., interview transcripts, audio/video recordings, laboratory or field notes). Student researchers in the data analysis/write-up phase of thesis research are required to maintain active IRB approval for their research activities for the duration of their affiliation with the University (e.g., through graduation)."

Only a few years ago (certainly as recently as 2005) these IRB expiration notices read like cease and desist orders: "We regret to inform you that IRB approval for your research Protocol has expired. Please note that research related activities (including interaction with human subjects, data collection, and/or data analysis) may not continue or be initiated until the IRB has approved the continuation of this research."

So, although there has been a softening of the rhetoric of these communications, I found myself wondering whether "cease and desist from all activities relating to research and scholarship on this project" continued to be its intended implication. Indeed when I received my latest IRB expiration notice for a non-federally funded student research project I found myself wondering about my responsibilities as a University of Chicago faculty member if the student in question were at that moment to show up in my office and were to ask me to assist her with an ongoing analysis of already collected data. Does the IRB actually expect me to permit them to intrude into the faculty-student relationship and the educational agendas of our university and bring conversation about research to a halt? I wondered: would they really expect me to cease and desist from doing the kinds of things I do by virtue of being a member of a great intellectual community dedicated to academic freedom?

So I wrote back to the Social Science IRB with this request: "I hereby request an official response to the following question: Is it the view of the IRB that if the student in question requests an appointment with me to discuss the analysis of their research data or wishes to show me a version of their write up for comment that it is my responsibility as a faculty member at the University of Chicago to refuse to speak to them?"

After several e-mails involving two different IRB representatives it now seems clear that ceasing and desisting from all research related work (including data analysis, conversations about the research project and writing) is precisely what the IRB has in mind. It was even suggested to me that if I don't like that state of play I should stop being the signatory P.I. on student research projects and let some other members of the faculty put their name on the student's IRB application.

I hope you can see the problems with this suggestion, which might well lead to an invidious distinction in the minds of social science students between those faculty members who are willing to have their names placed on student IRB applications and those who are not. Given the current state of play and the compromises of academic freedom involved I am not entirely sure which category of faculty would be viewed as the more principled investigators by our students.

I was also reminded by the representatives of our IRB that there are other things I have agreed to do by honoring the University authored requirement that even non-federally funded student research projects must have a faculty member as signatory P.I.

Some of these are things that many of the faculty in the social sciences (for example those who have advisees who conduct research alone in field settings at remote locations) cannot possibly do and certainly ought to know they cannot possibly do when they agree to have their name on the IRB application. For example, "I will obtain informed consent from all subjects unless a waiver or alteration of the informed consent process was approved by the IRB." With regard to this type of assumed responsibility the mandated signatory process is a mere charade. How can a faculty adviser know whether a student researcher in the field has actually followed the exact consent procedures approved by the IRB? I would wager that many ethically sensitive student field researchers in anthropology and sociology do things on the fly in a dynamic field context where they might well justifiably deviate from those formally approved consent procedures using their ethical common-sense; and I will wager they rarely report these deviations to the signatory faculty P.I. unless some problem arises. Basically the faculty member is being asked to make promises that everyone knows can't be kept.

Or, to cite another example, "I will gain IRB approval before altering the research protocol, recruitment materials, or consent forms." I hope you can see the problem here, given that much research in the social sciences is a matter of formulating questions while the research is underway and of discovering the correct or the most useful questions to ask. To faithfully and literally honor that "agreement" (mandating IRB approval before any new questions can be asked of the human beings with whom one is interacting) is to kill academic freedom, or at the very least stifle the very process of research for many social scientists.

Indeed when it comes to most research in the social sciences and humanities (and even some research in medicine) I hope you can see the problem with the current system, which seems to unnecessarily universalize a set of procedures, definitions and rules mandated by the federal agencies for application specifically to federally funded projects and which were instituted with certain forms of biomedical research in mind. Short of an actual finding of serious wrongdoing the very idea of an IRB presuming to tell faculty to stop speaking to students about data they already have in hand and telling them to cease and desist from writing about it ought to startle us into action about the regulatory regime we have brought upon ourselves by allowing the federal IRB regulations to penetrate the entire university.

The good news is that legally we are at liberty to reform the way we go about maintaining ethical research standards in the social sciences and we can certainly do so with an eye on our cherished tradition of academic freedom.

Zachary Schrag's book on the history of IRB regulation and its implications for social science research is not the only critical account of the current regulatory regime. And over the next several years a number of legal scholars and social scientists are sure to raise our consciousness about the collective failure on the part of those of us in the academy who say we cherish academic freedom yet were insufficiently vigilant in its defense when faced with federal guidelines and regulations concerning federally funded research in the biomedical sciences. But surely (given our history at the University of Chicago) if there is any academic institution in the country that one might expect to take the lead in reforming the system it is our own.

Reform in the social sciences is feasible; it is not an impossible dream. Approximately 80% of research projects in the Division of the Social Sciences are not federally funded (and many of those are entirely unfunded). The current University of Chicago system for ethical standards maintenance that is being applied to those non-federally funded projects (prior review and research permission granting by an Institutional Review Board for all research projects involving interactions with human beings regardless of funding source and regardless of research method or topic) mirrors a federal model for the review of federally funded research projects but is NOT mandated by federal laws or regulations for non-federally funded projects and is thus legally capable of being reformed by us in the light of our own traditions. With respect to the vast majority of research projects in the social sciences and humanities involving interactions with human beings the current system of regulations, definitions and mandated procedures and declarations is the product of local decision making and not something attached as a string to federal research funding or required by Washington. It is something we can change.

This is a long e-mail and I know all three of you are very busy. If you have read this far I am grateful for your attention. I have attached to this e-mail an essay I published in the American Ethnologist a few years ago titled "Protecting Human Subjects and Preserving Academic Freedom: Prospects at the University of Chicago." At the time I was hopeful that the University of Chicago might take the process of reform to a new level. This did not come to pass, despite some initial steps in that direction. (Over the years I have become aware of how easy it is to be risk averse; or to become habituated to regulatory regimes, even those that offend core academic values, if they can be made to run efficiently; and it is tempting to not be different and to just stay in the mainstream and keep a low profile; although these are not the qualities that historically have made us great).

CONCLUSION: DEATH BY
A THOUSAND CUTS?

Deep and difficult questions about the foundations of free inquiry must certainly be raised and debated in any conversation about the nature and purpose of academic freedom. Such questions as to whether academic freedom is a "natural right" (having its source in some transcendental good or in something you ought to desire because it is inherently good) or a "constitutional right" (having its source in some kind of penumbra or extension of the First Amendment of the U.S. Constitution, an amendment that never mentions academic freedom per se and facially applies only to acts of Congress abridging freedom of speech or the press) or a "positive right" (having its source in the legal instruments that incorporate and empower an institution to be an authentic academic institution and hence faithful to the mission of a genuine university or center of higher learning).

Of course, the different aspects of the way of life associated with the free university may have multiple or different sources. When a wealthy patron or member of the board of trustees of a private university instructs the president of that institution to make sure that a controversial or politically annoying junior faculty member is not retained on the faculty, the First Amendment protections of the U.S. Constitution are not going to be very helpful in defense of academic freedom. The relevance of that famous free speech amendment is far greater (and presumably would be decisive) if Congress itself ever passed a law requiring social science faculty members at private universities to submit their course readings and research proposals for content review by a committee of the Congress or to answer questions about the content of their lectures (as in the case of *Sweezy v. New Hampshire* discussed earlier). But one feels less sure what would happen in a court of law if that hypothesized federal statute simply conditioned the receipt of sought-after federal research funds on such a review but never required researchers at private universities to apply for those funds. Is there a constitutional protection against that type of indirect government coercion, or not?

Nevertheless, the fact that such questions about the justification and basis for academic freedom even get raised may just be one more sign of the times. It does not help matters that many of us find ourselves to be surprisingly inarticulate and at a bit of a loss trying to answer the question "What is academic freedom for?" It is noteworthy that the best and most readily persuasive defense that comes to mind when academics converse with politicians, benefactors, and the general public is some kind of instrumental appeal (precisely of the sort Edward Levi candidly set to the side, as discussed previously) to the collective material benefits (whether in the areas of technology, health, economics, or energy) that derive from discoveries and inventions originating within the walls of the academy. Demonstrating that the unintended social benefits of academic freedom at institutions of higher learning are great and far outweigh the costs to society is a great achievement (and here I hail Jonathan R. Cole for his magisterial book on that topic titled *The Great American University*).[39] I view such a showing, however, as a functional or practical account of the (for the most part) unintended (even if beneficial) consequences of the establishment of free universities and not necessarily as an account (or at least not a complete account) of what academic freedom is for. Aren't we able to say more about the telos of academic freedom and our intellectual motives as scholars? Might it not be true that those social benefits accrue largely because they are unintended and that the more they are intended or become part of our mission statement the less likely they are to actually accrue?

One of my favorite lines from a speech by a University of Chicago official is the one delivered by the chairman of our board of trustees on the occasion of our 100th anniversary in 1992. He too quoted our former president Robert Maynard Hutchins, who stated, "The faculty is not working for the trustees; the trustees are working for the faculty."

It is an observation that deserves to be true of any genuine institution of higher learning. The basic idea expressed by those words may seem counterintuitive to anyone who imagines that universities are (or ought to be) like other corporations, but it helps define the conditions that make for greatness in the academy (and, indirectly, as Felix Frankfurter imagined, for a vibrant and healthy society). Here is another way to make the point (quoting the philosopher Arthur Lovejoy, who helped found the AAUP): "The distinctive social function of the scholar's trade cannot be fulfilled if those who pay the piper are permitted to call the tune."[40] (And one would like to add: the scholar's trade also cannot be fulfilled if the piper creates and fashions his or her tune primarily with an eye on satisfying the tastes of those who pay him or her.) It is a splendid, and of course I realize it is a wishful, vision: the luminous image of enlightened patrons—merchants, investment bankers, politicians, trustees—who understand the virtue of free and unfettered inquiry, and who believe it is wise and dignifying to resist the natural temptation to try to use one's wealth and power to "call the tune." A few years ago I delivered the convocation address at the 480th convocation at the University of Chicago. It was a winter convocation, which happened to be packed with students from our business school campuses. I advised them: if you ever become very rich or very powerful, strive for that type of wisdom—and nobility.[41]

I hope it is not too much of an indulgence if I conclude this essay with a bit of a local conceit. Let me end by asking the reader (as I asked the students in that convocation address) if you remember the "fun index." It was a ranking of 300 American colleges and universities put together by some clever and mischievous Harvard students over twenty years ago. It got lots of publicity in the mainstream press. The University of Chicago was ranked 300 out of 300, just behind the U.S. Military Academy. Russell Baker, the *New York Times* humorist, immediately responded in an op-ed essay. He complained that his alma mater, Johns Hopkins University, which was ranked 296 on the fun index, should not have been outdone by Chicago. Yale University was ranked in the bottom ten. Florida State University had the distinction of being number 1.

That playful and prankish fun index—confirming the view that the University of Chicago just cannot compete in the same league with the fraternity parties and nightclubs at FSU—managed to make administrators at many colleges around the country, and even in Hyde Park, a bit nervous about public perceptions of their institutions and of course about their *U.S. News & World Report* ranking. So in recent years we have invested heavily in the life of the body as well as the life of the mind. We have a new swimming pool and a new award-winning dining hall. We have some new dormitories and a new Center for the Performing Arts. We have enlarged the Medical School complex. We have a new Business School campus right across the street from Rockefeller Chapel, which quite fortunately achieves part of its splendor by remaining in the shadow of Rockefeller Chapel rather than overshadowing it (as some had feared). And what was formerly a theological institute and the greatest academic bookstore in the United States (a symbol of the intellectual seriousness of the University of Chicago and a major civilizing site on campus) has now been renovated, expanded, spiffed up and re-consecrated as the "Becker Friedman Institute for Research in Economics." And by now the University of Chicago may even have nudged a bit ahead of Hopkins and United States Military Academy in providing those satisfactions in life that are abundant and readily available at FSU. Perhaps we are now 287 or even 252 on the going to college to have fun index, the type of fun they have at FSU.

It is possible I am just foolish to think it was actually an honor to have been placed at the very bottom of the fun index. Yet I do like to imagine that our real claim to fame at academic centers such as Columbia University and the University of Chicago is that we are mavericks, free-wheeling, tough minded, intellectually annoying, against the current, out there on the fringe, sometimes even a little beyond the pale (some of us even had our ancestral origins inside the Pale), and a bit perverse. I would like to believe *that* is what academic freedom is really for. Its teleology, its objective and worthy end in life, and its claim to fame is to make it possible for the creative imagination, critical reason, and the rational will to have some special place to play. Its purpose is to maintain and protect an intellectual environment in which it is always possible "to follow the argument where it leads." It will be a great irony in the history of the great American university if the boundaries between church, state, Madison Avenue, the marketplace, and the academy become so blurred (and the interest groups associated with political, moral, and commercial activism so influential) that instead of welcoming him to the academy (and giving him exile there) it is within the halls of the academy that Socrates suffers a death by a thousand cuts: without open debate, without even a trial, and most likely without a formal vote by any faculty ruling body. One contemplates the dawn of the great American university with a smile even as one has premonitions of the twilight of a great antiquarian tradition.

NOTES

1. Without implicating them in the judgments expressed in this statement about academic freedom I wish to thank several friends and colleagues (including some who are protagonists in the essay) for their generous, incisive and helpfully critical comments on an earlier draft of the manuscript, especially Jonathan R. Cole, Arthur Eisenberg, Hanna Gray, Benjamin Heineman Jr., Ralph Lerner, Steve Raudenbush, Geoffrey Stone, Richard Taub, and Robert Zimmer.
2. Sweezy v. New Hampshire, 354 U.S. 234 (1957).
3. The hazards and benefits of trying to separate inquiry and teaching at academically free universities has recently become a topic of intense debate at the University of Chicago, where with the aim of protecting academic freedom, the president, provost, and all the deans of the university have argued that faculty ruling bodies have jurisdiction and decision-making powers (a vote) only over the educational and teaching activities of the university but not over its research activities (including decisions about the creation of research centers and research institutes or the development of new directions of inquiry). I will discuss and try to interpret this apparent irony later in this essay.

4. Alexander M. Bickel, *The Morality of Consent* (New Haven, Conn.: Yale University Press, 1975), 127.

5. In recent decades many leading institutions of higher learning have in fact taken up such projects. One looks forward to reading dispassionate assessments of the effects of an institutional commitment to social problem solving (and to the ideological, political, and moral assumptions so entailed) on academic freedom as defined by Frankfurter and Bickel. This institutional commitment to social problem solving is exemplified, e.g., by the development of various kinds of identity politics programs and centers, by the creation at my own university of neighborhood charter schools with the aim and hope of discovering generalizable educational methods to eliminate racial and ethnic disparities in educational achievement, and, of course, by affirmative action policies. Concerns about "political correctness" and the chilling effect of accusations of sexism, racism, homophobia, and anti-Semitism on the ardor and fearlessness of scholars arise in the wake of these developments. In taking up such projects the university is far from neutral and commits itself via the programs its creates and policies it pursues to a particular ideological, political, or moral stance that is rarely questioned or treated as a topic for academic debate, in part because the type of social problem solving undertaken accords with the ideological, political, or moral views of a majority of members of the academic community or members of the board of trustees. All too frequently the result is a "big chill" or reduction in the public expression of viewpoint diversity for fear of stigmatization. In such an academic environment there is a premium on silence or acquiescence for members of the community who hold unpopular views.

6. Bickel, *The Morality of Consent*, 129.

7. Of course it is not just morally motivated student activists who want to enlist universities to solve social problems or further their own nonacademic ends (whether political, moral, or commercial). Threats to the academic freedom ideals described by Alexander Bickel can be even more serious and insidious when they come in the form of a Trojan horse of generous gifts or grants from patrons, board of trustee members, foundations, funding agencies, corporations, or even foreign governments. A gift becomes a Trojan horse–like threat to academic freedom when it does more than just enable ongoing academic inquiry but rather shifts the balance of influence among faculties or faculty members and shapes the character and direction of the questions asked at a university or the types of appointments that get made. This becomes especially serious when decision making about the character and shape of faculty appointments moves more and more into the hands of administrators who might be tempted to follow the money (rather than the argument) where it leads and can usually find some member of the faculty who is already on that path or is willing to go along for the ride and the possible benefit.

8. Sweezy v. New Hampshire, 354 U.S. 234 (1957).

9. For a discussion of the judicial restraint exercised by the liberal judges see Harry Kalven Jr., *A Worthy Tradition: Freedom of Speech in America* (New York: Harper & Row, 1988), 494–95. For further clarification of the narrowness of the decision and the problems with the procedural approach of the four liberal judges who, unlike Justices Frankfurter and Harlan, decided not to base their judgment on First Amendment

grounds, see the dissenting opinion in the case written by Justice Clark (with support from Justice Burton).

10. One is tempted to interpret "other sectional interests" to include commercial interests or the inducements associated with gifts and financial contributions from patrons and donors, at least to the extent that such interests and inducements are permitted to significantly influence the argument and where it leads.

11. And they might even exercise those liberties more effectively by actually debating and bringing evidence to bear on the court's ready assumption that affirmative action policies at institutions of higher learning truly serve the worthy and prized academic goal of increasing "viewpoint diversity." Surely that assumption is and should be open to skeptical challenges, and a debate on the topic is long overdue on college campuses. Although affirmative action is intuitively appealing to many advocates of social justice on grounds relating to various forms of group discrimination, the Supreme Court long ago rejected the argument that affirmative action can be constitutionally justified on the grounds of a history of social injustice toward racial or ethnic groups (e.g., the historical enslavement of the ancestors of contemporary African Americans). In the most pertinent judicial decision concerning legitimate versus illegitimate justifications for affirmative action policies, namely Regents of the University of California v. Bakke, 438 U.S. 265 (1978), the court did however leave open the door for a narrow justification in terms of maintaining a robust free thought environment at institutions of higher learning via admission policies that took race and ethnicity into account (as one among several other factors) so as to increase viewpoint diversity on college campuses. It may be a sign of the times that the actual empirical connection between viewpoint diversity and admission policies favoring particular ethnic and racial groups is not well documented or self-evident and the effects of those policies on the robustness of the free thought environment at universities is asserted far more often than it is scrutinized or even critically discussed. One must at least entertain and engage the alternative viewpoint or argument that on college campuses viewpoint diversity is in fact neither the real aim nor the actual outcome of affirmative action policies; and that the ready equation of racial and ethnic diversity with viewpoint diversity is little more than a politically convenient fiction and a legal loophole that has permitted institutions of higher learning to embrace affirmative action as part of a morally motivated social justice agenda aimed at correcting historical group injustices. Protecting the ardor and fearlessness of faculty and student scholars has not been an item on that social justice agenda. That alternative viewpoint on affirmative action policies suggests that one undesirable effect of those social justice policies has been to relax the demands of critical reason, reduce the expression of viewpoint diversity and eschew any real debate over the positive or negative effects of such policies on the expansive freedoms of speech and thought of the university environment. That argument invites us to consider the damage done to a free thought environment by the heightening of sensitivity to, and the greater sanctioning of, speech experienced as offensive or potentially disturbing to various interest groups on campus; by the damage done by self-censuring due to norms of political correctness that inhibit the expression of

challenges to received wisdom; and by any balkanization of groups that limits dialogue or debate and results in conversations primarily with those who already share your own ideological or identity politics viewpoint.

12. I would define a neo-antiquarian as someone who is prepared to see value in the past and to accept that history and change do not necessarily bring us closer to the Age of Truth, Beauty, and Goodness.

13. This invocation of a contrast between two discourses (of the dawn and of the twilight) is not meant to suggest that from an historical point of view the early days of the great American university (even at the University of Chicago) were always rosy with respect to the academic freedom ideals discussed in this essay. It is the resolve, promise, and sense of purpose associated with the articulation of those ideals by those of our academic ancestors who tried to bring those ideals to life that is connoted by the rhetorical contrast.

14. The University of Chicago originally opened as an institution of higher learning in 1892. The university holds several convocations each academic year, timed to its academic calendar's quarter system.

15. That conference was a launching point for this volume of essays.

16. See Robert Zimmer's essay in this volume.

17. On the history of academic freedom at the University of Chicago, see John Boyer, *Academic Freedom and the Modern University: The Experience of the University of Chicago*, Occasional Papers on Higher Education, X (Chicago: College of the University of Chicago, 2002). For a recent University of Chicago policy statement concerning free expression see Geoffrey Stone, "Statement on Principles of Free Expression," University of Chicago, www.uchicago.edu/about/statement_on_principles_of_free_expression.

18. It is, of course, one thing to (Madison Avenue–like) market oneself as a free and intellectually playful academic environment and quite another for any university to live up to that ideal. It might be instructive to survey the way the public relations/university news outlets of leading universities publicize the kinds of research and public policy ideas that circulate on campus. To what extent do they play safe and tend to avoid drawing attention to work that is against the current, provocative, or upsetting to the general public or to their own alumni?

19. It is ironic that this straightforward declaration of academic freedom is part of the preamble to a statute on patent policy, but it is the type of discourse one finds in several other official university documents. As noted previously (note 13) and for the sake of emphasis, in speaking of a discourse from out of the dawn of the great American university I do not mean to suggest that in yesteryears the University of Chicago always lived up to its ideals or was always a paragon of the academic virtues associated with a contentious free thought environment. Nevertheless, those who articulated those ideals offer us a particular kind of quest and invite us to have a particular kind of resolve, one that is defined by those virtues and stubbornly resistant to the discourse of the twilight.

20. The most recent variation of this official institutional review board communication, reminding faculty and students that from the point of view of the university administration faculty and students are not free to engage in inquiry involving the study of

human beings until they are given permission to do so by an administrative review board, reads as follows: "IRB Approval for the above-referenced submission will expire on [such and such date] . . . Please note that the University requires active IRB approval for all research activities involving human subjects, including participant recruitment, data collection, and analysis/write-up of data containing or linked to identifying information about individuals (including, e.g., interview transcripts, audio/video recordings, laboratory or field notes)."

21. Frankfurter's and Bickel's conceptions of academic freedom implied the desirability of a separation of things that might be separated from other things—inside from outside, scholarship from politics, perhaps even the ardor and fearlessness of those who follow the argument where it leads from the ardor of those within the university who have more practical concerns such as fund-raising or public relations or saving the world. Hence Frankfurter disallowed and Bickel disparaged external interference with the internal affairs of the university or the subordination of Socratic reasoning to either the ends of some moral crusade or the desires of those who are wealthy or politically powerful. They believed in the maintenance of boundaries between the professional duties and responsibilities of a genuine academic and the interests of that same person when he or she assumes the posture of a social activist or a concerned citizen. Presumably they would argue that members of the board of trustees of a free university have the same professional responsibility—to separate their role as trustee and guardian of an academic institutional tradition from their interests as social activists or concerned citizens or as nonacademic professionals in business, law, medicine, show business, or journalism. Although the particulars of trustee involvement in the affairs of the university are not always visible to members of the faculty, the University of Chicago appears to have been historically blessed by having many trustees who embraced that responsibility and worked in defense of the antiquarian view of the aim of academic freedom that is the theme of this essay. Nevertheless, the blurring of the boundaries between the world of the academy and the worlds of commerce, politics, celebrity, moral reform (typically in the form of social justice advocacy in the areas of race, gender, sexual orientation, and social class), local community or neighborhood development, and public relations is increasingly a fact of life at institutions of higher learning in the United States. Not everyone in the academy views the blurring of boundaries or the penetration of the academy by nonacademic interests as the twilight of the great American university or is prepared, even in their role as academics, to place academic freedom above other competing values, such as collective social responsibility or the promotion of educational, occupational, health, or income equality.

22. Available at this website (click on Appointment and Promotion Criteria [Shil's Report]: http://facultyhandbook.uchicago.edu/page/academic-appointments).

23. Edward H. Levi, "The University and the Modern Condition," in *Point of View: Talks on Education* (Chicago: University of Chicago Press, 2007).

24. A biographical memoir of the life and work of Edward Levi, written by Hanna H. Gray, can be found in the *Proceedings of the American Philosophical Society* 146, no. 3 (September 2002): 298–302.

25. Stephen W. Raudenbush, "The 511th Convocation Address: 'The Life of the Mind and Social Action,'" *UChicago News*, June 13, 2012, http://news.uchicago.edu/article/2012/06/13/511th-convocation-address-039the-life-mind-and-social-action039.

26. In the late nineteenth century, John Dewey, the famous philosopher and educational reformer, created the University of Chicago Laboratory School as a private university-run experiment in precollegiate education with potential implications for the design of public school education. John Dewey's time as a faculty member at the University of Chicago was quite brief. The institution he created remains today. It is a university-owned preschool through high school private school that is an attractive benefit for faculty and staff who have children but also has a large student applicant pool that extends beyond the university community. It is essentially a private pre-collegiate educational institution, one long freed of any official mission, if it ever truly had one, concerning public school reform in the city of Chicago, and it does not typically function as an experimental educational laboratory. Still, it would appear to be a fine topic for debate, whether the University of Chicago's official relationship during the early days of the Laboratory School to John Dewey's personal agenda for social action and reform was compatible with Edward Levi's conception of the mission of the university as intellectual not moral; and whether that official relationship (to the extent it ever existed and implied a University of Chicago endorsement of Dewey's visions of public educational progress and the character of democratic citizenship) can be squared with the spirit of institutional neutrality (to be discussed later) that has been at the heart of the University of Chicago's conception of academic freedom for many decades.

27. The text of the Kalven committee report can be found at: www-news.uchicago.edu/releases/07/pdf/kalverpt.pdf.

28. I told this story in a 1993 Aims of Education address titled "Fundamentalism for Highbrows," which was later published in a collection of essays. R. A. Shweder, *Why Do Men Barbecue?: Recipes for Cultural Psychology* (Cambridge, Mass.: Harvard University Press, 2003). Some of my thoughts about antiquarian conceptions of academic freedom at the University of Chicago are expressed in that speech and reiterated and expanded here in this essay.

29. A relevant case in point is the recent national uproar, negative publicity, and local institutional angst created by an off-the-cuff comment made by a tenured member of the University of Chicago faculty on his Facebook page in which he asked, based on his own reported personal observations, why physical attractiveness seemed to be in such short supply among female scientists at a large neuroscience meeting he was attending. This was a topic (physical attractiveness) about which he had previously written, engaging in Darwinian speculations. Physical attractiveness is a judgment about a perceived sensory quality (and a potentially beneficial interpersonal capacity for those able to elicit the judgment) that some Darwinians think is positively related to success in life (reproductive and otherwise); and the study of what makes for physical attractiveness, its functions and social benefits, has been a provocative (and popular) topic for research in the not always beautiful survival-of-the-fittest ideological world of evolutionary psychologists and among journalists who are themselves

attracted to Darwinian speculations. Whether one likes it or not, it is not hard to imagine a research program in evolutionary psychology designed to systematically document the distribution of physical attractiveness (in women and/or men) across social classes and occupations and across the various disciplines within the academy, posing the questions, for example, whether women in the humanities and social sciences faculties are more attractive than women in the physical and biological science faculties, and if so, why. At the same time this is a moment in the history of the academy when leading universities are keen to recruit and retain talented and academically accomplished women into the biological and physical sciences; and (for moral, legal, and reputational reasons) universities are highly alert to and sensitive about accusations of gender discrimination, sexual harassment, or intransigence in providing a supportive and welcoming work environment for women. That comment, a few lines written by a University of Chicago tenured professor reporting (and posing a why question) to his Facebook "friends" about what he perceived to be the relative absence of physical beauty among women who study the brain, was leaked and went viral on the Internet (which quickly took the form of an international cyber-stocks for transgressors). Almost instantly his comment was judged to be insensitive, stupid, impolitic, glib, puerile, egocentric, arrogant, snide, condescending, mean-spirited, callous, obnoxious, insulting, offensive, or infuriating by many of his colleagues, both men and women, locally and nationally. Some responders just dismissed him as a jerk. Other responders rushed to a dark and vilifying conclusion and labeled him with the epithet "sexist." Still others indignantly interpreted his observation as a sign that his only interest in his female colleagues at the conference (and women more generally, including his students) was as potential sex objects. The local uproar and national brouhaha unleashed by his Facebook entry was a perfect storm of disgust and outrage. The response included various types of calls for his resignation, censure, sanction, punishment, or removal from any leadership role in visible departmental activities. It is relevant in this discussion of the aim of academic freedom that the evolutionary psychologist's Facebook comment to his "friends" was not widely judged to be an example of the ardor and fearlessness of a research scholar: to follow a Darwinian argument where it leads regardless of the practical, moral, or political consequences or to challenge received pieties and make observations (or hypothesize the existence of facts) that might be embarrassing or even infuriating to some. Those who responded most forcefully did not do so in a spirit of the sort recommended by Geoffrey Stone in his explication of the implications of the Kalven committee report, one that is supportive of an academic environment in which one can speak freely about the right of Palestinians to destroy Israel or the moral legitimacy of murdering abortionists or the possibility that beauty and brains might not go together among women in the brainiest of the sciences. With a few exceptions his comment was not assessed (critically or otherwise) in terms of its descriptive truth; and most responders steered clear of actually trying to assess the truth or falsity of the (apparently) tabooed (and no doubt insensitive, impolitic, and perhaps deliberately provocative and even mischievously taunting) empirical claim addressed by a University of Chicago researcher to the readers of his supposedly private Facebook page. In some ways the tumultuous response was reminiscent of a far greater furor a few years ago, which precipitated the resignation of Lawrence Summers from the presidency of Harvard University. President Summers agreed to give a talk to what was supposed to be a private free-thinking seminar. He delivered an analysis of what he took to be the most likely explanations for the scarcity of female researchers in the physical sciences at the elite universities in the country. He listed personal preferences first on his list of possible explanations. He suggested that vicious gender discrimination was an overemphasized explanation and probably not the best explanation for the scarcity at the elite universities of the country (where in recent decades there has been a concerted effort to recruit talented and academically accomplished women into the biological and physical sciences). He left open the possibility that the intellectual capacities that were necessary for success in the physical sciences at the top universities were rare, in very short supply, and at the extreme tails of any normal distribution of talents and capacities; and that the frequency of such outliers may not be identical for males and females. This is a notion with a lineage that goes back to Darwin; and it is not unusual to hear Darwinians suggest that normally distributed characteristics typically show greater variance for men than for women, which implies that extreme or rare qualities (both good ones and bad ones) tend to be more likely in men than in women. In essence Lawrence Summers, the president of Harvard University and himself a somewhat assertive and impolitic member of both the faculty and the administration of that great university, was willing to entertain the possibility that most human beings (nearly all of them, men and women) are not capable of thinking the way top-level physical scientists think but that at the extreme tails of the distribution of the requisite rare qualities of mind that make for success in the physical sciences those qualities might be more prevalent among men than women. The rest is history. One or more of the participants in the seminar judged his comments to be ideologically and morally toxic for the cause of gender equality in the academy and leaked them to the press. Moral judgments and social agendas overwhelmed any academic debate. President Summers was forced to resign. Perhaps this is a special case: Lawrence Summers seemed to think that at the drop of a hat he could take off his president's cap and speak simply as a provocative or contentious member of the Harvard faculty, which may have been a naive and hazardous assumption; and while his seminar presentation on the gender gap in the physical sciences may have been the most salient and recent event leading to his resignation, discontent with his presidential interventions and with a confrontational interpersonal style that some experienced as a form of disrespect had been brewing for some time. Nevertheless, given the current dynamics of identity politics at universities in the United States, those who value academic institutions as assumption-questioning and provocative Socratic institutions and cherish them as homes for debates about controversial topics (conducted by fearless untenured junior faculty as well as tenured senior faculty) need to ask: What should the principles of academic freedom as expressed in the Kalven committee report require of the behavior (onstage and offstage) of administrators up and down the administrative hierarchy in instances such as the two I just described? How staunch and consistent can we count on our administrative leaders being in defense of academic freedom and the expressive liberties of research scholars (even research scholars who are irritating, snide, insensitive, or impolitic) when the going gets tough and unpopular for the institution and the offending or offensive scholar becomes a target of ridicule, disparagement, and calls for penalties in the context of hot-button political, moral, or ideological issues?

30. For critical discussions of what has been called regulatory "mission creep" on college campuses and the implications of the ethical review process at American universities for academic freedom, see Robert Digwall, "How Did We Ever Get Into This Mess?: The Rise of Ethical Regulation in the Social Sciences," in *Ethics in Social Research*, ed. Kevin Love, Studies in Qualitative Methodology, vol. 12 (Bradford: Emerald Group Publishing Limited, 2012); Philip Hamburger, "The New Censorship: Institutional Review Boards," *Supreme Court Review* 271 (2004); Zachary Schrag, *Ethical Imperialism: Institutional Review Boards and the Social Sciences, 1965–2009* (Baltimore: Johns Hopkins University Press, 2010); Richard A. Shweder, "Protecting Human Subjects and Preserving Academic Freedom: Prospects at the University of Chicago," *American Ethnologist* 33 (2006): 507–518; also the collection of essays in the "Symposium on Censorship and Institutional Review Boards" published in the *Northwestern University Law Review* 101, no. 2 (2007); the University of Illinois Center for Advanced Study white paper "Improving the System for Protecting Human Subjects: Counteracting IRB 'Mission Creep,'" www.law.uiuc.edu/conferences/whitepaper; and recent reports issued by the AAUP available online: e.g., Research on Human Subjects: Academic Freedom and the Institutional Review Board, June 25, 2005, www.aaup.org/AAUP/comm/rep/A/humansubs.htm; and www.aaup.org/AAUP/newsroom/2012PRs/irb.htm.

31. While the recent debates about faculty governance have been lively and intense among those involved, I am struck by the number of my colleagues who are entirely unaware of the administration's stance. Despite the fact that every regular faculty member received an e-mail with a link to the reports described in the text, it is astonishing how many faculty members do not realize these documents even exist. In earlier decades the minutes of the Council of the University Senate were distributed in hard copy. I believe they were read, or at least scanned for significant issues and discussions, by many of my colleagues. The advent of electronic means of distribution may have had the ironic effect of reducing the size of the faculty audience who are true readers of the minutes of council meetings. The implications of this type of disengagement for faculty governance should not be underestimated. I much preferred the old hard-copy system, and not just because I am a neo-antiquarian.

32. Historically, political pluralism has been a customary feature of governance at the University of Chicago, although the famous (or infamous) Robert Maynard Hutchins himself was frustrated by the norms of divided authority and precipitated a crisis of governance when he tried to centralize authority over educational policy and appointments in the hands of the president of the university. The current bylaws and formalized statutes of the University of Chicago are a by-product of that crisis. Perhaps the custom of political pluralism was based on the notion that a robust environment of

academic freedom is strengthened by a division of powers, the existence of multiple sovereignties, and a loose and sometimes even baffling federal system of decision making with a fair amount of decentralized authority and enumerated and un-enumerated powers that need to be negotiated over time. As noted earlier the appointment of a second faculty committee to address questions of faculty governance was motivated in part by the president's concern that the interests of local faculty ruling bodies (vis-à-vis the more centralized faculty Council of the University Senate) be appropriately represented. In practice, however, the issues are even more complex. According to the statutes the only local faculty ruling body in my own graduate region of the university is the Division of the Social Sciences, whose head is the dean of the social sciences, a faculty member who serves in the capacity of an administrator and is appointed by the central administration (after receiving recommendations from an elected faculty nominating committee). Yet that local ruling body—the faculty members in the Division of the Social Sciences—almost never meets; and over the past four decades I can recall only two occasions in which the members of that ruling body have had an issue placed before them for a vote (in both cases a vote to dissolve an academic department). Some matters of local concern such as hiring or promoting faculty members are made at the level of departments (which are not recognized as official ruling bodies in the university statutes) and sent directly to the dean of the social sciences and then on to the provost and board of trustees, while other matters of local concern, such as leave policy or the creation of a research center headed by some member of the faculty, seem to be decided largely by decisions made by the dean in consultation with the chairs of departments or individual faculty. With regard to the question of who controls the research agenda of the university and the creation of research centers and institutes, it thus seems to be an open question whether the structure of decentralized authority at the University of Chicago genuinely favors faculty governance at the local level or tilts instead in the direction of decision making by local administrators, namely deans. Some may argue that seen from this perspective it is not so surprising that all of the deans at the University of Chicago argue that the "educational work" of the university does not include decision making about research directions. In practice this kind of political pluralism can only really work if there is a sense of trust and a good deal of respectful deference between administrators and faculty, running in all directions.

33. In the air, as well, were controversial administrative initiatives of other sorts, in fashionable and applied areas of research and international outreach.

34. The meanings and uses of the distinction between gemeinschaft and gesellschaft in the social sciences literature are complex, but it is used here to connote the distinction between relationships grounded in a sense of duty and obligation to an historical ethical community or collective of some sort (a tribe, a caste, a family, a nation) and relationships based entirely on maximizing one's contemporary self-interest, the sacred/moral/sacrificial/visceral versus the profane/instrumental/hedonistic/calculated.

35. It is certainly possible I was naive or that it is utopian to imagine that viewpoint diversity is sustainable at institutions of higher learning and can be protected from subordination to politics or ideology.

36. Here too the jury is out. In general does the proliferation of research institutes and research centers strengthen or weaken the free thought and disputatious speech environment of our great universities? It would be helpful to know the answer to that question.

37. I say "perceived violations" because the instigation for the regulations was the four-decades-long Public Health Service research project investigating the natural course of untreated syphilis infections among already long-infected and noncontagious African American men in Macon County, Alabama, which was done in collaboration with African American doctors and researchers at Booker T. Washington's Tuskegee Institute and was reviewed and approved many times by panels of experts. For a detailed examination of the Tuskegee syphilis study and a critical discussion of the moral horror narrative that motivated the act of Congress creating the IRB regulatory system, see Richard A. Shweder, "Tuskegee Re-examined," published in the online magazine *Spiked*, January 8, 2004, www.spiked-online.com/newsite/article/14972#.U34LZNJdX7Q. My current discussion of the IRB regulations and their application at the University of Chicago reproduces several points from my essay "Protecting Human Subjects and Preserving Academic Freedom: Prospects at the University of Chicago" (see note 30).

38. Instructive in this regard is the University of Chicago convocation address (the 482nd) delivered in the summer of 2005 by Jonathan Moss, the chair at that time of the IRB in the biological sciences and the medical school. On other occasions, speaking in its defense, Dr. Moss sometimes voiced a very pragmatic view of the public relations and reputational advantages of the IRB process of research permission granting, e.g., its usefulness for subject recruitment in drug trial research. The nature and degree of his attachment to the value of academic freedom is expressed in one of his writings as follows: "Private universities are largely corporations. The respect for academic freedom within these corporations is desirable, but not indispensable" (see J. Moss, "If Institutional Review Boards Were Declared Unconstitutional, They Would Have to Be Reinvented," *Northwestern Law Review* 101 [2007]: 801–7). Nevertheless, he remarked as follows in his convocation address: "I have a growing concern about the barriers these regulations impose on new ideas—barriers that can be so daunting as to discourage innovation. As Institutional Review Board chair, I have seen many of our own young investigators drift away from clinical research because of these challenges. My experience is with medical research, but I suspect the problem of maintaining innovation in an increasingly regulated environment may well be a more general one." To read his convocation address, see Jonathan Moss, "The 482nd Convocation: Could Morton Do It Today?," *University of Chicago Record*, January 5, 2006, https://record.uchicago.edu/sites/reports.uchicago.edu/files/uploads/pdfs/40-2.pdf.

39. Jonathan R. Cole, *The Great American University: Its Rise to Preeminence, Its Indispensable National Role, Why It Must Be Protected* (New York: Public Affairs, 2012).

40. Arthur Lovejoy, "Professional Association or Trade Union?" *AAUP Bulletin* 24 (1938): 409, 414.

41. "The Fun Index" was a convocation speech delivered during the University of Chicago winter convocation on March 18, 2005. My concluding remarks here recapitulate some of the conclusions from that speech.

11

WHAT IS ACADEMIC
FREEDOM FOR?

ROBERT J. ZIMMER

A CADEMIC FREEDOM IS often taken as an unexamined given on university campuses and is often viewed from outside the academy with some bafflement. Both of these situations should be a cause of concern. Properly understood, academic freedom is of enormous importance to our society and to the well-being of our academic institutions, and it is central to the contributions universities can make. The threats to academic freedom come from both outside and within the academy. An examination of academic freedom, its meaning and purpose, can increase understanding outside the academy and also clarify its meaning within the academy, providing us all with better understanding for informed action.

Academic freedom is a complex subject with many aspects and a rich history. Focusing on the question "What is academic freedom for?" can help move us beyond the views of academic freedom as a near theological principle on one hand or as a peculiar entitlement for a privileged few on the other.

My own university, the University of Chicago, has been a significant player in the history and present-day issues of this subject, at least in part because of the particular role Chicago has played in the history of higher education in the United States. My remarks will use some examples from our experience in an effort to illuminate some of the issues.

Academic freedom is a particular feature of universities and colleges, and so a discussion of the purpose and value of academic freedom of necessity begins with the purpose and value of universities. Universities most often describe their missions as research and education and emphasize in addition the impact of this research and education for the benefit of society. Education, even organized education, and the ideas of discovery and understanding of the world have an ancient history across many cultures, far predating the modern university as we know it. Most date the birth of universities to around the end of the eleventh century, beginning with the early universities in Bologna, Paris, Oxford, Cambridge, and many others across Europe. Typically, they grew from specialized training schools. The name "university" reflects the emergence of institutions with some common whole while offering training in a variety of subjects. The evolution of universities over the ensuing centuries has a rich and fascinating history, full of challenges and debate, each of which must be understood in the context of the times. One of the central themes over the centuries has been the degree of independence from state, church, and other authorities.

A key moment in the history of universities and basic to our topic today was the founding of the University of Berlin in 1810. This was not just another addition to the by then long list of universities in Europe. The University of Berlin was to become the flagship for what became known as the German model of the university, and its founding represents the birth of the spirit of the modern research university as we know it today. The founder, Wilhelm von Humboldt, was deeply influenced by the ferment in thinking about universities taking place in Germany at that time. Moving beyond the idea of providing training in a multitude of crafts, the German model comprised three basic principles: first, that the goal of education was to teach students to think, not simply to master a craft; second, that research would play a role of central importance—and teaching students how to think would be accomplished through the integration of research and teaching; and third, that the university should be independent and not be in direct service to the state.

A prominent contemporary thinker who influenced Humboldt was the theologian and philosopher Friedrich Schleiermacher. Schleiermacher, writing in 1808, imagined universities going beyond training in crafts and described the goal of university education as enabling students "to become aware of the principles of scholarship, so that they themselves gradually acquire the ability to investigate, invent, and to give account. This," he writes, "is the business of the university."

This emphasis on developing independence of thought was accompanied by strong views about the relationship to the state. The recognition of the complexity of this relationship and the importance to universities of independence from the state was explicitly discussed by Humboldt, writing around 1809.

The founding of the University of Berlin and the gradual increase of influence of the German model in Europe during the nineteenth century are essential parts of the prehistory of the University of Chicago and its place in the story of academic freedom. As we know, most of the great research universities on the East Coast, Johns Hopkins excluded, began as small colleges. The University of Chicago began life very differently, as a research university that appeared almost whole from its start. Rather than taking its starting point to be a college for the training of future leaders, the University of Chicago took as its starting point a commitment to rigorous, intense, and open inquiry both in research and education, much along the lines of the University of Berlin, but added to it a spirit of openness and meritocracy derived from its particularly American roots.

At its inception, the University of Chicago purposefully distinguished itself within the landscape of higher education in the United States. It was intended from the start to be, and remains today, an institution where the culture supports open, rigorous, and intense inquiry as the highest value; where education and research are embedded in this culture of inquiry; where intellectual freedom is viewed as essential to open inquiry; and where we are open to all people and all perspectives that can stand the scrutiny of argument. Over the years, most of the universities on the East Coast gradually moved toward aspects of this model themselves, but resonance of the distinctiveness of Chicago remains both in its culture and in policies reflecting that culture.

The University of Chicago's first president, William Rainey Harper, was forceful in articulating his belief in the power of his university to have a profound impact on society and to improve the quality of human life. This has been true of all the major research universities that have emerged in this country since that time. And why is that? The issues society faces are complex without simple answers. And in general, it is universities' openness to ideas, to analytic debate, to rigor, and to questioning, and the provision of an umbrella, and in fact safe haven, for clashing thought and perspectives, that best illuminate societal, scientific, and humanistic issues. In a world that tries to overly simplify, universities should demand analysis of inherent complexity; in a world that has inevitable pressures to uniformity of views, we should embrace diversity of perspective; in a world that creates an "us-versus-them" approach to argument, we should support comfort with divergent views. This is the challenging environment, rather than a more intellectually chilled environment, that fosters the work of faculty, students, and ultimately alumni. The greatest contributions universities can make to society over the long run are the ideas and discoveries of faculty and students that emanate from the resulting intellectual ferment and the work of alumni across the scope of human activity—alumni whose capacity for invention has been dramatically enhanced through their education in this environment. Moreover, that universities are almost unique in making this type of contribution only highlights their importance to society.

If this is the purpose of universities, the purpose of academic freedom is precisely to preserve this openness of inquiry and freedom of thought. In other words, academic freedom is designed to protect and preserve for the long run the unique capacity of universities to contribute to society.

Most research universities would view the principles I have articulated as resonant with their own values, so how universities should act would seem relatively straightforward. But as usual, principles are easy to state, but both understanding what they mean in practice and how to realize them are much more complex. In particular, each university, even if it subscribes in general to the previously outlined principles, must ask itself what other values may intercede. How often will these principles be trumped by other considerations, whether externally or internally driven? This is where universities differ considerably in their approach and issues of academic freedom figure prominently. And this difference is as much a matter of the culture of the institution as it is of explicit policies, since the policies always need interpretation, and institutional culture will inevitably play a central role in that process. A feature of the University of Chicago's history is that it has been staunch in articulating the previously discussed values as our highest values. We strive to preserve and enhance a culture in which openness can be embraced, although this is a constant challenge. Because of our history, culture, and adherence to these values, we inevitably find ourselves as a focal point on issues of academic freedom.

The challenges to academic freedom can be directed at individuals or at the institution as a whole, and they can come from sources external or internal to the university. There are three categories I would highlight:

1. External forces on the university from the government, other formal authorities, media, financial supporters or alumni to take action against individual faculty members or students for their views; or external pressure directly against individuals themselves

2. Internal forces on faculty or students intended to stifle expression of individual views or perspectives that some deem objectionable (These can be explicit, but are often implicit because of an ambient culture of what is deemed acceptable.)

3. External and internal pressures on the university to take a political position that is widely perceived as just

A key underlying question in all these considerations is the relationship of an individual faculty member to the university as a whole. To what extent does a faculty member represent the university? What should the university expect from its faculty and what does it owe its faculty? The University of Chicago wrestled with this complex question for some time but came to a firm conclusion in the well-known Kalven report produced by a faculty committee led by Harry Kalven, a professor of constitutional law. This report, written in 1967, derives directly from a firm commitment to the principles I articulated a few moments ago regarding the importance of inquiry and the nature of our values and culture.

Before turning to the Kalven report itself, I want to read a statement that was made by University of Chicago faculty William Gardner Hale and Albion Small in 1899 in the discussion of a contentious matter regarding academic freedom. They say: "The principle of complete freedom of speech on all subjects has from the beginning been regarded as fundamental in the University of Chicago as has been shown by the attitude of both the President and the Board of Trustees; this principle can neither now nor at any future time be called into question; it is desirable to have it clearly understood that the University as such does not appear as disputant on either side of any public question; and the utterances which any professor may make in public are to be regarded as representing his own opinions only."[1] This remarkable statement, now 110 years old, is an indication of the culture of the University in which the Kalven report was produced and why its principles have resonated so strongly through the current day.

I will summarize the principles of the Kalven report, adding a few embellishments for emphasis.

First, the focus on rigorous, intense, and open inquiry carried out by the faculty and students of the University must be accompanied by the greatest possible intellectual freedom, in an environment that supports openness and avoids steps that lead to chilling the environment.

Second, it follows that the University, as an institution, should take no political positions and should remain neutral on such matters (except of necessity those in which it is a direct party), in order to ensure that we have a maximally open environment. Violations of neutrality are a mark against the maintenance of a non-chilling environment.

Third, this University neutrality provides a safe environment for faculty and students to express their own views and take whatever stance they like as individuals. Their views, in turn, never represent the University, which remains neutral.

Fourth, the University needs to protect the academic freedom of faculty and students both by its own neutrality and the protection from internal and external forces that would seek to dampen it.

Fifth, there is recognition of a possible exception. Kalven was a constitutional lawyer, and as such deeply appreciated that a competing interest could trump under unusual circumstances. The exceptions were not spelled out, but rather the emphasis was put on the strong presumption that the stated principles would govern. Much of the focus on the Kalven report in recent times is on understanding exactly where the exception clause applies. The report asserts a "heavy presumption against the university taking collective action or expressing opinions on the political or social values of the day, or modifying its corporate activities to foster social or political values however compelling and appealing they may be."[2]

This powerful statement, the culture in which it is embedded, and the way it has been implemented reflect the commitment of the University of Chicago not to have other values intercede in its commitment to academic freedom.

The external pressures applied by the state or other authorities can be extremely powerful. A most horrific example is that the University of Berlin itself was effectively destroyed by the Nazis in the 1930s, and then even after the defeat of Germany in World War II, became a shadow of its former self under the repressive East German regime. While this is a particularly grim example, there are many others in Eastern Europe. In addition, there have been very considerable political pressures on universities in this country. The demands for faculty to be fired for real or imagined connections to the Communist Party embodied a particularly dark moment, demands that some universities acceded to. While less dramatic than those episodes, there is always at least a low-level set of pressures in this direction that must be constantly confronted.

This type of external pressure is often quite explicit, and it is often evident to most of the academic community that the right course is to resist it. Even if dangerous and difficult, these issues can sometimes be conceptually more straightforward than dealing with other types of pressures. Most universities have struggled with issues created by internal pressures derived from broadly held perspectives, as well as with the pressures on universities to take a political position that is widely perceived as just. Calls for divestment as a means for universities to take a stand on various issues fall into this category. The Kalven report was the basis for the University of Chicago not agreeing with requests that we divest from companies doing business in South Africa or Sudan. There are certainly many ways other than divestment in which the University is encouraged to take a political position. The Kalven report continues to provide guidance for the University of Chicago on all matters related to the University taking a political position.

The Kalven report has most often been discussed as a policy document taken somewhat in isolation. But to understand it, why it has survived at the University of Chicago, and why other universities have gestured toward it but never fully adopted some such statement themselves, I believe it is necessary to contextualize the Kalven report within institutional culture. The commitment to maintain open, rigorous, intense inquiry in an environment of maximal intellectual freedom is not a simple one. It is difficult and to succeed demands a culture and community that will support it. The University of Chicago holds these as its highest values, and we seek to reinforce them at every turn. The Kalven report is a component of this culture. Many other institutions push other values forward as legitimate competing interests, and their culture may not support such a strong position on this particular set of values. Every institution needs to come to its own conclusion as to what it is and what it wants to be. It needs to decide how much weight to give to various competing interests. Kalven only works at the University of Chicago because of these common values at the University and can only be fully understood as a part of the realization of these values.

One of the interesting developments over time has been the way the presidents of the University have understood their own role. It is illustrative of how multiple interpretations and tensions always exist. Robert Maynard Hutchins, the University's fifth president, was a powerful defender of academic freedom. For years he confronted, with unwavering commitment, various calls, many by government, to curtail activities of University faculty and students. Hutchins took as part of academic freedom his own prerogative to speak freely and frequently of his own political views on a wide variety of issues. Were Hutchins's political activities an expression of academic freedom or were they chilling, given that he embodied the University as its president? Many today, including myself, would question this level of political engagement for a University president. While separating the University from its president in a legal sense is easy enough, it is problematic practically, and thus the potential chilling effect of a politically active president is something I and other of Hutchins's successors have tried to avoid.

Finally, let me give you a question to consider, one that has arisen recently (though not at the University of Chicago). Suppose there is a war that is very unpopular with the faculty of university X. A motion comes before the faculty governing body to the effect that the faculty of X declare themselves opposed to the war and call upon the government to end it immediately. What should happen? Is this faculty expressing their views? Or is it a chilling act that is inappropriate? What do considerations of academic freedom say?

I began with some historical comments about the evolution of the university, and I did that not only to contextualize our discussion but to emphasize another important point. Universities are institutions with a long history and the prospects for a very long future. It is essential to preserve their value, their capacity for inquiry, discovery, and education over time, which will inevitably far outlast any particular political issue of the day, no matter how important it is.

Academic freedom, fundamental to universities' capacity to effectively fulfill their mission, has a long history. It faces challenges both internal and external to the academy. It cannot be taken for granted. Establishing it has been a long struggle, and preserving it will always be a struggle. But for the contribution that we make to society and that we alone can make—for the integrity of inquiry and the quality of our education—vigilance is essential. Discussions and decisions will sometimes be unpopular, even within our own academic community; often difficult; and possibly even dangerous—they have been all of these in the relatively recent past. But all of us, in the academy or without, are stewards of this hard-won legacy, and its preservation and enhancement are incumbent upon us all.

NOTES

1. University of Chicago, *Report of the President* (Chicago, 1900), 208.
2. George Stigler, Harry Kalven, et al., "Report on the University's Role in Political and Social Action," November 11, 1967, www-news.uchicago.edu/releases/07/pdf/kalverpt.pdf.

12

ACADEMIC FREEDOM

Some Considerations

MATTHEW GOLDSTEIN AND FREDERICK SCHAFFER

THE PRINCIPLE OF academic freedom is so essential to colleges and universities that it could be said to be part of the genetic code of higher education institutions. It is a self-evident truth of a university's constitution. As Thomas Jefferson once said of the University of Virginia, "Here we are not afraid to follow truth wherever it may lead, nor to tolerate error so long as reason is left free to combat it."[1]

Less self-evident are its scope and application. Defining the concept of academic freedom has become a task shared by courts, colleges, and not a few constitutional scholars. The result has been something less than consensus and something more resembling an evolving conversation, shaped by actual practice.

CORE PRINCIPLES OF ACADEMIC FREEDOM

The principles of academic freedom in the United States were heavily influenced by the thinking and practice at German universities and the growth of nonsectarian American universities in the second half of the nineteenth century.[2] With the rise of ideological conflicts, especially those relating to economic theory, faculty began to feel the need for protection against trustees and/or administrators who sought the dismissal of faculty whose views they found unpalatable.

In 1915, the American Association of University Professors (AAUP) was founded, and the "Declaration of Principles on Academic Freedom and Academic Tenure" it set forth is still a cornerstone definition.[3] The "Declaration" states that academic freedom of the teacher "comprises three elements: freedom of inquiry and research; freedom of teaching within the university or college; and freedom of extramural utterance and action."

The "Declaration" considers these freedoms as deriving from the function of faculty "to deal first hand, after prolonged and specialized technical training, with the sources of knowledge; and to impart the results of their own and of their fellow-specialists' investigations and reflection, both to students and to the general public, without fear or favor." These principles come with corresponding obligations, both on the part of the individual scholar—to conduct inquiry with "a scholar's spirit"—and on the part of the scholarly body, to determine when violations of those obligations have occurred. All faculty members are subject to the judgment of their peers. In addition, decisions relating to appointments, tenure, and promotion are subject to laws prohibiting discrimination.

Ninety years later, in 2005, the City University of New York endorsed a statement by the First Global Colloquium of University Presidents that defined academic freedom in much the same way: "The freedom to conduct research, teach, speak, and publish, subject to the norms and standards of scholarly inquiry, without interference or penalty, wherever the search for truth and understanding may lead."

Universities, by definition, must seek to understand difficult ideas and answer complex questions. That requires rigorous inquiry, openness to all reasonable paths to illumination, and a willingness to challenge orthodoxy. Academic freedom protects the academy from efforts to impose restrictions on free inquiry, internally and externally. In turn, members of the academy are responsible for ensuring that such inquiry is pursued with integrity.

Through several decisions of the Supreme Court, and a number of decisions of lower courts, academic freedom was established as a legal principle, possibly with constitutional underpinnings, that protected faculty from termination based on ideological disagreement with their teaching, scholarship, political associations, or extramural utterances.

Notwithstanding this development, the concept of academic freedom has fared less well in the courts in the ensuing decades. The reasons for this are complex and relate to many issues considered elsewhere in this volume. It is sufficient to note at this point the comment of one scholar that the Supreme Court "has been far more generous in its praise of academic freedom than in providing a precise analysis of its meaning."[4] As Robert Post has noted, it is "a subject that has exceedingly fuzzy boundaries."[5] This poses challenges, particularly at public institutions, to university administrators dedicated to protecting and preserving academic freedom while operating increasingly complex institutions accountable to government, regulatory agencies, taxpayers, and students, among others.

The "1915 Declaration" ends its discussion with an important point that relates to all aspects of academic freedom: "It is, in short, not the absolute freedom of utterance of the individual scholar, but the absolute freedom of thought, of inquiry, of discussion and of teaching, of the academic profession, that is asserted by the declaration of principles." As Post has said, "[T]he protections of academic freedom are not best conceived as personal rights, but as freedoms and responsibility accorded to the corporate body of the faculty."[6]

In 1940, the AAUP and the Association of American Colleges (today the Association of American Colleges and Universities) agreed to a shorter version of the "Declaration," now known as the "1940 Statement of Principles on Academic Freedom and Tenure."[7] The basic purpose of academic freedom remained the same:

> Institutions of higher education are conducted for the common good and not to further the interest of either the individual teacher or the institution as a whole. The common good depends upon the free search for truth and its free exposition.
>
> Academic freedom is essential to these purposes and applies to both teaching and research. Freedom in research is fundamental to the advancement of truth. Academic freedom in its teaching aspect is fundamental for the protection of the rights of the teacher in teaching and of the student to freedom in learning. It carries with it duties correlative with rights.
>
> Academic freedom can serve the public good only if universities as institutions are free from outside pressures in the realm of their academic mission and individual faculty members are free to pursue their research and teaching subject only to the academic judgment of their peers.

ACADEMIC FREEDOM AND THE CITY UNIVERSITY OF NEW YORK

At the City University of New York, the nation's largest public urban university, the commitment to academic freedom is well established and firmly held. As a university that prides itself on diversity and access to opportunity, we hold in the highest regard policies and principles that guarantee open and tolerant academic inquiry and exchange. The freedom to conduct research, teach, speak, and publish is vigorously protected and defended.

At CUNY, as at other public institutions of higher education, the notion of a free exchange of ideas informs the entire academic community: students choosing a course of study; faculty pursuing scholarly research and teaching; and institutions admitting students, appointing faculty, and setting standards. Historically, this shared value, along with a condition of mutual respect, has enabled the existence of open scholarly research and discourse.

The university's governing board has recognized that value. The chair of CUNY's Board of Trustees, Benno C. Schmidt Jr., made clear the underlying principles that guide free discourse: "The university, true to its academic ideals, must treat each member of the community as a unique individual worthy of respect, to be judged solely by his or her actions, intellect, and character. A university does not stereotype its members; it does not permit them to be put into categories based on suspicion, ignorance, or prejudice; it does not deny to any of its members the full rights of academic freedom and engagement."

The board's recognition and support of the concept of academic freedom is important to a public institution that comprises different types of colleges, serves many constituencies, and is accountable to municipal and state governments that provide funding. CUNY is a system of 24 colleges and schools, with nearly 500,000 degree-seeking and continuing education students. The system comprises community colleges, baccalaureate colleges, and graduate and professional schools. Reminiscent of Clark Kerr's "multiversity" system described in the 1960 Master Plan for Higher Education in California, the CUNY system's many portals of entry are meant to ensure access and excellence for all students, opportunities for transfer, and, as Jonathan R. Cole put it in *The Great American University*, "a chance to realize the American dream."[8]

In fact, CUNY began as the Free Academy in 1847, an institution founded on the idea of democratizing higher education, as its first president, Horace

Webster, noted: "The experiment is to be tried, whether the children of the people, the children of the whole people, can be educated; and whether an institution of the highest grade, can be successfully controlled by the popular will, not by the privileged few." That principle still informs CUNY: 44 percent of students are first-generation college attendees, 38 percent report household incomes under $20,000, and more than 200 ancestries are represented.

Giving voice to all is a fundamental CUNY value. The university encourages informed discussion and expects its faculty members to pursue rigorous thinking and debate without restraint. As Robert Maynard Hutchins, former president of the University of Chicago and a champion of academic freedom, noted: "Education is a kind of continuing dialogue, and a dialogue assumes different points of view."[9] Of course, at public institutions the "freedom of external utterance and action" set forth by the "1915 Declaration" is not only qualified by what the "Declaration" calls "hasty or unverified or exaggerated statements" and "intemperate or sensational modes of expression," but is also subject to the First Amendment, which limits the scope of free speech afforded to public employees generally.

At CUNY, as elsewhere, the office of a chancellor, president, or other administrator cannot be used to compromise the principle of academic freedom. For intellectual freedom to flourish, the institution itself should remain neutral. Faculty and students do not speak on behalf of the university, and administrators should generally refrain from taking political positions. Fostering an environment conducive to open dialogue, free from hostility and repercussion, requires administrators to be protectors of, rather than participants in, debate. However, as protectors, they can and should advocate on behalf of the ideals that bind the academic community. For example, in 2009, in response to reports of suspensions, arrests, and investigations into university students, scholars, and curricula in Iran, a CUNY chancellor's statement was issued to address the troubling effort to quash dissent and nullify the very purpose of higher learning:

> At its core, a university operates as an open and civilized forum, one focused on increasing the capacity of our intellect and understanding. A university is dedicated to building an educated society, one composed of citizens who think deeply and broadly across a range of subjects—and that effort requires candid discourse and inquiry. . . . Higher education is not simply a high ideal but a necessary means of developing citizens and leaders who promote the peaceful advancement and co-existence of all societies. Our voices on behalf of our

academic colleagues in Iran, as well as our criticism of government actions in that country that restrict the pursuit of scholarship, dialogue, and advanced learning, must be amplified. . . . When the world's intellectual centers are imperiled, we lose more than the voices of a few; we risk the loss of an essential building block to a more stable and enlightened future and generations of human potential.

ACADEMIC FREEDOM AND FREE SPEECH

Of the three elements of academic freedom, the freedom of "extramural utterance and action" is surely the most problematic. Unlike freedom in research and teaching, it has no special connection to the university and no justification based on the special expertise of faculty members to judge the quality of the work of their peers based on academic standards. Indeed, both the "1915 Declaration" and the "1940 Statement" refer to the right of faculty to speak as citizens.[10] However, we do not ordinarily think of the right of citizens to speak and associate freely as a function of their professional or occupational status. Accordingly, in most contexts, the freedom of faculty "to speak publicly on matters of public concern reflects the permeation of the campus by general civil rights rather than an elaboration of a right unique to the university."[11]

This development has been a mixed blessing. The First Amendment limits the power only of government. Thus, private colleges and universities are not restrained by its terms, and their faculty members are not thereby protected.[12] Furthermore, the status of faculty at public universities subjects them to the narrower scope of free speech afforded to public employees generally. First, the protection afforded to a public employee's free speech depends on the application of a balancing test between the employee's interest in the expression and the interest of the employer in promoting efficiency of the public services it performs through its employees.[13] Second, the First Amendment protects the speech of a public employee only when he or she is speaking as a private citizen on a matter of public concern and not merely a matter of personal interest.[14] It is therefore doubtful under this test that constitutional protection exists for many aspects of faculty speech relating to internal university matters.[15] Finally, as the Supreme Court held in *Garcetti v. Ceballos*, public employees enjoy no freedom of speech when their speech or expression is made "pursuant to their official duties."[16]

In *Garcetti* the Supreme Court rejected the free speech claim of a prosecutor who had been fired allegedly in retaliation for his testimony on behalf of a criminal defendant to the effect that a sheriff's deputy obtained a search warrant by means of a false affidavit. The court held that "when public employees make statements pursuant to their official duties, the employees are not speaking as citizens for First Amendment purposes, and the Constitution does not insulate their communications from employer discipline."[17] Since the parties stipulated that the speech in question was made pursuant to the employee's duties, the court dismissed the complaint.

The *Garcetti* case presented a context that was quite different from a public university, and the court acknowledged that difference. In his dissenting opinion, Justice Souter expressed a concern that the decision might "imperil First Amendment protection of academic freedom in public colleges and universities, whose teachers necessarily speak and write 'pursuant to . . . official duties.'"[18] In response, Justice Kennedy wrote:

> Justice Souter suggests today's decision may have important ramifications for academic freedom, at least as a constitutional value. There is some argument that expression related to academic scholarship or classroom instruction implicates additional constitutional interests that are not fully accounted for by this Court's customary employee-speech jurisprudence. We need not, and for that reason do not, decide whether the analysis we conduct today would apply in the same manner to a case involving speech related to scholarship or teaching.[19]

In subsequent decisions lower courts have wrestled with the application of *Garcetti* to free speech claims of faculty members in public universities.[20] First, there is the question of when faculty members are speaking pursuant to their official duties. Most courts have interpreted this concept broadly, including speech related not only to activities that may be specified in a written job description or faculty handbook but also to pretty much everything that faculty traditionally do within the university setting, at least where the speech was directed to others within that setting.[21] By contrast, speech by faculty members directed to audiences outside the university, such as letters to the editor of a newspaper, articles for popular magazines, or speeches in nonacademic settings, have not been viewed as within their official duties.[22]

Second, there is the question of what significance should be given to Justice Kennedy's caveat and whether to carve out an exception from the *Garcetti* analysis for speech relating to scholarship or teaching. Some courts appear to have ignored the issue of academic freedom but did so in cases that did not involve speech relating to scholarship or teaching.[23] Others have explicitly held that speech relating to scholarship or teaching is protected by the First Amendment.[24] So far only a few courts have addressed a close question as to the meaning of "speech relating to scholarship and teaching." In one case the court interpreted that category rather narrowly, holding that a librarian's recommendation of a book for freshman reading in connection with orientation is not speech relating to teaching.[25] More recently, the Ninth Circuit held that a professor's plan concerning the faculty structure of a school of communications, written while he served on a committee that was debating some of the issues addressed by his plan, constituted speech related to scholarship or teaching because it was a proposal to implement a change "that, if implemented, could have substantially altered the nature of what was taught at the school, as well as the composition of the faculty that would teach it."[26]

This broader definition of speech relating to scholarship or teaching seems appropriate. If academic freedom is to be adequately protected, it would seem at a minimum that speech relating to scholarship and teaching should include not only what is written in scholarly articles and spoken in the classroom, but also statements made in connection with such activities as the evaluation of the scholarship of others, the establishment of curricula and academic standards, and the academic advising of students.

Moreover, apart from providing a fuller definition of "speech relating to scholarship and teaching," courts will need to define the scope of First Amendment protection. Such speech will always be pursuant to the official duties of faculty and will often not address matters of public concern. Thus, if there is to be meaningful protection for academic speech, those elements of the First Amendment analysis will have to be jettisoned.[27] However, it is likely that courts will continue to apply some sort of balancing test since not everything a teacher might say in a classroom deserves the protection of the principles of academic freedom. This includes speech that does not relate to the subject matter of the class and is profane, sexual, or otherwise objectionable.[28]

In due course the Supreme Court will undoubtedly have occasion to clarify the application of *Garcetti* to the public university faculty. In addition to the questions discussed above, the court may also consider whether to expand the categories enjoying greater protection for faculty speech to statements made in the course of performing their role in the academic governance of the university. Unlike other public employees, faculty members are expected to exercise independent thought and judgment on university governance rather than carry out the mandate of their agency head.[29]

However the courts eventually resolve these First Amendment questions concerning faculty speech at public universities, academic freedom is a concept independent of constitutional law. The question therefore arises whether the principles of academic freedom should establish norms within universities that are more protective of extramural speech than the First Amendment, even if they cannot be enforced by courts. At both private and public institutions of higher education, academic freedom should continue to protect speech in which faculty speak as citizens on matters of public concern. Although not directly related to the primary rationale for academic freedom, such freedom of expression is part of a long and valued tradition of universities as places committed to wide-ranging debate on such matters.[30] There is no good reason why any faculty, whether at private or public universities, should be subject to reprisals because colleagues, administrators, alumni, or politicians take umbrage at the expression of views on subjects of public concern.[31] Moreover, the boundaries of what constitutes matters of public concern should be interpreted broadly. At least some matters pertaining to university issues, such as presidential pay, conflicts of interest by trustees, and significant change in general education requirements or academic standards, are of real and legitimate interest to the larger community.

In addition, if the Supreme Court does not eventually recognize the need for expanded protection for speech relating to scholarship or teaching, or interprets those categories narrowly, or does not also include speech relating to academic governance as deserving of similar protection, a strong argument can be made for continuing to protect such speech under the umbrella of academic freedom as applied within the setting of the university itself.

Some would argue further that academic freedom should also protect speech unrelated to matters of public concern or to scholarship, teaching, or academic governance.[32] However, it is far from clear why such speech has value to the academic enterprise and should be protected by principles of academic freedom. Moreover, the recognition and enforcement of such a broad concept of academic freedom within universities would inevitably give rise to endless disputes and grievances as faculty claim retaliation for every adverse action. Internal procedures already exist at most universities to review decisions relating to reappointment, promotion, and tenure on the ground that they were based on extraneous factors and not on the quality of scholarship, teaching, and service. That seems not only appropriate but consistent with principles of academic freedom, which are premised upon the integrity of a system of academic judgment and peer review. However, academic freedom is in no way advanced by requiring the review of a morass of petty retaliation claims arising in contexts where there do not exist formal review procedures, such as departmental disagreements as to course content, class schedules, or the selection of department chairs,[33] and where there are no connections to the core values of scholarship or teaching.[34]

ACADEMIC FREEDOM AND THE RIGHTS OF STUDENTS

The principles of academic freedom do not apply to students as they do to faculty. As discussed previously, academic freedom serves to promote the public good by protecting the intellectual independence of faculty in their scholarship and teaching, subject to the professional judgment of their peers. Within the academic community, students are novices, under the intellectual tutelage of the faculty. Their freedom of speech is not properly understood as part of academic freedom because it has nothing to do with "the preservation of the unique functions of the university, particularly the goals of disinterested scholarship and teaching."[35] That is not to say, however, that students do not have any rights relating to the free expression of their views and opinions. Students at public universities are protected by the First Amendment against restrictions on their rights of free speech and association.[36] Indeed, in light of the limitations on the First Amendment rights of public employees discussed earlier, it may be that students at public universities have greater rights to free speech than faculty.

One of the most contentious areas of controversy concerning the First Amendment rights of university students relates to "speech codes," which have consistently been found unconstitutional.[37] Another area relates to the use of student activity fees. In *Southworth v. Board of Regents of the University of Wisconsin*,[38] the Supreme Court upheld the use of mandatory student activity fees to fund student advocacy having educational benefit against a claim that such a fee violates the First Amendment interest of students not to have their money used to promote ideas with which they disagree. The court reasoned that the university's educational interest in promoting speech by its students outweighed the students' interest as long as the university followed a strict policy of "viewpoint neutrality" in the allocation of the funds collected from the mandatory fee.[39]

As we noted in discussing the faculty's freedom of expression in extramural utterances, the university has come to serve an important function as a marketplace of ideas outside the realms of scholarship and systematic learning. It may be analytically correct to view this function as falling outside the protection of academic freedom. Nevertheless, it is a tradition worth protecting and preserving as long as it does not conflict with the core purposes of the university. Accordingly, students should enjoy rights to free speech and association whether or not they attend a public university and thus enjoy First Amendment protection. Both in the larger university setting and within the classroom, students should be free to express their views, and they should not be subject to reprisals because of their opinions.[40]

However, such freedom of expression by students is subject to two limitations. First, it may not interfere with the other activities of the campus or classroom. This commonsense limitation is an accepted part of First Amendment jurisprudence and serves as the justification for reasonable limitations on the time, place, and manner of protests and other expressive activities both on and off university campuses.[41]

Second, student speech and writing in the classroom context is subject to the academic authority of faculty to evaluate their course work with respect to factual accuracy, authority of sources, research methodology, organization, quality of expression, analytical rigor, and other legitimate academic factors. The Supreme Court has supported this limitation not only in *Southworth* but also in *Hazelwood School District v. Kuhlmeier*.[42] In that case the court upheld a high school principal's right to delete two pages from a newspaper produced by students in connection with a journalism class. The court held that "educators do not offend the First Amendment by exercising editorial control over the style and content of student speech in school-sponsored expressive activities so long as their actions are reasonably related to legitimate pedagogical concerns."[43] Of course, precedents from the K–12 context are not necessarily applicable to higher education, where the greater age and maturity of students and the stronger tradition of free inquiry militate in favor of greater student rights. Nevertheless, it remains true that in both contexts, students' right to free speech in the classroom setting is subject to the legitimate academic standards and concerns of the faculty and the institution.[44]

The authority of faculty, indeed their academic freedom, also extends to the design of curricula and the presentation of materials. This is not primarily a question of their individual rights as teachers but rather their collective authority as part of the academic governance of the institution. The purpose of teaching is not merely to impart knowledge, but to train students to think for themselves. The recent statement on "Academic Freedom and Educational Responsibility" by the Association of American Colleges and Universities puts it well: "Students do not have a right to remain free from encountering unwelcome or 'inconvenient questions.'"[45] At the same time, however, and as the "1915 Declaration" recognizes, faculty are expected to conform to professional norms with regard to avoiding controversial topics unrelated to the subject matter of a course and presenting relevant controversial materials in an academically thoughtful and rigorous way.[46]

Most of the litigated cases in this area pertain not to controversial subject matters or views but to the use of language by faculty that is profane or sexual. In several pre-*Garcetti* cases, the courts seem to have grasped the key principle here. On the one hand, courts have dismissed claims by faculty that their rights to free speech or academic freedom were violated because they were terminated for profane or sexual speech that was unrelated to the subject matter of the class and that served no valid educational purpose.[47] On the other hand, courts have reversed a university's discipline of a faculty member where they found that language, although objectionable to some, advanced his valid educational objectives related to the subject matter of his course.[48] Nevertheless, these cases are troubling to the extent that courts in some of them reviewed, and in one case reversed, the decision of a faculty committee as to what was appropriate, thereby intruding upon the university's autonomy in an area of academic judgment.[49]

As with many cases involving student speech, these cases often arise in the context of a university's enforcement of a policy against sexual harassment. One court has struck down such a policy because its language was unconstitutionally vague and therefore violated a faculty member's First Amendment rights.[50] However, where a professor's speech is reasonably regarded as offensive, is not germane to the subject matter of the course, and is sufficiently severe and pervasive as to impair a student's academic opportunity, there is no reason why antidiscrimination laws cannot be applied without violating faculty rights to free speech or academic freedom.[51]

Another area of contention relates to the introduction of religious texts or subjects. Where this has been done as part of an academic exercise and not to advance a particular religious view, the courts have upheld the university's actions against claims that they violated the Establishment or Free Exercise Clauses of the First Amendment.[52] Conversely, one court has upheld limitations on a faculty member's speech about his religious views within a classroom that appeared unrelated to the subject matter of the course.[53]

In sum, it is inconsistent with principles of academic freedom for faculty to have to censor their speech within the classroom because of student objections where such speech is related to the subject of the course. If their speech is not so related and is offensive to a reasonable person, faculty may be appropriately restrained or disciplined. In either case, it is helpful in dealing with these types of controversies for universities to have internal procedures to review complaints by students concerning faculty behavior in classrooms. Such procedures should involve faculty in the review of student complaints and should provide explicit protection for the principles of academic freedom.[54]

ACADEMIC FREEDOM AND UNIVERSITY GOVERNANCE

The emphasis on the independence of faculty in the "1915 Declaration" applies not only to their individual work as researchers and teachers, but also appears to have implications for the shared governance of the institution: "A university is a great and indispensable organ of higher life of a civilized community, in the work of which the trustees hold an essential and highly honorable place, but in which the faculties hold an independent place, with quite equal responsibilities—and in relation to purely scientific and educational questions the primary responsibility." However, *how* governance and responsibility are shared—and how that connects to academic freedom—is not always clear, and the distinctions drawn in practice often depend on institutional traditions and mission.

The "1915 Declaration" is explicit that academic freedom requires the faculty to play the central role in making academic judgments about scholarship and teaching and in disciplining faculty for failure to meet appropriate standards. The "1940 Statement" is silent on issues of governance. However, in 1966 the AAUP adopted a "Statement on Government of Colleges and

Universities" (the "Statement on Government") that it had jointly formulated with the American Council on Education and the Association of Governing Boards of Universities and Colleges.[55] The "Statement on Government" emphasizes the need for shared responsibility by boards, faculties, and administrators. It notes that the role of each group and the form of their cooperation will vary depending on the area in question. Like the "1915 Declaration," it gives the faculty primary responsibility for academic matters based on their expertise and goes on to define those matters as "curriculum, subject matter and methods of instruction, research, faculty status, and those aspects of student life that relate to the educational process."

In 1998 the Association of Governing Boards issued its own "Statement on Institutional Governance."[56] The AGB statement notes "a widespread perception that faculty members, especially in research universities, are divided in their loyalties between their academic disciplines and the welfare of their own institutions" and the belief of many governing boards, faculty, and chief executives that "internal governance arrangements have become so cumbersome that timely decisions are difficult to make, and small factions often are able to impede the decision-making process." While acknowledging the important role of faculty regarding academic matters, the AGB statement emphasizes "the ultimate responsibility" of governing boards, the role of other constituencies, such as students, non-faculty staff, and external stakeholders, and the need for the fiscal and managerial affairs of universities to be "administered with appropriate attention to commonly accepted business standards." The variations between the AAUP statement and the AGB statement reflect not only the different perspectives of the associations that issued them but also the differing practices of the many universities and colleges within the United States. Nevertheless, as a matter of practice it is fair to say that faculty generally have strong but not dispositive authority over such critical academic matters as curricula and appointments.[57]

Notwithstanding its recognition of the policy arguments in favor of such shared authority, in *Minnesota State Board for Community Colleges v. Knight*,[58] the Supreme Court held that faculty have no First Amendment right to participate in academic governance at a public institution of higher education.[59] Where does this leave the idea of shared governance as a component of academic freedom? It seems clear that a substantial faculty role in the academic governance of the university is a sine qua non for academic freedom even if it is not a matter of constitutional right and may not be subject to judicial enforcement.[60] However, there will continue to be considerable disagreement as to the exact contours of that role. The AAUP "Statement on Government" maintains that the president and the board should overrule the faculty "only in exceptional circumstances, and for reasons communicated to the faculty" and goes on to identify financial constraints or personnel limitations as the kinds of factors that might justify the rejection of a faculty recommendation.[61]

Nevertheless, many university presidents are members of the faculty and have deep experience in exercising academic judgment. Moreover, even if one were to agree that presidents should generally defer to the faculty on academic matters (and boards even more so), it seems entirely appropriate for them to review faculty decisions where there is evidence that they may not have rested on academic judgment.

For public institutions subject to review and oversight by governmental entities, the notion of shared governance and its relation to academic freedom is further complicated. For example, legislatures in several states have enacted legislation mandating articulation policies that rely on the establishment of a common core curriculum. Ensuring ease of transfer among the state's higher education institutions—from community colleges to baccalaureate colleges in particular—is cited as a particular mandate by such legislative bodies. Likewise, accrediting agencies review a university's policies to ensure that institutional operations are conducive to student learning. For institutions like CUNY, in which governance is shared among the system, individual colleges, and discipline-based departments, the path to compliance is not always clear.

For example, in 1967, a Middle States report on the organization of the City University of New York noted that "articulation between the two-year and four-year colleges is a pressing problem. . . . The goal should be the acceptance by the four-year colleges of the entire block of transfer work taken in a university two-year college, without examination of specific course titles or credits except to establish prerequisites for more advanced work." New York's Education Law specifies that CUNY is one university and must have clear transfer paths and curricular alignment across its colleges. Nowhere is CUNY's unique structure of two-year and four-year institutions with individual faculties and traditions within a confined geographical area more pronounced than in its vast network of articulation agreements and transfer decisions. Today, more than 50 percent of graduates from the baccalaureate colleges are transfer students (from CUNY and non-CUNY campuses), and many students graduate with more credit than required for their degrees and take a longer time to graduate, jeopardizing financial aid availability, often because of transfer issues.

Nonetheless, there has been disagreement about CUNY's current efforts—forty-plus years after the Middle States report—to create a general education framework and transfer system for the entire university. While faculty conceive, develop, review, approve, and teach the core courses, it is the CUNY board that passed a resolution to create an efficient transfer system. Some faculty have questioned the board's actions. (This is not entirely surprising; as Cole notes, Clark Kerr's California master plan "did meet with resistance. . . . Paradoxically, individual university faculty members tend to be liberal, but when they are brought together to discuss educational reform, they become highly conservative.")[62]

Clearly, it is the function of the faculty corpus, as the "1915 Declaration" says, to "deal first hand . . . with the sources of knowledge; and to impart the results of their own and of their fellow-specialists' investigations and reflections." But where does the *impetus* for structural change originate? How does an institution create necessary—and, in some cases, legally mandated—system-wide change in the absence of faculty unanimity and cohesion? Administrators may feel justifiably compelled to generate an operational framework to improve the educational experience and progress of students, while remaining committed to the faculty prerogative to make decisions about the development of curricula. Likewise, it is the entire faculty body—from all campuses, across the entire system—that share in governance. As Kerr said, "A multiversity is inherently a conservative institution but with radical functions. There are so many groups with an interest in the status quo, so many veto groups; yet the university must serve a knowledge explosion and a population explosion simultaneously. The president becomes the central mediator among the values of the past, the prospects for the future and the realities of the present."[63] It is often the case that the more faculty who participate in issues of governance, the stronger the concept, and practice, of shared governance becomes, especially when the faculty body is large and diverse. Administrators and faculty together must ensure that decisions about a core curriculum are guided by a commitment to upholding academic rigor and disciplinary standards and ensuring a structure conducive to student learning—not by workload issues or efforts to boost enrollment in underutilized departments.

As Stanley Fish has pointed out, such disagreements about what constitutes "participation" in shared governance are often viewed outside of the academy as petty academic squabbles.[64] And indeed, they risk reducing the ideals of a scholarly community to procedure and politics. Ideally, this must be avoided; robust disagreement is often useful to an institution, but such discourse should aim to be a model to students and citizens of open-minded, fairly considered, and deeply felt inquiry. Over the years, the term "academic freedom" has been applied to contentious opposition of all kinds. But disagreement alone does not necessarily threaten—or necessarily relate to— academic freedom; on the contrary, it is often indicative of an active and free exchange of ideas. In practice as in theory, it is an institution's insistence on academic freedom that makes possible progress on the academy's most difficult and important task: the creation and dissemination of knowledge.

USES AND ABUSES OF ACADEMIC FREEDOM

In the ninety-five years since the AAUP issued the "1915 Declaration," the principles of academic freedom have gained greater acceptance than its originators could have imagined. There is hardly a university that does not at least profess its commitment to academic freedom, although conformance to its principles, as always, tends to ebb and flow with the phases of the political moon. Indeed, so widespread is the acceptance of academic freedom that some use it to advance claims or proposals that have little or no connection to its principles—or in fact are inconsistent with them. Some such claims border on the silly.[65] However, two examples from opposite ends of the spectrum are worth considering in more detail.

In his Academic Bill of Rights,[66] David Horowitz proposes principles to address what he claims is a lack of intellectual and political diversity among university faculty and a resulting tendency of faculty to use the classroom for indoctrination.[67] Several of those principles consist of restatements of the traditional view of academic freedom. These include the principles that (1) faculty should be evaluated based on their competence and knowledge in their field of expertise; (2) students should be graded on the basis of their reasoned answers and appropriate knowledge of the subjects and disciplines they study; and (3) neither faculty nor students should be judged on the basis of their political or religious beliefs.

Others are consistent with the principles of academic freedom, but create pressures against the exercise of intellectual independence or originality. For example, it is a valid objective that curricula, reading lists, and classroom teaching should expose students to a range of significant scholarly opinion. However, it is not a simple matter to determine precisely what that should include in order to protect faculty from charges of "indoctrination" from their students or outside groups. As several scholars have commented, the Academic Bill of Rights threatens to "snuff out all controversial discussion in the classroom" by presenting faculty "with an impossible dilemma: either play it safe or risk administrative censure by saying something that might offend an overly sensitive student."[68]

Moreover, the Academic Bill of Rights seeks to implement its goal of neutrality in teaching by requiring universities to recruit faculty "with a view toward fostering a plurality of methodologies and perspectives," thereby creating a risk that faculty will be hired based on their political beliefs, notwithstanding the bill's own prohibition on precisely such behavior. This risk is exacerbated by modern telecommunications technology. In the past, most scholarship was published in academic journals and books that were not widely available, and criticism (generally from scholars) appeared in similar venues. Now, however, almost everything that faculty write is available online, and commentary by both other scholars and the public (including highly ideological segments of the public) is distributed widely through social media, blogs, and other electronic outlets. Although such commentary, even when vitriolic and unfair, is not itself a violation of academic freedom, its widespread availability, including occasional appearances on mainstream media, may well serve to intimidate some faculty.

Finally, by seeking (so far unsuccessfully) the enactment of laws similar to the Academic Bill of Rights by Congress and several state legislatures, its supporters invite the kind of outside interference, from both legislatures and courts, that is inconsistent with academic freedom. Here, as in so many debates concerning academic freedom, the issue is not only what the proper principles are, but who gets to enforce them. Academic freedom is based on the institutional autonomy of universities. The Academic Bill of Rights, in its purported effort to strengthen academic freedom, would in fact weaken if not destroy it.[69]

Coming from the other direction, the AAUP's vision of academic freedom has been encumbered by the addition of multiple policies, procedures, rules, and prohibitions, as a ship accumulates barnacles. The AAUP, of course, deserves great credit for having put academic freedom on the map and having investigated and reported on a number of important cases involving significant violations of its principles. However, there is hardly any aspect of university life on which the AAUP has not expressed an opinion and which, according to the AAUP, is not an aspect of academic freedom. These include such diverse matters as detailed procedures relating to the renewal or nonrenewal of appointments, dismissal and suspension, including the permissible grounds for such action, standards for notices of non-reappointment, the use of collegiality as a criterion for faculty evaluation, posttenure review, the status of part-time faculty, non–tenure track appointments and the status of such faculty, the use of arbitration in cases of dismissal, operating guidelines for layoffs in cases of financial exigency, and so on.[70] This development is understandable as the AAUP has worked over many years to further the interests of faculty.

Nevertheless, to link to academic freedom every policy and procedure that a professional association or labor organization might want for its members is to drain the concept of all meaning and to lend credence to the unfortunate view of some that academic freedom is no more than special pleading on behalf of a privileged elite. Because there are and will continue to be real and serious threats to academic freedom, it is important to all who care about universities to be as clear as possible about its meaning, to exercise restraint in its invocation, and to support true claims with vigor.

NOTES

1. Jefferson to William Roscoe Lipscomb, in *The Writings of Thomas Jefferson*, ed. Andrew A. Lipscomb and Albert E. Bergh (Washington, D.C.: Thomas Jefferson Memorial Association of the United States, 1903–1904), 15: 303.

2. The literature on the history of academic freedom is large. One of the best works is Richard Hofstadter and William P. Metzger, *The Development of Academic Freedom in the United States* (New York: Columbia University Press, 1955).

3. American Association of University Professors, "1915 Declaration of Principles," in *Policy Documents and Reports*, 10th ed. (Washington, D.C.: AAUP, 2006), 291–301, www.aaup.org/AAUP/pubsres/policydocs/contents/1915.htm (hereafter referred to as *AAUP Documents*).

4. J. Peter Byrne, "Academic Freedom: A 'Special Concern of the First Amendment,'" *Yale Law Journal* 99 (1989): 257.

5. Robert Post, "Academic Freedom: Its History and Evolution Within the UC System," (paper presented at the Academic Freedom Forum, June 11, 2003), www.universityof-california.edu/senate/committees/ucaf/afforum/post.pdf.

6. Ibid.

7. *AAUP Documents*, 3–7, www.aaup.org/AAUP/pubsres/policydocs/contents/1940statement .htm.

8. Jonathan R. Cole, *The Great American University: Its Rise to Preeminence, Its Indispensable National Role, and Why It Must Be Protected* (New York: Perseus, 2009), 135.

9. Statement of Robert M. Hutchins, associate director of the Ford Foundation, November 25, 1952, in Hearings Before the House Select Committee to Investigate Tax-exempt Foundations and Comparable Organizations, pursuant to H.Res. 561, 82d Cong., 2d Sess.

10. There is a tension in the "1940 Statement" on this point. On the one hand, it states that when faculty "speak or write as citizens, they should be free from institutional censorship or discipline." On the other hand, it states that "their special position in the community imposes special obligations" and that "as scholars and educational officers, they should remember that the public may judge their profession and their institution by their utterances" and therefore "should at all times be accurate, should exercise appropriate restraint, should show respect for the opinions of others, and should make every effort to indicate they are not speaking for the institution." The 1940 interpretations to the statement do nothing to resolve this tension, stating that "if the administration of a college or university feels that a teacher has not observed the[se] admonitions . . . and believes that the extramural utterances of the teacher have been such as to raise grave doubts concerning the teacher's fitness for his or her position, it may proceed to file charges," but in doing so "the administration should remember that teachers are citizens and should be accorded the freedom of citizens." It then concludes with the following warning: "In such cases the administration must assume full responsibility, and the American Association of University Professors and the Association of American Colleges are free to make an investigation." However, the 1970 interpretive comments go on to provide further limitations on the enforcement of those "admonitions," including the following quotation from a 1964 Committee A statement: "The controlling principle is that a faculty member's expression of opinion as a citizen cannot constitute grounds for dismissal unless it clearly demonstrates the faculty member's unfitness for his or her position. Extramural utterances rarely bear upon the faculty member's fitness for the position. Moreover, a final decision should take into account the faculty member's entire record as a teacher and scholar." *AAUP Documents*, 5–6. It thus appears that the current position of the AAUP is that a faculty member's extramural utterances as a citizen should very rarely be the basis for disciplinary charges.

11. Byrne, "Academic Freedom: A 'Special Concern of the First Amendment,'" 99 Yale L.J. 251, 264 (1989). Professor Byrne argues more generally that the meaning and purposes of academic freedom are distinct from those of the First Amendment, although he supports constitutional protection of academic freedom to the extent necessary to protect universities from political interference with their academic judgments. See also William Van Alstyne, *The Specific Theory of Academic Freedom and the General Issue of Civil Liberty*, revised and reprinted in *The Concept of Academic Freedom*, ed. E. Pincoffs (1975), 60.

12. But see Cal. Educ. Code §9436, which protects students (but not faculty) at private colleges and universities from any rule or disciplinary sanction based solely on

conduct or speech outside the campus or facility that would be protected from governmental restriction under the First Amendment of the U.S. Constitution or article 1 of the California Constitution.

13. See Pickering v. Bd. of Ed., 391 U.S. 563, 568 (1968). Many of the public employee cases, like *Pickering,* involve primary or secondary school teachers. Courts generally recognize that such schools present a different context from universities, if for no other reason than the age of the students. Accordingly, in applying the balancing test, they generally accord greater First Amendment rights to faculty (and students) in university settings than in public schools. What courts often miss, however, is the fact that only university faculty, and not public school teachers, enjoy academic freedom. Accordingly, it should rarely be the case that speech by university faculty on matters of public concern can be seen as disruptive of the efficient administration of the institution.

14. See Connick v. Myers, 461 U.S. 138, 146–47 (1983). The court defined a matter of "public concern" as one "fairly considered as relating to any matter of political, social, or other concern to the community." Ibid. at 146. This requirement reflects "the common sense realization that government offices could not function if every employment decision became a constitutional matter." Ibid. at 143. However, as discussed later, the application of this principle to concrete facts has produced widely different results.

15. See, e.g., Gorum v. Sessoms, 561 F.3d 179, 185–86 (3d Cir. 2009) (statements in connection with counseling students and student activities); Savage v. Gee, 716 F.Supp.2d 709, 718 (S.D. Ohio 2010) (librarian's recommendation of a book for freshman orientation); Isenalumhe v. McDuffie, 697 F.Supp.2d 367, 378–79 (E.D.N.Y. 2010) (faculty member's complaints to union representatives and grievance officer, accusations that another professor interfered in committee matters, and other complaints about internal matters to higher-ups within department, college, and university); Munn-Goins v. Bd. of T. of Bladen Cmty. College, 658 F.Supp.2d 713, 728 (E.D.N.C. 2009) (faculty member's request for and distribution of salary information). But see Jackson v. Leighton, 168 F.3d 903, 910 (6th Cir. 1999) (professors' comments on administrative decisions regarding university resources held to be matters of public concern); Yohn v. Coleman, 639 F.Supp.2d 776, 786 (E.D. Mich. 2009) (dentistry professor's comments on alleged lowering of academic standards held to be a matter of public concern).

16. Garcetti v. Ceballos, 547 U.S. 410, 421 (2006).

17. Ibid.

18. Ibid., 438 (internal quotes omitted).

19. Ibid., 425.

20. There have been a considerable number of lower court decisions applying *Garcetti,* but only a small number have dealt with faculty at public universities. For a summary of those cases, see Leonard M. Niehoff, "Peculiar Marketplace: Applying Garcetti v. Ceballos in the Public Higher Education Context," *Journal of College and University Law* 35 (2008): 75. For a pre-*Garcetti* case that provides a strong endorsement of the right of a faculty member to speak on a controversial matter without reprisal by his college, see Levin v. Harleston, 52 F.3d 9 (2d Cir. 1995).

21. See, e.g., Demers v. Austin,___ F.3d__,____, Slip op. at 11-13 (9th Cir., Jan. 29, 2014); *Gorum*, 561 F.3d at 187; Renkin v. Gregory, 541 F.3d 769, 774 (7th Cir. 2008) (dispute over research grant); Hong v. Grant, 516 F. Supp. 2d 1158 (C.D. Cal. 2007) (criticism of department chair and dean); *Isenalumhe*, 697 F.Supp.2d at 378; Ezuma v. City Univ. of N.Y., 665 F.Supp.2d 116, 129–30 (E.D.N.Y. 2009) (transmittal of complaint about sexual harassment). Cf. Fusco v. Sonoma County Junior College Dist., 2009 U.S. Dist. LEXIS 11 91431, at *6 (N.D. Cal. Sept. 30, 2009) (court refused to dismiss faculty member's First Amendment claim where complaint did not establish that her attempts to place certain matters on the agenda for department meetings were pursuant to her official duties). Courts have generally held that speech by teachers in the K–12 context was made pursuant to their official duties. See Weintraub v. Bd. of Educ., 593 F.3d 196 (2d Cir. 2010) (complaints about the handling of student discipline in public secondary school); Fox v. Traverse City Area Pub. Sch. Bd. of Educ., 605 F.3d 345, 348–350 (6th Cir. 2010) (elementary school teacher's complaints about workload); Lamb v. Booneville Sch. Dist., 2010 U.S. Dist. LEXIS 9728 (N.D. Miss. Feb. 3, 2010) (special education teacher's complaints about corporal punishment). But see Reinhardt v. Albuquerque Pub. Sch. Bd. of Educ., 595 F.3d 1126, 1137 (10th Cir. 2010) (complaints of wrongdoing by speech pathologist in public school system not made pursuant to her duties); Evans-Marshall v. Board of Education of Tipp City Exempted Village School, 428 F.3d 223, 230 (6th Cir. 2005) (teacher comments on curricular and pedagogical decisions protected by First Amendment).

22. See Adams v. Tr. of Univ. of North Carolina, 630 F.3d 550, 561–62 (4th Cir. 2011) (non-scholarly columns and articles published outside the university are protected by the First Amendment even though they were subsequently submitted by faculty member in support of application for promotion). See also Niehoff, "Peculiar Marketplace," 82–84. This distinction creates an odd incentive for faculty members at public universities (and other state employees) to voice their complaints outside of the university (or chain of command), rather than within. If the statements relate to a matter of public concern, the faculty are more likely to be protected by the First Amendment. Furthermore, this distinction seems arbitrary in other ways. It suggests that faculty members are speaking pursuant to their official duties when they write an article in a scholarly journal or give a speech at a professional gathering, but not when they write an article in a popular magazine or give a speech at a political meeting.

23. See, e.g., *Renkin*, 541 F.3d at 774; *Hong*, 516 F.Supp.2d at 1166.

24. In some of these cases, the court held that the speech related to scholarship and teaching. See *Demers*, *Slip* op. at 13–16; *Adams*, 640 F.3d at 562–64; Kerr v. Hurd, 694 F.Supp.2d 817, 843 (S.D. Ohio 2010); Sheldon v. Dhillon, 2009 U.S. Dist. LEXIS 110275, at *12 (N.D Cal. Nov. 25, 2009). In others, the court recognized the exception for speech relating to classroom teaching but held it was not applicable. Pigee v. Carl Sandburg College, 464 F.3d 667, 672 (7th Cir. 2006); *Savage*, 716 F.Supp.2d at 718.

25. *Savage*, 716 F.Supp.2d at 718. In a pre-*Garcetti* case, one court held that faculty members had engaged in speech related to matters of public concern, and therefore were protected by the First Amendment, in connection with objects displaced in a history

exhibit. See Burnham v. Ianni, 119 F.3d 668, 679–80 (8th Cir. 1997). However, in a secondary school context, a court held that an art teacher's statements to his class about the portfolio requirements of college art programs, including the necessity for providing sketches of male and female nudes, were not protected by the First Amendment. *Panse v. Eastwood*, 2007 U.S. Dist. LEXIS 55080, at *12–13 (S.D.N.Y. July 20, 2007).

26. *Demers*, Slip op. at 23.

27. In *Adams*, 640 F.3d at 564–66, the Fourth Circuit easily concluded that the speech involved a matter of public concern, since the speech in question was writings and advocacy on clearly public issues, not the typical sort of scholarship or classroom teaching. In one pre-*Garcetti* case, a court held that there was no First Amendment protection for faculty speech in the classroom, because it did not relate to a matter of public concern. See Rubin v. Ikenberry, 933 F.Supp. 1425, 1443 (C.D. Ill. 1996). Another court reached the opposite conclusion. See Hardy v. Jefferson Community College, 260 F.3d 671, 679 (6th Cir. 2001).

28. See discussion at pp. 258–259 below.

29. For a thoughtful argument in favor of extending the protection of the First Amendment to faculty speech relating to its role in the academic governance of universities, see Judith Areen, "Government as Educator: A New Understanding of First Amendment Protection of Academic Freedom and Governance", 97 *Geo. L.J.* 945, (2009), 985–1000. As that argument makes clear, however, such protection requires a careful analysis of whether or not a particular kind of speech relates to academic governance—a task that is far from easy. We believe that the Supreme Court is more likely to protect speech relating to such governance issues as the evaluation of scholarship and curriculum by finding it within the exception for scholarship and teaching rather than creating a new and separate protected category for speech relating to academic governance.

30. As the Supreme Court recognized in upholding the free speech rights of students: "The college classroom with its surrounding environs is peculiarly the 'marketplace of ideas,' and we break no new constitutional ground in reaffirming this nation's dedication to safeguarding academic freedom." Healy v. James, 408 U.S. 169, 180–81 (1972), quoting Keyishian v. Bd. of Regents, 385 U.S. 589, 603 (1967).

31. See, e.g., Levin v. Harleston, 966 F.2d 85 (2d Cir. 1992) (college violated professor's right to free speech in creating alternative section of his class and investigating his conduct as a result of articles and speeches arguing that blacks are less intelligent than whites).

32. Areen, supra note 28, at 987 n. 240.

33. See Jeffries v. Harleston, 52 F.3d 9, 14–15 (2d Cir. 1994) (distinguishing removal of department chair from dismissal of tenured professor).

34. It is precisely in such areas as these where universities most resemble governmental agencies and where the need for managerial authority to achieve effective and efficient administration becomes paramount. See Areen, supra note 28, at 989; Clarke v. Holmes, 474 F.2d 928, 931 (7th Cir. 1972); *Ezuma*, 665 F.Supp.2d at 130–31.

35. Byrne, "Academic Freedom: A 'Special Concern of the First Amendment,'" 262; see also Byrne, supra note 28, at 100 ("Student free speech rights against universities reflect political values rather than academic ones.").

36. See, e.g., Rosenberger v. Rector and Visitors of the Univ. of Virginia, 515 U.S. 819 (1995) (State university, which pays for the printing expenses of other student publications, violates the First Amendment rights of students in refusing to pay for the printing expenses of a student publication because it primarily promotes or manifests a particular belief in or about a deity or an ultimate reality.); Widmar v. Vincent, 454 U.S. 263 (1981) (State university, which makes its facilities generally available for the activities of registered student groups, violates First Amendment rights of students in closing its facilities to a registered student group desiring to use the facilities for religious worship and religious discussion.); Healy v. James, 408 U.S. 169 (1972) (State university violates First Amendment rights of students in refusing to recognize student political organization because of its views.). Students have similar, although somewhat more circumscribed rights in public schools. See, e.g., Bd. of Educ. v. Pico, 457 U.S. 853 (1982) (Local school boards violate the First Amendment rights of students in removing books from library shelves solely because they dislike the ideas contained in those books and seek by their removal to prescribe what shall be orthodox in politics, nationalism, religion or other matters of opinion.); Tinker v. Des Moines Indep. Comty. Sch. Dist., 393 U.S. 503 (1969) (School policy violates First Amendment rights of students in prohibiting junior and senior high school students from wearing armbands in protest of the Vietnam War.).

37. See, e.g., DeJohn v. Temple Univ., 537 F.3d 301 (3d Cir. 2008); Bair v. Shippensburg University, 280 F.Supp.2d 357 (M.D. Pa. 2003); Booher v. Bd. of Regents, 1998 U.S. Dist. LEXIS 11404 (E.D. Ky. Jul. 21, 1998); Dambrot v. Cent. Mich. Univ., 55 F.3d 1177, 1182–85 (6th Cir. 1995).

38. Board of Regents of the University of Wisconsin System v. Southworth, 529 U.S. 217 (2000).

39. Ibid. at 233.

40. The Joint Statement on Rights and Freedoms of Students, issued by the AAUP, the United States Student Association, the Association of American Colleges and Universities, the National Association of Student Personnel Administrators, and the National Association for Women in Education, includes the following provisions:

> The professor in the classroom and in conference should encourage free discussion, inquiry, and expression. Student performance should be evaluated solely on an academic basis, not on opinions or conduct in matters unrelated to academic standards.
>
> 1. *Protection of Freedom of Expression* Students should be free to take reasoned exception to the data or views offered in any course of study and to reserve judgment about matters of opinion, but they are responsible for learning the content of any course of study for which they are enrolled.
>
> 2. *Protection Against Improper Academic Evaluation* Students should have protection through orderly procedures against prejudiced or capricious academic evaluation. At the same time, they are responsible for maintaining standards of academic performance established for each course in which they are enrolled. (*AAUP Documents*, 262)

41. See, e.g., Grayned v. City of Rockford, 408 U.S. 104, 117–21 (1972); *Tinker*, 393 U.S. at 513.
42. Hazelwood School District v. Kuhlmeier, 484 U.S. 260 (1988).
43. Ibid. at 273.
44. See Brown v. Li, 308 F.3d 939 (9th Cir. 2002), where the court upheld the refusal of a faculty committee to approve a master's thesis unless the student removed the "disacknowledgements" section because it did not meet professional standards. The court applied to a university setting the principles of Hazelwood, holding that "the First Amendment does not require an educator to change the assignment to suit the student's opinion or to approve the work of a student that, in his or her judgment, fails to meet a legitimate academic standard." Ibid. at 949.
45. Association of American Colleges and Universities Board of Directors, "Academic Freedom and Educational Responsibility," January 6, 2006, www.aacu.org/about/statements/academic_freedom.cfm (internal quotes omitted). See also Axson-Flynn v. Johnson, 356 F.3d 1277 (10th Cir. 2004). In that case, a Mormon student objected to certain language she was required to say in connection with classroom acting exercises. The District Court granted summary judgment in favor of the defendants and dismissed the case. The Court of Appeals held that the *Hazelwood* standard requires only that restrictions on a student's right to free expression in the classroom be reasonable and that courts will not override a professor's judgment unless it is a substantial departure from accepted academic norms or "where the proffered goal or methodology was a sham pretext for an impermissible ulterior motive." Ibid. at 1293. The Court of Appeals remanded the case to the District Court because there was a genuine issue of material fact as to whether the department requirement that the script be strictly adhered to was based on legitimate pedagogical reasons or was a pretext for religious discrimination. Ibid. at 1295.
46. For a summary of the case law involving the tension between faculty and student rights, see Cheryl A. Cameron, Laura E. Meyers, and Steven G. Olswang, "Academic Bills of Rights: Conflict in the Classroom," *Journal of College and University Law* 31 (2005): 243.
47. See, e.g., Bonnell v. Lorenzo, 241 F.3d 800, 823–24 (6th Cir. 2001); Martin v. Parrish, 805 F.2d 583, 584 n.2, 586 (5th Cir. 1986); *Rubin*, 933 F.Supp. at 1442.
48. See, e.g., *Hardy*, 260 F.3d at 679 (Instructor used and solicited from students derogatory expressions pertaining to race, sex, and sexual orientation in connection with a lecture and discussion in a communications class about words that have historically served the interests of the dominant culture in violation against policy prohibiting the use of offensive language in class.); Silva v. University of New Hampshire, 888 F.Supp. 293, 313 (D.N.H. 1994) (Writing instructor used sexually suggestive language and metaphors in explaining aspects of writing in violation of sexual harassment policy.)
49. Consider the following example that does not involve profanity, sex, religion, or other hot-button issues. A professor's style of questioning and criticizing students is harsh, and many of them find it difficult if not impossible to learn from him. Students complain bitterly. Those who can avoid his classes do so. Those who cannot perform poorly compared with their peers in other classes. Despite efforts to counsel him by

other faculty and administrators, the faculty member refuses to change, arguing that his pedagogical method is entirely legitimate. His department's personnel committee eventually decides not to reappoint him. Would not judicial second-guessing of that result violate the core principles of academic freedom?

50. See, e.g., Cohen v. San Bernardino Valley College, 92 F.3d 968, 972 (9th Cir. 1996). In light of its holding on the vagueness issue, the court declined "to define today the precise contours of the protection the First Amendment provides the classroom speech of college professors." Ibid. at 971. The opinion contains no reference to any of the case law relating to the First Amendment rights of public employees. See also *Dambrot*, 55 F.3d at 1182–85, where the Sixth Circuit upheld a First Amendment challenge to the university's discriminatory harassment policy brought by both a basketball coach and students. Nevertheless, the court went on to hold that the termination of the coach for use of the word "nigger" in a locker room pep talk was permissible, because his speech did not involve a matter of public concern and was not protected by academic freedom. Ibid. at 1185–91.

51. For example, in Hayut v. State Univ. N.Y., 352 F.3d 733 (2d Cir. 2003), the court found that a professor's classroom comments to a female student were sufficiently offensive, severe, and pervasive that a reasonable person could conclude that he had created a hostile environment. The professor repeatedly called the student "Monica" because of a purported resemblance to Monica Lewinsky and would ask her in class about "her weekend with Bill" and make other sexually suggestive remarks such as "be quiet Monica, I will give you a cigar later." The professor did not argue that his classroom comments were protected by academic freedom, and thus the court did not express a view on the availability of such a defense. Ibid. at 745. The AAUP, in its "Report on Sexual Harassment—Suggested Policy and Procedures for Handling Complaints," offers the view that sexual harassment may include classroom speech that is reasonably regarded as offensive, substantially impairs the academic opportunity of students, is persistent and pervasive, and is not germane to the subject matter. *AAUP Documents*, 209.

52. See, e.g., Yacovelli v. Moser, 2004 WL 1144183 (M.D.N.C. May 20, 2004) (upheld university's assignment of a book about the Qu'ran in freshman orientation program); Calvary Bible Presbyterian Church of Seattle v. Univ. of Washington, 436 P.2d 189 (Wash. 1967) (upheld university's course in the Bible as Literature).

53. See Bishop v. Aronov, 926 F.2d 1066 (11th Cir. 1991), where the court upheld restrictions on the speech of an assistant professor of health, physical education, and recreation prohibiting him from interjecting his religious beliefs and/or preferences during instructional time periods or conducting optional classes in which a "Christian perspective" of an academic topic is delivered. The court held that the First Amendment right to free speech of the faculty member, which it found did not include a distinct right to academic freedom, was outweighed by the authority of the university to establish curriculum. The court declined to reach the Establishment Clause issue. Although the decision does not specifically state that plaintiff's speech was not related to the subject matter of the course, it would appear to underlie its reasoning;

otherwise, it is hard to see why the general authority of the university to establish curriculum allows it to prohibit certain classroom speech of a faculty member consistent with the First Amendment.

54. For a recent example, see the procedures established at the City University of New York: www.cuny.edu/about/administration/offices/la/PROCEDURES_FOR_HANDLING_STUDENT_COMPLAINTS.pdf.

55. *AAUP Documents*, 135–40. Although jointly formulated by the three organizations, each took a different action with respect to the "Statement on Government." The AAUP's council adopted it, and the AAUP's membership endorsed it. The board of directors of the American Council on Education issued a statement in which it "recognizes the statement as a significant step forward in the clarification of the respective roles of governing boards, faculties, and administrations" and "commends it to the institutions which are members of the Council." Similarly, the Executive Committee of the Association of Governing Boards issued a statement in which it "recognizes the statement as a significant step forward in the clarification of the respective roles of governing boards, faculties, and administrations," and "commends it to the governing boards which are members of the Association."

56 http://agb.org/statement-board-responsibility-institutional-governance. The statement was revised and updated as the AGB's "Statement on Board Responsibility for Institutional Governance" in 2010, to which the above citation refers. However, the language quoted in the text appears in both the 1998 and 2010 statements.

57. Areen, *supra* note 28, at 964–66.

58. Minnesota Board for Community Colleges v. Knight, 465 U.S. 271 (1984).

59. The issue arose in an unusual context. Minnesota law required public employees to bargain over the terms and conditions of employment and further required their employers to exchange views on subjects relating to employment that were outside the scope of mandatory bargaining only with the exclusive representatives selected by the employees. The law was challenged by faculty members at a community college who wanted to discuss academic matters directly with their college administration. Although again recognizing the arguments in favor of the value of faculty participation in governance, the court held there was no constitutional right to do so. Ibid. at 288.

60. Quite apart from what is necessary for academic freedom, faculty participation in governance is an appropriate way to reach the best and most informed decisions, to ensure the necessary support from those who actually deliver the services provided by universities, and to create an atmosphere conducive to the enthusiastic pursuit of scholarship and teaching. These reasons also support some faculty participation in such "nonacademic" matters as budget and facilities, where the expertise of the faculty may not always be relevant and a more corporate style of governance may seem appropriate. In addition, decisions in even such financial and managerial areas often have a direct and significant impact on scholarship and teaching.

61. *AAUP Documents*, 139.

62. Cole, *The Great American University*, 136

63. Cole, *The Great American University*, 136, as quoted from Clark Kerr, *The Uses of the University*, 5th ed. (Cambridge: Harvard University Press, 2001), 28.

64. Stanley Fish, "Faculty Governance in Idaho," *New York Times*, June 6, 2011, http://opinionator.blogs.nytimes.com/2011/06/06/faculty-governance-in-idaho.

65. See, e.g., Carley v. Arizona Bd. of Regents, 153 P.2d 1099 (Ariz. Ct. App. 1987) (rejecting claim by faculty member that the university violated his constitutional rights by taking into account negative student evaluations of his teaching in deciding not to renew his contract).

66. American Historical Association, *The Academic Bill of Rights*, www.studentsforacademicfreedom.org/abor.html.

67. Similar student bills of rights have been introduced in Congress and in several state legislatures. See Cameron, Meyers, and Olswang, "Academic Bills of Rights: Conflict in the Classroom," 243–47. So far none has been enacted.

68. David Beito, Ralph E. Luker, and Robert K. C. Johnson, "The AHA's Double Standard on Academic Freedom," *Perspectives on History* (March 2006), www.historians.org/Perspectives/issues/2006/0603/0603vie2.cfm.

69. For a more detailed critique of the Academic Bill of Rights, see the "Statement on the Academic Bill of Rights of Committee A of the AAUP," www.aaup.org/AAUP/comm/rep/A/abor.htm.

70. See, generally, *AAUP Documents*, passim. Many of the AAUP's recommendations are thoughtful. However, the connection of many such recommendations to academic freedom is not always clear or well established. Moreover, where there is little or no link between particular AAUP policies and academic freedom, it does not seem appropriate for it to enforce them through investigations, reports, and ultimately censure, especially at universities that established different procedures and policies in consultation or collective bargaining with their own faculty.

13

ACADEMIC FREEDOM AND THE BOYCOTT OF ISRAELI UNIVERSITIES

STANLEY FISH

1

T HE BOOK-LENGTH STUDY from which this chapter is excerpted begins by noting that the literature of academic freedom is a literature of persistent and basic questions.

Is academic freedom a subset of the First Amendment and therefore something that affords legal protection to those who qualify as academics? Or is academic freedom a subset of freedom in the larger philosophical sense and therefore a political rather than a legal project? Or (a third possibility) is academic freedom a less exalted concept, neither a legal right nor a philosophical imperative, but the name of a guild desire, the desire to be free from external monitoring and discipline in the workplace. (This, of course, is the desire of all professions.) If that is all there is to it—a claim of special privilege—what, if anything justifies affirming the claim? Do academics who work in public universities enjoy a status superior to that of other public employees? Are academics, unlike other employees, free to criticize their superiors without fear of retaliation? Does academic freedom attach to the university or to the individual professor? Do students have academic freedom rights? Do classroom teachers have an academic freedom right to depart from strictly academic concerns?

As I explored these questions, each of which has a literature of its own, I noticed that the answers to them varied depending on whether academic freedom was conceived narrowly—as a freedom conditioned by the particular obligations of the academic task—or conceived expansively as a general obligation to support the cause of freedom wherever it is under threat. Is academic freedom intelligible only within the confines of a singular profession—is it a professional norm?—or it is a norm that guides, or should guide, the actions of all right-thinking men and women, whether they are standing in front of a classroom or standing in front of the barricades. These alternate conceptions, and the gradations between them, can be captured by a simple formula: as one moves from a restrictive to an expansive notion of academic freedom—as one moves from right to left—the force of "academic" as a limiting adjective is less and less felt, and the scope of the word freedom more and more enlarged. Hence the subtitle of the book: "From Professionalism to Revolution."

In my analysis one moves from professionalism to revolution in five stages, and I call these stages the five schools of academic freedom. Here they are.

First, the "it's just a job" school. This school is deflationary; it regards higher education not as a vocation or holy calling, but as a provider of services. Colleges and universities offer disciplinary knowledge and skills to students who wish to receive them. Faculty members are trained to impart that knowledge, demonstrate those skills, and engage in research that adds to the body of what is known. They are professionals, not moralists or therapists or change agents, and when they are engaged in professional activities, narrowly defined, they should be accorded the latitude—call it freedom if you like—necessary to their proper performance. When they depart from their professional responsibilities they merit blame, not freedom.

Second, the "for the common good" school. This school has its origin in the "1915 Declaration of Principles on Academic Freedom and Academic Tenure" of the American Association of University Professors (AAUP) and it shares some arguments with the "it's just a job school," especially the argument that the freedom accorded academics is conditioned on their hewing to academic responsibilities and not using their position in the university as a "shelter . . . for uncritical and intemperate partisanship." However, the "for the common good school" departs from the severe professionalism of the "it's just a job" school when it links the performance of responsible scholarship to the flourishing of democracy. The reasoning is that democracy requires credentialed experts in order to check "the tyranny of public opinion" and thus "train" the less expert citizenry. By using an external measure—the health of democracy—to justify the academy, this school opens the way to the de-emphasizing of "academic" in favor of the more abstract value of freedom.

Third, the "for uncommon beings" or "academic exceptionalism" school. If academics are charged not merely with the task of adding to our knowledge but with the task of providing a counterweight to common popular opinion, they must themselves be uncommon, not only intellectually but morally. They must be, in the words of the "1915 Declaration," "men of high gift and character." Such men (and now women) not only correct the errors of popular opinion; they escape popular judgment and are not to be held accountable to the same laws and restrictions that constrain ordinary citizens.

Fourth, the "academic freedom as critique" school. If academics have the special capacity to see through conventional public wisdom and expose its contradictions, exercising that capacity—the capacity of critique—is their real job. While the "it's just a job" school and the "for the common good" school insist that the freedom academics enjoy is limited by the norms of the profession, those who identify academic freedom with critique insist that professional norms should be interrogated and regarded as objects of critical scrutiny rather than as the unexamined parameters within which scrutiny is performed. Schools 1, 2, and 3 elevate and celebrate professionalism, albeit in different ways; this fourth school is deeply suspicious of professionalism and of all established structures of authority.

Fifth, the "academic freedom as training for revolution" school. This school takes the obligation of critique seriously and turns the suspicion of established structures into a program for overturning them. If school 4 urges us not to accept professional norms without inquiring into their source, members of school 5 know in advance where that inquiry will lead—to the discovery that professional norms have their source in the corrupt motives of agents who are embedded in the corrupt institutions that serve and reflect the corrupt values of a corrupt neoliberal society. With the emergence of this school, the shift from "academic" as a limiting adjective to freedom as an overriding and global concern is complete; frankly political actions takes the place of actions performed within professional constraints. "Academic freedom" is still a phrase that can be invoked, but its meaning is radically changed, as it is when Grant Farred declares that "academic freedom has to be conceived of as a form of political solidarity."[1] If that is what academic freedom really is, adhering to a narrowly professional view of one's responsibilities in the classroom amounts to a betrayal of both one's political being and one's pedagogical being. One can be true to the academy only by breaking free of its ideologically based constraints.

The poster boy for this fifth school is Denis Rancourt, a professor of physics at the University of Ottawa who was dismissed from his position for practicing what he calls "academic squatting." You perform academic squatting when you occupy the space of an assigned course in a traditional discipline and turn it into a course on political activism; not, Rancourt is quick to say, a course *about* political activism—that would be perfectly ordinary—but a course that trains students to *be* political activists. You appropriate the university's resources in an effort to bring the university down, and you do this with a sense of moral righteousness." "Academic squatting," Rancourt explains, "is needed because universities are dictatorships . . . run by self-appointed executives who serve capital interests."

Rancourt continues to raise the banner of academic freedom but in a way that reverses its traditional professional meaning. He defines academic freedom as "the ideal under which professors and students are autonomous and design their own development and interactions."[2] You might ask, what are professors and students autonomous *from*, and the answer is given when Rancourt contrasts his definition of academic freedom with another, which he rejects: "The institutions, however, define academic freedom to mean that the universities are not accountable to elected governments." In Rancourt's view, the trouble with this second definition is that under it professors and students are accountable to the universities rather than being free to "design their own development and interactions." What professors and students should be autonomous from is the monitoring by the university of whatever they choose to do. In short, *academic freedom means freedom from the academy.*

When I wrote briefly about Rancourt in the *New York Times*, some readers chided me for focusing on so extreme an example and presenting it as if his was a position held by more than a few cranks. But while Rancourt's pronouncements are theatrical and perhaps exaggerated for effect, the view underlying them is not so uncommon and has in fact been ratified in 2008 by an arbitrator commissioned by the University of Ottawa and the Association of Professors of the University of Ottawa. Although he had critical things to say about the behavior of both parties, on the main point arbitrator Michel Picher came squarely down on the side of Rancourt: "It is difficult for this arbitrator to conclude that it was inappropriate or beyond the bounds of academic freedom for Professor Rancourt to have framed the description of the course in the terms he chose." This is as much to say what Rancourt had been saying: academic freedom has no bounds at all.

The merit of the Rancourt case is that it puts on display the steps by which taking a certain view of academic freedom leads to the expansion and consequent emptying out of the concept: if you begin by assuming that academic freedom attaches to the individual professor rather than to the institution (a position Robert Post and Matthew Finkin term "antinomian" in their book *For The Common Good*), the exercise of your freedom might well involve flouting the institution's protocols in the name of a higher obligation; and once you begin to do that, you are more than halfway to deciding that what academics are free and obligated to do is critique and oppose arrangements that impede the advancement of social progress. It will then seem obvious to you that universities, tied as they are to the interests of the state and corporate capitalism, do just that kind of bad work. Therefore, in order to stand up for true freedom, you must burst the bounds of merely *academic* freedom and turn your energies against the structures that house you in the hope that, in time, they will be reformed and align themselves with the project of social justice. Academic freedom, in this logic, is appropriately exercised only when it transcends the academy and is no longer academic in any narrow sense.

2

Something very much like this sequence is enacted by those who have in recent years advocated a boycott of Israeli universities. They argue that because Israeli universities are funded by a rogue state and because the policies of that state have the effect of abrogating the academic freedom of Palestinian professors and students (by denying them materials, access, funding, and mobility), it is an expression and not a violation of academic freedom to refrain from engaging in intellectual commerce with Israeli universities or with Israeli scholars unless they actively repudiate the policies of their government. (I should note that the question of whether the boycott should extend to individual scholars is a matter of dispute within the movement.) Pointing out that "Israeli universities are . . . heavily involved in tailored teaching for the military and security services," boycott supporters conclude that the "academic freedom of Israel has generated illegal, racist, and oppressive behavior . . . , complicity in [the] government's expansionist and oppressive policies;

and in response to the suffering imposed on the Occupied Territories and the violation of Palestinian academic freedom—deafening silence."[3] How, asks University of California–Los Angeles Professor Sondra Hale, "can we discuss academic freedom in the absence of basic human rights?" How will the invocation of academic freedom be received by Palestinian academics who live under conditions that make the phrase "meaningless":

> The destruction of infrastructure, civil society, and cultural and intellectual life cannot be separated from the question of academic freedom. The ability of teachers, researchers and students to deliver and access teaching cannot be separated from the question of academic freedom. The right to be free from arbitrary detentions and delays, and from the threat of an occupying force backed by the threat of violence cannot be separated from the question of academic freedom.[4]

The basic argument is that while academic freedom, conceived of narrowly as the freedom to engage in "scientific and scholarly discourse," is undoubtedly an "attractive" principle, it cannot be allowed to function as an alibi for the violation of principles of equal, and perhaps superior, importance. The point is made forcefully by Maximilian Forte, associate professor of anthropology at Concordia University, in his essay "Canadian Academic Boycott of Israel: Why We Need to Take Action."[5] Forte begins by wondering "how institutions that boast of enhancing and developing the individual's capacities for citizenship, for appreciation of diversity, and sensitivity to humanity, can so quickly turn a cold face to genocide." The path to the conclusion he wishes to reach is opened up the moment universities are made instrumental to extra-academic purposes. If individual growth, the formation of citizens, and the broad needs of humanity are identified as the university's core concerns, the freedom to teach, say, Byzantine art and to publish scholarly monographs about it will seem pretty small potatoes; and a focus on such esoteric matters in a time of geopolitical urgency will be seen as a dereliction of duty.

In response to a University of Ottawa professor's concern that a boycott would violate academic freedom, Forte deplores what he calls "a selfish and narrow way of thinking." Academic freedom, he declares, does not "trump everything else on earth." While in some respects academic freedom is "vital," it is not "so paramount that it rises above the interests of human beings subject to genocidal practices." Indeed, if given a choice, he "would rather live in a world with justice, and no concern with academic freedom, rather than the reverse." He cannot, he says, accept "the notion that out of concern for academic freedom, all other freedoms must be drowned." Political freedom must come before academic freedom, and any version of academic freedom that would draw a bright line separating academic work from political work must be rejected.

Forte correctly identifies the narrowness of an academic freedom understood as the freedom to engage in professional projects that stop at the water's edge of politics and address large-scale social concerns indirectly if at all. (What will a new account of *Paradise Lost* or of the doctrine of consideration in contract law do to alleviate human misery?) If the test universities must pass measures their contributions to world peace or universal justice, a university that sticks to its academic knitting will fail it, and Forte will be right to say "We should be serving humanity, be concerned for humanity, and [a university] ought to show more sensitivity and respect for humanity if it is to be taken seriously and to be protected as an institution worth preserving in very uncertain times."

In this argument, academic institutions deserve protection only if they detach themselves from merely professional academic imperatives and join the political struggle everyone should be engaged in. Like Rancourt, who, not surprisingly, is a boycott supporter, Forte is willing to invoke academic freedom so long as it is extended to everyone and not clung to as a guild privilege: "If academic freedom is what really mattered in this discussion, it would be made to matter for all, and not just held as the inviolable, paramount, and absolute right of a privileged few." This cannot mean that everyone should be an academic, festooned with degrees and assigned an office in a university building. It must mean, rather, that everyone should enjoy the privileges and respect now accorded only to academics; everyone should be regarded as an equal partner in the struggle for social justice; everyone's contribution should be taken seriously; and everyone should be guaranteed the freedom to speak out without fear of retaliation. Needless to say, this utopian vision would spell the end of academic freedom as a doctrine responsive to the distinctive conditions—there would not be any—of academic labor.

Still, it is not difficult to understand the appeal of this vision. The contention that in the end human freedom trumps academic freedom, if only because absent the security of human rights academic rights can neither flourish nor be protected, seems intuitively right. It is a matter of what comes first, isn't it? If an oppressive regime makes daily life miserable for an entire population, including its students and teachers, and if you determine that fellow academics flourishing under that regime are either passive or complicit, is it not your duty—both as a professor and as a human being—to apply what leverage you have in an effort to provoke your delinquent colleagues to rouse themselves and do the right thing? If you fail to do so, do you not join them in their complicity? Isn't it simply wrong to hunker down in the academic trenches, writing your essays and teaching your sanitized classes, while millions are denied the freedom you take for granted?

On the other side—the side I favor—there is only one thing to say and it amounts largely to a reaffirmation of the independence and priority of professional academic values. I don't mean that professional values take precedence over more general human values, but that more general human values should not be the ones dictating your behavior when you are acting as a professional. In 2002, Mona Baker, a professor of translation studies at the University of Manchester in England, removed two Israelis from the editorial boards of the journals *Translator* and *Translation Studies Abstracts*. She told a reporter that she was not boycotting Israelis, just "Israeli institutions," and in an e-mail to Gideon Toury, one of those she had "unappointed," she declared that she continued to regard him as a friend, and said that her decision was "political, not personal." (All too true.) Toury replied, "I would appreciate it if the announcement made it clear that 'he' (that is I), was appointed as a scholar and unappointed as an Israeli. That is, when you invited me it was by virtue of my scholarly credentials with no concern for my nationality or religious affiliations, and now you disinvite me for political reasons, reasons that are not relevant to the doing of academic business."

Baker and Toury are not really in disagreement: each is aware that the wall separating academic judgments and political judgments—between academic reasons for appointing a board member and political reasons for appointing a board member—has been breached. It is just that while Toury continues to insist on the independent integrity of the academic community—a community that knows no geography but the meta-geography of professional recognition and cooperation—Baker would claim that the community's integrity could not possibly be independent of the material conditions without which contemplative leisure would be impossible. In her view, one must act politically so that those conditions and the leisure they bring with them can be restored.

Judith Butler makes the same point: "If the exercise of academic freedom ... is actively thwarted, that freedom is lost, which is why checkpoints are and should be an issue for anyone who defends a notion of academic freedom."[6] Butler's statement allows us to see clearly why the word "freedom" in the phrase "academic freedom" is the source of so much confusion. Freedom is obviously a political concept, and it is easy to make the mistake of thinking that something called academic freedom is a political value in competition with other political values to which it must, on occasion, yield.

But the fact that academic freedom cannot flourish in a political space that denies the conditions necessary for its exercise does not mean that academic freedom is a political value. It is an abstract value—the value of the unfettered search for truth—and it is defined independently of the political circumstances that might attend or frustrate its implementation. Those circumstances, whether encouraging or discouraging of the value, are not essential to it as distinct from being essential to its realization. Butler says that "it makes no sense to value the doctrine in the abstract if we cannot call for its implementation." But it makes the same sense as valuing universal health care apart from the question of whether the political/economic situation of a particular nation is such that the care can actually be delivered. If it were determined that the actions of Nation X had the effect of undermining the health care of Nation Y's citizens, would we then think it right to refuse to sell medical supplies to Nation X in the hope that the damage to *its* citizens would provoke a reconsideration of policy? The value—whether it be academic freedom or universal health care—is one thing, the context of its instantiation another; and when one context has been rendered inhospitable to the value (perhaps by an occupation), the conclusion cannot be to abandon it by surrendering it to politics. Boycotters who say "because the Israelis deny academic freedom to the Palestinians, we're going to deny it to them" are also denying it to themselves. They reason that given the present circumstances we cannot continue to respect the distinctiveness of academic work—a distinctiveness defined by its difference from political work—and we are morally obligated to use the leverage provided by our academic positions to perform political acts. They congratulate themselves for doing a good deed while happily paying the price for their virtue of abandoning the academic integrity they continue to claim.

Needless to say, Butler would resist this critical account of the boycotters' logic. "We could say," she says dismissively, "that these are terrible circumstances and ought to be addressed by other means, but that, strictly speaking, these are not matters of academic freedom." "Strictly speaking" in Butler's vocabulary means speaking within a pinched, narrow position in which the discourse of academic freedom proceeds merrily and airily along while entire populations are unable to exercise the freedom being celebrated. (A version of Nero fiddling while Rome burns.) That is the position held to by those (like me) for whom academic freedom is a professional concept that is not enlarged but hollowed out when it becomes the freedom (and the duty) to act in extra-academic ways. Butler is quite precise in her characterization of both what is asked and perhaps lost by such strict speaking: "If to enter the debate on academic freedom is precisely to bracket out both the material devastations characteristic of the Occupation . . . , then what form of political constriction is performed through constricting the discourse of academic freedom to a narrow liberal conception?" The assertion of her dependent clause ("If to enter") is correct, although the bracketing out need not be self-consciously performed. That is, as an academic you do not have to say to yourself: I am now going to put aside the devastations of the Occupation (or of Sudan or of Syria or of a hundred other places) and just focus on medieval metrics or the Hundred Years War. Once you step into the world where topics like these are the basis of a lifetime of scholarly work, the putting aside (at least for the period of professional labor) has already occurred, not as an act of the will— you do not pledge to close your eyes to the suffering of peoples—but as the consequence of your having committed yourself (again for certain specified times, not all the time) to a necessarily limited project, the project of engaging in the practices that typically take place in universities.

Of course, this is a choice—no one forced you to become an academic— and one could argue that the choice is a political one. You could decide, as many have, that life is too short to spend a significant amount of it worrying over something perhaps only 500 other people in the world care about. You could decide to leave the academy and devote all your energies to, say, the redressing of injustice and the alleviation of misery. But if you decide to stay, you should actually do it and not sail under false colors by appropriating the machinery and prestige of the academy for political purposes as Rancourt frankly urges and Butler urges in effect.

The answer to Butler's question—"What form of political constriction is performed through restricting the discourse of academic freedom to a narrow liberal conception?"—is "no form at all." Restricting the discourse of academic freedom to a "narrow conception" is simply to recognize that academic work, like every other kind of work, *is* narrowly conceived. No kind of work does everything, and a task whose limits are expanded far beyond what appropriately belongs to it (and I know that "appropriateness" is precisely what is in dispute) is no longer what it is. Choosing to perform a limited task and determining to respect its limits is not a political statement; it is a professional statement. The politics, as I have already said, comes in when you decide to perform this task rather than another. Fidelity to your decision, not a constriction of your politics, is what is being practiced.

Nor will it do to say (as Butler sometimes seems to) that demarcating a space where analysis and description but not politics (in the partisan sense) are done is itself a political act for which one must take responsibility. This argument, which continues to be popular in certain quarters, gets its apparent force by enlarging the category of politics until it includes everything: urging specific policies is political and ruling out the urging of specific policies is political. But expanding the meaning of politics in this fashion is just like expanding the meaning of academic freedom until it encompasses anything an academic might think right to do: the concept loses its usefulness as a way of making distinctions (which is of course the strategy of those who equate academic freedom with critique and revolution). When Butler calls for a "more robust conception of academic freedom," one that does not bracket out geopolitical considerations, she is calling for the end of the academy as a place where a distinctive activity is performed and plumping instead for a place indistinguishable at bottom from the ballot box, the parliamentary debate, and the street rally.

Now an argument that there should not be an academy and that society's resources and the energies of citizens would be better expended elsewhere is an argument I am always ready to entertain. I have never been a hard-core defender of the educational experience or of disinterested inquiry as a value that must be protected at all costs. All I would say is that if we are going to have an academy we should really have it in all its glorious narrowness and not transform it into an appendage of politics, even when—no, especially when—the politics is one that we affirm and believe in with all our hearts

3

As a way of bringing our discussion to a close, let us revisit the taxonomy of the schools of academic freedom and ask what each of them would say about the boycott of Israeli universities and scholars. (Much of the answer has already been given.)

The "it's just a job" school would see the boycott as a perfect example of what happens when the narrowly professional conception of academic work is enlarged so that its exercise can be directly linked to real-world problems and their possible solutions. Even the apparently innocuous tying of academic freedom to democracy leads to an alteration in the direction of justification, for rather than asking how a proposed project contributes to the furthering of knowledge, one asks how the project furthers the goals of democracy. Sooner or later, that question will be seen as legitimizing any action taken by academics in the name of social justice, and boycotting Israeli universities will be regarded as the fulfillment of academic freedom rather than as its violation (precisely the argument of the boycotters).

The boycott presents a difficult problem for the "it's for the common good" school, which is in many ways a "swing" school. As I observed earlier, the shift from the professional good to the common good opens the door to the transformation of academic freedom into an agenda of political activism, and that is a door members of the "it's for the common good" school are reluctant to walk through. So they are pulled in two directions, affirming professional norms while leaning toward the norms and imperatives of a progressive politics. Thus the split message of the AAUP's 2006 statement on academic boycotts.

The statement begins by reaffirming its 2005 resolution: "We reject proposals that curtail the freedom of teachers and researchers to engage in work with academic colleagues, and we reaffirm the paramount importance of the freest possible international movement of scholars and ideas." But then the statement goes on to acknowledge candidly that the AAUP's practices have not always been faithful to its own severe standard. In 1970 the organization engaged in a debate about whether a university should "take a position on disputed public issues" like the Vietnam War. One side said no, reasoning that a university should not "become an instrument of indoctrination." The other side argued that there should be an exemption for "extraordinary situations." The question of dealing with German universities under the Nazis was raised: "Can one plausibly maintain that academic freedom is inviolate when the civil freedoms of the larger society have been abrogated?"

Fifteen years later the same issues surfaced in the context of the movement to divest from companies doing business with South Africa. In a 1985 resolution, the AAUP called on colleges and universities to "oppose apartheid" by declining "to hold securities in banks which provide loans to the government of South Africa." This, it was said, "did not constitute an academic boycott," because it kept open "lines of communication among scholars." The claim was that by thus splitting hairs, "the AAUP carefully distinguished between economic and academic boycotts largely on matters of principle" (although one could argue that the so-called principle failed the test of "indirect effect": an economic boycott is likely to have an adverse impact on teachers and researchers).

It is in the context of this ambiguous history that the organization confronted the calls for a boycott of Israeli universities. This time, it appeared to come down squarely against boycotts: "In view of the Association's longstanding commitment to the free exchange of ideas, we oppose academic boycotts." But then the report concluded with a curious sentence, the two halves of which are much closer together than its syntax suggests: "We understand that threats to or infringement of academic freedom may occasionally seem so dire as to require compromising basic precepts of academic freedom, but we resist the argument that extraordinary circumstances should be the basis for limiting our fundamental commitment to the free exchange of ideas and their free expression." Huh? The argument "we" resist after the "but" is the argument whose force we acknowledge in the part of the sentence before the "but." We concede X, but we resist X.

The fence-sitting this sentence performs is characteristic of the 2006 statement as a whole, especially its list of alternative "sanctions and protest" that might be considered by the university community as a response to Israeli aggression—"resolutions by higher education organizations condemning violations of academic freedom whether they occur directly by state or administrative suppression of opposing points of view or indirectly by creating material conditions such as blockades, checkpoints, and insufficient funding of Palestinian universities, that make the realization of academic freedom impossible." The adverb "indirectly" lets in everything the firm stand against boycotts supposedly bars. If universities can legitimately issue condemnations and sponsor protests whenever the actions of a state indirectly affect academic freedom adversely, the line separating academic and political actions has been irremediably blurred.

The same blurring of the line occurs in a widely read essay by Martha Nussbaum, an AAUP-style liberal. Nussbaum writes "Against Academic Boycotts,"[7] but she too believes that there are "a number of options open to those who want to express strong condemnation." She lists a number of them, beginning with "censure": "a professional association might censure an academic institution that violates the rights of scholars." (That of course is the job of AAUP Committee A.) That seems straightforward enough, as does the option of "organized public condemnation." Nussbaum illustrates this tactic by declaring that "if Martin Heidegger had been invited to the University of Chicago, I would have been one of the ones conducting a public protest of his appearance and trying to inform other people about his record of collaboration with the Nazi regime." A public protest is one conducted in public by individuals who come together for a cause; it is precisely not a protest conducted by the university, which should hold itself aloof from the constitutionally protected activities of its employees no matter what side of the political aisle they are on. So far so good. I probably would not have been one of those protesting Heidegger's appearance, but the decision of a professor to do so is not a departure from the norms of academic freedom; it is in fact protected speech under the First Amendment.

But the slide down the fabled slippery slope has already begun when Nussbaum announces, as another "option" (short of boycotting) open to a university, the "failure to reward." The institution, she says, "might decide that [an] individual does not deserve special honors," such an honorary degree. Her example is Margaret Thatcher who, she says, was understandably denied an honorary degree from Oxford because by "conferring an honorary degree, a university makes a strong statement about its own values." No, it does not. By conferring an honorary degree, a university recognizes the significance—in the sense of magnitude—of the recipient's labors; it does not endorse them. A university that awarded a degree to either Antonin Scalia or Ruth Bader Ginsburg would not be indicating approval of the honoree's decisions; it would be recognizing that in their professional capacities these justices have played a significant role in shaping the nation's legal culture. Failure to make this distinction informed the opposition at Southern Methodist University to housing the George W. Bush library; the protestors confused the question "Is the tenure of a two-term U.S. president a worthy subject of academic study?" with the question "Do we politically and morally approve of the president's policies?" When Nussbaum declares that Thatcher's "assault on basic scientific research" in addition to her "ruin of the national medical system" were "values that the Oxford faculty believed that it could not endorse," she falls into the same confusion. Oxford faculty members would not be endorsing Thatcher's policies by acquiescing in the awarding of a degree to her; they would be testifying to her immense and undoubted stature as a national and world figure. At this point one might object that the same could be said about Al Capone or Adolf Hitler; but Capone and Hitler were criminals and (in different ways and scales) mass murderers. One can still hold on to the category of "significant figure" as a basis for selection while excluding from it the performance of significant criminality. (To be sure, the distinction isn't always perspicuous; while some regard Henry Kissinger as an exemplary statesman, others think of him as a war criminal.)

Nussbaum gives the game away when she declares that under the "failure to reward" rubric "one might in some cases of competition for merit grants, refuse to reward Israel, without endorsing a boycott." Surely that is a distinction without a difference; excluding Israeli academic institutions from a competition for funds is just a boycott by another name. Nussbaum's alternative options, like those listed in the AAUP's 2006 statement, illustrate how easy it is for the members of the "it's for the common good" school to transgress the boundary that separates academic from political advocacy.

There is no straight line from the third school, that of academic exceptionalism ("academic freedom is for uncommon beings") to any position on the boycott of Israeli institutions and scholars. Exceptionalism is typically asserted in the context of employment disputes; the claim is that academics should be exempt from regulations and limitations to which other workers are bound. One could affirm that claim and have any view, or no view, of the boycott.

The relationship between the "critique" school of academic freedom and the approval of the boycott is much closer and is indeed inherent in the notion of critique itself. Critique, at least as it is urged by members of this school, is inseparable from the quest for social justice. Henry Giroux's name for this quest, as it is conducted in the university, is "critical pedagogy": "Critical pedagogy is about providing the conditions for students to be agents in a world that needs to be interrogated as part of a broader project of connecting the search for knowledge, truth, and justice to the ongoing tasks of democratizing both the university and the larger society."[8] It is important for this school that the "interrogation" not be merely academic as it is in some safely theorized versions of postmodernism. The relevant distinction is made by Sophia A. McClennen: "The key nuance between postmodern political critique and postmodern apolitical critique is that in the former questions are posed in the service of struggle and vision, and in the latter, the questions are an end in themselves."[9] Questions about justice and injustice should not be posed merely to elucidate the shape of political conditions; rather the aim should be the altering of those conditions, and that, of course, is what the boycott is intended to do. Academic freedom, in this view, cannot be invoked as an argument against the boycott because, properly conceived, academic freedom demands the boycott: "There can be . . . no demand that Israeli academics not be denied academic freedom when such freedom is routinely, deliberately, and as a matter of state policy, denied to their Palestinian colleagues."[10] Once again academic freedom is "saved" by refusing to limit its scope and obligations to the academy. Grant Farred, in the statement I quoted at the beginning of this chapter, identifies the imperative that follows from the installation of active, not merely intellectual, critique at the center of academic freedom: "Academic freedom has to be conceived as a form of political solidarity."

Once that conception is in place, the school of "academic freedom as revolution" has been fully realized. In fact, it would be no exaggeration to say that the boycott of Israeli institutions *is* the realization of this school; for it involves a deliberate and unapologetic turning of the energies of the academy *against* the academic project, at least insofar as that project confines itself to asking and answering narrowly professionally questions. The boycott, as Farred's pronouncement makes clear, represents the overwhelming of traditional academic concerns by blatantly political concerns. The boycott is academic squatting writ large: not just a single course but the entire project is hijacked for political ends.

4

By reaching that conclusion I invite the argument that is always made (I have made it myself) against any claim that a realm is or could be purged of politics, the argument that no area of experience, not even a supposedly politics-free zone, escapes politics. Here is R. Radhakrishnan's version:

> Is the world out there and is academia an interior space? Isn't the world somehow always already in, and isn't academia always in a relationship of heteronomous exteriority to the world of which is a representation/mediation? Aren't outsides and insides always reciprocally relational and mutually constitutive such that there can be no absolute and non-negotiable forms of exteriority and interiority?[11]

I cheerfully stipulate to the assertions implicit in Radhakrishnan's questions. If the academy is an interior space, it is so only by permission of the outside it defines itself against; and, moreover, that outside—the world with all its political/economic/cultural forces and biases—rather than being excluded from the interior space from which it only rhetorically withdraws, configures it and everywhere marks it. The outside owns the inside and, therefore, the claim of the academy to *be* an inside—to be sharply distinguishable from what it pushes away, to be an independent, pure thing—cannot be maintained. There is no "intrinsic" form of the academy, only the form that emerges when some historically limited, contestable definitions and demarcations are put in place by an act of the will. There is, therefore, no reason in nature for the category of academic work not to include the direct taking up of charged political questions with a view to pronouncing on them and prompting students to action. The academy I defend in these pages—narrowly professional and resistant to calls for "relevance"—cannot be defended down to the ground; it rests on foundations no firmer than its self-assertion.

Butler, then, is right when, in a critique of Kant, she insists that philosophy's "claim to transcendental status"—its claim to rise above politics—can only be maintained "by virtue of its implication in politics."[12] She asks, "Is it a transcendental ground that conditions philosophy's difference . . . , or is it precisely the way that line of demarcation is drawn that produces the transcendental effect upon which the disciplinary self-definition of philosophy depends?" The question could be rephrased. "Is it a transcendental ground that conditions the academy's difference, or is it precisely the way that line of demarcation is drawn that produces the effect of difference upon which the academy's self-definition depends?" Both Butler and I would affirm the second alternative in our respective questions. It is "the particular political power of delimitation"—the bald declaration that there politics is and here it is not—and nothing more foundational that produces the differences that then offer themselves as essential.

We disagree, however, in our assessment of whether this production of an artificial difference is a good or bad thing. For Butler it has the unfortunate effect of creating an area "in which critique ought not to go." The academy gains its internal coherence at the price of being unable either to interrogate its boundaries or to move beyond them to a direct engagement with the world. "If, according to the Kantian scheme, philosophy has held itself exempt from state commands and policies, then philosophy has been instrumental in limiting the scope of critique." To which I would reply, "Yes, and it does that in order to be what it is." What Butler complains about—the limitation of critique in the academy to the realm of thought—I see as the necessary founding gesture of the academic realm. If, in Kant's words, it is essential that there be a learned community that "having no commands to give is free to evaluate everything," the only way to establish that community is to declare it into existence and then to enforce the distinctions that sustain its entirely arbitrary vision.

It is because the vision is arbitrary—not motivated by an authority higher than itself—that its maintenance is entirely an internal responsibility. If members of the academy wish to continue doing what they have been trained to do, it is up to them to monitor the conditions—the list of professional dos and don'ts—that ensure the health of their practice. That practice is not underwritten by any theory of truth or justice and it will not survive an interrogation that demands an independent corroboration of its cogency. It is underwritten only by its own protocols, and if they are flouted or actively rejected, the activity they make possible will disappear. The narrowly professional definition of academic freedom is not merely a rival account of the academy. It *is* the academy.

NOTES

1. Grant Farred, "The Art of Politics Is to Divide," *Works and Days* 26/27 (2008/2009): 355.

2. Denis Rancourt, "Dismissing critical pedagogy: Denis Rancourt vs. University of Ottawa," interview by Jesse Freeston, January 12, 2009, http://rabble.ca/news/dismissing-critical-pedagogy-denis-rancourt-vs-university-ottawa.

3. British Committee for the Universities of Palestine (BRICUP), *Why Boycott Israeli Universities?* (London: BRICUP, 2007), 18–19, www.bricup.org.uk/documents/WhyBoycottIsraeliUniversities.pdf.

4. BRICUP, *Why Boycott Israeli Universities?*, 14.

5. Maximilian Forte, "Canadian Academic Boycott of Israel: Why We Need to Take Action," *Zero Anthropology*, February 4, 2009, http://openanthropology.wordpress.com/2009/02/04.

6. Judith Butler, "Israel/Palestine and the Paradoxes of Academic Freedom," *Radical Philosophy* 135 (2006): 8–17.

7. Martha Nussbaum, "Against Academic Boycotts," *Dissent* 54 (2007): 30–36.

8. Henry Giroux, "Academic Unfreedom in America," in *Academic Freedom in the Post-9/11 Era*, ed. E. J. Carvalho and D. B. Downing (New York: Palgrave Macmillan, 2010), 31.

9. Sophia A. McClennen, "The Crisis of Intellectual Engagement," in *Academic Freedom in the Post-9/11 Era*, ed. E. J. Carvalho and D. B. Downing (New York: Palgrave Macmillan, 2010), 209.

10. Farred, "The Art of Politics Is to Divide," 354.

11. R. Radhakrishnan, "Is Freedom Academic?," *Works and Days* 26/27 (2008/2009): 505.

12. Judith Butler, "Critique, Dissent, Disciplinarity," *Critical Inquiry* 35 (2009): 782.

14

EXERCISING RIGHTS

Academic Freedom and Boycott Politics

JUDITH BUTLER

O NE MIGHT BEGIN by asking whether there are conditions under which academic freedom can be exercised. The thesis that academic freedom *is conditioned* presupposes that there are institutional structures that make academic freedom possible and protect its ongoing exercise. What does it matter if there are such conditions? Is academic freedom not separable from the conditions of its exercise? My suggestion is that academic freedom is a conditioned freedom and that it cannot rightly be thought or exercised without those conditions. So when we defend academic freedom, we defend the complex institutional conditions that make its exercise possible, and we understand those conditions and its exercise as bound up with one another; if the conditions fall away, the exercise becomes impossible. This may seem like a reasonable position, and yet it is often forgotten when debates on academic freedom get underway. Indeed, we take the durable support of educational institutions for granted in most academic debates, and we defend the right to education as if it were a separate matter from the right to academic freedom. And yet, if it is only on the condition that institutions prove durable, that the exercise of academic freedom becomes possible, it follows that when and if those institutions prove precarious, then the possibility of exercising the right of academic freedom is correspondingly imperiled. If there are conditions without which there can be no exercise of that right, then those conditions ought to be understood as components of the right itself. In this way, the right to academic freedom presupposes a right to education,[1] and a broader social commitment to making educational institutions accessible, affordable, and durable. Otherwise, the exercise of academic freedom proves to be an abstract right. Further, we might begin to understand checkpoints, erratic closures of universities, and the indefinite detention of students and faculty for espousing political viewpoints as relevant to both the right to education and academic freedom itself.

But what does this argument have to do with the politics of the academic boycott? PACBI, the Palestinian Campaign for the Academic and Cultural Boycott of Israel,[2] calls for a boycott against Israeli cultural and academic institutions that fail to call for an end to the occupation, understood as an abrogation of international law. In fact, the broader goals the boycott hopes for include the support of the international community to boycott those institutions that fail to (1) oppose the discrimination against non-Jewish citizens of the State of Israel, (2) oppose the occupation of the West Bank as a violation of international law, and (c) support the rights of return for Palestinian refugees in the diaspora who lost homes and lands through illegal confiscation and forcible expulsion.

So a paradox is already underway insofar as the dominant debates suggest that it is the boycott that poses a threat to academic freedom. In fact, the unjust conditions that the boycott opposes prove to abrogate academic freedom more fully than the boycott itself. The isolation, underfunding, and episodic closing of Palestinian universities, the detention of students and faculty who espouse, or who are perceived to espouse, political views inimical to the Israeli regime, surely undermines the right to education that is, I will argue, not only a precondition of academic freedom but part of its very definition.

Of course, we are used to identifying academic freedom as the right that faculty have to espouse various points of view, and most consistent liberals claim that views that are critical of the state of Israel or its policies ought be freely articulated by those in Israel, the United States, or elsewhere without censorship. But surely, equally important to consider as a violation of academic freedom is the isolation, underfunding, and episodic closing of Palestinian universities, the checkpoints that make it sometimes impossible to arrive at the university at all, and the detention and imprisonment of those whose views are considered controversial. All of these conditions characterize the contemporary state of Palestinian universities, and singly and together they threaten and weaken the infrastructure of educational institutions and, hence, the exercise of academic freedom.

A critical rejoinder might nevertheless insist on the distinction that I am calling into question. One could argue that a sufficient infrastructure to educate students and sustain faculty and rights of access and mobility are contingent preconditions of academic freedom, but constitute no proper part of academic freedom itself. My response: the right of academic freedom is its exercise, and when it cannot be exercised, the right is correspondingly diminished. Thus, I would like to redefine academic freedom so that its institutional conditions are part of its very definition. Further, I want to suggest that once we undertake this redefinition, the political issue of academic freedom in Israel/Palestine will look very different, and the rights to academic freedom and freedom of assembly, for instance, will then be tied to a struggle for affordable and accessible education. Indeed, if we consider demonstrations at contemporary U.S. and European universities that oppose tuition increases and decreased funding by the state (as we have been witnessing over the last few years, for example, on the University of California campuses, Montreal, Chile, and Athens, Greece), we can see that sometimes the right to academic freedom is exercised in support of the idea of a durable, accessible, and affordable university. In these cases, those whose educations and futures are imperiled by high costs and cancelled courses oppose those conditions at the same time that their opposition is in some ways supported by what is left of those conditions. When those students or faculty leave the university and continue their protest, they exercise rights of free speech, but they are no longer protected by academic freedom.

Indeed, we are used to identifying academic freedom as a right that presupposes membership in an identifiable and enduring institution of higher education, but how do we name the struggle to achieve or retain membership itself? In the name of academic freedom, we oppose the kinds of assaults on academic freedom that have been threatened against those who hold controversial political views, and we oppose the kinds of control over the curriculum exercised by funding sources (public or private) that try to tie their donations to curricular or ideological outcomes. Such concerns would seem to imply that those concerned with academic freedom ask about censorship and ideological control within Israel and the land it occupies. And yet, when we debate the relation between the academic boycott of Israel and rights of academic freedom, we tend to imagine first those Israeli academics and cultural workers who may be disadvantaged by the boycott, and very often the debate pivots on whether that disadvantage can rightly be construed as the denial of a right to academic freedom for Israeli citizens (by which we generally assume Israelis with full citizenship, that is, Jewish Israelis and not Palestinian Israelis). This is an important point worth debating, and I will return to it later when I attempt to make the distinction between a boycott focused on institutions that ratify and normalize the occupation and individuals who happen to work in those institutions. The boycott does not discriminate against individuals on the basis of their citizenship, but only against institutions that refuse to actively and consistently oppose the conditions of occupation.

So my immediate concern is not to adjudicate the question of whether academic freedom conflicts with boycott politics, but rather to ask whether the aims of the boycott draw attention to the unacceptable debilitation of the infrastructure of Palestinian universities, inaccessibility by roads controlled by moving and stationary checkpoints, and the regulation of speech that has culminated in the detention and imprisonment of hundreds of students and faculty every year. Let us remember that more than 9,000 students at An-Najah University alone pass through checkpoints (internal to the West Bank) to get to the university, and 64 percent report having been abused at checkpoints; 91 percent report having missed classes by virtue of being delayed at checkpoints; 84 percent claim that they have put off traveling because of checkpoints.[3]

My question is whether our conception of academic freedom is broad enough to understand these two sorts of rights violations: the one happens when an already established institution sets limits on its curriculum or faculty speech for political reasons; the other happens when the infrastructural conditions are destroyed or debilitated and render impossible the exercise of the right of academic freedom (and other rights as well, including the right to assembly and rights of mobility, presupposed by rights of access).

My point is to say that the academic boycott is, at least in part, a way of objecting to abridgements of academic freedom, a way of calling for an equal right to education, and a way of opposing a systematic and militarily enforced inequality and subjugation. So the academic boycott against Israel signals an unwillingness to lend recognition or support to those institutions that participate in the destruction of the livelihood of populations or fail actively to oppose that destruction.

This very point of the boycott is not legible when we hold to a fully abstract conception of rights and assume that if only explicit forms of censorship and prohibition were lifted, rights would be exercised. That can only be true if the institutional conditions for the exercise of rights are in place. Hence, we need a distinction: rights can be prohibited from being exercised or they can be rendered "unexercisable" by virtue of the absence of destruction of workable and durable infrastructures. What we require is a concept of academic freedom that can conceptualize those two ways of negating a right: the violation of existing rights and the preemptive foreclosure of the exercise of rights.

How does such a formulation affect how we think about sanctions, boycotts, and divestment? Does it tell us whether to be for or against the boycott? I will suggest that although some people have clearly argued that boycotts set one set of principles (moral, economic, or political) against the principles of academic freedom, they remain restricted to the version of academic freedom that assumes that positive rights have already been established and that institutions are in place. When and where the infrastructural conditions of a university, including its economic isolation and devastation, make something like "freedom of exchange" impossible or expose the exercise of that freedom to systematic failure, we are actually referring to a second dimension of academic freedom, namely the situation in which certain privations preclude and preempt the exercise of rights themselves. Indeed, many of the arguments about divestment and sanctions fail to grasp that these two dimensions of academic freedom are in tension with one another, and so many of the debates use one side of academic freedom to argue against the other, without realizing that both dimensions are essentially linked to one another and must be reconciled with one another.

There are two striking features to current debates about academic freedom and about the politics of boycotting that point to the persistently one-sided conception of academic freedom as an abstract right. With respect to academic freedom, we actively worry that certain rights, presumptively established and durable, are abrogated when there is an inappropriate intervention into academic research and teaching by funding sources, whether state or private. We also worry whether rights, conceived as belonging to the individual, are honored or not. In such cases, we have as a background assumption that academic institutions are functioning; that they are adequately funded; and that there are classrooms, meeting times, books, and discussions. Similarly, when we talk about boycotting as a political principle, we imagine that those who are boycotted are deprived of their rights of academic freedom, since boycotts do usually imply the withholding of funds and of forms of intellectual exchange and mobility. These last two, in particular, belong to the domain of academic freedom, and when one objects to the withholding of funding, it is precisely because the loss of funding paralyzes modes of academic exchange. So, in the last argument, we see the link between funding and the exercise of rights, but they are still considered to be two different kinds of concerns.

In the boycott politics that has emerged in response to the continuing occupation of the West Bank and the military bombardment and economic siege of Gaza, we are confronted with yet another argument that has less to do with academic freedom than with forms of discrimination. A boycott, divestment, or sanctions campaign against the state of Israel is sometimes construed as a discriminatory act, most especially when it adversely affects individuals and does so apparently on the basis of their citizenship. But recent efforts to formulate a new boycott politics (since 2005, to be sure) overcome this objection by focusing on cultural and political institutions that fail to oppose the occupation. It is this failure rather than any group membership or national citizenship that becomes the salient basis for boycott. In addition, one also hears the argument that boycotts are justified against Israeli institutions since Israeli institutions have been effectively boycotting Palestinian educational institutions for a long time. By this claim is meant that the Israeli control over checkpoints and the Palestinian economy more generally have led to the deterioration and destruction of institutions of higher education in Palestine. This claim uses "boycott" to designate an economic embargo, if not an economic and military siege, references police raids on Palestinian universities, roadblocks, administrative detentions, and imprisonment for political viewpoints. The point is not only that individuals cannot exercise academic freedom, but that academic institutions cannot fully function, or indeed, in some cases academic institutions are invaded by police or become military targets.[4]

My first point is to suggest that most of the debates on academic freedom not only assume that universities have funded and functioning infrastructures, including buildings and classrooms, but also that students and faculty have (1) unimpeded mobility to arrive at a classroom and (2) material means to pursue their studies. These assumptions form the background of most of the debates that consider, for instance, whether funding organizations ought to be proscribed from intervening in strictly academic affairs or whether state-supported schools are protected from state-initiated efforts to control the curriculum or speech on campus.

Academic freedom is not just the name for the freedom we exercise when we teach and write, but also the name for this entire conundrum: we are dependent on a funded infrastructure to exercise academic freedom at the same time that academic freedom requires protection against the incursions by those very funding sources into the domain of teaching, writing, and scholarship. It is this knot of dependency and independence that cannot be overcome. On the one hand, we ask how it is that any educational institution can preserve open inquiry under conditions of institutional, legal, and economic constraint.[5] We worry about incursions from funding sources. On the other hand, we also have to worry about whether institutions themselves remain viable and accessible in order to guarantee the exercise of rights. For the most part, our debates are biased in favor of the first concern and neglect the equal importance of the second. But if, following Hannah Arendt, to have a right only becomes meaningful if one has the power to exercise that right, then there is no way to think of the right of academic freedom apart from its exercise and, indeed, the right to education itself.

But what about the situation where there is no dependency on state or private funds precisely because the university has been abandoned by such funding or because the university persists in an underfunded way. Hence, the problem is not how to broker dependency but how to survive and combat abandonment or destitution. The conventional view of academic freedom assumes that there is funding and that the infrastructural conditions for the exercise of academic freedom are secured. The question is not only how to keep funders from imposing their views, but for an institution radically defunded, the question is how to create the conditions under which academic freedom can be exercised at all.

My reflections here are meant to raise the question of what happens when the problem is *not* that the funding sources on which we depend fail to protect the independence of our academic research and teaching. Rather, what happens when there are no funding sources, or when funding sources are radically imperiled, and the infrastructural conditions for the exercise of rights become impossible? This is not an intervention into the domain of freedom that otherwise should be protected from such interventions. Rather, it is the decimation of the conditions under which alone the domain of academic freedom can be constituted. When there is insufficient institutional and economic support, the right to academic freedom cannot be exercised. To exercise academic freedom as a right is to some extent the exercise of a power secured through economic means and, in this sense, an economic power. In this sense, it is important to distinguish between the *abrogation* of rights by public or private sources that ought to protect the autonomy of academic life and the *preemptive foreclosure* of the right to academic freedom by depriving students and faculty of the effective power to exercise that right.

Many of the arguments that seek to think about academic freedom in light of these various strategies are concerned with what I earlier called the exercise of privative rights rather than infra- and extrastructural conditions that condition or foreclose that exercise. But if we consider both dimensions of academic freedom, how finally do we broker the question of the cultural and academic boycott against Israel? Ultimately, many of us outside the region have come to wonder whether the devastation of the university system in the West Bank and most brutally in Gaza is not also an issue of academic freedom, as it is in other parts of the globe where war, famine, or government negligence has devastated university structures.

Although not usually acknowledged as an issue of academic freedom, it is doubtless worth noting that more than 400 students at Birzeit University have been incarcerated on the basis of espousing political views or belonging to political associations.[6] Interestingly, even membership in the student council at that university served as grounds for administrative detention. In February of 2012, students there undertook a hunger strike to protest temporary checkpoints and harassment at the entry to the university as well as widespread practices of administrative detention. Needless to say, incarcerated students are denied their freedom to hold to political views that may not be acceptable to the occupying state, but they are also denied an education. Deprivation of an education takes place through the restriction of the mobility to get to class, something that happens as well by delays at the checkpoint, which can last for several hours. Since 2006 (the year in which the blockade against the West Bank took hold after the popular election of Hamas), thousands of Palestinians with foreign passports have been denied the right to visit, work, or study at Birzeit. At An-Najah University, 9,100 students depend on open checkpoints to reach class, and some students pass through a total of five checkpoints. Since 2004, no students from Gaza are have been permitted to travel to study in the West Bank, and in Hebron, more than 1,100 students were denied petitions to study abroad. In Hebron as well, over 80 percent of students reported difficulty in reaching campus. Israel has explicitly banned Gaza residents accepted at Israeli institutions of higher education from entering Israel to pursue their studies.

All these statistics pertain to rights of mobility and, in some cases, political association, but also, clearly, to the military administration of "collective punishment" explicitly prohibited by international law. What is most striking is the level of poverty that effectively preempts the possibility of gaining access to a sustained education. At Birzeit alone, 3,000 students since 2006 have been unable to pay university fees. But in Gaza, where conditions are acute, over 70 percent of the total population lives below the poverty line, and 32.5 percent are unemployed.[7] Birzeit lost over 1.2 million U.S. dollars after the 2006 blockade was imposed, and the Islamic University has not been able to gain access to materials to rebuild its university, destroyed by the Israeli assault of 2008–2009.

On the one hand, it is clear that embargoes, incarceration, siege, closed or intermittently open borders (depending on whether we are referring to the West Bank or Gaza), legal restrictions on travel, and administrative detention are all economic and military means to preempt and paralyze the exercise of academic institutions and even academic freedom. On the other hand, the claim that boycotts unjustly use economic power to undermine academic freedom relies on the presumption that economic power should be used *to support* academic freedom. In a sense, the boycott uses economic power to show that economic power is an invariable dimension of academic freedom. If one claims that academic freedom depends on the separation of economic power and academic activity, then we fail to understand that the "separation" such an argument has in mind is one that presumes that conditions of material support are adequate and ongoing and can thus be "separated" from academic freedom itself. In other words, economic power and academic life ought to be separated only as long as economic power supports academic life. But where academic life is itself threatened with paralysis or destruction by the military organization of economic life, the operative presumption of academic freedom debates proves limited and calls for reformulation.

Boycotts presume that both state and economic power condition university life and are essential to the reproduction of the institutional life of the university. In turn, and more importantly, the reproduction of institutional life of the university is essential to the reproduction of the state; thwarting the operation of the one is a way of registering political opposition to the other. If there were no link between them, the point of boycott would be lost. On the surface, it would seem that the absolute distinction no longer holds between the economic conditions by which the university runs and the academic activity that constitutes the core mission of the university. This would also be the case with any strike that sought to halt the usual operations of the university. So the strategy of boycott seems minimally to draw upon and expose the link between the economic and academic dimensions of the university and to situate both within a larger political frame; the strategy is often opposed on grounds of academic freedom when the strategy is seen to conflate the academic, economic, and political domains. But is the intervention that academic freedom opposed by economic and political powers the same kind of intervention undertaken by boycott strategists who seek to make use of economic power to highlight the political implications of the university in problematic political practices or institutions? Only if the link that boycott draws between these two domains is the same as the one that academic freedom seeks to sever do we really have a problem. If they are the same, then we might well conclude that academic boycott is in fact an abrogation of academic freedom. If they are not the same, however, we have to be able to distinguish them and then to evaluate whether there is, in fact, an abrogation of academic freedom at issue.

Omar Barghouti has suggested that boycotts may well abrogate academic freedom but that academic freedom is not the only public good at issue under the conditions of occupation.[8] He points out that values such as equality and justice may well have to trump academic freedom. And though he may well be right, my concern is that if we accept that argument, we have conceded that academic freedom is separable from the right to education, and this is a consequential error. To understand why, we have to return to the question of why academic freedom is not the same as freedom of expression, and why it is not the same as those rights to enter into contract that might exist within the presumption of free market economics. We could say that economic boycott is precisely an effort to use economic power to affect what happens in the state and even the academy, but that would not quite be right, since a boycott withdraws support and collaboration but does not seek to use any funding capacity to alter or influence curriculum. Unlike other state or corporate pressures that sometimes do seek to purchase curriculum changes or use state power over public funding to promote or deny politically controversial tenure cases, boycott does not seek to affect intra-university deliberations or decisions. In fact, there seems to be a certain studied indifference to whether or not individuals have particular political points of view, since individuals are not the focus of the boycott, but institutions are, especially when they are understood to provide cultural support and alibi for the state. The individual faculty member is considered part of an institution that is itself considered part of a state, and it is this institutional link that is most important but also most difficult to understand. But it is crucial to understand in order to distinguish between individuals who are actively representing their institutions and individuals who are not. The recent effort to boycott institutions rather than individuals seeks to overcome the presumption that individuals are simply symbolic representatives of cultural institutions and of states. This is why a collaboration with an individual who is representing an institution may not be possible, but that same individual may enter into a collaboration when clearly not representing that institution. Boycotts that focus on institutions tend to think that institutions, rather than individuals, have the power to appeal to the state, to withdraw their tacit support from state operations, including military ones. They call on individuals to persuade institutions to break with the state and to expose their illegal and unjust activities.

There are different versions of boycott, and they are not always in agreement with one another. Indeed, many activities are called "boycott" when they are not boycotts, and others are called "divestment" when they really are not. So take the case of a public statement that was critical of the alliance of the Toronto International Film Festival with the city of Tel Aviv, as a result of a "Brand Israel" campaign that sought to produce a positive and benign public image for the state, setting aside those images that show the Israeli assault on Gaza or report on the allegations of war crimes committed there. The public statement, signed by hundreds of artists and intellectuals did *not* call for a boycott of the Toronto International Film Festival. It called only for public criticism of that particular alliance. And yet, articles in the *Jerusalem Post* and *Ha'aretz* (September 6, 2009) objected to the public letter as an instance of "boycott." This is only one example of the limits on public audibility that emerge in relation to issues such as these. The term "boycott" serves as a rhetorical scare tactic, inciting paranoia ("they are against us" or "they seek to destroy us"), thus confounding a nonviolent mode of resistance with a violent one. And this can and does happen regardless of whether the version of boycott has the more limited aim of opposing the explicit violence and illegality of the occupation or the more expansive aims to oppose discrimination against Palestinian Israelis and call for a right to return for exiled Palestinians.

Similarly, even conversely, there was a certain rush to judgment with the so-called Hampshire College divestment episode a few years ago.[9] Hampshire College decided to divest from certain companies that were engaged in the making of war materiel, because such practices were in violation of their long-standing policies on socially responsible investment. They had already divested from companies outside of Israel for these same reasons, and in this most recent instance, they divested from some companies in Israel, but they did not divest from all Israeli companies. We might reasonably conclude that they implemented their policy across the board and without reference to the nation in which the company worked. A student group then enthusiastically claimed that Hampshire was embracing boycott, divestment, and sanctions against Israel, when actually something different had taken place: the implementation of a socially responsible investment policy regardless of the national status of the company in question. To implement a policy that would affect Israel as it would affect any other country that housed such industries refused to exempt Israel or Israeli companies from its consideration. It neither singled out that country nor did it accept its exceptional status—and this was, apparently, difficult to understand. Accusations of backtracking ensued, but the conditions for misapprehension were already in place. But did this confusion emerge in part because we are not exactly sure what qualifies as divestment strategy? If an institution were to say that it would not divest from a company that clearly violates its socially responsible divestment policy because it operates in a given state, that would be to set national limits on the application of the policy. If an institution were to apply its socially responsible divestment policy only to a certain state, then we might also say that certain national limits are imposed on the application of the policy. At this point, the policy would be determined no longer in light of the socially irresponsible practices of companies but in light of the broader state politics.

Neither of the two instances I just mentioned (Toronto, Hampshire) actually engaged in boycott, according to any of the standard definitions. And yet, the first was criticized as boycott, and the second was prematurely celebrated as boycott, or as BDS, the acronym for this current political metonymy of boycott, divestment, and sanctions. How then do we unravel such quick misunderstandings? In the example of the Toronto film festival, we have to distinguish public criticism from boycott (one cannot, for instance, say that all public criticism is effectively boycott, especially if one wants to say that free and open public criticism is the alternative to boycott). In the second, we have to see that there are a number of different ways of conducting divestment, and that this particular one did not target any and all Israeli companies; indeed, Hampshire never ceased to invest in some Israeli companies and never said it would divest from all; it continues to invest in those same companies that, in its view, did not violate its standards governing socially responsible investment.

Of course, things may change. At what point do selective divestments targeting certain kinds of companies in accord with an established policy on socially responsible investment become tantamount to a national boycott? It is one thing to say that there are companies making weapons or building walls, like Elbit, boycotted by the state of Norway, that do not deserve to be invested in. But if the analysis extends to other companies, and then to state actors, at what point does the boycott extend to both companies and to states actively engaged in this same sort of production? One tactic is to target those companies and even state actors who actively contribute to the occupation, and it is yet another tactic to target those companies, institutions, and state actors who fail to oppose the occupation and whose failure to act in this instance is complicitous with the occupation. Most of the boycott efforts against universities in Israel take this second form.

Similarly, with divestment, at what point does the selective application of socially responsible investment policies become interpreted as "divestment." If investments are withdrawn from specific companies because of their production of military materiel, regardless of where they are situated, then the policy does not take aim at the state but only at companies that make certain kinds of products that are used by states for certain kinds of ends (the destruction of homes, the building of the separation wall). But if it is not possible to distinguish that company from the state where the military products are used because of binding contracts or shared personnel, and if those military products are used for the purposes of instating a segregation of populations on the basis of ethnicity or religion, or if those military goods are used to commit repeated violations of international law, then new criteria for responsible divestment have been added to the old, and instead of proceeding on a case-by-case basis, a more systematic analysis would have to ensue. An effective divestment strategy would not only target companies actively contributing to the occupation but also state and cultural institutions that fail to actively oppose this unjust and protracted condition disenfranchisement.[10]

If a policy were then to emerge that resolved not to invest in that state, it would be based on the claim that any investment in the state would be socially irresponsible. One can see how an incremental divestment could become a general divestment from a state over time, but that can only happen when it could be established that companies engaging in socially irresponsible actions are no longer distinguishable from a state whose general activities are socially irresponsible or from the condition of injustice that precipitated the divestment effort to begin with; and, of course, that systemic link would have to become persuasive to those who make and implement investment policy.

Of course, as we know, once the state itself—and in its apparent totality—becomes the object of BDS, the issue is raised whether such actions discriminate against companies, institutions, and individuals on the basis of national identity or national belonging. But this question misunderstands the aims and terms of the boycott, which are to target those companies, institutions, and corporations because they support certain violent or unjust state practices. There has to be more to this distinction than considering two sides of a coin. In fact, there are strong distinctions to be made between a boycott that discriminates on the basis of *citizenship* and one that focuses more precisely and in a differentiated fashion on *institutions* that are actively involved in reproducing unjust and criminal conditions, precluding the rights of citizenship for others, or manifesting complicity by refusing to take a stand.

When the example is Israel, the argument can and does emerge that the undifferentiated BDS strategy is discriminatory because it "singles out" the Jewish state, and for some this is a sign of its implicit or explicit anti-Semitism. But for others, the fear is that Israelis will be barred from academic events or exchanges on the basis of their citizenship. Of course, there is an undifferentiated version of BDS that was made controversial by some faculty members in the United Kingdom who argued that papers from Israeli scholars ought not to be accepted at journals and e-mails from Israeli colleagues ought not to be returned—one I would describe as a misguided and self-righteous micropolitics.[11] Confronted with the fact that some Israelis actively oppose the occupation, these faculty members took it upon themselves to distinguish between righteous and unrighteous Jews, going so far as to provide lists, arguing that the righteous ones who passed their own private moral test might be exempted from boycott. The making of lists was incendiary, stoking those who suspected the anti-Semitic character of the movement, recalling more gruesome lists from the Nazi regime or South American dictatorial regimes, and generally provoking moral revulsion across the political spectrum.[12] Interestingly enough, some of the very people who revolted against the Manchester version of boycott now stand in favor of a different version of boycott. Indeed, even Neve Gordon, the political theorist from Ben-Gurion University, originally thought that progressive Israelis were unfairly discriminated against by the Manchester version of BDS, but has found a new approach to boycott that helped to reopen the topic for a more serious consideration.[13] Perhaps even more importantly, the PACBI itself issued several statements making clear its policy to oppose ties of normalization, but refusing discrimination on the basis of nationality.

Some of the positions on boycott that have made it more available within public discourse maintain some distance from the PACBI positions. And although it is important for boycott politics to be more broadly discussed and debated, it is most important to remember that the boycott campaign belongs to the larger political movement of Palestinian self-determination. Hence, any revision or reworking of the boycott position that works against or disregards Palestinian self-determination undermines the larger political goals of that movement. In publishing her view on boycott, author Naomi Klein reiterated the 2005 PACBI position, making clear that the boycott was not against Israeli citizens, but rather against institutions. She opposed what she called the "stupid" tactics of failing to accept articles by Israelis to journals, and sought to replace the moral self-righteousness of the Manchester advocates with a politically oriented analysis. In an interview, she made clear "this is not a boycott of Israelis. It's a boycott of pretending that everything is normal." She remarked further, "It's true that some academics won't agree to accept an article by an Israeli for publication in a journal. There aren't many of them, and they make stupid decisions. This is not what the boycott committee has called for. The decision isn't to boycott Israel but rather to oppose official relationships with Israeli institutions." Moreover, she objects not to the Israeli state as such, but to the condition of occupation (and so limits herself to the first of the three aims that PACBI articulates). And although she seeks recourse to the boycott of apartheid South Africa to develop strategies, she does not argue that Israel is the same as South Africa. In refusing to do business with organizations and institutions that think they can do business as usual, that they can separate Israeli cultural institutions, for instance, from the occupation, Klein herself separates the state of Israel from Israeli institutions, but for her the reason to exercise economic and cultural boycott is to pressure Israeli institutions to oppose the specific policies of the Israeli state. She nowhere calls into question the legitimacy of the Israeli state—and this will make her position too weak for some, whereas the focus on the occupation will make it too strong for others. For those for whom the boycott entails an insistence on the right of returns for Palestinians expelled in 1948, Klein's version of the boycott will be regarded as limited in its scope and targets. For those who hope to separate Israel from its conflict (the aim of Brand Israel and the Israel Beyond the

Conflict organizations), the presumption is that something called Israeli life and culture can be held separate from the occupation, and this would be a position opposed by BDS advocates. It is probably important to keep this all in mind as we try to navigate this particular scene. Since boycott does not take one form, its "object" is hardly singular.

Klein agrees to work with those Israeli organizations and institutions that take a firm stand against occupation and who demonstrate that opposition, and she refuses to work with those who do not, those she considers to be normalizing Israeli life in the midst of the occupation. As much as Klein sought to distinguish between citizens and institutions, some of her Israeli allies nevertheless thought the boycott should extend to the treatment of individuals insofar as they represent universities and cultural institutions. The slogan Boycott Me! was repeated by Anat Matar,[14] an Israeli philosopher, and Yael Lerer, the publisher of Andalus, the only bilingual publisher in Palestine, and was recently recited by Neve Gordon.

Clearly, the call to "boycott me" is not a call to discriminate against the "me" on the basis of national citizenship, but rather to disrupt normalized relationships with the Israeli institutions with which each is identified. This point is explicitly made by the organization Boycott! Supporting the Palestinian BDS Call from Within. The "me" who is referenced as the object of the boycott is clearly an institutional actor.[15]

Obviously, Naomi Klein did not refuse to be published by Andalus, her bilingual Israeli publishing house. The point of this selective version of boycott is to pressure institutions to take a stand against the occupation and to work only with those organizations that actively oppose those conditions. Although PACBI gave its support to Klein's visit to Israel in order precisely to discuss this version of boycott, it takes another tack. And it is important to note that the BDS National Committee[16] focuses primarily on economic sanctions and pressures in light of what is understood as a failure of the United Nations and the international community more broadly to implement its own resolutions and findings. The BDS committee was formed in 2005 and has the support of more than 170 organizations in Palestine. It does not stipulate the right way to impose boycott and sanctions, but it does describe itself as an "anti-normalization" politics that seeks to force a wide range of political institutions and states to stop compliance with the occupation. It is also worth noting, to be sure, that BDS is the major nonviolent movement for Palestinian self-determination under conditions of occupation, disenfranchisement, and exile. For Klein, it is not the fundamental structure of the state of Israel that is called into question, but the occupation, its denial of basic human rights and international law, and the brutality of its conditions. Of course, for this distinction to hold, we would have to date the occupation to 1967 rather than to 1948, a claim that continues to be controversial, to be sure, and precisely not the framework that Klein invokes. And yet, that framework is precisely at work in the third demand of the boycott movement (BDS and PACBI alike), namely, the right of return for those dispossessed of lands and rights by the Nakba.

It is important to understand that the boycott movement is an appeal from Palestinians who are seeking to strengthen rights of self-determination, and it is an appeal to a global community to lend support to that struggle for self-determination. It is not an appeal to the international community to determine the fate of the Palestinians for them, but to find ways to lend support and solidarity as Palestinians decide the terms of their own struggle. Those who complain that Palestinians are "setting the terms" for boycott politics forget that setting the terms is yet another name for self-determination, and that that right has not yet been acquired under conditions of occupation, subjugation, and exile.

The Israeli pro-boycott philosopher Anat Matar has suggested that academic freedom has a suspect history. She writes,

When the flag of academic freedom is raised, the oppressor and not the oppressed is usually the one who flies it. What is that academic freedom that so interests the academic community in Israel? When, for example, has it shown concern for the state of academic freedom in the occupied territories? (*Ha'aretz*, September 11, 2009)

Omar Barghouti similarly writes,

"The claim is very biased in that it privileges Israeli academic freedom over any other, so they completely ignore that by denying Palestinians their basic rights—all of our freedoms, including academic freedom—Israel is also infringing deeply on our academic freedom. That doesn't count, it seems. We never heard those liberal voices when Israel shut down Palestinian universities during the first intifada [uprising]—Birzeit University was shut down for four [consecutive] years, for example. We haven't heard much of an outcry among those liberals who are now shouting academic freedom. Is academic freedom a privilege to whites only? Do we global southerners deserve academic freedom? Are we equally human or not? So those people who are shouting academic freedom are either hypocrites or racists, I'm sorry to say it. They are either hypocritical in that they only care about academic freedom for Israelis and they consider them white, European, Jewish, civilized and not for us Palestinians who are southern-ers and brown—this is at a theoretical level. In principle the academic boycott that PACBI is calling for and all our partners are adopting is institutional; there-fore, it does not infringe on the rights and privileges of Israeli academics to go out and participate in conferences and so on so long as this is not the product of an institutional link—we are calling for cutting all institutional links, not to cut off visits by individual academics, or artists, or cultural figures to participate in events and so on—they can and they do and that will not stop—so it's really very hypocritical and deceptive to call the academic boycott a form of infringement on academic freedom." (*Electronic Intifada*, June 6, 2009)

I want to respond to these well-earned criticisms of academic freedom by recapitulating the view that in any adequate and responsible conception of academic freedom the devastation of universities must count as a decimation of academic freedom, and this principle must be applied to Palestine.

In conclusion, I hope to have shown two different ways in which eco-nomic power is a precondition of the exercise of academic freedom. We doubtless understand within prevailing frameworks that academic freedom is supposed to protect against the intrusion of those funding sources, state or private, on which academic institutions are fundamentally dependent. True enough, but academic freedom is not an abstract right, but a constant strug-gle to establish academic independence in the midst of both economic and political dependency. Under conditions of privatization, regimes of value become established, however, that call into question those values within the academy, especially those that cannot quickly or indeed ever be justified according to market rationale. The rights of research are separate from the responsibilities of institutions. And yet, the idea of socially responsible invest-ment again links economic rationale to questions of value that cannot be reduced to market terms.

This mode of undermining or explicitly attacking educational institutions is not quite the same as boycott, but the accusation is meant to expose the link between economic conditions that imperil the very possibility of teach-ing and research that are the action and effect of the political conditions of occupation. One cannot talk about rights of cultural exchange when laws and walls restricting mobility make those issues abstract. One cannot talk about freedom of expression when modes of publishing are not available. And it is not only the question of the material condition for the expression of rights, as if the two were distinct, but of the right to a material condition for institutional life, a right to education.[17] Can we think of academic freedom apart from the right to education? I think not, especially if we have a conception of rights that must be exercised and so must become the exercise of a certain power. Nothing less than the critique of abstract rights is necessary to understand the ways in which the very operation of an institution is called into question by the economic siege that is the occupation.

On the one hand, the economic is to be separated from the academic (it cannot control academic values, nor can it control curriculum and research); on the other hand, there is no academy apart from the economics by which it is sustained. If academic freedom pertains only to that situation in which funding is adequate, then the doctrine not only fails to apply to the most dire situations within higher education but leads to a misunderstanding of the key term by which it operates: "freedom."

If academic freedom is a conditional right, as I have tried to suggest, then we need to be able to understand its "conditions" in order to know both the situations under which the claim can be made and the limits of that claim. We say, for instance, that a hostile environment sets a limit on academic freedom within the classroom. We say as well that discriminatory actions, which may involve verbal conduct, also set a limit to academic freedom. These are limits on the freedom that we understand to be justified, and that establish academic freedom as a conditional right within academic institutions. One way to say this is that academic freedom is a good under those conditions when it does not conflict with greater goods. And this means that those greater goods are preconditions for the exercise of academic freedom. If those preconditions are not met—a nonhostile and nondiscriminatory educational environment—then the exercise of academic freedom is impossible. Can we not go further and claim not only (1) that certain privative economic conditions also thwart the exercise of academic freedom, but also (2) that adequate economic conditions are necessary for the exercise of this right? This would again be to further delineate those conditions under which the exercise of such rights first becomes possible. To take this last step is to agree that economic conditions are a precondition for the exercise of rights, and that as a result, certain rights to economic viability precede and inform rights to academic freedom. The precondition is not fully separable from the exercise of rights, since the "exercise" of the right is the enactment of power that makes it possible, drawing from the precondition and, in that sense, its very realization.

We have to rethink the political obligation that establishes the economic dependency that is the first part of our definition of academic freedom. Academic freedom is the name for the paradox that we are fundamentally dependent on institutions from which we require independence (in the sense of protection from incursion). But what happens when we are not utterly dependent, when the very conditions of dependency are lost? What happens to the formulation of academic freedom when economic dependency turns to economic destitution, when support is withdrawn, or when universities are devastated by conditions of siege and forced restriction? Do we still ask to be independent of those economic powers by which we have been abandoned, or has the point of the struggle changed? The traditional formulation that assumes adequate funding cannot cover these kinds of cases, and we can see that the very possibility of exercising a right requires the sustained economic power to do so: the exercise is the realization of the power. Without that power, there is no exercise of the right, and then there are surely no freedoms left either to protect or to exercise.

As for boycott politics, it seems to me that objecting to the destroyed infrastructural conditions of life would include objecting to the destroyed infrastructure of the university, which would include not only its buildings, but roads of access and ability to move freely on such roads, and the right to attend university and academic meetings without being thwarted by military police or checkpoints, including access to archives and research institutions. In other words, institutions must be financially maintained as free and self-governing, not as sanctuaries from police control. In this way, academic freedom is bound up with the conditions of the survival of educational institutions, considered as an integral component of Palestinian livelihood. To engage the boycott is simply to say that there can be no relationship to Israeli institutions that do not actively oppose the destruction of Palestinian livelihood. In this way, the boycott affirms the right of academic freedom and reminds us that there is no academy without sustainable lives and livelihoods. We cannot—and must not—commit to the one without the other.

So even as internationals must oppose the state crackdown on dissenting Israeli scholars—scholars within the borders of Israel as well as the barred entry of Noam Chomsky from Israel—we must make sure that our efforts to

defend the academic freedom of those individuals does not end up subscrib-
ing to a limited version of academic freedom. As important as it is to defend
the right to express and publish those controversial viewpoints, and not to
lose employment by virtue of the political viewpoints one holds, it is equally
important to think about the differential way that access to academic freedom comes about in that region. Who actually can "appear" as an individual
within the reigning discourse of academic freedom? None of us "appear" as
individual scholars or students without sustained and recognized institutions
that ratify our individual status. What would it mean to develop a view of
academic freedom that focused not only on the unjust punishments that citizens receive for espousing controversial views, but also on the administrative
detention of students who enjoy no rights of citizenship, have limited access
to global media, and are deprived of access to educational institutions? When
institutions are deratified or become inaccessible to students and faculty,
then there can be no academic freedom—those rights are actively withheld,
if not systematically foreclosed. Most important, then, is to link the struggle
for academic freedom across those various borders and elsewhere on a clear
understanding that the right to education is constitutive of academic freedom
and the struggle for academic freedom requires alliance. Indeed, it may well
be that, paradoxically, only through a large-scale boycott strategy is alliance
finally possible in these times and against this persisting injustice.

NOTES

This chapter was written in 2010.

1. The "right to education" was established as a universal right in 1948 by the Universal
   Declaration of Human Rights. The United Nations has argued that the right to education is essential to the exercise of all other human rights.
2. Palestinian Campaign for the Academic and Cultural Boycott of Israel home page,
   www.pacbi.org.
3. Right2edu: Studies and Research, p. 3, http://right2edu.birzeit.edu/news/article495.
4. Consider in this respect the bombing of the University Teachers Association of Palestine in Gaza on January 16, 2009, as well as the bombing of two five-story university
   buildings at the Islamic University of Gaza on December 29, 2008.
5. See my exchange with Robert Post on academic freedom in *Critical Inquiry*. Robert
   Post, "Debating Disiplinarity," *Critical Inquiry* 35, no. 4 (2009): 749–72; and Judith
   Butler, "Critique, Dissent, Disciplinarity," *Critical Inquiry* 35, no. 4 (2009): 773–97.
6. This statistic and those that follow in this paragraph are based on the website, right2@
   edu, operated by the Birzeit University Right to Education Campaign.

7. www.haaretz.com/news/diplomacy-defense/.premium-1.559530.
8. Omar Barghouti writes: "Freedom to produce and exchange knowledge and ideas was deemed sacrosanct regardless of the prevailing conditions. There are two key faults in this argument. It is inherently biased—regarding as worthy only the academic freedom of Israelis. The fact that Palestinians are denied basic rights as well as academic freedom due to Israel's military occupation is lost on those parroting it. And its privileging of academic freedom as a value above all other freedoms is antithetical to the very foundation of human rights. The right to live, and freedom from subjugation and colonial rule, to name a few, must be of more import than academic freedom. If the latter contributes in any way to suppression of the former, more fundamental rights, it must give way. If the struggle to attain the former necessitates a level of restraint on the latter, then so be it." (PACBI website, www.badil.org/ar/annual-al-awda-award/item/915-academic-freedom-in-context-the-boycott-of-israeli-universities-remains-a-moral-imperative)
9. www.jta.org/2009/02/15/news-opinion/united-states/mass-college-denies-israel-divestment. Hampshire made clear its own views when it posted on its website the following claim: "This review did not include Israel, its interaction with the Palestinians, nor its presence on the West Bank as tests for the stocks in this fund. Moreover, Hampshire currently holds investments in funds that include many hundreds of companies that do business in Israel and in at least three actual Israeli companies: Amdocs, Teva Pharmaceuticals and Check Point Software. No other college or university should use Hampshire as a precedent for divesting from Israel, since Hampshire has refused to divest from Israel. Anyone who claims otherwise is deliberately misrepresenting Hampshire's decision and has no right to speak for the college." www.hampshire.edu/news/11321.htm August 14, 2009.
10. Amira Hass in *Ha'aretz* made the following remarks on the Norwegian divestment from Elbit in September 2009: "Elbit developed equipment used specifically in the construction of the separation barrier. The council extended this conclusion to other companies involved in building the separation barrier that also benefited from Norwegian investment. In this way it corresponds indirectly with left-wing Norwegian activists, and with Palestinian and Israeli anti-occupation activists, providing a basis for their suspicions that the fund's ethics guidelines have been violated. Those guidelines forbid investment in companies that 'contribute to serious or systematic human-rights violations,' and are in blatant contradiction to the will or pretense of moving Israel and the Palestinians toward a just agreement." She continues her analysis and asks why, if Norway is willing to hold to such standards, they restrict themselves to that one company, when others do the same kind of business with Israel and with other sites of military conflict? She supplies a list of worthy targets.
11. www.buzzle.com/editorials/7-15-2002-22427.asp.
12. Naomi Klein makes clear the focus of boycott in her interview with *Ha'aretz*: "It's true that some academics won't agree to accept an article by an Israeli for publication in a journal. There aren't many of them, and they make stupid decisions. This is not what the boycott committee has called for. The decision isn't to boycott Israel but rather to

oppose official relationships with Israeli institutions." See also Jon Pike's philosophical argument against boycotting Israel in which he assumes the 2002 Manchester version of boycott as the relevant model: Jon Pike, "Academic Freedom and the Limits of Boycotts: Some Kantian Considerations," *Engage* 1 (January 2006), www.engageonline. org.uk/journal/index.php?journal_id=5&article_id=25.

13. Neve Gordon, "Boycott Israel," *Los Angeles Times*, August 20, 2009.

14. Anat Matar, *Ha'aretz*, September 11, 2009; but see also "Words and Deeds," a letter to *The Guardian* signed by dozens of Israeli intellectuals. "Words and Deeds in the Middle East," *The Guardian*, January 17, 2009.

15. "Boycott! Supporting the Cairo Declaration," Boycott! Supporting the Palestinian BDS Call from Within, http://boycottisrael.info/content/boycott-supporting-cairo -declaration.

16. The BDS National Committee, or "BNC," consists of 170 member groups including: Council of National and Islamic Forces in Palestine (all major political parties); General Union of Palestinian Workers; Palestinian General Federation of Trade Unions; General Union of Palestinian Women; Palestinian NGO Network (PNGO); Federation of Independent Trade Unions; Palestine Right of Return Coalition; Union of Palestinian Farmers; Occupied Palestine and Golan Heights Initiative (OPGAI); Grassroots Palestinian Anti-Apartheid Wall Campaign (STW); Palestinian Campaign for the Academic and Cultural Boycott of Israel (PACBI); National Committee to Commemorate the Nakba; Civic Coalition for the Defense of Palestinian Rights in Jerusalem (CCDPRJ); Coalition for Jerusalem; Union of Palestinian Charitable Organizations; Palestinian Economic Monitor; Union of Youth Activity Centers–Palestine Refugee Camps.

17. See Judith Butler, "Israel/Palestine and the Paradox of Academic Freedom," *Radical Philosophy* 135 (2006): 8–17.

15

ISRAEL AND ACADEMIC FREEDOM

JOHN MEARSHEIMER

F REEDOM OF SPEECH lies at the heart of American academic life.[1] It means that scholars and students can say what they want on virtually any subject and bring controversial speakers to campus. Universities go to great lengths to promote open discourse and not endorse or discriminate against any particular perspective. Academic freedom is easy to support in principle, but not always easy to embrace in practice. At times, individuals and groups both within and outside the academy dislike what is being said on campus and try to silence the voices they find offensive.

A major threat to academic freedom today comes from the Israel lobby.

Universities are the one place in the United States where Israel tends to be treated like a normal country. Although Israel has many defenders on college campuses, it gets criticized there for its past and present behavior in ways that rarely happen in the mainstream media or among politicians and policy makers in Washington. Thus, it is not surprising that Natan Sharansky, the head of the Jewish Agency for Israel, remarked in January 2011, "I believe that the most important battlefield which we have, and the most difficult one, is American universities."[2]

Many hard-line supporters of Israel—both inside and outside universities—find this situation deeply troubling, which causes them to work assiduously to suppress criticism leveled at either Israeli policy or America's "special relationship" with Israel. Of course, they also work to promote a positive image of Israel on campuses. To achieve their goals, pro-Israel forces not only seek to marginalize or silence critics of Israel in the academy, but to limit their numbers as well.

The aim of this chapter is to analyze this situation in more depth by describing the strategies the lobby employs to achieve its goals on college campuses. I will then attempt to explain why Israel's supporters are so deeply committed to trying to make sure that Israel—and its special relationship with the United States—is always portrayed in a positive light.

Before delving into these matters, however, I want to emphasize that in principle there is nothing wrong with the lobby trying to influence campus life.[3] The key proviso, however, is that it should be done in legitimate ways. For example, it is acceptable for pro-Israel donors to give money to establish a chaired professorship in Israel studies, or even to establish an Israel studies program. Moreover, a donor can give money to set up a speaker series that brings pro-Israel speakers to campus or help fund a college magazine that seeks to be Israel-friendly.

Individuals and groups outside the academy can also write articles and books that are critical of particular professors as well as universities, as Martin Kramer did in *Ivory Towers on Sand*.[4] But my concern is not with these kinds of activities, which are legitimate and consistent with the way business is conducted at colleges and universities across the United States. Instead, my focus is on the illegitimate strategies that the lobby employs to foster a one-sided discourse about Israel.

MINIMIZING THE NUMBER OF ACADEMIC CRITICS

The Israel lobby tries to influence the hiring and promotion process as a way of limiting the number of Israel's critics at American colleges. Probably the most well-known case was DePaul University's June 2007 decision to deny tenure to Norman Finkelstein, who has long been an outspoken critic of Israeli policies toward the Palestinians. Pro-Israel groups and individuals put significant pressure on DePaul to fire Finkelstein. Harvard law professor Alan Dershowitz led the charge, sending professors in DePaul's law school and political science department what he described as "a dossier of Norman Finkelstein's most egregious academic sins, and especially his outright lies, misquotations, and distortions."[5] Nevertheless, the political science department voted 9–3 to give him tenure and a college-level tenure committee voted unanimously in his favor. His promotion was nixed, however, at the highest levels of the university.

Another prominent promotion case involved Nadia Abu El-Haj, an anthropology professor at Barnard College who came up for tenure in 2007. A 1982 Barnard graduate, who is an Israeli settler on the West Bank, organized a campaign to pressure Barnard and Columbia University to deny her tenure. The opposition was angered by Abu El-Haj's critique of efforts by Israeli archaeologists to find evidence of an ancient Jewish presence in Palestine. Critics claimed that her book, *Facts on the Ground,* is a polemic against the state of Israel. The campaign against Abu El-Haj was aided by the *New York Sun,* which has since gone out of business, but which at the time monitored Columbia closely and vehemently criticized it whenever someone at the school said or did something that was considered hostile to Israel. However, the lobby's efforts failed in this case, as Abu El-Haj was awarded tenure in November 2007.[6]

Pro-Israel forces also interfere in the hiring process at universities. Consider what happened in the early 2000s, when Columbia was recruiting Rashid Khalidi, who was then teaching at the University of Chicago. According to Jonathan R. Cole, the Columbia provost at the time, "when it became known that we were recruiting Khalidi to Columbia the complaints started flowing in from people who disagreed with the content of his political views." Princeton faced much the same problem a few years later when it tried to woo Khalidi away from Columbia. Nevertheless, both Columbia and Princeton made offers to Khalidi, which shows the lobby does not win every fight.[7]

Of course, not every case has a happy ending, as Finkelstein's firing make clear. Also consider that in 2006 the history and sociology departments at Yale voted an appointment for Professor Juan Cole, a distinguished historian at the University of Michigan, who is a sharp critic of many Israeli policies. Pro-Israel columnists at the *Wall Street Journal* and the *Washington Times* attacked Cole's appointment, and *Jewish Week* reported that several prominent Jewish donors had called Yale officials to protest the decision, which was subsequently overturned by the university's appointments committee. The actual impact of donor pressure is unknown, but the incident underscores the importance some supporters of Israel place on shaping discourse on campus.[8]

SMEARING CRITICS

The lobby also seeks to marginalize critics within academia by smearing them. This strategy was employed at Columbia in 2004, when the "David Project," a Boston-based pro-Israel group concerned with campus issues, produced a propaganda film alleging that faculty in the Middle Eastern studies program were not only anti-Semitic, but were also intimidating Jewish students who defended Israel. Columbia was raked over the coals in pro-Israel publications like the *New York Sun*, but a faculty committee assigned to investigate the charges found no evidence of anti-Semitism. The only incident worth noting was the possibility that one professor had "responded heatedly" to a student's question.[9]

The David Project apparently has changed its mind about the utility of smearing scholars by labeling them anti-Semites. In early 2012, it published a "white paper" that called for rethinking how to do Israel advocacy on American campuses. In particular, the report's authors maintained that:

> Accusing faculty members who propagandize against Israel of "academic malpractice" is likely to be a much more effective strategy than challenging specific allegations or invoking anti-Jewish bigotry. Rightly or wrongly, the current campus atmosphere is much more sympathetic to charges that teachers are not satisfactorily teaching their subject than to complaints of anti-Jewish bias and Israel supporters will likely have a greater practical impact by framing their concerns in this manner.[10]

Another example of the lobby smearing Israel's campus critics took place at the University of California–Los Angeles in January 2009. The Center for Near Eastern Studies sponsored a panel discussion dealing with the implications of Israel's war against Gaza (Operation Cast Lead) for human rights and international law. As reported in *Tikkun* by one of the panel members and a professor in the audience at the event, "The talks by the four speakers were largely uneventful, being interrupted by pro-Israeli jeers just once and briefly. The question and discussion period grew a bit more heated and contentious. But it was hardly uncivil, save for a mostly irrelevant rant read by an insistent member of the Socialist Workers Party."

Israel's supporters, however, misrepresented what happened at the panel, and some went so far as to accuse the panelists of leading the audience into chanting, "Zionism is Nazism" and "F-ck, f-ck Israel." One article written by a member of Stand With Us, a key organization in the lobby, ran under the headline: "Reviving 1920's Munich Beer Halls at UCLA, Courtesy of California Taxpayers." The panel was also described as "an academic lynching of Israel" and a "Hamas recruiting rally." Regarding these various charges, the authors of the *Tikkun* article write: "Both of us were present throughout the entire event, we have listened in the wake of these absurd accusations to the publicly available podcasts of the talks, and we have checked with others present. Nothing could be further from the truth."[11]

Smearing outspoken professors is not merely designed to silence or marginalize them. It also has a powerful deterrent effect. Specifically, it sends a clear message to other scholars who might be inclined to criticize Israel or American policy toward Israel that if they speak out, the lobby will make a concerted effort to damage their reputations and marginalize them within and outside the academy. This is a potent threat that can strike fear into the hearts of many academics.

STOPPING THE PRINTING PRESSES

Another strategy that pro-Israel forces employ is attempting to suppress the publication of scholarly works that make arguments they deem wrongheaded and dangerous. For example, in 1998, the Anti-Defamation League (ADL) called on the publisher of Norman Finkelstein and Ruth Bettina Birn's *A Nation on Trial* to halt its release. *A Nation on Trial* is a sharply worded critique of Daniel Goldhagen's controversial best seller *Hitler's Willing Executioners*, which argues that the Holocaust was not mainly the product of Nazi ideas and Hitler's own madness, but was instead rooted in a pervasive "eliminationist ideology" in German society that predated the Nazi period. Like the Goldhagen book, *A Nation on Trial* elicited praise as well as criticism from respected scholars. Yet ADL head Abraham Foxman maintained that *A Nation on Trial* should not have been published, claiming that the issue was not "whether Goldhagen's thesis is right or wrong but what is 'legitimate criticism' and what goes beyond the pale." Fortunately, Foxman's campaign failed and *A Nation on Trial* was published as planned.[12]

A similar episode took place in 2003, when lawyers representing Alan Dershowitz sent threatening letters to the University of California Press in an attempt to halt publication of Finkelstein's book, *Beyond Chutzpah*, which is an extended critique of Dershowitz's own book, *The Case for Israel*. Dershowitz also wrote to California governor Arnold Schwarzenegger as part of his campaign against Finkelstein. Dershowitz subsequently claimed that he was not trying to suppress publication, but that is certainly not how officials at UC Press interpreted his actions. They resisted these pressures, however, and issued Finkelstein's book anyway.[13]

Four years later in 2007, the lobby put significant pressure on the University of Michigan Press not to distribute Joel Kovel's book, *Overcoming Zionism*, which originally had been published in Britain by Pluto Press. Not only did the press initially cave in to the pressure, it also decided to end its long-standing arrangement to distribute Pluto Press books in the United States. There was an outcry, however, as soon as these controversial decisions became public knowledge, and the University of Michigan Press reversed itself and said it would distribute Kovel's book. However, it severed its ties with Pluto Press in 2008, when the contract between the two presses expired.[14]

KEEPING CRITICS OFF CAMPUS

The lobby also works to limit criticism of Israel by keeping outside voices from speaking on campuses. A case in point is the decision in the spring of 2007 by the University of St. Thomas in Minnesota to cancel a speech by the Nobel laureate, Archbishop Desmond Tutu. The move was prompted by pressure from members of the local Jewish community, who were offended by the archbishop's criticism of Israel's treatment of the Palestinians and his comparison of Israeli behavior in the Occupied Territories with the apartheid policies of white-dominated South Africa. The mainstream media naturally said little about Tutu being disinvited from St. Thomas. However, the story was posted on Muzzle Watch, a website run by Jewish Voice for Peace (JVP) that tracks efforts by the lobby to stifle debate about Israel. The ensuing publicity, which included an e-mail campaign encouraged by JVP, forced St. Thomas to reverse field in October 2007 and re-invite the archbishop to speak.[15]

A few years earlier in 2002, Hanan Ashrawi, an articulate Palestinian moderate who had worked for Yasser Arafat, was invited to Colorado College to be a keynote speaker at a symposium looking at the events of September 11 one year later. Pro-Israel forces were up in arms about the invitation; indeed, the Zionist Organization of America described Ashrawi as an "apologist for terrorism" and said she "should be disinvited" from the forum. Cooler heads prevailed, however, and she was allowed to speak, although the president of the school made sure that an Israeli was invited to be the keynote speaker the night after Ashrawi's address.[16]

This outcome illustrates that when the lobby cannot prevent a speaker from appearing on campus, its fallback position is invariably to demand "balance," which means also inviting someone to speak who has impeccable pro-Israel credentials. That politically correct person might be paired with the speaker on the same stage or appear separately after the critic has spoken. When Jimmy Carter appeared at Brandeis in January 2007 to talk about his controversial book, *Palestine: Peace Not Apartheid*, Alan Dershowitz wanted to be present to debate him. The sponsors of the event, as well as Carter, wanted the former president to be on stage alone. So arrangements were made for Dershowitz to speak after Carter spoke.[17]

More recently, the controversial Israeli historian, Ilan Pappe, was scheduled to speak in February 2012 at three California campuses: California Polytechnic State University in San Luis Obispo, California State University–Fresno, and California State University–Northridge. The Amcha Initiative, a newly formed organization that "endeavors to inform the California Jewish community about manifestations of harassment and intimidation of Jewish students on colleges and university campuses across the state," led an effort to prevent Pappe from speaking at those schools. It asked the president of each university to "rescind all . . . sponsorship and support from the Ilan Pappe events."

To their great credit, the presidents refused to cave in to the pressure. Instead, they reminded the Amcha Initiative that "our universities do not endorse any particular position, but emphatically support the rights of people to express and hear all points of view. For these reasons, it is not appropriate for our universities, as public institutions, to decide whether speakers are permitted to appear on campus based on the ideas they hold. Others are always welcome to invite speakers and create events that offer opposing views."[18]

WAGING LAWFARE FOR ISRAEL

In some of its other cases, the Amcha Initiative has employed a relatively new strategy for dealing with criticism of Israel. Under pressure from the lobby, Secretary of Education Arne Duncan mandated in October 2010 that Title VI of the 1964 Civil Rights Act, which was designed to fight racial segregation in the South, could be extended to include religious discrimination. This decision allows Jewish individuals and groups to file complaints either in the courts or with the Office for Civil Rights in the Department of Education. Specifically, it allows them to try to make the case that criticizing Israel is tantamount to anti-Semitism, and thus any school that tolerates such criticism is creating a hostile environment for its Jewish students and should be punished.

A good example of this strategy at work is the case filed against the University of California–Santa Cruz by Tammi Rossman-Benjamin, a cofounder of the Amcha Initiative. Her twenty-nine-page brief to the Office for Civil Rights concludes with these words:

> The anti-Israel discourse and behavior in classrooms and at departmentally and College-sponsored events at UCSC is tantamount to institutional discrimination against Jewish students, which has resulted in their intellectual and emotional harassment and intimidation, and has adversely affected their educational experience at the University . . . The institutional discrimination against Jewish students has shown no signs of abating, and has in some ways worsened with time.

So far, it appears that nine cases involving anti-Israel activity have been filed under Title VI. None have been successful, although it is too early to know whether the lobby will be able to make this strategy work either in the courts or with the Office for Civil Rights. There is little doubt that if this approach is successful, it will have a chilling effect on academic freedom.[19]

CO-OPTING STUDENTS

The lobby commits a large amount of time and resources to influencing students on campus. The American Israel Public Affairs Committee (AIPAC), which is surely the most powerful pro-Israel organization, has been doing this since at least the late 1970s. In the early 2000s, when Israel was being widely criticized on college campuses, it moved aggressively to "take back the campuses." But AIPAC was hardly the only group to participate in this effort. Indeed, the Israel on Campus Coalition, which was founded in 2002 "to create positive campus change for Israel," includes thirty-three organizations.

These various groups target Jewish as well as non-Jewish students. The objective with Jewish students is to motivate them to support Israel enthusiastically and fearlessly and also instruct them on how to sell Israel on campus.

An important element in the strategy is instructing Jewish students on how to win non-Jewish students over to Israel's side.

Aside from the fact that there is something disturbing about an outside lobbying group waging a wide-ranging campaign to influence how students think about a foreign country, many of the tactics the lobby employs are antithetical to core academic values. Consider the advice that is proffered to students in the *Hasbara Handbook: Promoting Israel on Campus*. They are told that two approaches can be used to sell Israel on campus: "point scoring" and "genuine debate." Point scoring aims "to give the impression of rational debate, whilst avoiding genuine discussion." The goal, in other words, is to manipulate the facts in clever ways to make Israel's case. The *Hasbara Handbook* goes on to note, "Point scoring can irritate audiences who are genuinely committed to thinking about their views on a subject." One would hope so. But more importantly, universities are committed to discouraging point scoring and instead teaching students to think critically and engage in genuine debate.

The lobby also pays careful attention to winning over non-Jewish students by co-opting them. This strategy is clearly laid out in the David Project's 2012 white paper on how to advocate for Israel on campus. It starts with the assumption that today's college students are easy to manipulate, because they "are largely politically apathetic" and most of them are not serious about their studies. For the most part, they see college "as a time to focus on recreation and self-exploration." This situation is abetted by the fact that "many universities and colleges are not academically rigorous environments for many of their students."

Given this fertile recruiting ground, the white paper emphasizes that "campuses should first be 'mapped' by student leaders," which "means identifying campus influencers, whether individuals or groups." Then, an effort should be made to win them over to Israel's side. "Co-opting them into pro-Israel efforts is an opportunity for a significant 'win' by Israel advocates." The David Project goes so far as to suggest that particular groups, like Indian Americans, "have a potential for natural affinity," in part because India and Israel are both "primary targets of Islamist terrorism [and] suffer from protracted border disputes with majority Muslim populations." "Other Asian groups" like Chinese and Korean students are also said to be good prospects for Israel's cause.

Pro-Israel forces also place a high premium on molding student thinking by influencing what is written about Israel in college newspapers. "Campus Israel advocates," says the white paper, "should work to achieve leadership roles on these publications themselves or at least develop relationships with those who do positively impact their coverage of Israel." Although there is nothing wrong with trying to foster positive media coverage on campus, this strategy shows that the lobby leaves no stone unturned in its crusade to shape how college students all across the United States think about Israel.[20]

HITTING COLLEGES AND THE POCKETBOOK

Finally, the lobby attempts to shape the campus discourse about Israel by monitoring what professors say and threatening to curtail financial support from outside sources—individual donors, foundations, and the government—when Israel is criticized. In September 2002, for example, Daniel Pipes established Campus Watch, a website that posted dossiers on suspect academics and encouraged students to report comments or behavior that might be considered hostile to Israel. This transparent attempt to blacklist and intimidate scholars prompted a harsh reaction and Pipes later removed the dossiers, but the website still invites students to report alleged anti-Israel behavior at American colleges. Turning students into snitches is hardly consistent with core academic values.

Pipes's campaign to stamp out criticism of Israel on college campuses did not stop there. Together with Martin Kramer, an Israeli American scholar who is a fellow at the Washington Institute for Near East Policy and president of Shalem College in Jerusalem, Pipes began encouraging Congress to curtail or at least closely monitor Title VI money that the federal government gives to Middle East and other area studies programs at major universities. The aim is to silence critics of Israel and hopefully force universities to hire scholars whose views are more in line with those of Kramer and Pipes.[21]

Even more importantly, when Israel gets seriously criticized in a university setting, some Jewish donors invariably call administrators to complain and in some cases threaten to stop donating to the school. This could have significant consequences for a college if those donors are wealthy and if large numbers of them stop giving gifts. A good example of this strategy at work occurred in February 2012, when the University of Pennsylvania hosted a Boycott, Divestment, and Sanction (BDS) conference. BDS is a bête-noire of the pro-Israel community, which was deeply upset that the conference was being held at an Ivy League university. Not surprisingly, the school newspaper ran a story just before the conference started with a headline saying: "BDS Conference

Arrives This Weekend: Alums Are Threatening to Cease Donations for Allowing the Conference on Campus."

Unsurprisingly, the university went to great lengths to assure Israel's supporters that "it does not support sanctions or boycotts against Israel." In particular, the president of Penn and the chairman of its board of trustees wrote a joint op-ed in the school newspaper in which they said: "We want to be absolutely clear . . . the University has repeatedly, consistently and forcefully expressed our adamant opposition to this agenda. Simply stated, we fundamentally disagree with the position taken by Penn BDS."

University administrators, however, are not supposed to take a position on the ideas expressed by their professors or at conferences held on their campuses; they are supposed to remain neutral so as not to prejudice the discussion in any way. When individuals in positions of power and authority pass judgment on ideas that are under debate, it cannot help but have a chilling effect on what professors and students say. But Penn's leaders violated that norm, surely because they feared there would be negative financial consequences if they did not make clear that they loathed BDS and wished that the conference was not being held on their campus. Nevertheless, the conference was held at Penn without incident.[22]

In sum, pro-Israel individuals and groups have been especially active on campuses in recent years, working hard to silence criticism of Israel and promote a positive image of the Jewish state. Unfortunately, they have often employed strategies that are illegitimate and threaten open discourse in the academy.

ISRAEL AND THE DANGER OF OPEN DISCOURSE

There are two related reasons why defenders of Israel think that criticism of Israel is so dangerous and thus relentlessly labor to police academia. First, the case for America's special relationship with Israel is weak. Second, contrary to the claims of Israel's strongest backers, support for that relationship among the American people is neither wide nor deep. Americans do have a generally favorable image of Israel, but most of them do not think the United States should back Israel unconditionally.

This means that if there is an open and freewheeling discussion of Israeli history, Israeli policy in the Occupied Territories, and the U.S. relationship with Israel, it would probably lead more Americans to pressure their leaders in Washington to abandon the special relationship and treat Israel like a normal country, much the way it treats other democracies like Britain, France, and India. The lobby wants to make sure that this does not happen, and thus it works 24/7 to shape the discourse so that Israel is portrayed in a favorable light.

Israel's relationship with the United States has no counterpart. Indeed, as the late Yitzhak Rabin once said, U.S. support for Israel is "beyond compare in modern history."[23] To be more specific, the special relationship means that Washington gives Israel consistent diplomatic backing and more foreign aid than any other country, and gives it nearly unconditionally. In other words, Israel gets this aid even when it does things that the United States opposes, like building settlements in the Occupied Territories.

Many of Israel's supporters maintain that this special relationship is based on the fact that Israel is a vital strategic asset for the United States, and moreover, that it shares core American values.[24] Viewed objectively, however, these arguments cannot explain why Washington gives Israel so much aid and diplomatic support with so few strings.

Israel may have been a strategic asset during the Cold War, but that conflict is over. Today, giving Israel nearly unconditional support is one of the reasons the United States has a terrorism problem, and it makes it harder to address a range of other problems in the Middle East. Support for Israel is not the only source of anti-Americanism, of course, and our problems in the Middle East would not disappear if the United States had a more normal relationship with Israel. And Washington does benefit from some forms of strategic cooperation with Israel. But it is hard to argue that giving it nearly unconditional backing is making the United States more popular around the world or making American citizens more secure. On balance, it is now a strategic liability.[25]

As for the claim that Israel is a democracy that shares our values, yes, Israel is a democracy, but so are many other countries, and none gets anywhere near as much support, and they certainly do not get it unconditionally. Furthermore, the United States is a liberal democracy that goes to great lengths not to discriminate against its citizens on the basis of religion, ethnicity, or race. It is certainly not a Christian state. Israel, on the other hand, is a Jewish state that discriminates against its Palestinian citizens in theory and in practice. Moreover, its cruel treatment of the Palestinians living in the Occupied

Territories is sharply at odds with American values. There is a strong moral case for Israel's existence—based on the long history of anti-Semitism—but its survival is fortunately not in jeopardy, and past crimes against the Jewish people do not justify giving Israel a blank check today.[26]

THE AMERICAN PEOPLE AND ISRAEL

Some of Israel's staunchest defenders recognize that both the strategic and moral rationales do not carry much explanatory weight on close inspection, and argue instead that the United States backs Israel because there is broad and deep support for the special relationship among the American people, and politicians are just doing what the public wants.[27]

This argument is not persuasive for several reasons. Americans do have a generally positive image of Israel—in part because of the lobby's efforts to promote favorable media coverage and stifle negative commentary—but most of them do not think their country should give Israel unconditional or one-sided aid. A survey conducted for the ADL in 2005 found that 78 percent of Americans think the United States should favor neither side in the Israeli–Palestinian conflict; and another survey conducted by the University of Maryland in 2003 found that over 70 percent of "politically active" Americans favored cutting aid to Israel if it refused to settle that conflict. A poll taken in August 2011 by the University of Maryland found that just 56 percent of Americans surveyed have a favorable view of Israel, and only 27 percent want the United States to "lean toward Israel" over the Palestinians.

The Pew Research Center for the People and the Press has been asking Americans for many years whether they sympathize more with Israel or the Palestinians. There has always been much more sympathy for Israel, but from 1993 through 2006, the number sympathetic to Israel only went above 50 percent once—it was 52 percent during the second Lebanon war in 2006—and was as low as 37 percent in July 2005. The American public's sympathies have changed hardly at all since 2006, according to subsequent Pew surveys.

Furthermore, most Americans recognize that the United States pays a price for its unyielding support of Israel. A Pew survey conducted in November 2005 found that 39 percent of the American public said that Israel was "a major cause of global discontent." Among opinion leaders, the numbers were substantially higher. Indeed, 78 percent of members of the news media,

72 percent of military leaders, 72 percent of security experts, and 69 percent of foreign affairs specialists believe that backing Israel seriously damages America's image around the world. More recently, a BBC poll released on March 7, 2011, found that 43 percent of Americans thought that Israel's influence on the world was "mainly positive," while 41 percent said it was "mainly negative."[28]

So while Americans have a generally favorable image of Israel and want it to exist and be secure, they are not insisting that Washington back it no matter what. But that is pretty much what U.S. policy is, and this gap is due largely to the political influence of the Israel lobby.

In sum, the strategic and moral justifications for the U.S. special relationship with Israel are weak, and there is no evidence that the American people are in favor of it. These basic facts mean that the lobby has to work hard to shape the discourse about Israel and make sure the American public thinks there are good reasons for maintaining that unique relationship. Its task, of course, is not easy in the halls of academia, where free speech and open discourse are core values. Nevertheless, Israel's supporters have mounted a full-court press on campuses across the country and have scored some notable successes. But thankfully they have not won every fight.

BIGGER TROUBLE AHEAD

In all likelihood, this situation will get worse, not better, in the foreseeable future. There is little reason to think that Israel will abandon the West Bank and allow the Palestinians to have a viable state of their own. Instead, Israel is likely to continue colonizing the West Bank while denying the Palestinians basic human rights and keeping them trapped in enclaves on the West Bank and Gaza. What this means is that there is going to be a Greater Israel between the Jordan River and the Mediterranean Sea, not a Palestinian state and an Israeli state living side by side.

Greater Israel, however, will be an apartheid state. Former Israeli prime minister Ehud Olmert made this point in November 2007, when he said that if there is no two-state solution, Israel will "face a South-African-style struggle." He went so far as to argue that "as soon as that happens, the state of Israel is finished." Former prime minister Ehud Barak, who later became Israel's defense minister, said in February 2010 that "as long as in this territory west of the Jordan River there is only one political entity called Israel it is going to be either non-Jewish, or non-democratic. If this bloc of millions of Palestinians cannot vote, that will be an apartheid state."[29]

The critical problem that Greater Israel's defenders will face is that it is impossible to defend apartheid, because it is antithetical to core Western values. How does one make a moral case for apartheid, especially in the United States, where democracy is venerated and segregation and racism are routinely condemned? It is hard to imagine the United States having a special relationship with an apartheid state for very long. Indeed, it is hard to imagine Americans having much sympathy for one. It is much easier to imagine the United States strongly opposing that racist state's political system and working hard to change it. Many other countries around the globe would surely follow suit. This is why former prime minister Olmert said that going down the apartheid road would be suicidal for Israel.

Given Israel's trajectory, there is not likely to be any letup in criticism of Israel inside and outside of the United States in the years ahead. Indeed, it is likely to intensify, because the discrimination and repression that are the essence of apartheid will be increasingly visible to people all around the world. Israel and its supporters have worked hard with considerable success to keep the mainstream media in the United States from telling the truth about what Israel is doing to the Palestinians in the Occupied Territories. The Internet, however, is a game changer. It not only makes it much easier for opponents of apartheid to get the real story out to the world, but it also allows Americans to learn the story that the *New York Times*, the *Wall Street Journal*, and the *Washington Post* have been hiding from them. Over time, this situation might even force those media institutions to cover the story more accurately themselves.

Naturally, the threat of even more pronounced criticism of Israel, and consequent criticism of America's support for an apartheid state, will motivate the lobby to work harder to defend Greater Israel. This surely means that hardline defenders of the special relationship will intervene even more forcefully in academia and do everything possible to silence Israel's critics. They simply cannot allow an open discourse about Israel in the United States without placing the special relationship at risk.

In short, the lobby is likely to increase its already substantial presence on campuses and in the process do serious harm to the core principle of academic freedom that makes American colleges and universities so successful.

NOTES

1. This chapter is a revised version of a talk given at the Freedom and the University Symposium held at Columbia University on October 30, 2007.

2. Quoted in David Epstein, "We Need All of You," *Israel Campus Beat*, January 21, 2011. Also see Robert Wiener, "Sharansky Sees Campuses as Jewish Battleground," *New Jersey Jewish News*, May 25, 2011.

3. For a discussion of the Israel lobby, see John J. Mearsheimer and Stephen M. Walt, *The Israel Lobby and U.S. Foreign Policy* (New York: Farrar, Straus and Giroux, 2007), chap. 4.

4. Martin Kramer, *Ivory Towers on Sand: The Failure of Middle Eastern Studies in America* (Washington, D.C.: Washington Institute for Near East Policy, 2001).

5. Jennifer Howard, "DePaul Rejects Tenure Bid by Finkelstein and Says Dershowitz Pressure Played No Role," *Chronicle of Higher Education*, June 8, 2007. Also see Patricia Cohen, "Outspoken Political Scientist Denied Tenure at DePaul," *New York Times*, June 11, 2007.

6. Karen W. Arenson, "Fracas Erupts Over Book on Mideast by a Barnard Professor Seeking Tenure," *New York Times*, September 10, 2007; Annie Karni, "After Battle, Barnard Professor Given Tenure," *New York Sun*, November 2, 2007.

7. Jonathan R. Cole, "The Patriot Act on Campus: Defending the University Post 9/11," *Boston Review* 28, no. 3/4 (Summer 2003): 16–18; Chanakya Sethi, "Khalidi Candidacy for New Chair Draws Fire," *Daily Princetonian*, April 22, 2005; Chanakya Sethi, "Debate Grows Over Khalidi Candidacy," *Daily Princetonian*, April 28, 2005.

8. Liel Liebovitz, "Middle East Wars Flare Up at Yale," *Jewish Week*, June 2, 2006; Steve Lipman, "Opening the Ivy Doors," *Jewish Week*, December 22, 2006; Philip Weiss, "Burning Cole," *The Nation*, July 3, 2006.

9. Robert Gaines, "The Battle at Columbia University," *Washington Report on Middle East Affairs* (April 2005): 56–57; Nathaniel Popper, "Columbia Students Say Firestorm Blurs Campus Reality," *Forward*, February 11, 2005; Scott Sherman, "The Mideast Comes to Columbia," *The Nation*, April 4, 2005; "Columbia University Ad Hoc Grievance Committee, Final Report, New York, 28 March 2005 (excerpts)," in *Journal of Palestine Studies* 34, no. 4 (Summer 2005), 90–100.

10. David Project, *A Burning Campus? Rethinking Israel Advocacy at America's Universities and Colleges* (Boston, Mass.: 2012). Also see Julie Wiener, "The New Israel Campus Strategy," *Jewish Week*, February 14, 2012.

11. David Theo Goldberg and Saree Makdisi, "The Trial of Israel's Campus Critics," *Tikkun*, September/October 2009.

12. Ralph Blumenthal, "Cries to Halt Publication of Holocaust Book," *New York Times*, January 10, 1998; Norman G. Finkelstein, *Beyond Chutzpah: On the Misuse of Anti-Semitism and the Abuse of History* (Berkeley, Calif.: University of California Press, 2005), 55–56.

13. Jon Weiner, "Giving Chutzpah New Meaning," *The Nation*, July 11, 2005; "Dershowitz, Prof Spar Over Plagiarism," *New York Times*, July 14, 2005; Jennifer Howard,

"Calif. Press Will Publish Controversial Book on Israel," *Chronicle of Higher Education*, July 22, 2005; Jon Wiener, "Chutzpah and Free Speech," *Los Angeles Times*, July 11, 2005.

14. Scott Jaschik, "A Book on Hold," *Inside Higher Ed*, September 11, 2007; Scott Jaschik, "Michigan Severs Ties to Controversial Publisher," *Inside Higher Ed*, June 18, 2008; Michal Lando, "Israel Critique on Campus," *Jerusalem Post*, November 4, 2007.

15. Scott Jaschik, "Desmond Tutu, Persona Non Grata," *Inside Higher Ed*, October 4, 2007; Scott Jaschik, "St. Thomas Agrees to Invite Tutu," *Inside Higher Ed*, October 11, 2007; Jeff Shelman, "Oct. 10: About-face: Tutu Gets St. Thomas Invite," *Minneapolis Star Tribune*, October 22, 2007; Cecilie Surasky, "Archbishop Tutu Barred by U. of St. Thomas Because of Criticism of Israel," posted on *MuzzleWatch*, October 3, 2007, http://muzzlewatch.com/2007/10/03/bishop-tutu-barred-by-u-of-st-thomas-because-of-criticism-of-israel.

16. Michael Janofsky, "Invitation to Palestinian Draws Protest at Colorado College," *New York Times*, August 30, 2002; Michael A. de Yoanna, "Palestinian Activist Equated with 'Terror' in Fliers at U. Colorado," *New York Times*, September 6, 2002; Valerie Richardson, "College Rapped for 9/11 Speaker; Palestinian Pick on Anniversary Draws Outrage," *Washington Times*, August 30, 2002; Zionist Organization of America, "Hanan Ashrawi, Apologist for Terror, Should Be Disinvited from Colorado Symposium on 9/11 Anniversary," press release, August 30, 2002.

17. Pam Belluck, "At Brandeis, Carter Responds to Critics," *New York Times*, January 24, 2007; Nathaniel Popper, "Carter Wins Over Student Crowd at Brandeis, Receives Ovation," *Forward*, January 26, 2007; "Jimmy Carter Ducks Dershowitz, Open Questions," *Newsmax.com*, January 23, 2007.

18. Cecilie Surasky, "State University Hosts Israeli Historian Ilan Pappe—Says No to McCarthy Campaign," posted on *MuzzleWatch*, February 18, 2012, http://muzzlewatch.com/2012/02/18/state-university-hosts-israeli-historian-ilan-pappe-says-no-to-mccarthyite-campaign. On the Amcha Initiative's mission, see its website at http://amchainitiative.org. For its letter to the three presidents, see http://amchainitiative.org/pappe_at_csu.

19. Naomi Zeveloff, "Coming Up Empty on Title VI," *Forward*, March 16, 2012; Naomi Zeveloff, "College Leaders Balance Israel and Speech," *Forward*, January 20, 2012; Zionist Organization of America, "ZOA Praises Office for Civil Rights—Opening Title VI Investigation of Anti-Semitic Environment at UC Santa Cruz Arising from Israel-Bashing," press release, March 14, 2011. A copy of Tammi Rossman-Benjamin's brief can be found at http://brandeiscenter.com/images/uploads/cases/complaint_ucsc.pdf.

20. David Project, *A Burning Campus*; World Union of Jewish Students, *Hasbara Handbook: Promoting Israel on Campus* (Jerusalem: World Union of Jewish Students, March 2002); Mearsheimer and Walt, *The Israel Lobby*, 178–79.

21. Mearsheimer and Walt, *The Israel Lobby*, 179–82.

22. Amy Guttman and David L. Cohen, "Protecting Speech We May Not Like," *Daily Pennsylvanian*, February 1, 2012; Sarah Smith, "BDS Conference Arrives This

Weekend: Alums Are Threatening to Cease Donations for Allowing the Conference on Campus," *Daily Pennsylvanian*, February 3, 2012; Shelli Gimelstein, "From 'Water Buffalo' to BDS, Penn Faces Free Speech Question," *Daily Pennsylvanian*, February 14, 2012.

23. Mearsheimer and Walt, *The Israel Lobby*, 23.

24. Robert D. Blackwill and Walter B. Slocombe, *Israel: A Strategic Asset for the United States* (Washington, D.C.: Washington Institute for Near East Policy, November 2011).

25. Mearsheimer and Walt, *The Israel Lobby*, chap. 2; Stephen M. Walt, "News Flash: WINEP Defends the 'Special Relationship'," *Foreign Policy* (blog), November 9, 2011.

26. Mearsheimer and Walt, *The Israel Lobby*, chap. 3.

27. For a sophisticated version of this argument, see Jerome Slater, "The Two Books of Mearsheimer and Walt," *Security Studies* 18, no. 1 (January–March 2009): 4–57. For a rebuttal, see John J. Mearsheimer and Stephen M. Walt, "Is It Love or the Lobby? Explaining America's Special Relationship with Israel," *Security Studies* 18, no. 1 (January–March 2009): 58–78.

28. British Broadcasting Corporation, "BBC World Service Country Rating Poll," press release, March 7, 2011, 19–20; Mearsheimer and Walt, *The Israel Lobby*, 108–10; Pew Research Center for the People and the Press, "Views of Middle East Unchanged by Recent Events," June 10, 2011; Steven Kull and Shibley Telhami (principal investigators), "The American Public on the 9/11 Decade" (program on International Policy Attitudes, University of Maryland, September 8, 2011), 15; Stephen M. Walt, "Do the American People Support the 'Special Relationship'?," *Foreign Policy* (blog), June 3, 2011.

29. Barak Ravid et al., "Olmert to Ha'aretz: Two-State Solution, or Israel Is Done For," *Ha'aretz*, November 29, 2007; Rory McCarthy, "Barak: Make Peace with Palestinians or Face Apartheid," *Guardian*, February 2, 2010.

16

ACADEMIC FREEDOM AND THE SUBSERVIENCE TO POWER

NOAM CHOMSKY

THE SUBJECT OF this brief essay is the decision by the DePaul administration to deny tenure to Norman Finkelstein, a remarkable teacher and outstanding scholar, whose work has received the highest praise from some of the most distinguished scholars in the many fields in which he has worked, notably the founder of Holocaust studies and its most respected figure, the late Raul Hilberg. And also the denial of tenure to another fine scholar, Mehrene Larudee, whose crime appears to have been her honorable support for Finkelstein. I will not review this sordid affair. The basic facts are clear enough in easily accessible sources. Instead, I would like to say a few words about the general background for the ongoing assault on academic freedom, of which this is an ugly example.

Perhaps a good place to start is with an observation by a prominent University of Chicago professor, Hans Morgenthau, one of the founders of the realist school of international relations, who condemned the intellectual classes for what he called "our conformist subservience to those in power." Power comes in many forms, typically state or economic power, though one should not ignore the power of the defamation industries and depraved individuals associated with them who can lie, slander, and vilify with impunity, thanks to media that tolerate and even encourage such behavior.

The assault on academic freedom is broad, but it has specifically targeted Middle Eastern departments and peace studies programs. That makes sense. State power is focused on war in the Middle East, so impediments must be removed and "conformist subservience to those in power" must be assured in these areas.

The matter goes far beyond purifying academic institutions of faculty who reveal unwanted truths. Subordination to power can take many other forms. Let us take a very recent case that has elicited a huge public outcry: the appearance of Iranian president Ahmadinejad at Columbia University. In the background is the frenzied government-media campaign to demonize Iran and its relatively powerless president, the "new Hitler" if not worse. New Hitlers have been a familiar refrain in the doctrinal system over the years, though the cast of characters changes depending on current plans for subversion and aggression. The propaganda campaign about alleged Iranian iniquity is accompanied by the threats of war that resound across the political spectrum, including every viable Democratic candidate. The threats are a serious violation of the UN Charter if anyone still cares about such marginalia. The campaign may also lay the basis for further U.S. aggression in the region, probably with even more catastrophic consequences than the invasion of Iraq.

Demonization is a conventional preliminary to aggression, and therefore is not to be regarded lightly, particularly when it is carried out in an academic setting, which in a free society should be as untainted as possible by the conformist subservience to power that Morgenthau deplored. Before turning to Columbia University's instructive contribution, a few more words about the context.

Wars are almost always defensive wars in the eyes of the perpetrators — at least in their words — as when the original and authentic Hitler invaded Poland in self-defense against the "wild terror" of the Poles. And right now the ground is being prepared for a war of *self-defense* against Iran, in a manner that tells us a lot about the dominant intellectual and moral culture. Speaking for a very large segment of articulate opinion, the editors of the *Washington Post* thundered that Iran "is waging war against the United States and trying to kill as many American soldiers as possible" so that we must "fight back."[1] Iran's aggression is its alleged support for Iraqis resisting U.S. invasion, occupation, and virtual destruction of their country, right on Iran's borders.

The propaganda campaign illustrates an important difference between totalitarian and democratic propaganda systems. In totalitarian systems, the party line is openly announced: obey it, or else. The mailed fist takes care of the rest. In more democratic systems, that will not work. The party line is not articulated, hence is protected from easy refutation. Rather, it is insinuated, presupposed as the framework for debate. And lively debate is then encouraged, within that framework. That has the double advantage of making it appear that the society is free and open, while also instilling the party line even more deeply, as the precondition for responsible discussion. It is adopted as unchallengeable reality, like the air we breathe.

True to form, the current charges about Iran's crimes elicit a lively debate. The hawks say they we must bomb them in self-defense. The doves respond that the evidence is not entirely clear, so perhaps we should delay before we obliterate them.

By the prevailing logic, Russia would have been justified in bombing the U.S. in the 1980s, when Washington was quite publicly supporting resistance to the Russian invasion and occupation of Afghanistan. The CIA station chief in Pakistan in 1981, Howard Hart, reported that "I was the first chief of station ever sent abroad with this wonderful order: 'Go kill Soviet soldiers.' Imagine! I loved it." "The mission was not to liberate Afghanistan,"[2] so Tim Wiener writes in his recent history of the CIA, repeating the obvious, but it was noble anyway, he says. Presumably the nobility includes support for Reagan's favorites, who amused themselves by such acts as throwing acid in the faces of women in Kabul they regarded as too liberated, and after the withdrawal of the Russian forces turned to tearing the country to shreds, creating such havoc and terror that the population actually welcomed the Taliban.

Killing Russian invaders and supporting crazed Islamic fundamentalist murderers was noble, but providing aid to forces resisting a U.S. invasion would be a shocking crime, which justifies military action in self-defense. The stand is arguable, on the tacit assumption that the United States owns the world; hence a U.S. invasion is by definition right and just. It may be a mistake, too costly to us, a quagmire. But it cannot be criminal, like comparable acts by enemies. Withdraw the assumption that the United States owns the world and the entire debate about Iranian interference in occupied Iraq is simply ludicrous.

Demonization as a preliminary to violence is standard operating procedure. The reason is that the population is generally opposed to war and has to be whipped into hysteria about the ultimate evil that threatens its existence. In this case the task is not easy, so the propaganda efforts must be fierce. Seventy-five percent of Americans are opposed to even threats against Iran and prefer entering into normal relations. Roughly the same percentage believe that Iran has the right to nuclear energy and call for a nuclear weapons–free zone in the entire region, including Iran and Israel, an idea that is virtually unmentionable in respectable society. Though few of the respondents in polls are likely to know it, they are endorsing UN Security Council Resolution 687 of April 1991, to which Washington selectively appealed in its efforts to justify the invasion of Iraq: the resolution calls for "establishing in the Middle East a zone free from weapons of mass destruction and all missiles for their delivery."[3] Rather interestingly, Iranians and Americans are in almost complete agreement on these matters and in radical opposition to the government and articulate opinion in the United States.

Let us turn to Columbia University's contribution. Columbia's President Lee Bollinger introduced Ahmadinejad with a tirade that has no precedent I can think of. Bollinger adopted without question the charge that Iran has committed the shocking crime of supporting resistance to U.S. aggression on its borders, thereby adopting the familiar tacit premise that the United States owns the world. And he went on with the familiar refrain that has been trumpeted through the loyal media, which there is no need to repeat.

The most apt comment I have seen on this performance was in the *Asia Times*:

> An even more appalling measure of Western arrogance . . . is the diatribe with which the president of Columbia University, Lee Bollinger, chose to "greet" his guest, a head of state . . . Were President Bush to be greeted in the same manner in any university in the developing world—and motives would abound also to qualify him as a "cruel, petty dictator"—the Pentagon would have instantly switched to let's-bomb-them-with-democracy mode. [4]

To which we may add that Bush's crimes vastly exceed anything attributed to Ahmadinejad, by a huge margin in fact.

The hysteria had its comical aspects—or what would be comical if it were not so serious. Since Ahmadinejad kept from being too offensive, the media and commentators leaped on his silly statement about homosexuality in Iran, which deeply offended Westerners, who have such a stellar record in defending gay rights ever since gaining independence centuries ago. Who can imagine that President Bush could have been governor of a state that outlawed sodomy, for example. And there is much more to say. Since we are discussing universities, we might recall the murder of the very distinguished mathematician and computer scientist Alan Turing by the British government, which forced him to undergo hormone therapy for his "disease," which led to his suicide. The year was 1953, which has a certain significance in U.S./UK–Iranian relations.

It also worth remembering the reaction in the media and at Columbia University to the events of that important year, in which the United States–Britain instigated a military coup to overthrow the Iranian parliamentary system, imposing the iron rule of a brutal tyrant and torturer. The *New York Times* editors were full of praise for the achievement. In their words, "Under-developed countries with rich resources now have an object lesson in the heavy cost that must be paid by one of their number which goes berserk with fanatical nationalism,"[5] seeking to control its own resources. Columbia University played its part by inviting the shah to deliver the university's 1955 Gabriel Silver Lecture Dedicated to International Peace, also granting him an honorary degree. In his lecture, the shah urged, "We must be strong enough internally and externally so that the temptation of subversion from within, supported from without, can be obliterated."[6] The *New York Times* report records no embarrassment. Its headline reads: "Shah Praises U.S. for Peace Policy; Iran's Ruler Calls on West to Bolster Independent Nations" — as the United States and Britain had just done with such grace and nobility in his country.

Columbia's delicate taste with regard to visiting dignitaries was revealed again when Pakistan's military dictator Pervez Musharraf visited recently. His country of course not only developed nuclear weapons and refused to sign the Non-Proliferation Treaty, but also provides refuge to the world's champion proliferator, Abdul Qadeer Khan, who "did more damage in 10 years than any country did in the first 50 years of the nuclear age," according to James Walsh, executive director of Harvard's Managing the Atom project.[7]

President Bollinger opened his fulsome welcome to the dictator by saying, "Rarely do we have an opportunity such as this to greet a figure of such central and global importance. It is with great gratitude and excitement that I welcome President Musharraf and his wife . . . to Columbia University. . . . Mr. President, as you share your thoughts and insights you will give our students, the leaders of tomorrow, firsthand knowledge of the world their generation will inherit. President Musharraf, we thank you for being with us today. And we welcome you to Columbia University."[8]

To enhance the imagery, while Bollinger was once again conforming to state doctrine by berating Ahmadinejad, Musharraf's riot police were firing tear gas and beating lawyers and human rights activists protesting Musharraf's plans to have himself reelected while serving as chief of the military.

A few hours before Ahmadinejad's arrival at Columbia, the university welcomed the president of Turkmenistan, another vibrant democracy with a stellar human rights record—and plenty of natural gas, which the United States covets.

This is just a sample, but perhaps enough to remind us that conformist subservience to power takes many forms in the academic world.

The current assault on academic freedom traces back to the activism of the 1960s and the elite reaction to it. This "time of troubles," as it is called, had a dangerous civilizing effect on American society and culture in many domains: civil and human rights, opposition to criminal aggression, concern for the environment, critical analysis of dominant institutions and ideology, and many more. That aroused deep concern and elicited a backlash that has taken many forms. A good indication of how the problems were perceived is given in a 1975 publication of the Trilateral Commission called *The Crisis of Democracy*. This is a view from the liberal internationalist end of the political spectrum. The Carter administration was largely drawn from the ranks of the commission. The "crisis of democracy" that troubled the liberal internationalist commentators was that 1960s activism was making the country too democratic. It was mobilizing formerly passive special interests to enter the political arena to advance their concerns: women, the young, the elderly, working people, minorities, majorities—in simple terms, the population. The commission called for more "moderation in democracy" so that the natural rulers would not be disturbed by "ignorant and meddlesome outsiders," the population, to borrow the phrase used years earlier by Walter Lippmann, the leading public intellectual of the twentieth century, expressing the same rather conventional thoughts.

One specific concern of the commission was what they called the institutions responsible for "the indoctrination of the young"—schools, universities, churches, and the like. They were not carrying out this task with sufficient rigor and must act more vigorously to inhibit the freedom and opportunity they provide for independent thought. That is the liberal end of the spectrum.[9] At the other end we have today the attack by statist reactionaries who are outraged by the "liberal bias" that subjects "conservative students" to punishment and instills anti-American, pro-Palestinian, and other left-liberal dogma, to quote press commentary. The press reports that "Congress is taking the first steps toward pressuring colleges to maintain ideological balance in the classroom" by overcoming this extreme bias, claims that scarcely merit ridicule in the light of the realities of the academic world.

The attack is quite real, however. The press also reports that the House of Representatives "unanimously passed a bill that could require university international studies departments to show more support for American foreign policy or risk their federal funding."[10] The resolution was aimed particularly at Middle Eastern programs, which, as I mentioned, are the main targets, along with peace studies programs. The late Baruch Kimmerling, one of Israel's leading scholars, warned of the dangerous consequences of "this assault on academic freedom by a coalition of neocons and zealous Jewish students supported by some Jewish 'mainstream' organizations," inspired by David Horowitz's "crusade." The title of his essay was: "Can a 'Patriotic' Mob Take Over the Universities?"[11] His article was rejected by the *Chronicle of Higher Education.* Writing in the *London Review of Books*, Harvard University Middle Eastern scholar Sara Roy quotes Horowitz's attack on 250 peace studies programs in the United States, which he asserts "teach students to identify with America's terrorist enemies and to identify America as a Great Satan oppressing the world's poor and causing them to go hungry . . . The question is: how long can a nation at war with ruthless enemies like bin Laden and Zarqawi survive if its educational institutions continue to be suborned in this way?"[12]

It is pointless to debate such lunacy. But it is wrong to disregard it. The goal of the statist reactionaries is not to tell the truth, but to shift the range of admissible options even more toward the conformist subservience that Morgenthau condemned. It is understandable that Middle Eastern departments and peace studies programs should be the primary targets. Peace studies are inherently threatening to power, if they are at all serious. The common term "peacenik" insinuates the attitudes that serious people should hold toward the subversives who seek peace; there is no word "warnik." And Middle Eastern departments might expose the truth about the region and U.S. policies there, as Norman Finkelstein has done with scrupulous documentation and penetrating analysis. Truth poses a serious barrier to the policies carried out by state power and supported by all too many among the educated classes — whether invading Iraq to establish a client state and base for U.S. power in the region, or restoring Iran to the happy days under the shah, or destroying Palestine under the pretext of defense and democracy promotion, or a series of other crimes too long and familiar to mention.

These crimes are likely to persist into the future in the region that President Eisenhower described as "the strategically most important area" of the world, which contains two-thirds of the world's energy resources. Sixty years ago, the State Department recognized that these resources constitute "a stupendous source of strategic power and one of the greatest material prizes in world history."[13] What is more, they are a lever of world control, a matter that has been understood by planners from the early postwar period until the present day. A successful conquest of Iraq, for example, would provide the United States with "critical leverage" over industrial rivals, Zbigniew Brzezinski observed at the outset of the war, echoing remarks of George Kennan when he was a leading planner right after World War II, and explained that control of Middle Eastern oil would provide Washington with "veto power" over allies.[14] The George W. Bush administration understood the point very well. Control over pipelines can provide "tools of intimidation and blackmail," Dick Cheney warned. Control by others, that is. Control by us is, by definition, for the benefit of the world, another tacit presupposition that provides the framework for discussion in polite society

The assault on academic freedom has deep roots and ominous portent. It should be resisted with the steadfastness and courage that has been shown by the students at DePaul University who have courageously and honorably protested its manifestations at their own university. In a free society, there should be zero tolerance for institutions responsible for "the indoctrination of the young" or for the rest of the array of attacks on democracy under the cynical pretext of defending freedom.

NOTES

1. "Tougher on Iran," *Washington Post*, August 21, 2007.
2. Tim Weiner, *Legacy of Ashes* (New York: Doubleday, 2007), 484.
3. United Nations Security Resolution 687, April 3 1991, www.fas.org/news/un/iraq/sres/sreso687.htm.
4. Pepe Escobar, "'Hitler' Does New York," *Asia Times*, September 26, 2007, www.atimes.com/atimes/Middle_East/II26Ako1.html.
5. *New York Times*, August 21, 1953.
6. Khwajah Kamal al-Din, ed., *Islamic Review* 45/46 (1958): 15.
7. Stephen Fidler, *Financial Times*, May 22, 2005.
8. Lee Bollinger, Introduction to "Pakistan: Meeting the Challenge of Peace and Development," September 16, 2005, Columbia University presentation transcript archive, http://ccnmtl.columbia.edu/projects/wlf/ta/introduction_musharraf.html.

9. Michel Crozier, Samuel Huntington, and Joji Watanuki, *The Crisis of Democracy* (New York: New York University Press, 1975), www.trilateral.org/download/doc/crisis _of_democracy.pdf.

10. Michelle Goldberg, "Osama University?," *Salon*, November 6, 2003, www.salon. com/2003/11/06/middle_east_5.

11. Baruch Kimmerling, "Can a 'Patriotic' Mob Take Over the Universities?," *Dissident Voice*, March 29, 2005, www.dissidentvoice.org/Mar05/Kimmerling0329.htm.

12. Sara Roy, *London Review of Books*, February 15, 2005.

13. Walter Hume Long, cited by Ian Rutledge in *Addicted to Oil: America's Relentless Drive for Energy Security* (London: Tauris, 2005).

14. Zbigniew Brzezinski, "Hegemonic Quicksand," *National Interest* 74 (Winter 2003/2004).

17

ACADEMIC FREEDOM

A PILOT STUDY OF FACULTY VIEWS

JONATHAN R. COLE, STEPHEN COLE, AND CHRISTOPHER C. WEISS

These pages need not be burdened with proof, based on the testimony of a cloud of impressive witnesses, of the dependence of a free society on free universities. This means the exclusion of governmental intervention in the intellectual life of a university. It matters little whether such intervention occurs avowedly or through action that inevitably tends to check the ardor and fearlessness of scholars, qualities at once so fragile and so indispensable for fruitful academic labor.

—FELIX FRANKFURTER, *SWEEZY V. NEW HAMPSHIRE,*
CONCURRING OPINION, 354 U.S. 234 (1957)

THE OVERWHELMING MAJORITY of faculty members at America's leading colleges or universities would fully embrace the concepts of academic freedom and free inquiry. The same is apt to be true for faculty members throughout the nation's more than 4,000 colleges and universities. But if you were to ask the same faculty members what academic freedom was, or how it differed from the more general form of freedom that is called "freedom of speech" or "freedom of expression," or if you were to ask them what academic freedom was for, they might pause before formulating an answer, and their answers might be highly varied.

In fact, academic freedom and the protection of free inquiry *are* two of the core values of great universities. As Harvard literary critic Louis Menand has said, academic freedom "is the key legitimizing concept of the entire [academic] enterprise. It is the underlying basis of the mechanism that establishes who alone may, with any justification, have control and authority over the critical decisions of the university. It places in the hands of highly trained, competent professors, who have met standards set by the disciplines, the power to create criteria for entrance into the profession, to set standards for admissions, to establish what is and what is not valued or labeled as 'high quality work,' to determine standards for hiring and promotion to coveted positions, to construct the examinations, and to determine what will or will not be taught in classes run by those professors."[1]

Despite the centrality of academic freedom in the institutional and intellectual life of our universities, little has been done to explore empirically what faculty members believe academic freedom is, what behavior they think it protects, what its limits and boundaries are, and how it is related to the fundamental structure of universities and colleges. How do they conceive of the relation between academic freedom and free speech and expression? Do they see the former as a special instance of the latter, or do they, as Yale's dean of the Law School, Robert Post, has argued, see the former as having more to do with the rights and obligations of faculty members in relation to their employers than with free speech?[2] Would they think that the boundaries of academic freedom are controlled by the judgments of a professional guild, rather than by each individual scholar herself? Or would they argue that academic freedom is a limited extension of the political liberty of the individual, as David Bromwich suggests in his essay in this volume?[3] Faculty members may not be able to cite any higher educational system in the world that has thrived without the internalization of these norms and values—because there may not be a single example of a great university system operating without these freedoms—but that does not mean that they have a clear idea themselves about the functions and scope of academic freedom. Furthermore, we have no empirical evidence of whether faculty members at universities, such as Columbia, have a hierarchy of values. Are some values more sacred than others? When academic freedom and free inquiry come into conflict with other values faculty members associate with the university, which one is given priority?

As is widely known in the academy, the core values of free inquiry and academic freedom have periodically come under attack in the United States.[4] The assaults on academic freedom have been associated with elevated levels of anti-intellectualism and, perhaps more often, at times of perceived external threats (such as our recent obsession with and fear of terrorism). The quality of teaching and research at our colleges and universities have suffered when these values are attacked, as they were, to cite only a few examples, during the Lockner age[5] at the turn of the twentieth century (when employers had enormous power to fire employees arbitrarily), during the time surrounding World War I with American fears of anarchism and Bolshevism running high, and during the 1940s and the period of McCarthyism.[6] The protection of faculty employment rights (not to be mistaken for free speech protections) can be traced back to the "Declaration of Principles on Academic Freedom and Academic Tenure" of the formation of the American Association of University Professors in 1915. Since the "Declaration" (modified in 1940), there have been many essays and books written about academic freedom and free inquiry, including of course those in this volume.[7] In a number of landmark decisions, the Supreme Court has reinforced the idea of academic freedom as being essential for the independence and fulfillment of the missions of universities.[8] In *Sweezy*, Justice Frankfurter noted the "grave harm resulting from governmental intrusion into the intellectual life of a university." Thus, it is somewhat surprising that quantitative data on faculty views about academic freedom remain scarce. This pilot study attempts in a limited way to increase our understanding of these views among full-time faculty members at Columbia University.

Most research on university and college faculty members has focused on their political views, not on academic freedom. The best known of those inquiries that have included questions about academic freedom was *The Academic Mind*, which was published more than fifty years ago by Columbia sociologists Paul F. Lazarsfeld and Wagner Thielens Jr. They examined the behavior and levels of apprehension of more than 2,400 social scientists who worked at these colleges and universities during the witch hunts that focused on universities, among other institutions, during the McCarthy era.[9] While most empirical studies have been interested principally in the political interests and voting patterns of academics,[10] the Lazarsfeld survey focuses on the effects of McCarthyism on the intellectual life of colleges and universities — as much as what was not said or taught as what was.

Far more recently, two sociologists, Neil Gross, then at Harvard, and Solon Simmons, at George Mason University, examined faculty political views, but their 2006 survey also reproduced questions related to academic freedom that had appeared in the Lazarsfeld study. Remarkably, the two studies, separated by a half-century, show roughly the same level of faculty apprehension about intrusive outsiders undermining academic freedom. The 1955 survey described in *The Academic Mind* found that 21 percent thought that in the past few years, their own academic freedom has been threatened in a significant way. Gross and Simmons, using different sampling methods and drawing upon more universities than the earlier study, found that 28 percent of faculty respondents answered either "a lot" or "some" to the same question that Lazarsfeld and Thielens used. Gross and Simmons concluded: "Although the samples are not strictly comparable . . . we can still reasonably say that social scientists today perceive as much if not more of a threat to academic freedom than during the McCarthy era."[11] While a substantial proportion of faculty members then and now are apprehensive about threats to their academic freedom, only about a quarter claimed to feel personally threatened.

In *The Academic Mind*, Lazarsfeld and Thielens did try to identify correlates of variations in faculty opinions regarding intolerance and violations of free inquiry and academic freedom. However, while these studies were informative and valuable for those interested in these values, they both used the loaded term "academic freedom" in their questions. Since it is normatively appropriate for faculty members to be concerned about and supportive of academic freedom, few are apt to admit a lack of concern with abridgements of academic freedom, even if they really do not care about it. Thus, we ought to find ways to reduce, if not eliminate, normatively appropriate responses to our survey questions. We tried to do that in our Columbia pilot survey by excluding any mention of the term "academic freedom" and to obtain reactions of faculty to hypothetical situations in which some might feel academic freedom was at stake.

METHODS

We surveyed Columbia University's 1,610 full-time faculty members in the Arts and Science disciplines and its professional schools, as well as a sample of faculty in the biomedical sciences departments at the medical school campus. We omitted the clinical faculty from the study. Because this was a pilot study, no effort was made to sample faculty members at other universities for comparative purposes. As you can see from examining the survey questions (see the appendix), we used the term "free inquiry," but never mentioned academic freedom explicitly in an attempt to avoid normative responses. Rather than ask directly whether faculty members believe in academic freedom or whether it was being threatened at Columbia, we presented them with fourteen short hypothetical vignettes, or situations, and asked them to assess the action taken by the professors, administrators, and outside actors portrayed in the vignette. Each situation was based on an actual academic case. These vignettes ranged from actions involving congressional interference with research on HIV/AIDS street workers, to treatment of students in class, to appropriate subjects to discuss in class, to the role of institutional review boards (IRBs) in limiting research,[12] to action outside the university taken by faculty members, and to the appropriate treatment of faculty members whose research does not conform to the existing paradigm of the field. We also asked the respondents a set of general questions about the idea of a university, a few questions about their own values and politics, and for some demographic information.

The Columbia administration supplied us with their most current list of full-time faculty, and we e-mailed faculty members a request to respond to the survey through an Internet link to an anonymous, Web-based survey instrument.[13] We pretested the survey by sending it to 100 of the 1,610 full-time faculty members. The response rate for the pretest was 27 percent. We asked those in the pretest to complete the survey and to offer us their criticisms of the instrument.[14] The final survey was sent to 1,510 faculty members who included those in all of the arts and sciences departments, the Morningside Heights campus professional schools, and the full-time faculty on the medical campus in biochemistry and molecular biology, physiology and cell biophysics, pharmacology, pathology and cell biology, neuroscience, microbiology, and genetics and development. Three hundred and nineteen faculty members, or roughly 21 percent, responded to the final survey, although not all faculty members, of course, answered all of the questions.

We were interested in whether the faculty members thought that the action represented in the fourteen short vignettes was justified or not, and whether it should be protected or not. If they felt the action was inappropriate, they were asked whether the administration of the university should administer "soft" or "hard" sanctions, or do nothing. Soft sanctions might include "a request not to repeat the behavior" or "a freeze of the professor's salary for a year or two"; hard sanctions might include "temporary suspension," or "a formal reprimand," or "action to dismiss the professor" from the university.[15] Finally, if the response categories failed to capture a professor's beliefs about how to handle the situation, we provided the faculty member with an opportunity to tell us in qualitative terms what they would do. Again the response rate, after two follow-up requests to the initial mailing of the survey, was only 21 percent, which may be standard for online surveys but, nonetheless, allows for the possibility of significant levels of self-selection bias in the results obtained.[16]

We compared the returned surveys with the distribution of the population of the faculty by school, by disciplinary categories, and by age. The results showed that the arts and sciences faculty was overrepresented in the responses to the questionnaire: those departments represented roughly 47 percent of the population of faculty members, but 71 percent of the respondents. It follows, of course, that faculty members in both business and engineering and the other professional schools were underrepresented in the final totals, as were the members of the pre-clinical biological faculty at the medical school. The professional schools made up 40 percent of the population and only 26 percent of the respondents. The pattern of underrepresentation of medical school faculty members is equally striking: they represented only 3 percent of the respondents, but 13 percent of the population.[17]

Here we present some preliminary results from the survey that may be of interest to those who are concerned with academic freedom and free inquiry at universities. Our survey questions allow others to assess whether similar types of studies are worth carrying out at other colleges and universities. We refer to specific vignettes and both quantitative and qualitative results in the body of the essay, but not to all of them. We will provide the marginal results associated with each category of response for each of the situations as part of the appendix.

RESULTS

From the outset of this study, we were unsure whether survey questions would yield any significant variation in the responses of Columbia's faculty members. This apprehension was, in fact, warranted for some critical independent variables, for which we found very little variation. For example, when asked whom they voted for in the 2008 presidential election, 231 faculty members, or 75 percent, voted for Barack Obama compared with only 8, or less than 3 percent, for John McCain. That skewed percentage in favor of Obama would be even higher had we excluded the 15 who refused to answer the question and the 43 who said they were not eligible to vote in that election—most of them, we presume, are scholars who were not American citizens. The overwhelming proportion of faculty members defined themselves as Democrats ($n = 203$) or Independents ($n = 50$); very few as Republicans ($n = 7$). The rest identified themselves with some other political party or refused to respond to the question. Similarly, on a few questions used to examine the values of the faculty, the overwhelming majority considered themselves as "pro-choice" (270) compared with a mere 18 who identified themselves as "pro-life." Few of the faculty favored the death penalty ($n = 16$). In response to a question about appropriate punishment for first-degree murder convictions, the majority ($n = 146$) supported "life in prison without parole" and another 86 supported "parole after 25 years for good behavior." Finally, the overwhelming majority of the faculty who responded identified themselves as Caucasian (82 percent; $n = 255$), only 14 percent ($n = 45$) as members of a racial or ethnic minority group. In terms of basic political self-identification and attitudes, we did not find much variance among the Columbia faculty. Since these represent some of the small number of independent variables we introduced into the survey, we knew from the outset that we were not going to be able to develop models that would explain the variations in faculty responses to the vignettes.

The absence of variance in the study's independent variables proved unfortunate, since there turned out to be significant variation in the faculty's responses to many of the vignettes themselves and to a number of other substantive questions. One conclusion that we can reach from this effort is that in any follow-up study, more attention needs to be paid to a larger set of independent variables that might help us understand better the variations in faculty responses to the substantive questions about academic freedom. That said, with the data in hand, we are not going to be able here to *explain* what accounts for these differences of opinion toward the actions described in the fourteen situations that we describe. At the end of the day, what we present here, then, is a description of the quantitative responses to the vignettes and additional questions about free inquiry, along with anecdotal qualitative responses of the faculty to the situations presented. We can also speculate about whether there is any discernable pattern to the responses to different types of academic freedom situations.

THE HYPOTHETICAL SITUATIONS

We will report the results of a number, but not all, of the fourteen situations that we presented to the faculty. The first hypothetical, situation 1, which deals with efforts by members of Congress to interfere with a study of prostitutes and HIV/AIDS by social scientists interested in the transmission of the virus, offers an example of a fairly high level of consensus on what faculty believe should be done. Eighty-six percent of the faculty thought that the university should do nothing, since the faculty had a right to conduct this National Institutes of Health–funded, peer-reviewed research. The situation also elicited a substantial number of comments by faculty members about what the university should do beyond "nothing." Roughly 10 percent of the respondents thought that none of the categories adequately captured their views. The majority of the qualitative comments expressed the view that the university should be more proactive in denouncing the interference by Congress and should actively defend the researchers. Among these admittedly anecdotal responses, one faculty member put it this way:

> I would suggest writing to the members of Congress saying politely that while we appreciate your point of view, and that not everyone, including not everyone in the University, will think that this is valuable or appropriate research, the research has been approved by a federal agency, and violates no law, and the university cannot sanction faculty members for engaging in a project that violates no law or rule, simply because 'some' members of Congress disapprove.

Another said:

> The University president should make a public speech on academic freedom, excoriating the congressmen for McCarthyism. The University's three most influential trustees should ask for a meeting with Senator Feinstein and demand her support for the research, the university, and the principle of academic freedom.

Finally, another put it this way:

> The university should commend them for their work. It is impossible to learn about risky behavior by interviewing saints.

In situation 3, the university administration discovers that a "distinguished professor . . . uses his office computer to download explicit adult sexual materials," although he does not share the materials with anyone else. The majority (167 or 55 percent) of faculty members thought the university should do nothing about this behavior, while 22 percent favored some form of "soft sanctions" or "hard sanctions." Thirteen percent felt that none of the categories captured their views and provided us with an amplification of what they thought the proper response should be. Many of these respondents were, perhaps correctly, more interested in how the university obtained information about what the professor was downloading onto his computer, and some had responses that were contingent on what the university's policy was about the use of office computers for personal use. One professor who favored sanctions put it this way:

Tell the jerk that he should have some common sense and he should realize he has created a situation that could seriously embarrass himself and the institution.

Another faculty member said:

The response must be serious, because anytime explicit materials are on an office computer in a university there is potential for exposing students or employees to the content. What if someone is trying to repair the office computer and an open file is visible in the process? What if the person doing the repair is [a] student hired as an assistant?[18]

Faculty members offered widely varying opinions on this case when they filled in what they thought about the professor's behavior. Consider just two:

If the material downloaded was legal, there should be no strong sanctions, at least at first. However, depending on how the issue came to light and who knows about it, how blatant the behavior is, etc., it might [be] important to explain that such behavior could make other members of the university (including staff and esp. students) uncomfortable, and that such behavior in the office place is inappropriate and could contribute to an unwelcoming atmosphere. For example, if a faculty member views porn on his computer such that students arriving at his office or walking by can see it, this would be much more problematic than something done that affects no one else directly.

Another professor expressed the following view:

Since the viewing of such material is legal, no crime is being committed. The key issues are whether the university had a policy prohibit[ing] accessing of certain classes of material in a university setting, especially when those materials might be considered recreational; and, if it has none, whether one should be instituted. Few, if any universities have such policies, and the drafting of one that does not blatantly suppress academic freedom might be very difficult. The matter is confounded by the blurred boundaries between a typical professor's private and public life . . . In the absence of a prior policy, this is not an actionable case. The creation of a policy would be very controversial, as it would be perceived as restricting academic freedom and privacy.

In situation 2, a tenured professor in a university with a speech code is dismissive and disdainful of an African American student's question in a social science class. The student complains to the dean after the teacher says that he/she "is a product of affirmative action and really doesn't belong at the college." Almost no faculty members thought that the speech code was relevant to actions that should be taken in the case. Only 6 percent of the faculty said that the university should do nothing, while 35 percent thought the university should apply either soft or hard sanctions (roughly equally divided between soft and hard sanctions). Fully 41 percent "punted," that is, they said they would leave it up to a faculty committee without prior opinions to assess the case and recommend appropriate action(s) to be taken. Here is a sample of responses from the 44 faculty members who did not believe any of the categories described their beliefs, which ranged from rather informal action to more dramatic action:

> Have someone talk to the faculty member privately about proper treatment of students both minority and nonminority.

Another faculty member said:

> [The] faculty member should be "brought up on charges" with an attempt to carefully evaluate whether and how this incident reflects her/his usual behavior. In other words, it should be handled with the utmost seriousness, but not necessarily with the intent of immediate dismissal. [The] faculty member should be reminded of university policy and should accept responsibility for wrongdoing. Additional violations will result in "harder" sanctions including possible dismissal.

And two other faculty members varied in the way they would handle the case. The first said, "No sanctions should be taken without faculty review. A formal warning is the strongest reasonable sanction for a first offense." The second was more emphatic: "Dismissal is appropriate for unequivocally racist speech in the classroom."

In a number of the situations, we asked faculty if their response to an action by a professor would be influenced by whether the professor was tenured or not. There were almost no differences in the responses based on academic rank, but where slight differences obtained, they suggest that the faculty would be somewhat harsher on nontenured or adjunct faculty members.

In situation 4, a highly regarded, tenured faculty member in the chemistry department, who has a distinguished record as a researcher and teacher, belongs to a group that denies the Holocaust. What should the university do when some students complain about the faculty member discussing his views about the Holocaust in class? Almost a third of the faculty responding to this question wanted to refer it to a faculty committee rather than express their own views on the case. However, an equal proportion argued that either soft or hard sanctions ought to be applied. About 11 percent of the faculty responding would: "Do nothing or ignore the incident," while another 9 percent would have had the administration actively defend the faculty member's right to make his remarks even if they had nothing to do with the subject matter of the course. But a third of the faculty thought that the university ought to apply soft or hard sanctions for this behavior. A few of the responses of faculty members who did not find the categories that we provided adequate follow.

A contrasting perspective can be found in the following views of one faculty member:

> First, appoint a committee. Second, speak to the professor. Third, take the position that opinions are open to all but facts are not individually manufactured. A fact-based culture requires fact-based discussion. Inability to accept facts means inability to teach.

Another faculty member expressed the following view:

> Free speech must be protected, but there are two difficult issues here. First, why is a chemist talking about the Holocaust in class? This is not a political science class, and so we can safely conclude that no matter what he has to say about

the Holocaust, he is using his classroom as a political pulpit, and no matter what his views are, that is inappropriate. Of course, if we applied this criterion across the board to all professors, we would probably have to discipline most of the faculty, many of whom see their mission as political indoctrination rather than education. Second, any scientist who teaches facts that are wrong in class, and persists in doing so after being corrected, should be exposed by his/her fellow faculty and by the administration. In other words, it is one thing to protect free speech; it is another thing to ignore lies. Faculty and administrators should counter this professor's actions with actions of their own, which do not require official university action.

Finally, here are two additional responses:

He is paid to teach chemistry not social science. If he persist[s] drop salary as you do if he started talking about, say Australian geography.

He shared a controversial opinion in class. He is not teaching from this perspective. As long as he doesn't use his classroom time to try and recruit students to his position and doesn't jeopardize the students' evaluation[s] (grades) for the course and he is open to having his ideas challenged and debated the university should do nothing.

Consider now a different type of situation—one involving the legitimacy of an institutional review board's (IRB) intervention into the research of a team of anthropologists and geneticists. There has been a good deal of controversy surrounding the role of IRBs, especially among social scientists and members of professional schools who do research without federal government support. The issue of whether IRBs are intrusions on a professor's academic freedom is taken up in this volume in the essay by Columbia Law School professor Philip Hamburger. In the survey situation presented to the faculty, the researchers were studying "a rare but deadly hereditary disease in Venezuela." There was a very high incidence of the disease in a small fishing town where there was significant intermarriage within the fishing village community. It was a deeply Catholic community. The researchers, who had been working in this village for over 20 years, would provide villagers with birth control information, but only on request. The IRB, in reviewing a grant proposal from the group, told the researchers that they "cannot carry out the research unless they have mandatory

sessions explaining the heritability of the disease and how birth control methods could reduce the incidence in the community." The researchers, who had
made major genetic discoveries about the disease through their prior research,
refused to comply with the IRB requirement, claiming that the IRB was being
insensitive to the religious beliefs of the community and that the IRB's rejection
of the proposal was violating their rights of free inquiry. The responses of the
faculty to this scenario showed significant variation: 49 percent of the faculty
agreed with the researchers that the IRB was interfering with the right to free
inquiry, but 37 percent supported the position of the IRB. (Fourteen percent of
the faculty had qualitative responses to the situation, since they did not feel that
the two response categories captured their views.)

Here is an unsystematic sample of these qualitative views. It is worth noting that a substantial number of professors did not know what an IRB was, presumably those who are in disciplines that do not apply typically for research
grants from the federal government.[19] One professor said:

> The IRB system is a mandatory requirement of the US Federal medical funding
> system created to prevent exploitation of human research subjects. A common
> criticism of the IRB system is that it was designed to handle medical research in
> US hospitals and that its rules are unsuited for other types of research, especially
> social science research abroad . . . This is a good argument for social science
> professional societies working towards changing the rules. However, until that
> time, the university has no legal option but to follow the advice of its IRB. Any
> student of academic bureaucracies knows that a review board will issue ridicu-
> lous ruling[s] in at least a small percentage of cases. Get used to it!

Another faculty member expressed a somewhat different point of view:

> It seems to me that the researchers have an obligation to share their results, but
> in a way that is culturally sensitive and assessed by them rather than imposed
> by the IRB.

Yet another faculty member thought some form of compromise was
appropriate:

> The University Institutional Official should work with the IRB and the PI and
> move toward a middle ground—explaining the heritability of the disease may

be done without needing to jump to prescribing birth control for all—disentangle these two steps. This is complex. As a former IRB chair, I believe it warrants the University's attention and problem solving.

Another faculty member was inclined to look at the situation in terms of risk assessment:

> The key is that the intervention of the researchers does not increase risk to community members. If the rest of their research does not expose community members to increased risk, I don't see why the researchers must hold sessions on the impact of birth control.

And another, who was weighing the response in terms of the relative importance of two values:

> I don't know. IRB's job is to weigh ethical concerns against one another, so in principle I support the position of the IRB as the proper arbiter to these issues, but I don't want to select that because it would suggest that I reflexively think reproductive rights obviously trump respect for religious traditions, which is a different question and would require more details.

And, finally, the not infrequent response:

> What is an IRB?

Consider one more vignette, situation 10, which like the others is based on an actual case. An undergraduate at a highly prestigious university is working on a senior thesis that involves performance art. Her advisor approved the project. Her project consists of repeatedly inseminating herself with donated sperm and inducing abortions by using herbs. The display of her project features a large cube wrapped in sheets covered with blood from the abortions, as well as video images of her inducing the procedures. Word of the project got out and there was substantial public outrage about it, including angry letters from scores of alumni criticizing the university for allowing the project to be done and then possibly displaying the results publicly. The dean of the undergraduate college was "appalled" by the project and decided not to allow the performance art project to be shown, while promising to reexamine what constitutes an appropriate senior art project. The question put to the faculty receiving the survey is: What ought to be done about this project? The responses to this vignette revealed significant variability in reactions by the faculty. Twenty-eight percent thought that the administration should do nothing, since it was not their business "to determine what 'appropriate' art is even if it does offend the community." A quarter of the responding faculty agreed with what the dean did; another 11 percent not only agreed with the dean's action, but "would also publicly sanction the advisor of the student." Thirteen percent would have referred the case to a faculty committee to decide; another 15 percent offered qualitative responses because their responses did not fit into any of the given categories; and about 6 percent of the faculty said: "I don't know what should be done."

Expressed opinions varied with this issue as with the others. One faculty member said:

> I am disgusted by the performance, even though I am not against abortion per se. I do agree that they should reassess what constitutes an appropriate senior art project, but given that the student was approved for this project, she cannot be reprimanded now. I would recommend engaging a discussion between the faculty mentor and the administration, as well as other faculty members.

Another put it slightly differently:

> I believe the Dean's public statement was appropriate, but not the decision to prohibit the performance. "Appalling" does not mean illegal.

Yet another expressed somewhat different concerns:

> I may not agree with the dean's handling of the situation or even the verdict (a committee of faculty members would be the appropriate mechanism), but the university has the obligation and right to determine what is in the interest of the university, its educational mission, and reputation. In this case . . . the student is using university property and resources to produce potentially deeply offensive art.

It remains, of course, an open question how far this faculty member would be willing to go to allow the university administration to define for the faculty what is in the "interest of the university" and "its educational mission, and reputation."

Health concerns of the student was another theme raised in the qualitative responses. For example:

> In general, the administration of a university should avoid any censorship of students' creative work. I therefore tend to agree most with the first option ["do nothing"]: The administration should not determine what "appropriate" art is even if it does offend the community . . . In this instance, however, the situation is complicated by the fact that the student's work—involving repeated insemination and self-induced abortion—is very likely dangerous to her health. There's also the question of whether the university is liable to prosecution for sanctioning or turning a blind eye to such a quasi-medical procedure. The university has no obligation to censor projects it finds morally offensive. But the administration would need to take legal advice to ensure that it is fulfilling its duty of care to its student, and that it is not exposing itself to legal risk by allowing the student to go ahead with her project. A competent advisor would bring these questions before his/her supervisor as soon as he/she learned about the project.

And finally, another faculty member tersely said:

> Get the poor kid some help.

As we noted, this was not a fictitious hypothetical. In the actual case, extreme pressure was placed on the student to withdraw the project from public view and to admit, as it turns out to have been the case, that the abortions were simulated and not real. Under protest and possibly some threat, the student went public and admitted these facts.

■ ■ ■ ■

We asked a series of other questions related to academic freedom and the institutional nature of universities. Let us review a number of the responses to these questions in terms of the variability of responses. For some of the questions, there was a high level of faculty consensus. For example, in response to the prompt: "When politically controversial issues like abortion come up in class discussions, faculty members . . . ," 73 percent said that the faculty should be allowed to "express their personal opinion but allow students who disagree to express their views without those views affecting their grades in the course." Almost a fifth said that they "should keep their opinions to themselves."

An even higher proportion of the faculty, 86 percent, agreed with the statement: "A fundamental role of a professor is to challenge orthodoxies and the presuppositions and biases of his/her students even if this results in unsettling feeling among the students." When the issue of challenging orthodoxies that students believe are biased was presented as a question about the right of students (without prior administration approval) "to organize and boycott and picket a professor's class if they believed he or she presented biased views on important subjects," the faculty was virtually evenly divided: 46 percent of the faculty said that they agreed that the students should be allowed to boycott and picket the class, while 45 percent disagreed. Clearly, the performance art vignette also elicited differences of opinion among the faculty.

We also found variable responses to a question stating that "the university should not interfere with the behavior of faculty if it is conducted off campus." Fifty-nine percent felt that "the university is not responsible for what its faculty do off campus. If the faculty member violates the law it is up to the police authorities to sanction him." But almost 30 percent felt differently and thought that even "if an act is done off campus by a university employee, it still reflects on the reputation of the university and the university has to be concerned with it even if it would prefer not to [be]." In response to the statement that "universities should not accept grants or contracts that stipulate restrictions related to the publication of research," we found the 45 percent of the faculty agreed, but slightly more than a third disagreed.

BRIEF DISCUSSION OF THE RESULTS

Given the variations in the responses by the Columbia faculty to the vignettes and other questions, can we find *any* patterns to these responses? Do the vignettes cluster and form a set of distinct types of responses to academic freedom or free inquiry situations? Are there patterned differences between men and women faculty members, those of different ages, and among the faculty in different schools and disciplines? In order to determine whether any patterns exist, we examined the relationship between these demographic variables and responses to the situations and other questions by simply creating a dichotomy out of the situation responses: those who would do nothing and those who would be in favor of some form of sanctions. We already know that the absence of variation in the faculty members' political views and on some of the vignettes means that political attitudes and identification, and demographic characteristics, such as gender, age, or field, will not help us explain variations in responses by the faculty to the situations we presented in the survey. Let us look therefore at some of the vignettes and questions where there was significant variation and see whether these demographic characteristics are patterned in any way.

Do male and female faculty members respond similarly to the vignettes and other questions?[20] In the majority of cases, there were in fact small and insignificant differences between men and women. However, where some differences obtained, faculty members reflected national patterns: Women tend to be more politically liberal, and in response to the academic freedom vignettes, somewhat more supportive of doing nothing against the action represented in the cases. They also were somewhat more likely than male faculty members to opt for referring the case to a faculty committee. There were a few exceptions to this pattern. For example, 60 percent of men compared with 47 percent of women would do nothing about the faculty member who downloaded adult sexually explicit materials on his office computer.[21] In the case involving the IRB's insistence on providing birth control information to members of the Catholic community with a high level of a heritable disease, almost half of the women compared with 30 percent of the men disagreed with the researchers who would only provide this information if it were requested by the subjects of the study.[22] Situation 14 produced differences between male and female faculty members. Women, by roughly 20 percentage points,[23] were more likely to side with a professor's right in the following situation:

> A professor works on problems of immunology—trying to find vaccines for diseases like plague. He works with toxic and other select agents that could be used potentially by bioterrorists in creating biological weapons. His work could contribute significantly to finding cures or prevention for these diseases. He may not allow any graduate or postdoctoral student to work in his laboratory if that student comes from certain nations that the government has defined as supporting terrorism—even if there is no evidence that the student is a security risk. The papers that the scientist writes are subjected to prepublication review by members of the boards of leading scientific journals in his field for possibilities

that sections of the paper would have to be omitted before publication because in the opinion of the board, the methods section or other results could fall into the wrong hands. Given this situation, how do you feel about the following: The professor should have the right to bring into his laboratory students on the basis of his belief in their talent rather than their national origin and that any restrictions on his doing so is a violation of his rights as a researcher and a violation of the restricted students' rights.

We found some variations in responses to the cases by both age and department or school affiliation. In this survey, when we examine age effects, we cannot be sure if the differences in responses are a result of aging per se, period effects (the effects, for example, of living through the 1960s), or cohort effects. In general, where we did find variations in opinion, faculty members who came of age in the 1960s and 1970s tended to have somewhat more liberal academic freedom views than those who were born later. A few illustrations will suffice. For example, on the issue of supporting the researcher or the IRB's position on requiring contraceptive advice for participants in the study of the heritable disease, those faculty members who were older were about 20 percentage points more likely to side with the researcher.[24] This is not an extremely strong correlation, but the pattern is clear: the younger scholars tended to favor the IRB position over the researcher's position. Similarly, the faculty members who came of age in the 1960s were somewhat more likely to say that professors should be permitted to express their opinions on controversial issues, like abortion. On the other hand, perhaps because they lived through the campus wars of the 1960s and 1970s, those faculty members who were teaching in that era are less permissive than younger faculty about allowing students to boycott or picket a professor's class when they believe that the instructor is presenting a biased point of view. They were also less likely than their younger colleagues to approve of accepting research grants or contracts that potentially restrict publication. Again, the difference in both of these questions is roughly 20 percent.[25]

Finally, we considered whether there were any patterned differences to those questions for which there was variance among faculty members of different schools and departments. For the purpose of comparison, we divided the faculty into membership in one of six disciplinary or professional schools. The arts and sciences were subdivided into three groups: sciences, social sciences, and humanities. The responses of the faculty in the business and engineering schools were lumped together as a single group, because we hypothesized that those two faculties were apt to have more conservative views on the academic freedom issues than members of other professional schools. Faculty members in all the other professional schools were grouped together. Finally, we looked at the bioscience departments at the medical school as a single group. As we might have expected, business and engineering faculty members tended to be a bit tougher in terms of sanctions for faculty whose behavior they found opprobrious. They were more likely, again a roughly 20 percent point difference, to embrace soft or hard sanctions, although a majority of those in favor of sanctions opted for soft sanctions. Roughly two-thirds of the faculty members in the arts and sciences would simply do nothing or ignore the situation in which a faculty member downloads adult sexually explicit materials, while around 45 percent of the professional school faculty would do nothing in this case.[26] Interestingly, members of the faculties of business, engineering, and the natural and biological sciences were more likely (20 percent) than their colleagues in the other professional schools and in the humanities and social sciences departments to agree that scientists should not talk about political issues in a science class.[27]

In light of the greater than expected variation in responses to the academic freedom and free inquiry situations, we decided to construct an "index of commitment to academic freedom." To do this, we dichotomized the responses to each of the fourteen situations in terms of the degree of commitment to freedom of inquiry. If faculty members thought that the university should do "nothing" in the situation (that is, enact no sanctions against the faculty member and not even discuss the situation with her/him), we coded that as strongly in favor of academic freedom. All other responses, such as suggesting soft or hard sanctions or disagreeing with the faculty member's claim to the right of free inquiry, we coded as a lesser commitment to the norm. We omitted from the index all qualitative responses in which the faculty members felt that none of the categories fit their responses to the situation. We did that because there was wide variability in these qualitative responses, as you can see from those quoted previously. We then added up all the "highly committed" responses so that the range of scores could run from 0 (lowest level of commitment) to 14 (highest possible commitment). We also created a second form of the index: the percentage of responses that indicated a deep commitment to academic freedom. As it turned out, these two forms of the index were, as we might expect, highly correlated ($r = .83$).

Did the index allow us to better understand a faculty member's response to the other questions in the survey and were there any differences by the demographic and locational variables in the survey? We begin with the somewhat surprising result that the mean index score for the entire set of responding faculty was 7.22 with a standard deviation of 2.44. This suggests that a faculty reputedly as liberal on academic freedom issues as Columbia's were, on average, scoring in the middle range of the index—deep commitment was demonstrated in their responses about half of the time. What this also means is that other norms that the faculty valued trumped the academic freedom value in a significant proportion of the cases.[28] In percentage terms, 62 percent of the responses indicated a strong commitment to academic freedom when we looked at the scenarios in their totality.

When we examined the relationship between scores on the index and other independent variables, we found little predictive value in either of the two forms of the index. There were a few relationships that are suggestive, however. For example, and not unexpectedly, those who believe that the university should stay out of the sanctioning of behavior of faculty conducted off campus score higher (mean = 7.9) on the academic freedom index than those who believe that the university has a responsibility for the behavior of its faculty off campus because it affects the reputation and standing of the university with the public and alumni (mean = 6.4). This may not be substantively a large difference, but it is statistically significant at the .001 level. On the questions of whether students should have the right to picket and boycott a class whose professor is believed to be biased, there were only minor differences in terms of their commitment to academic freedom of those who were supportive of the students' rights and those who disagreed with their right to protest in this manner. And there were only minor differences in their commitment to academic freedom among those faculty members who did or did not feel that professors in science courses should not discuss political issues such as capital punishment or abortion rights. There was a significant difference in commitment to free inquiry values between those faculty members who felt that the university should not accept grants or contracts that included any restrictions on the publication of results, with those highly supportive of academic freedom and free inquiry more likely (mean = 8.13) than those less supportive of these values (mean = 6.54) believing that the university ought to reject such grants and contracts ($p < .01$).

Faculty members' race or gender had no significant relationship with their attitudes toward their scores on the academic freedom index. However, academic rank was associated with attitudes toward these values. Those faculty members with tenure scored significantly higher on the academic freedom and free inquiry index (mean = 7.14) than assistant professors without tenure (mean = 6.05) ($p < .01$). This could be a consequence of the protections that tenure brings, or it could be an age or cohort effect, as suggested earlier in this essay. This remains an open question, although the survey yields a bit of data that suggest it is not tenure per se and its protections that lead to these differences—since associate professors and full professors without tenure score much the same on the index as full professors with tenure.[29]

■ ■ ■ ■

Consider a few tentative observations about how the faculty responded to the various vignettes, since the patterns would seem to suggest how they feel about various aspects of academic freedom and free inquiry. For most faculty members, academic freedom is associated with freedom of expression. There was a higher level of consensus among the faculty when they considered basic freedom of speech vignettes—with the overwhelming majority favoring doing nothing to hinder open discourse and expression of opinions by faculty members, even when the subject of their speech was on highly controversial topics.[30] However, one of the objectives in creating these vignettes was to place the faculty members in situations where they might find themselves having to evaluate conflicting norms. For example, faculty members might support the right of a colleague to say anything in class, but they might also believe strongly that political statements should be limited to courses about political subjects, or should be articulated outside the classroom. The reactions to free speech vignettes were more varied when we introduced what some might feel were inappropriate settings for the speech. So, we found less faculty consensus when a chemistry professor was using his/her chemistry class to discuss a political subject. In short, in situations involving conflicting norms, the level of consensus went down substantially.

For example, faculty members who felt that a tenured member of the faculty's response to a student about an African American's qualifications for admission to the college was inappropriate were more likely to recommend some form of sanctions—both hard or soft sanctions for the professor.

Only 6 percent responded: "Do nothing or ignore the incident." The faculty responses were more varied when the vignettes turned to the conduct of research under conditions of potentially conflicting norms. When the government attempts to intervene in research projects funded through the peer-review process of federal granting agencies, the faculty objected strongly and almost without dissent. But when other conditions were added, such as whether it was acceptable to have prior review and prior restraint on publications that could, hypothetically, help terrorists create biological weapons, the faculty members were far more divided in their opinions. When vignettes posed questions about the appropriate role of IRBs at the university, opinions also varied widely. The norm to support the IRB is based on the idea that it exists to ensure that human subjects are protected from harm during a federally sponsored research project. This conflicts with the gains to be obtained from the genetic and anthropological work being done and the respect for local cultural norms in a highly Catholic setting.[31]

Faculty members were almost exactly equally divided on the question of whether students had the right to picket and boycott a class because they believed the professor was presenting a biased point of view. Here the conflicting norms involved the right of students to protest and to make their opinions known (as well as appropriate location of the protest and whether the boycott and picketing could go on without the approval of the administration), against the norm that faculty autonomy in the classroom is virtually sacred and that the faculty and students are not in a symmetric relationship: faculty members determine what is on a reading list, how a class is organized, and how the discourse takes place inside the classroom. Furthermore, since these protests took place outside the classroom, without the permission of the dean, the action violated the accepted norm of *where* protest can take place on campus, as well as the institutional processes required for protests on campus. In short, the responses to the vignettes not only varied but also suggest that there may be different types of actions by professors that elicit very different responses among their peers in terms of the limits or boundaries of academic freedom.

If an erosion of the norms of academic freedom and free inquiry has taken place at American universities and colleges, it may well be the result of abridgements of the freedom of speech that we have seen on university campuses over the past several decades. The restrictive nature of speech codes, the willingness to forbid speakers to talk at universities because their speech might offend some members of the community, the hundreds of cases of abridgments of free speech on campus that have been chronicled by scholars like David Bromwich,[32] Cass Sunstein,[33] Kent Greenawalt,[34] and Greg Luki-anoff,[35] may have led the faculty to devalue academic freedom compared with other core values of the university. In fact, the unwillingness to accept the idea that speakers have a right to hurt others, feelings and offend their sensibilities may lead faculty members to think of academic freedom and free inquiry as just another value of the university without any special place among this hierarchy of values. This devaluation, if confirmed by additional research, could have dangerous consequences for the university, including a greater willingness among faculty and students to limit free discourse and free research inquiry.

It also seems to be true that relatively few faculty members, even at a place like Columbia, have given much time to thinking about the limits and conse-quences of restraints on academic freedom, despite the consequences that it may have for free inquiry at the university. In our survey, this becomes most apparent in the situation involving the IRB's actions regarding a long-standing and highly successful research program carried out in Venezuela. We can be reasonably certain that the vast majority of faculty do not view the IRB as a form of licensing that involves prior restraint on speech and research. But Philip Hamburger, in his essay in this volume, argues that the IRBs are actu-ally unconstitutional violations of the First Amendment and that in the name of protecting human subjects, they do far more harm than good—and they are more intrusive than restrictions on speech in seventeenth-century Eng-land. Whether or not one agrees with Hamburger, this subject has not been the subject of proper debate within the framework of academic freedom— despite the considerable subterranean complaints one hears all of the time on campus about the intrusiveness and power of the IRBs to control both the protocols of research and its publication. When roughly 40 percent of the Columbia faculty support the IRB position in response to situation 5 and simply accept the IRB structure because it is a requirement for receiving gov-ernment grants and do not weigh the effects of the IRBs on academic freedom and free inquiry, then it suggests far more discussion needs to take place about the effects of various forms of government intrusion into the operation of free inquiry on university campuses.

Whether or not there exists a hierarchy of core values at great universities also remains unknown. The essays by President Robert Zimmer and Pro-fessor Richard Shweder suggest that at the University of Chicago, following the repeated reinforcement of the principles set out by Robert Maynard Hutchins, Edward Levi, other presidents of Chicago, and later briefly codified in the 1968 Kalven committee report, academic freedom and free inquiry trumps all other norms within the university. But to what extent is this true among all of the great universities and is it still true at Chicago?—a question raised by Richard Shweder in his essay. The data from the Columbia survey suggest that we may be witnessing an erosion of the centrality of the norm of academic freedom within the existing hierarchy of values. This is disquieting to us, since we cannot conceive of a great university without an absolute commitment to both academic freedom and free inquiry. Yet many of the faculty members who are younger and tenured at these places have not experienced a McCarthy period or other forms of repression from government sources and therefore may devalue the norms compared with others.

We do know from the responses to this survey as well as from the views expressed in other essays in this volume that there are many ways of looking at academic freedom and free inquiry. There is no agreement on what it is for, what it does or does not protect, whether or not it is a protection of civil liberties that differs from those afforded members of the general population, or how the meaning of these core values have changed over time. When we chart the history of the First Amendment, there are clear indicators of changes in the central dogma of the court on cases that deal with free expression. But when we deal with academic freedom and free inquiry, absent an arbiter such as the Supreme Court, there remain many different definitions and beliefs about its role in the American university.

■   ■   ■   ■

In short, the pilot survey results have created a puzzle. We can describe phenomena in which faculty members hold significantly different opinions about the appropriateness of different actions taken by their colleagues, differences in whether they believe these actions are covered by the norms of academic freedom and free inquiry, differences in the extent to which they would sanction the behavior of the faculty member. We can speculate when we are apt to obtain consensus among the faculty about the appropriateness of the action of their colleagues. But we do not have an understanding of what causes these differences. That remains an open question for future inquiry. Generating as many questions as answers is a hallmark of the way science is done. And this pilot has done just that. If ignorance drives science, as Columbia biologist Stuart Firestein argues in his lively 2012 book, then we have managed to generate a good deal of continued ignorance—and perhaps a set of interesting questions to be explored further.[36]

APPENDIX. FREE INQUIRY AT AMERICAN UNIVERSITIES: A SURVEY OF COLUMBIA FACULTY OPINION

In recent years Columbia and other universities around the nation have witnessed incidents where students and faculty members have acted in a way that their colleagues and or students have found to be inappropriate.[37] How do faculty members feel about these incidents and the ways in which they have been handled by the administration? This questionnaire will help us find out the views of Columbia faculty in regard to various hypothetical incidents (most of which are based on real cases), and what, if any, sanctions you believe would be appropriate for the university administration to impose. The questionnaire will take about twenty minutes to complete. Your answers will be completely anonymous.

Here are 14 situations that we would like to have your opinions about. Please assume that all of the situations described below are factually correct.

SITUATION 1

Social scientists working on the transmission of HIV/AIDS in San Francisco are interviewing street workers about their sexual behavior as it relates to the spread of the virus. The NIH supports the work and it went through the peer review process including an Institutional Review Board (IRB) review. Some members of Congress question the value of the research and call on the NIH to rescind the grant. The congressional members who opposed the grant call on the university where the social scientists are employed to sanction them if they do not stop their research immediately.

What do you think the administration should do?

○ The university who employs these scientists should do nothing as they have a right to conduct research which peers thought was important.

○ The university should ask these scientists to temporarily halt their research and see if some agreement can be reached with the congressional critics.

○ If the researchers refuse to halt their research the university should administer "hard" sanctions like
1. temporary suspension
2. a formal reprimand

○ Bring the faculty member(s) up on charges in an attempt to dismiss them from the university.

○ Refer the case to a faculty committee of members who do not have strong prior opinions on the matter and who will assess the case and make a judgement about appropriate action(s) to be taken.

○ I don't know what the administration should do.

○ If none of the above responses adequately captures your opinion, please briefly tell us in the box below what you believe the university should do in this situation:

SITUATION 2

A university institutes a speech code for students and faculty members. It stipulates that:

Speech or other expression constitutes harassment if it is intended to insult or stigmatize an individual or a small number of individuals on the basis of their sex, race, color, handicap, religion, sexual orientation, or national and ethnic origins.

In response to an African American student's question in a social science class, his tenured professor is dismissive and disdainful and says that the student is a product of affirmative action and really doesn't belong at the College. The student complains to the Dean.

What should the university do?

○ Do nothing or ignore the incident. Speech codes are unconstitutional and violate both faculty members' and students' right to free speech.

○ Actively defend the faculty member's right to engage in this behavior.

○ Administer "soft" sanctions such as:
   1. a request for him not to repeat this behavior
   2. freeze his salary for one or two years

○ Administer "hard" sanctions such as:
   1. temporary suspension
   2. a formal reprimand

○ Bring the faculty member up on charges in an attempt to dismiss him from the university.

○ Refer the case to a faculty committee of members who do not have strong prior opinions on the matter and who will assess the case and make a judgement about appropriate action(s) to be taken.

○ I don't know what the administration should do.

○ If none of the above responses adequately captures your opinion, please briefly tell us in the box below what you believe the university should do in this situation:

What if the faculty member engaging in the behavior described was either a non-tenured or an adjunct professor. Then what should the administration do?

○ Do nothing or ignore the incident. Speech codes violate both faculty members' and students' right to free speech.

○ Actively defend the faculty member's right to engage in this behavior.

○ Administer "soft" sanctions such as:

    1. a request for him not to repeat this behavior

    2. freeze his salary for one or two years

○ Administer "hard" sanctions such as:

    1. temporary suspension

    2. a formal reprimand

○ Bring the faculty member up on charges in an attempt to dismiss him from the university.

○ Refer the case to a faculty committee of members who do not have strong prior opinions on the matter and who will assess the case and make a judgement about appropriate action(s) to be taken.

○ I don't know what the administration should do.

○ If none of the above responses adequately captures your opinion, please briefly tell us in the box below what you believe the university should do in this situation:

SITUATION 3

A distinguished professor at the university uses his office computer to download explicit adult sexual materials. He does not share these materials with anyone else. The university administration finds out about this practice.

    What should the administration do?

○ Do nothing or ignore the incident. The right to view explicit adult sexual materials is protected by the first amendment.

○ Actively defend the faculty member's right to engage in this behavior.

○ Administer "soft" sanctions such as:

    1. a request for him not to repeat this behavior

    2. freeze his salary for one or two years

○ Administer "hard" sanctions such as:

　1. temporary suspension

　2. a formal reprimand

○ Bring the faculty member up on charges in an attempt to dismiss him from the university.

○ Refer the case to a faculty committee of members who do not have strong prior opinions on the matter and who will assess the case and make a judgement about appropriate action(s) to be taken.

○ I don't know what the administration should do.

○ If none of the above responses adequately captures your opinion, please briefly tell us in the box below what you believe the university should do in this situation:

What should the administration do if the instructor viewing explicit adult sexual materials on their university computer was a non-tenured or an adjunct professor?

○ Do nothing or ignore the incident. The right to view pornography is protected by the first amendment.

○ Actively defend the faculty member's right to engage in this behavior.

○ Administer "soft" sanctions such as:

　1. a request for him not to repeat this behavior

　2. freeze his salary for one or two years

○ Administer "hard" sanctions such as:

　1. temporary suspension

　2. a formal reprimand

○ Bring the faculty member up on charges in an attempt to dismiss him from the university.

○ Refer the case to a faculty committee of members who do not have strong prior opinions on the matter and who will assess the case and make a judgement about appropriate action(s) to be taken.

○ I don't know what the administration should do.

○ If none of the above responses adequately captures your opinion, please briefly tell us in the box below what you believe the university should do in this situation:

SITUATION 4

Suppose there is a tenured faculty member who is a chemist and a member of a group that denies the Holocaust. He is a highly regarded research scientist and has an excellent teaching record.

When some students complained about this faculty member discussing his views about the Holocaust in class, what do you think the university should do?

○ Do nothing or ignore the incident.

○ Actively defend the faculty member's right to say what he wants in class even if it has nothing to do with the subject matter of the course.

○ Administer "soft" sanctions such as:
  1. a request for him not to repeat this behavior
  2. freeze his salary for one or two years

○ Administer "hard" sanctions such as:
  1. temporary suspension
  2. a formal reprimand

○ Bring the faculty member up on charges in an attempt to dismiss him from the university.

○ Refer the case to a faculty committee of members who do not have strong prior opinions on the matter and who will assess the case and make a judgement about appropriate action(s) to be taken.

○ I don't know what the administration should do.

○ If none of the above responses adequately captures your opinion, please briefly tell us in the box below what you believe the university should do in this situation:

Suppose the Holocaust denier was a non-tenured or an adjunct professor. Then what do you think the administration should do?

○ Do nothing or ignore the incident.

○ Actively defend the faculty member's right to say what he wants in class even if it has nothing to do with the subject matter of the course.

○ Administer "soft" sanctions such as:
    1. a request for him not to repeat this behavior
    2. freeze his salary for one or two years

○ Administer "hard" sanctions such as:
    1. temporary suspension
    2. a formal reprimand

○ Bring the faculty member up on charges in an attempt to dismiss him from the university.

○ Refer the case to a faculty committee of members who do not have strong prior opinions on the matter and who will assess the case and make a judgement about appropriate action(s) to be taken.

○ I don't know what the administration should do.

○ If none of the above responses adequately captures your opinion, please briefly tell us in the box below what you believe the university should do in this situation:

SITUATION 5

A team of anthropologists and geneticists who hold faculty positions at a major research university are conducting a study of a rare but deadly hereditary disease in Venezuela. There is a high level of the disease in the fishing town and a great deal of family formation within the community. It is a deeply Catholic community. The researchers offer birth control information for those who ask for it, but otherwise do not. The efforts of the team have led to the discovery of the gene responsible for the hereditary disease. They receive a grant from the NIH to continue their work, but the local IRB says that they cannot carry out the research unless they have mandatory sessions explaining the heritability of the disease and how birth control methods could reduce its incidence in the community. The researchers refuse and claim that the IRB is being insensitive to the religious beliefs of the community and in refusing to allow them to conduct the research is violating their rights of free inquiry.

- ○ I agree with the researchers that the IRB is interfering with the researchers' rights as faculty members.
- ○ I disagree with the researchers and support the position of the IRB.
- ○ If none of the above responses adequately captures your opinion, please briefly tell us in the box below what you believe the university should do in this situation:

SITUATION 6

A brilliant, young, and iconoclastic biologist comes up with a new theory of disease—a theory that lies completely outside of the current paradigm of his field. Most of the leaders of this field believe that the scientist is either a genius or completely misguided but conclude that his work is too far outside of what is currently accepted in the biological sciences that he should not receive financial support for his work and that he does not deserve an appointment at a major research university.

Which of the following is closest to your opinion on this subject?

○ The academic community should welcome innovative work that contradicts the current research paradigm.

○ The academic community is right in denying this professor research support and a position at a major research university because legitimating his work would help create a situation of intellectual chaos.

○ I have no opinion on this topic.

○ If none of the above responses adequately captures your opinion, please briefly tell us in the box below what you believe the university should do in this situation:

SITUATION 7

A tenured professor in the biology department has developed a weblog featuring postings that mostly focus on issues related to her research, but also cover a wide range of current events. One of the most controversial postings on her blog was entitled "Evolutionary Benefits of Homophobia" and offered a biologist's perspective on how homophobia could logically stem from natural selection and mating preference. Some readers of this blog complain to the administration and two weeks after it is posted the professor receives a request from the provost's office to remove the posting.

Which of the following comes closest to your opinion on this topic?

○ The provost's request that the professor remove the blog on homophobia constitutes a violation of the professor's right of free expression and she has a right to ignore it.

○ The provost is right in requesting that a blog on homophobia be removed from the website if this blog disturbs a significant number of readers.

○ If the scientist refuses to take down the parts of her blog that others find offensive, the university should administer strong sanctions against her like:

1. temporary suspension

2. a formal reprimand

○ Bring her up on formal charges and attempt to dismiss her from the university.

○ Refer the case to a faculty committee of members who do not have strong prior opinions on the matter and who will assess the case and make a judgement about appropriate action(s) to be taken.

○ I have no opinion on this topic.

○ If none of the above responses adequately captures your opinion, please briefly tell us in the box below what you believe the university should do in this situation:

SITUATION 8

A faculty member is a former member of the Palestinian Liberation Organization and continues to make speeches strongly critical of the Israeli government's policies and actions. He advocates that Israel return all land to the Arab countries that they held prior to the 1967 war. He also condones suicide bombings by Palestinians. His views are well known but he does not discuss his opinions in his literature classes where the conflict in the Middle East is not part of the curriculum. Some Jewish students at the university complain to the administration that by continuing to employ this faculty member they were giving implicit support to his positions. They petitioned the administration to sanction him.

Which of the following comes closest to your views of what the administration should do?

○ The administration should do nothing and tell the Jewish students who complained that a faculty member has the right to his political views even if they are unpopular.

○ The administration should tell the faculty member that his public support for the Palestinians reflects badly on the university and he should refrain from making public speeches on the topic or face more serious sanctions.

○ Refer the case to a faculty committee of members who do not have strong prior opinions on the matter and who will assess the case and make a judgement about appropriate action(s) to be taken.

○ I don't know what the administration should do.

○ If none of the above responses adequately captures your opinion, please briefly tell us in the box below what you believe the university should do in this situation:

SITUATION 9

Suppose a faculty member belonged to an environmentalist group that advocated that protection of the environment was a more important priority than economic development. He participated in violent demonstrations at International Monetary Fund (IMF) meetings and other places where they felt people of power were not sufficiently focusing on environmental concerns. A photographer took a picture of this faculty member throwing a stone at the participants in one of these meetings. A student group asked the administration to sanction this faculty member.

What do you think the administration should do?

○ Do nothing or ignore the incident. The faculty member has a right to engage in political demonstrations and if he threw a stone it was the business of the police to sanction this behavior not the university.

○ Administer "soft" sanctions such as:

1. a request for him not to repeat this behavior

2. freeze his salary for one or two years

○ Administer "hard" sanctions such as:

1. temporary suspension

2. a formal reprimand

○ Bring the faculty member up on charges in an attempt to dismiss him from the university.

○ Refer the case to a faculty committee of members who do not have strong prior opinions on the matter and who will assess the case and make a judgement about appropriate action(s) to be taken.

○ I don't know what the administration should do.

○ If none of the above responses adequately captures your opinion, please briefly tell us in the box below what you believe the university should do in this situation:

SITUATION 10

A senior at a prestigious university is working on a performance art project as part of her senior thesis. For the project, which was approved by her advisor, she has repeatedly inseminated herself with donated sperm and then induced abortions by using herbs. The display of her project will feature a large cube wrapped in sheets covered with blood from the abortions, as well as video images of her inducing the procedures. After substantial public outrage and external criticism of the University, the Dean of the Undergraduate College responds that he is "appalled" by the project. The Dean of the School of Art and the College Dean reassess what constitutes an appropriate senior art project and the manner in which those projects are mentored. The College Dean decides not to allow the performance art project to be displayed.

What do you think should be done about this project?

○ Nothing. The administration should not determine what "appropriate" art is even if it does offend the community.

○ I agree with what the College Dean did.

○ I agree with what the College Dean did but would also publicly sanction the advisor of the student.

○ I would bring the advisor up on charges in an attempt to dismiss her from the university.

○ Refer the case to a faculty committee of members who do not have strong prior opinions on the matter and who will assess the case and make a judgement about appropriate action(s) to be taken.

○ I don't know what should be done.

○ If none of the above responses adequately captures your opinion, please briefly tell us in the box below what you believe the university should do in this situation:

SITUATION 11

A white professor is teaching a course on race and ethnic relations. In the introduction to the course the professor presents the class with what he takes as facts: African Americans are more likely than other racial and ethnic groups to have children out of wedlock. African Americans are more likely to be in prison. African Americans are more likely to be on welfare. African Americans score lower than whites and Asians on SAT tests. The professor said that the class would address the reasons for these differences; but some African American students who were taking the course go to the Dean and complain that the professor was racist and shouldn't be allowed to teach the class. The Dean removed the professor from the class and said that he would not be allowed to teach this course again. The administration said that it was just not acceptable for a professor to hurt the feelings and self-image of African American people in his class even if what he said was all based upon documented facts.

Which of the following statements would you be most likely to agree with?

O The dean was right in removing the professor from the class.
O The dean was wrong in removing the professor.
O I don't know what is right in this situation.
O If none of the above responses adequately captures your opinion, please briefly tell us in the box below what you believe the university should do in this situation:

SITUATION 12

A tenured professor in an undergraduate course pointed out that women don't score as well as men on quantitative tests like the math SAT and stated his opinion that one cause of this difference might be genetic differences between the sexes. Based on these remarks, a group of women students in his class complained to the Dean that the professor was a sexist and was making them feel very uncomfortable in his class.

What do you think the administration should do?

○ Nothing, even if the comment was not related to the topic of the course, because sanctioning the professor would violate his rights as a faculty member.

○ Ask the professor to be more sensitive to the feelings of women students.

○ Remove him from the class.

○ Bring the professor up on charges in an attempt to dismiss him from the university.

○ Refer the case to a faculty committee of members who do not have strong prior opinions on the matter and who will assess the case and make a judgement about appropriate action(s) to be taken.

○ I don't know what the administration should do.

○ If none of the above responses adequately captures your opinion, please briefly tell us in the box below what you believe the university should do in this situation:

SITUATION 13

A popular non-tenured lecturer at a prestigious university is a "person of interest" in a murder case involving one of the University's students. The professor is never indicted and, therefore, according to our law is assumed to be innocent. Nonetheless, the University decides to terminate his contract because he is a suspect in the case.

What is your opinion about the University's actions?

○ The University has a responsibility to protect its students and did the correct thing in terminating the professor.

○ The University acted prematurely and violated the rights of the professor.

○ I don't know what the University should do.

○ If none of the above responses adequately captures your opinion, please briefly tell us in the box below what you believe the university should do in this situation:

SITUATION 14

A professor works on problems of immunology—trying to find vaccines for diseases like plague. He works with toxic and other select agents that could be used potentially by bioterrorists in creating biological weapons. His work could contribute significantly to finding cures or preventions for these diseases. He may not allow any graduate or post-doctoral student to work in his laboratory if that student comes from certain nations that the government has defined as supporting terrorism—even if there is no evidence that the student is a security risk. The papers that the scientist writes are subjected to prepublication review by members of the boards of leading scientific journals in his field for possibilities that sections of the paper would have to be omitted before publication because in the opinion of the board the methods section or other results could fall into the wrong hands. Given this situation, how do you feel about the following:

A. The professor should have the right to bring into his laboratory students on the basis of his belief in their talent rather than their national origin and that any restrictions on his doing so is a violation of his rights as a researcher and a violation of the restricted students' rights.

○ Agree
○ Disagree
○ I don't know.
○ If none of the above responses adequately captures your opinion, please briefly tell us in the box below what you believe the university should do in this situation:

B. Open communication of ideas is a core value of scientific work. Scientists should not be subjected to principles of "prior restraint" in publishing their work even if some of the publications might help terrorists in planning their attacks.

○ Agree
○ Disagree
○ I don't know.
○ If none of the above responses adequately captures your opinion, please briefly tell us in the box below what you believe the university should do in this situation:

OTHER QUESTIONS

Q1. Do you think that a university confronting these situations should first research how other universities have dealt with similar problems in the past, and with what consequences and reactions, before making a decision on which of the above responses to adopt?

O Yes
O No
O I don't know.

Q2. If the argument is made that the university should not interfere with the behavior of faculty if it is conducted off campus, what would you think of the following statements?

O I agree with that position. The university is not responsible for what its faculty do off campus. If a faculty member violates the law it is up to the police authorities to sanction him.
O I disagree with that position. Even if an act is done off campus by a university employee, it still reflects on the reputation of the university and the university has to be concerned with it even if it would prefer not to.
O I have no opinion about this topic.
O I prefer not to answer this question.

Q3. When politically controversial issues like abortion come up in class discussions, faculty members:

O should keep their opinions to themselves.
O express their personal opinion but allow students who disagree to express their views without those views affecting their grades in the course.
O I have no opinion about this topic.
O I prefer not to answer this question.

Q4. Below are a group of statements related to issues in higher education. Please indicate whether you agree with each statement, disagree with it, or have no opinion on it.

A. Without prior administration approval students should be allowed to organize a boycott and picket a professor's class if they believe he or she presents biased views on important subjects.

○ Agree
○ Disagree
○ I have no opinion on this subject.
○ I prefer not to answer this question.

B. Science professors should not discuss political issues like abortion or capital punishment in their science courses.

○ Agree
○ Disagree
○ I have no opinion on this topic.
○ I prefer not to answer this question.

C. A fundamental role of a professor is to challenge orthodoxies and the presuppositions and biases of his/her students even if this results in unsettling feelings among students.

○ Agree
○ Disagree
○ I have no opinion on this topic.
○ I prefer not to answer this question.

D. Universities should not accept grants or contracts that stipulate restrictions related to the publication of research.

○ Agree
○ Disagree
○ I have no opinion on this question.
○ I prefer not to answer this question.

E. If a student group follows all appropriate rules, it should be permitted to invite to the campus any speaker regardless of the content of his or her views even if the speaker holds views which are generally rejected by the overwhelming majority of the university community like Ku Klux Klan members.

○ Agree
○ Disagree
○ I have no opinion on this question.
○ I prefer not to answer this question.

Below are a group of questions that we need for statistical analysis of the data:
  Your sex:

○ Female
○ Male

  In what year were you born?

_____

  What is the highest degree you have earned?

_____

  In what year did you get your highest degree?

_____

  Field of highest degree:
○ Biological and Biomedical Sciences
○ Humanities
○ Physical and Mathematical Sciences
○ Social and Behavioral Sciences
○ Architecture, Planning & Preservation
○ Arts
○ Business
○ Continuing Education
○ Engineering
○ International & Public Affairs
○ Journalism

○ Law
○ Social Work
○ Teachers College
○ Dental Medicine
○ Medicine
○ Nursing
○ Public Health

For how many years have you been employed in colleges and universities?

_____

For how many years have you been employed at Columbia University?

_____

In which department do you hold your major position?

_____

What is your academic rank?

_____

What is your race or ethnicity?

○ American Indian/Alaska Native
○ Asian
○ Black/African American
○ Caucasian
○ Hispanic/Latino/Spanish
○ Middle Eastern
○ Pacific Islander
○ Other

In the 2008 US presidential election, did you vote for:

○ Barack Obama
○ John McCain
○ Some other candidate
○ I did not vote.
○ I was not eligible to vote in that election.
○ I prefer not to answer this question.

Do you usually think of yourself as a:

○ Democrat
○ Republican
○ Independent
○ Other
○ I prefer not to answer this question.

On the issue of abortion would you consider your opinion to be closest to:

○ Pro Life
○ Pro Choice
○ I have no opinion on this issue.
○ I prefer not to answer this question.

In cases where a person has been convicted of first-degree murder and has exhausted all appeals would you favor:

○ The death penalty
○ Life in prison without parole
○ Parole after 25 years for good behavior
○ A lesser sentence
○ I prefer not to answer this question.

Thank you for taking the time to answer this survey.
If you would like to read the Informed Consent Document, please click here.

NOTES

1. Louis Menand, ed., *The Future of Academic Freedom* (Chicago: University of Chicago Press, 1999). See Menand's essay "The Limits of Academic Freedom," p. 4.

2. See Jon Elster's essay in this volume for a significantly different perspective on the positive and negative consequences of academic freedom in the academy. See also, Judith Butler, "Academic Norms, Contemporary Challenges: A Reply to Robert Post on Academic Freedom," in Beshara Doumani, ed., *Academic Freedom After September 11* (New York: Zone, 2006). Butler raises a critical question in her essay: If academic freedom depends on the evaluation of a set of certified experts in a particular discipline who work within the constraints of certain norms and values, are the norms themselves subjects for attack as biased or wrongheaded? Is academic freedom part of an evolving, dynamic system, or must it be wedded to the views of those currently in positions of power who control the norms and their application?

3. As Bromwich says: "Professors come to be considered as authorities in part because they are licensed by a qualified parochial community of scholars in a given field of study. They are not licensed as political authorities; and when they speak of political matters, their opinions ought to carry only the same weight and to enjoy the same protection as the opinions of ordinary citizens. No more, no less."

4. In Jonathan R. Cole's recent book, *The Great American University: Its Rise to Preeminence, Its Indispensable National Role, Why It Must Be Protected* (New York: Public Affairs, 2010), twelve core values of great universities are identified. These include, among others, meritocracy, organized skepticism, free and open communication, disinterestedness, and academic freedom and free inquiry. For a discussion of these values, see pp. 61–70.

5. The Lockner age takes its name from the Supreme Court case, Lockner v. New York, 198 U.S. 45 (1905). The court gave employers a great deal of latitude to hire and fire employees at will. It symbolized the age of contracts. Academic institutions acted like other institutions during this period. Presidents and trustees felt they could unilaterally fire professors for their political and social views—and they did precisely that. Faculty members had little if any power to protect themselves from the arbitrary opinions of the administration and trustees. Stanford University's firing of the distinguished economist/sociologist E. A. Ross is a notable case in point. Lockner was later challenged in Muller v. Oregon, 208 U.S. 412 (1908), from which we get the famous Brandeis brief that argues on the basis of empirical evidence (the famous Pittsburgh studies) for restrictions on the absolute right of contract—essentially for public health reasons. For those unfamiliar with the Brandeis brief, Brandeis was one of the plaintiff's lawyers in Muller and presented to the Court, for the first time, systematic empirical data, collected by others, on the negative health effects on women of working excessively long hours as a result of contract. The result in Muller, which today has the sound of an extremely paternalistic set of majority opinions, was to limit work hours and to give employees some basis for defending themselves against the

work rules set down solely by employers. The initial American Association of University Professors "1915 Declaration of Principles" was, in fact, in part a response to the arbitrariness in hiring and firing at universities by presidents and trustees. American Association of University Professors, "1915 Declaration of Principles," in *Policy Documents and Reports* (Washington, D.C.: AAUP, 2006), 297.

6. Qualitative examples exist in abundance about the harm to teaching and research, and these are recounted in Cole, *The Great American University*, as well as in books on academic freedom by Paul Lazarsfeld and Wagner Thielens, Ellen Schrecker, and Sigmund Diamond. Here, as elsewhere, there are few quantitative studies to reference. Most of the examples are represented through qualitative data and historical examples.

7. Among the scores of books and essays on the subject, the best introduction to the history of the idea of academic freedom can still be found in Richard Hofstadter and Walter P. Metzger, *The Development of Academic Freedom in the United States* (New York: Columbia University Press, 1955); Robert M. MacIver, director, *Academic Freedom in Our Time: A Study Prepared for the American Academic Freedom Project at Columbia University* (New York: Columbia University Press, 1955); Sigmund Diamond, *The Compromised Campus: The Collaboration of Universities with the Intelligence Community, 1945–1955* (New York: Oxford University Press, 1992); Ellen W. Schrecker, *No Ivory Tower: McCarthyism and the Universities* (New York: Oxford University Press, 1986); Menand, *The Future of Academic Freedom*; David Bromwich, *Politics by Other Means* (New Haven: Yale University Press, 1992); Cole, *The Great American University*; Matthew W. Finkin and Robert C. Post, *For the Common Good: Principles of Academic Freedom* (New Haven: Yale University Press, 2009).

8. The following Supreme Court cases, among others, are important for their attention to academic freedom: Sweezy v. New Hampshire, 354 U.S. 234, 250 (1957); Keyishian v. Board of Regents, 385 U.S. 589, 603 (1966); Adler v. Board of Education of City of New York, 342 U.S. 485 (1952). In the Sweezy case, one should look particularly at the concurring opinions of Justices Frankfurter and Harlan about the central role of academic freedom in a free society.

9. Paul F. Lazarsfeld and Wagner Thielens Jr., *The Academic Mind* (Glencoe, Ill.: Free Press, 1958).

10. See, e.g., the many studies by Seymour Martin Lipset and Everett Carl Ladd Jr., including, as one example, Everett Carl Ladd Jr. and Seymour Martin Lipset, *The Divided Academy: Professors and Politics* (New York: Norton, 1976). In that volume, you will find references to many other books on academic politics, authored separately or jointly by Lipset and Ladd.

11. Neil Gross and Solon Simmons, "The Social and Political Views of American Professors," Working Paper, September 24, 2007.

12. For those unfamiliar with IRBs, the federal government instituted a review of the research protocols of all federally sponsored grants and contracts that involved human subjects. This followed *The Belmont Report* and the Kennedy hearings, which focused on the now famous Tuskegee syphilis study of African American men. Although the

researchers followed standard practices at the time in carrying out this research on syphilis, there was no requirement for "informed consent" before participating in the study. The Kennedy hearings led to the establishment of institutional review boards, or IRBs, located at universities, that had the power to deny researchers the right to conduct their research if the review board felt that there was some threat to the human subjects. As is made abundantly clear in Philip Hamburger's essay in this volume, the IRBs have become a bone of contention at universities and their power, licensing practices, and scope are matters of dispute. For example, we had to go through extensive IRB review and changes in order to carry out this survey, even when faculty members at Columbia could simply delete, as no doubt many did, the e-mail message or the survey if they did not wish to participate in the survey. Subfields, such as social-psychology, which depended on small-scale experiments (mostly with students) and on some form of deception, have been virtually put out of business by the inability of the researchers to get by IRBs.

13. This project, which was supported by a grant from the Ford Foundation, was the result of an RFP that the foundation put out that asked a number of universities to submit one proposal for possible funding. Columbia and Ford selected our proposal. In this sense, this was a grant made to the university (as all are technically) that we carried out. That is why the provost's office, which we thank for its cooperation, permitted us to use its mailing list. We particularly want to thank Roxie Smith and Stephen Rittenberg for their cooperation with the pilot study.

14. We found that if faculty members actually went so far as to go to the linked survey, roughly 60 percent answered the questions, but obviously most faculty members did not move from the e-mail to the survey instrument. This pattern proved similar in the responses to the final survey.

15. There was some disagreement among the faculty about what we defined as a "soft" versus a "hard" sanction. For example, some faculty members thought that freezing a faculty member's salary for one or two years was hardly a "soft" sanction as we had defined it. A number of faculty members who responded to the pretest and the actual survey also felt that the vignettes were too short to provide enough information to know how to respond. While longer descriptions of the cases might have been valuable, we did not lengthen the vignettes, because it would have increased the time required to respond to the entire survey—and we were fearful that this would lower even further an anticipated low response rate to the Web survey.

16. There are now many studies that have examined response rates to different types of surveys that are conducted in Web format, via regular mail, and through in-person interviews. There are variations that are examined using each mode of collecting data. For one example, a survey of Michigan State University students, somewhat comparable to our own effort, see, Michael D. Kaplowitz, Timothy D. Hadlock, and Ralph Levine, "A Comparison of Web and Mail Survey Response Rates," *Public Opinion Quarterly* 68, no. 1 (Spring, 2004): 94–101. In their study, the response rate was 21 percent to a Web-based survey that was preceded by an e-mail notice of the survey with a link to the Web-based survey, which is the method that we used. They also found that

if you preceded the sending of the survey with a regular mail notice of the forthcoming receipt of the survey, response rates went up significantly, as did the cost.

17. We were somewhat surprised by the underrepresentation of the medical school biological science departments in the final set of respondents and are not entirely sure whether this reflects less interest in these issues or some technical problems in distributing the survey. We also decided not to weight the responses despite the differences between the population of faculty members and the respondent population. This would probably result in false precision, since on many of the questions there was little variance and for those questions weighting would not have made a difference. Since the arts and sciences represents a higher proportion of the faculty who responded compared with their numbers in the population, there is a slight bias toward their collective views for those questions for which we report variations between the faculty in the different schools—but weighting even in these instances would not have made a great deal of difference in the results reported.

18. Interestingly, some faculty members actually believe that students are less familiar with this type of material than they are, when in fact they may well have had more experience with it than the faculty members. Had the comment included a phrase that students who find these kinds of material abhorrent might inadvertently discover the sexually explicit material on the professor's office computer, then there might have been a basis for sanctions—beyond the possibility of the action violating clear university rules.

19. There is a good deal of ignorance about IRB regulations among the faculty. For example, researchers who do not receive federal research grants, or who do their research without funding, do not have to submit their proposals through the IRB, unless the individual university has mandated that they do so. But there is a provision that allows universities to opt out of using IRBs for unfunded work and work not funded by the federal government. Our understanding is that the University of Chicago has, in fact, opted out of these reviews for non–federally funded grants. Columbia does require all grants to be reviewed by the IRB, even surveys and experiments that proceed without funding. That is a local choice that was never adequately explained to the faculty, and the faculty at Columbia were never given a voice in that decision. This is a classic case of the lawyers at universities, who tend to be risk averse, dictating behavior regardless of whether or not it is mandated by federal or other regulations.

20. Most questions had roughly 310 responses, although there was some variation in the number of faculty members who responded to each question. Roughly 35 percent of those who responded to the survey were women; 65 percent were men.

21. $p < .05$. Significance levels were tested using t tests (when a predictor variable had two categories) or ordinary least-squares regression (when a predictor had three or more categories). We have presented some indication of whether these differences are statistically significant, or, in short, whether they were likely to be a result of chance variation. We are not making claims that the statistical tests indicate that any particular result is of substantive significance, since sample size will often be a key factor in statistical tests of significance, regardless of whether the results are of substantive importance on the basis of some conceptual or theoretical ideas.

22. $p < .001$.

23. $p < .01$.

24. $p < .05$.

25. $p < .05$.

26. $p < .01$.

27. $p < .05$.

28. It would be of interest to see whether, in a comparative analysis, the scores on these indexes were different at different universities. For example, one has the sense from President Robert Zimmer's essay in this volume, as well as the one by Richard Shweder, that the value or norm of academic freedom at the University of Chicago trumps virtually all other values. But is that fact or fiction? And what would the scores be at some of the other great American universities as well as at some lesser ones?

29. There are only a few full professors at Columbia who do not have tenure. Most often they are located at the medical school in the clinical departments. There may be a few who received the survey in the biomedical departments who have clinical appointments; also there are a few professors in the professional schools who do not have tenure.

30. This does not mean that most faculty members understood the current doctrine on the First Amendment: that speech can be restricted in certain circumstances, but the legislation that restricts speech must be content neutral. Other forms of unprotected speech include libel and slander, commercial advertising, fighting words, etc. For a fuller explanation of the evolution of First Amendment doctrine, see Lee C. Bollinger and Geoffrey R. Stone, eds., *Eternally Vigilant: Free Speech in the Modern Era* (Chicago: University of Chicago Press, 2002). We are putting aside here that Columbia University is a private school and therefore is not bound by the current court's views on the scope of protection under the First Amendment.

31. In fact, the research on which this case was built did discover the gene that causes the disease that was being studied. Both the anthropological and the genetics research contributed to this discovery.

32. David Bromwich, *Politics by Other Means*.

33. Cass Sunstein, *Why Societies Need Dissent* (Cambridge, MA: Harvard University Press, 2003).

34. Kent Greenawalt, *Fighting Words: Individuals, Communities, and Liberties of Speech* (Princeton: Princeton University Press, 1995).

35. Greg Lukianoff, *Unlearning Liberty: Campus Censorship and the End of American Debate* (Philadelphia: Foundation for Individual Rights in Education, 2012).

36. Stuart Firestein, *Ignorance: How It Drives Science* (New York: Oxford University Press, 2012). Firestein, who began his adult life as a theatrical producer, turned to science at a rather late age and has reached distinction as a biologist and chair of Columbia's Biological Sciences Department. This book ought to be read by nonscientists for a better understanding of how science actually is carried out. By "ignorance," Firestein means that at the core of science is the creation of ignorance out of knowledge—the production of new, interesting, yet unanswered questions.

37. We would like to thank Jon Elster, Akeel Bilgrami, and Peter Bearman for their helpful critiques of various forms of the survey instrument.

CONTRIBUTORS

AKEEL BILGRAMI is the Sidney Morgenbesser Professor of Philosophy at Columbia University. After completing a degree in English literature from Bombay University, he went to Oxford University as a Rhodes Scholar and there received another bachelor's degree in philosophy, politics, and economics. He has a PhD from the University of Chicago.

Professor Bilgrami has two relatively independent sets of intellectual interests—in the philosophy of mind and language and in political philosophy and moral psychology, especially as they surface in politics, history, and culture. In the former, he has published *Belief and Meaning* (Blackwell, 1992) and *Self-Knowledge and Resentment* (Harvard University Press, 2006). In the latter, he has published *Secularism, Identity, and Enchantment* (Harvard University Press, 2013). He is presently working on a book on the relations between agency and practical reason and on two small books entitled *Gandhi's Integrity* (Columbia University Press) and *What Is a Muslim?* (Princeton University Press).

He teaches courses and seminars regularly in the department, on Philosophy of Mind and Language, and also for the Committee on Global Thought and Political Science, on issues in Politics and Rationality as well as Religion and Politics in a Global Context.

DAVID BROMWICH is Sterling Professor of English at Yale University. His books include *Moral Imagination*, *A Choice of Inheritance*, and *Politics by*

Other Means. He is the editor of Edmund Burke's selected writings *On Empire, Liberty, and Reform,* and has written on politics and culture for the *New York Review of Books,* the *Nation,* and other journals.

JUDITH BUTLER is Maxine Elliot Professor in the Department Comparative Literature and a founding director of the Program of Critical Theory at the University of California, Berkeley. She received her PhD in philosophy from Yale University in 1984. She is the author of several books, including *Subjects of Desire: Hegelian Reflections in Twentieth-Century France* (Columbia University Press, 1987), *Gender Trouble: Feminism and the Subversion of Identity* (Routledge, 1990), *The Psychic Life of Power* (1997), *Giving an Account of Oneself* (1997), *Antigone's Claim: Kinship Between Life and Death* (Columbia University Press, 2000), *Frames of War: When Is Life Grievable?* (2009), and *Parting Ways: Jewishness and the Critique of Zionism* (Columbia University Press, 2012), as well as several coauthored volumes, including *Is Critique Secular?* (2009), *The Power of Religion in Public Life* (2011), and *Dispossessions* (2013). She is also active in gender and sexual politics, human rights, and anti-war politics, and is on the advisory board of Jewish Voice for Peace. She recently held the Andrew Mellon Fellowship for Distinction in the Humanities.

NOAM CHOMSKY was born on December 7, 1928, in Philadelphia, Pennsylvania. He received his PhD in linguistics in 1955 from the University of Pennsylvania. From 1951 to 1955, Chomsky was a junior fellow of the Harvard University Society of Fellows. The major theoretical viewpoints of his doctoral dissertation appeared in the monograph *Syntactic Structure* (1957). This formed part of a more extensive work, *The Logical Structure of Linguistic Theory,* circulated in mimeograph in 1955 and published in 1975.

Chomsky joined the staff of the Massachusetts Institute of Technology in 1955, and in 1961 was appointed full professor. In 1976 he was appointed institute professor in the Department of Linguistics and Philosophy.

Chomsky has lectured at many universities here and abroad and is the recipient of a number of honorary degrees and awards. He has written and lectured widely on linguistics, philosophy, intellectual history, contemporary issues, international affairs, and U.S. foreign policy. Among his more recent books are *New Horizons in the Study of Language and Mind; On Nature and Language; The Essential Chomsky; Hopes and Prospects; Gaza in Crisis;*

How the World Works; 9–11: Was There an Alternative?; Making the Future: Occupations, Interventions, Empire, and Resistance; The Science of Language; Peace with Justice: Noam Chomsky in Australia; and *Power Systems.*

JONATHAN R. COLE is the John Mitchell Mason Professor of the University at Columbia University. For fourteen years, from 1989 to 2003, he was provost and dean of faculties at Columbia. Prior to becoming provost, he was vice president for arts and sciences for two years. His scholarly work has focused principally on the development of the sociology of science as a research specialty, and he has written extensively about the reward and stratification system of science, peer review, and women in science. In recent years, he has turned his scholarly attention to issues of higher education. His latest book is *The Great American University: Its Rise to Preeminence, Its Indispensable National Role, Why It Must Be Protected.* He lectures around the world on topics related to higher learning. He received his BA in American history from Columbia College in 1964 and his PhD in sociology from Columbia in 1969. He has spent his entire scholarly career at Columbia. Among the awards and honors he has received are election to the American Academy of Arts and Sciences and the American Philosophical Society, and being named a Fellow of the American Association for the Advancement of Science and a member of the Council on Foreign Relations. He is a recipient of a Guggenheim Fellowship and has spent time at the Center for Advanced Study in the Behavioral Sciences and at the Russell Sage Foundation. He is currently completing a book on what great universities ought to look like 25 or 30 years from now.

STEPHEN COLE is Distinguished Professor of Sociology at the State University of New York, Stony Brook. He studied with Robert K. Merton and Paul F. Lazarsfeld at Columbia University. He has published extensively in the following areas: the sociology of science, the sociology of education, gender, and medical sociology. He is also the author of a best-selling research methods text. In 1991, he published an edited collection of essays critical of the current state of sociology, *What's Wrong with Sociology?* (Transaction Publishers). In January 2003, Harvard University Press published his monograph, *Increasing Faculty Diversity: The Occupational Choices of High Achieving Minority Students.* Recently, with Mark Schneider, Cole taught an interdisciplinary graduate seminar in educational policy. He is currently working on a book tentatively titled *Fixing Education*. When that is completed, he intends to put together his lectures on medical care into a book highly critical of the current way in which medicine is practiced in the United States. In May 2007, Professor Cole was named a Distinguished Professor.

JON ELSTER is the Robert K. Merton Professor of the Social Sciences at Columbia University. Before moving to Columbia University, he taught in Paris, Oslo, and Chicago. His publications include *Ulysses and the Sirens* (1979), *Sour Grapes* (1983), *Making Sense of Marx* (1985), *The Cement of Society* (1989), *Solomonic Judgements* (1989), *Local Justice* (1992), *Alchemies of the Mind* (1999), *Ulysses Unbound* (2000), *Closing the Books: Transitional Justice in Historical Perspective* (2004), *Explaining Social Behavior* (2007), *Alexis de Tocqueville: The First Social Scientist* (2009), and *Securities Against Misrule* (2013). His research interests include the theory of individual and collective choice and the theory of distributive justice. He is currently working on a comparative study of the Federal Convention and the first French constituent assembly of 1789–1891.

STANLEY FISH is the Floersheimer Distinguished Visiting Professor at Cardozo School of Law at Yeshiva University, the Davidson-Kahn Distinguished University Professor and Professor of Law at Florida International University, and a world-renowned literary theorist and legal scholar. He began his academic career in the English department at the University of California, then became the Kenan Professor of English and Humanities at Johns Hopkins University, where he taught from 1974 to 1985, before becoming arts and sciences professor of English and professor of law at Duke. He was dean of the College of Liberal Arts and Sciences at the University of Illinois from 1999 to 2004. Professor Fish is a prolific author, having written over 200 scholarly books and articles. Professor Fish is a contributor to *The Opinionator* blog for the *New York Times*.

MATTHEW GOLDSTEIN is chancellor emeritus of the City University of New York (CUNY). He served as CUNY chancellor from September 1999 to June 2013, the first CUNY graduate to lead the nation's most prominent urban public university, with 24 colleges and professional schools throughout the five boroughs of New York City.

Under Dr. Goldstein's leadership, CUNY experienced a widely lauded transformation. The university raised academic standards, improved student performance, increased enrollment, built its faculty corps, created new colleges and schools, and expanded its research capacity.

Prior to serving as chancellor, Dr. Goldstein held senior academic and administrative positions, including president of Adelphi University, president of Baruch College, president of the Research Foundation, and acting vice chancellor for academic affairs of CUNY. He has also held faculty positions at several colleges and universities and has written extensively in mathematics and statistics.

Currently, Dr. Goldstein is chair of the board of trustees of the J.P. Morgan Funds and a member of the Executive Committee of the Business–Higher Education Forum. He is also a member of the board of trustees of the Museum of Jewish Heritage, as well as a director of the Lincoln Center Institute for the Arts in Education, ex officio. By appointment of Governor Andrew M. Cuomo, he is chair of the New York City Regional Economic Development Council and a member of the New NY Education Reform Commission. He served as chair of the 2010 New York City Charter Revision Commission by appointment of former mayor Michael R. Bloomberg.

Dr. Goldstein is a fellow of the American Academy of Arts & Sciences and a fellow of the New York Academy of Sciences. Among his honors are the 2011 Association for a Better New York Spirit of ABNY Award, the 2007 Carnegie Corporation of New York's Academic Leadership Award, the 2005 John H. Finley Award, the 2005 Medal of Honor "Austrian Cross of Honor for Science and Art, First Class," the 2002 Ellis Island Medal of Honor, and the 2000 Townsend Harris Medal.

Dr. Goldstein earned his doctorate from the University of Connecticut in mathematical statistics, and a bachelor's degree with high honors in statistics and mathematics from the City College of the City University of New York.

PHILIP HAMBURGER is the Maurice and Hilda Friedman Professor of Law at Columbia University. His scholarship focuses on constitutional law, and his publications include *Is Administrative Law Unlawful?* (University of Chicago Press, 2014), *Law and Judicial Duty* (Harvard University Press, 2008), *Separation of Church and State* (Harvard University Press, 2002); "Getting Permission" (*Northwestern Law Review*, 2007); and "Liberality" (*Texas Law Review*, 2002).

Before moving to Columbia, Hamburger was the John P. Wilson Professor at the University of Chicago Law School, where he was the director of the Bigelow Program and the Legal History Program. Earlier, he was the Oswald Symyster Colclough Research Professor at George Washington University Law School and a professor at the University of Connecticut Law School. He has been a visiting professor at the University of Virginia Law School and at Northwestern Law School, where he was the Jack N. Pritzker Distinguished Visiting Professor of Law.

JOHN MEARSHEIMER is the R. Wendell Harrison Distinguished Service Professor of Political Science and the codirector of the Program on International Security Policy at the University of Chicago, where he has taught since 1982. He graduated from West Point in 1970 and then served five years as an officer in the U.S. Air Force. He then started graduate school in political science at Cornell University in 1975. He received his PhD in 1980.

Professor Mearsheimer has written extensively about security issues and international politics more generally. He has published five books: *Conventional Deterrence* (1983), *Liddell Hart and the Weight of History* (1988), *The Tragedy of Great Power Politics* (2001), *The Israel Lobby and U.S. Foreign Policy* (with Stephen M. Walt, 2007), and *Why Leaders Lie: The Truth About Lying in International Politics* (2011).

He has also written many articles that have appeared in academic journals such as *International Security* and popular magazines such as the *London Review of Books*. Furthermore, he has written a number of op-ed pieces for the *New York Times* and the *Los Angeles Times* dealing with topics like Bosnia, nuclear proliferation, American policy toward India, the failure of Arab–Israeli peace efforts, and the folly of invading Iraq.

MICHELE MOODY-ADAMS is Joseph Straus Professor of Political Philosophy and Legal Theory at Columbia University, and served as dean of Columbia College and vice president for undergraduate education at Columbia from 2009 to 2011. Moody-Adams has published broadly in ethics, political philosophy, and the history of philosophy, and is the author of a widely cited book on moral relativism and moral objectivity, *Fieldwork in Familiar Places: Morality, Culture and Philosophy*. Her current work is in two areas: on the associative duties and civic virtues that make democracy possible and on the moral demands that history makes through calls for reparations, reconciliation, national apologies, and forgiveness.

ROBERT POST is Dean and Sol & Lillian Goldman Professor of Law at Yale Law School. Before moving to Yale, he taught at the University of California, Berkeley, School of Law. Dean Post's subject areas are constitutional law, the First Amendment, legal history, and equal protection. He has written and edited numerous books, including *Democracy, Expertise, Academic Freedom: A First Amendment Jurisprudence for the Modern State* (2012), *For the Common Good: Principles of American Academic Freedom* (with Matthew M. Finkin, 2009), *Prejudicial Appearances: The Logic of American Antidiscrimination Law* (with K. Anthony Appiah, Judith Butler, Thomas C. Grey, and Reva Siegel, 2001), and *Constitutional Domains: Democracy, Community, Management* (1995).

He is a member of the American Philosophical Society and the American Law Institute and a fellow of the American Academy of Arts and Sciences. He has an AB and a PhD in history of American civilization from Harvard and a JD from Yale Law School.

JOAN W. SCOTT is Professor Emerita in the School of Social Science at the Institute for Advanced Study in Princeton, New Jersey. Her most recent book is *The Fantasy of Feminist History*. She has had a long affiliation with the American Association of University Professors as a member of its Committee on Academic Freedom and Tenure.

FREDERICK SCHAFFER is general counsel and senior vice chancellor for legal affairs of the City University of New York. In this position, he is responsible for providing legal counsel to the board of trustees, the chancellor, and the university on a wide range of issues, and for supervising a legal department of twenty lawyers. Mr. Schaffer also serves as general counsel to the CUNY Construction Fund, a public authority that finances capital construction at the university. Previously, Mr. Schaffer was a litigation partner in the law firm of Schulte Roth & Zabel LLP, where he specialized in commercial and securities litigation and employment law. Earlier in his career, Mr. Schaffer served as counsel to Mayor Ed Koch, chief of litigation in the Office of the Corporation Counsel of the City of New York, and assistant U.S. attorney in

Manhattan. He also was an associate professor at the Benjamin N. Cardozo School of Law. Mr. Schaffer recently served as chairman of the Legal Aid Society and is currently a trustee of the Practising Law Institute and a director of Citizens Union, where he also cochairs the Municipal Affairs Committee. He has previously served as chairman of NYC Public/Private Initiatives, Inc., and as a director of the University Settlement Society. He is also active in the New York City Bar Association, where he currently serves as a member of the Committee on Government Ethics. He previously served as a member of a number of committees, including the Executive Committee and the Nominating Committee, and as Chairman of the Committee on Education and the Law. Mr. Schaffer received his BA degree summa cum laude from Harvard College and his JD degree magna cum laude from Harvard Law School, where he was an editor of the *Harvard Law Review*. Following law school, he clerked for the Honorable Francis L. Van Dusen, circuit judge on the U.S. Court of Appeals for the Third Circuit. Mr. Schaffer was a recipient of one of the 2011 Awards for Excellence in Public Service from the New York State Bar Association.

RICHARD A. SHWEDER is a cultural anthropologist and the Harold Higgins Swift Distinguished Service Professor in the Department of Comparative Human Development at the University of Chicago. His recent research examines the scope and limits of cultural pluralism in Western liberal democracies.

GEOFFREY R. STONE is the Edward H. Levi Distinguished Service Professor at the University of Chicago. A member of the law faculty since 1973, Mr. Stone has served as dean of the Law School (1987–1994) and provost of the University of Chicago (1994–2002). After graduating from the University of Chicago Law School in 1971, where he was editor-in-chief of the *University of Chicago Law Review*, Mr. Stone served as a law clerk to Justice William J. Brennan Jr. of the Supreme Court of the United States.

Mr. Stone is the author or coauthor of many books on constitutional law, including *Speaking Out: Reflections of Law, Liberty and Justice* (2010), *Top Secret: When Our Government Keeps Us in the Dark* (2007), *War and Liberty: An American Dilemma* (2007), *Perilous Times: Free Speech in Wartime* (2004), and *Eternally Vigilant: Free Speech in the Modern Era* (University of Chicago Press, 2002). He is also the lead coauthor of two casebooks, one on constitutional law and the other on the First Amendment, and since 1991 he has been an editor of the *Supreme Court Review*.

Mr. Stone is currently chief editor of a twenty-volume series, Inalienable Rights, which is being published by Oxford University Press. Mr. Stone's next major book, *Sexing the Constitution*, will explore the history of sex from ancient Greece to contemporary constitutional law.

Mr. Stone is a Fellow of the American Academy of Arts and Sciences, a member of the American Philosophical Society, former chair of the board of the American Constitution Society, and a member of the Advisory Council of the American Civil Liberties Union.

CHRISTOPHER C. WEISS is senior research analyst at Langer Research. He has nearly 20 years of experience in research design, execution, and analysis. An expert in quantitative methods, he specializes in modeling contextual and environmental effects, techniques of causal inference, and epidemiological and demographic studies.

Weiss has extensive experience designing and implementing rigorous research training programs. He joined Langer Research from New York University, where he served as clinical associate professor of sociology and director of the Applied Quantitative Research MA program. Weiss previously spent a decade as lecturer of sociology and director of the Quantitative Methods in the Social Sciences MA program at Columbia University.

A former program chair of the New York Chapter of the American Association for Public Opinion Research, Weiss has served on the editorial board of the journal *Statistics, Politics, and Policy* and the external editorial board of *American Journal of Education*, and on a technical advisory committee that evaluated the Transportation Security Administration's behavioral profiling program for the American Institutes for Research.

Weiss earned his doctorate in sociology and demography from the University of Pennsylvania, where he designed and carried out a number of survey-based research studies. He is a cum laude graduate of Trinity University in San Antonio.

ROBERT J. ZIMMER is president of the University of Chicago. Prior to his appointment as president, Zimmer was a University of Chicago faculty member and administrator for more than two decades specializing in the mathematical fields of geometry, particularly ergodic theory, Lie groups, and differential geometry. As a University of Chicago administrator, Zimmer served as chairman of the Mathematics Department, deputy provost, and vice president for research and for UChicago Argonne National Laboratory. He also served as provost at Brown University from 2002 to 2006, returning to Chicago in 2006 to become president of the university.

President Zimmer earned his AB summa cum laude from Brandeis University in 1968 and a PhD in mathematics from Harvard University in 1975. He joined the Chicago faculty as an L. E. Dickson Instructor of Mathematics in 1977. He was also on the faculty of the U.S. Naval Academy from 1975 to 1977 and has held visiting positions at Harvard, Berkeley, and at institutions in Israel, France, Australia, Switzerland, and Italy.

INDEX

AAC. *See* Association of American Colleges

AAUP. *See* American Association of University Professors

abortions, 8, 131, 356–58, 380

Abrams v. United States, 25n1

abrogation of rights by public or private sources, 299

Abu El-Haj, Nadia, 318

abuses, of academic freedom, 28–30, 103–6, 263–65, 274n69, 344–45

academic authority, 106; disciplinary, 107–8, 127–30, 145n31, 266n12; scholarly, 29–30; Williams on, 108–9

Academic Bill of Rights, of Horowitz, 263–64

academic boycotts. *See* boycotts

academic conduct, 43, 77, 138, 248, 250; grievances filed for, 49, 99; licensing of, 169–70; public judgment for, 30; responsibility for, 68–69; right to risk offense, 111–12

academic dishonesty, 18, 22, 26n8

academic exceptionalism school, 277, 289

academic exclusion, 19

academic freedom: abstract value of, 283, 297, 310–11; abuses of, 28–30, 103–6, 263–65, 274n69, 344–45; as conditioned value, xv–xvi, 293–94, 311–12; contemporary challenges to, 98; CUNY and, 250–52; Dewey on university and, 124–25; fundamentals of, 101–3; German university influence on, 3, 4–5, 247; imbalance in, 24, 30; intellectual diversity, 117–19, 122n50; justifications for, 11–12; legal principle of, 248; licensed expertise, 31–32, 39; limits, intellectual freedom limits and, 27; natural, constitutional or positive right to, 225; overtly coercive activity, 103; political values and, 281, 283, 284–85; principles of, 247–49; social benefits from, 226

academic freedom, exercising rights of, 293–316; abrogation of rights by public or private sources, 299; for affordable and accessible education, 295; Arendt on, 299; Barghouti on, 302; BDS, 297, 298; curriculum limits for political reasons, 296; divestments, 304–5;